W9-BRP-719

WILDE'S WOMEN

*How Oscar Wilde Was Shaped
by the Women He Knew*

ELEANOR FITZSIMONS
is a researcher, writer, journalist and occasional broadcaster
specialising in historical and current feminist issues. She has an MA in
Women, Gender and Society from University College Dublin. Her work
has been published in a range of newspapers and journals including
The Sunday Times, *The Guardian*, *History Today* and *The Irish Times*, and
she is a regular radio and television contributor.

WILDE'S WOMEN

*How Oscar Wilde Was Shaped
by the Women He Knew*

Eleanor Fitzsimons

OVERLOOK DUCKWORTH
New York • London

First published in the United States and the United Kingdom in 2016 by
Overlook Duckworth, Peter Mayer Publishers, Inc.

NEW YORK
141 Wooster Street
New York, NY 10012
www.overlookpress.com
For bulk and special sales please contact sales@overlookny.com,
or to write us at the above address.

LONDON
30 Calvin Street, London E1 6NW
T: 020 7490 7300
E: info@duckworth-publishers.co.uk
www.ducknet.co.uk
For bulk and special sales please contact sales@duckworth-publishers.co.uk,
or write to us at the above address.

© 2015 by Eleanor Fitzsimons

Cataloging-in-Publication Data is available from the Library of Congress

A catalogue record for this book is available from the British Library

ISBN: 978-1-4683-1266-9 (US)
ISBN: 978-0-7156-4936-7 (UK)

CONTENTS

List of Illustrations

ILLUSTRATION ACKNOWLEDGEMENTS

The portrait of Lillie Langtry by Edward John Poynter is included courtesy of the Jersey Heritage Collections.

The watercolour portrait of Lady Jane Wilde by Bernard Mulrenin; the image of the envelope containing strands of Isola Wilde's hair; the sketch of Florence Balcombe by Oscar Wilde; the watercolour of *View from Moytura House* by Oscar Wilde; the photograph of Constance Lloyd before her marriage; the letter from Oscar Wilde to Constance, written on 16 December 1884; the photograph taken at the home of Jean and Walter Palmer in 1892; and the photograph of Lady Jane Wilde in old age are all included in the Merlin Holland Picture Archive and are used with the kind permission of Merlin Holland.

The image of the Warner Brothers Trade Card depicting Oscar Wilde looking on as a cherub presents a corset was kindly supplied to me by Michael Seeney of the Oscar Wilde Society.

The portrait of Ellen Terry as Lady Macbeth, painted by John Singer Sargent 1889, is included in the Tate collection (currently on loan to the National Portrait Gallery, London) and is used with the kind permission of Tate Images.

The image of *Salome Dancing before Herod* by Gustave Moreau, 1876, is included in the Armand Hammer Collection, Gift of the Armand Hammer Foundation, Hammer Museum, Los Angeles and is used with the kind permission of the Hammer Museum, Los Angeles.

The photograph of Sarah Bernhardt is from the Folger Shakespeare Library.

The photograph of Constance's grave in Genoa is used with the permission of Outi Määttänen-Bourke/G is for Genoa.

The photograph of Dolly Wilde dressed as Oscar Wilde is the property of Joan Schenkar and is used with her kind permission.

INTRODUCTION

Given the nature and magnitude of the monstrous injustice perpetrated against him, Oscar Wilde's life is often examined in terms of his relationships with men, Lord Alfred Douglas in particular. Yet, he was genuinely fond of many women and this affection was usually reciprocated. As Oscar's friend Vincent O'Sullivan confirmed in *Aspects of Wilde*, his warm and frank biography:

> I have always found, and find today, his [Wilde's] warmest admirers among women. He, in his turn, admired women. I never heard him say anything disparaging about any woman, even when some of them required such treatment![1]

Ever since I first encountered Lady Jane Wilde, Oscar's flamboyant mother and an enduring heroine in his native Ireland, I have been intrigued by the influence she had on her son's life and work. This fascination led me to examine his attitude towards women in the context of a society that was determined to keep them down, something that was anathema to both Oscar and his mother. As an individualist who believed that few limits should be placed on anyone's life, man or woman, Oscar chose, as some of his closest friends, freethinking, influential, enterprising and intelligent women who challenged conventional gender roles and operated in the public sphere.

Jane Wilde was deeply unconventional and determined to shine bright. Oscar admired her brilliance and her appetite for life, and it was she who taught him that a woman could be as intuitive and inventive as any man. Yet, she was contradictory in her approach to what we label feminism. While she campaigned vociferously for women to be granted access to education and the professions, and welcomed progressive legislation such as The Married Women's Property Act (1870), she also believed that a loyal wife should accommodate any indiscretions perpetrated by her husband, particularly if he was a genius as Oscar's father was. This contradictory approach surely influenced Oscar's choice of wife and his subsequent behaviour during their marriage.

Oscar Wilde is, quite correctly, held up as a gay icon who railed against the ignorance and prejudice of those who would deny the authenticity and appropriateness of love between two men. Yet, like every aspect of his life, his sexuality is complex. It seems that from the early 1890s onward, he was attracted exclusively to men. Yet, before this, he was involved with several women. Oscar lost his first girlfriend, Florence Balcombe, to Bram Stoker, but won her back as a friend. His wife, Constance Lloyd, was highly accomplished, politically active and hugely supportive of him. She held strong proto-feminist views and advocated the adoption of rational clothing that would allow women to lead more comfortable and effective lives. Throughout their marriage, she supported Oscar emotionally and financially and she gave birth to their two beloved sons. Although deeply saddened by his duplicity, she did everything she could to help him after his arrest and imprisonment. He loved her and he mourned her deeply when she died.

Oscar also had dozens of women friends, among them socialite and astute businesswoman Lillie Langtry; and acclaimed actresses Ellen Terry and Sarah Bernhardt. He provoked extraordinary loyalty in women we have largely forgotten today: the witty and vivacious Ada Leverson and the hugely popular and influential Henrietta Eliza Vaughan Stannard, who published her bestselling novels as 'John Strange Winter'. He traded witticisms with women, promoted their work, collaborated with them on theatrical productions and drew inspiration from their lives. Many of the most outspoken and memorable characters in his plays are women.

Nowhere was the support of powerful women more important than in America, where Oscar toured in 1882 as a young poseur with only a poorly reviewed collection of poetry to his name. Dozens of wealthy and influential women who could make or break the reputation of a young writer delighted in his compelling personality and promoted him with enthusiasm. One of them even married his brother.

One of the most illuminating periods in Oscar's life in terms of his attitude towards women was his tenure as editor of proto-feminist magazine *The Woman's World*. Under his editorship, he insisted, this publication would concern itself 'not merely with what women wear, but with what they think, and what they feel'. He encouraged contributors to write about women in the public sphere and he demonstrated a nuanced and progressive attitude towards gender expectations and control.

Oscar acted as a conduit for women's ideas and used his social comedies to expose the deep-rooted hypocrisy that prevailed in patriarchal Victorian society. He facilitated the introduction of female-centric European culture to a London audience by collaborating with Polish actress Helena Modjeska and American actress Elizabeth Robbins, who brought the plays of Ibsen to England. He encouraged and gave practical assistance to progressive New Woman and feminist writers, including E. Nesbit, Olive Scrivener and Amy Levy. He harnessed the epigrammatic language used by women such as novelist Ouida (Marie Louise Ramé); his work was often compared to hers. His women friends often put him into their novels.

Prominent women friends, many of them members of 'The Souls', an influential clique of literary aristocrats, funded and informed his plays, poems and stories, and used their influence to give him access to vital publicity. He delighted society women with his stories, which he later dedicated to them. O'Sullivan understood that:

> In the upper reaches of English society it was not the men, who mostly did not like him, who made his success, but the women. He was too far from the familiar type of the men. He did not shoot or hunt or play cards; he had wit, and took the trouble to talk and be entertaining.[2]

Yet most of these women abandoned him when he needed their help.

Naturally, Oscar was not drawn to every woman he met and he could be cutting in his condemnation of those whose attitudes differed from his. He reserved his most biting commentary for puritanical women who, rather than campaigning for a relaxation in the moral strictures imposed on them, insisted instead that these restrictions be applied equally to men. Characters such as Hester Worsely in *A Woman of No Importance* and Gertrude Chiltern in *An Ideal Husband* exemplify this sort and are judged harshly as a result.

What follows are the compelling accounts of the many fascinating and brilliant women who influenced, inspired and collaborated with Oscar Wilde throughout his life, an aspect of Wilde that is often neglected. The impact of each one on the life and work of one of the most written-about men in the world is profound.

Chapter 1

THE REAL MRS ERLYNNE

Besides, my dear Windermere, how on earth could I pose as a
mother with a grown-up daughter? Margaret is twenty-one, and
I have never admitted that I am more than twenty-nine, or thirty
at the most. Twenty-nine when there are pink shades, thirty
when there are not.
OSCAR WILDE, *Lady Windermere's Fan*

On Saturday evening, 20 February 1892, a lively throng, numbering
close to twelve hundred, filed through the ornate foyer of the St James's
Theatre in the heart of London's 'clubland'. That first-night crowd,
described by *The New York Times* as 'the most brilliant audience that had
gathered for years in the St James's Theatre', included family and friends
of the playwright, critics, writers, and those eager to witness what would
undoubtedly be one of the most talked about nights in the theatrical season.[1] As each patron took his or her seat in anticipation of curtain-up, the
excitement was palpable. George Alexander, the dynamic actor-manager
who was to play the male lead, must have experienced more than his
usual measure of first night jitters, as it was he who had commissioned
this 'modern play' almost two years earlier. Since then, it had come close
to being abandoned several times: 'I can't get my people real', the author
complained in a letter that offered the return of the £50 advance he had
received.[2] Six months later, he wrote to say: 'I am very much disappointed
I have not been able to write the play'.[3]

In the weeks running up to its glittering debut, Alexander worked tirelessly on the staging of this potentially controversial new comedy, written
by one of the most talked about men in London. He rehearsed it exhaustively and endured incessant interventions from the playwright, who was
present at every rehearsal. Up until the moment his audience streamed
in, and beyond, he and the play's exacting author remained locked in
disagreement as to the timing of a shocking disclosure. Their animosity
had peaked with the arrival of a strongly worded letter earlier that month:
'. . . had I intended to let out the secret, which is the element of suspense
and curiosity, a quality so essentially dramatic, I would have written the

play on entirely different lines', fumed its author, Oscar Wilde.[4] For him, it was vital that the audience would admire the selfless actions of his unconventional female protagonist without interpreting them as the duties of motherhood.

Alexander gave up. On the opening night of *Lady Windermere's Fan*, Mrs Erlynne's secret was revealed during the final act, just as its author had wished. This fleeting victory prompted Clement Scott, the irascible but influential theatre critic from *The Daily Telegraph* to accuse Oscar of making his audience work far too hard:

> for two-thirds of the evening, people were asking one another: "Who is she? What is he? Why does she do this? How does he come to do that? Is this adventuress a mistress, or can she be a mother?"[5]

Scott, a first night fixture whose pithy reviews could make or break a production, had conspired with Alexander and was acting on a letter in which the theatre manager had raged about his inability to persuade 'this conceited, arrogant and ungrateful man of his stupidity'.[6]

Oscar capitulated and moved his revelation to Act II, insisting that he had not been swayed by the critics but by 'a small number of personal friends' who had joined him for a post-performance supper and convinced him that 'the psychological interest of the second act would be greatly increased by the disclosure of the actual relationship existing between Mrs Erlynne and Lady Windermere'.[7] Absent from that gathering was Oscar's wife, Constance, who had watched his play from a private box. Neither planned to return home that night: owing to the unpleasantness of faulty drains at their Tite Street house, Constance and the couple's elder son, Cyril, were staying with an elderly relative of hers; their younger son, Vyvyan, was with friends in Reading. Pleading the necessity of staying close to the theatre, Oscar had taken rooms at the Albemarle Hotel, but he did not return there alone: with him was Edward Shelley, an impressionable young clerk with The Bodley Head publishing house. He was, by then, leading a complex and exhausting double life.

That first night audience was not as confused as Clement Scott suggested, since they applauded enthusiastically as the curtain fell. The artist Louise Jopling, a close confidante of Oscar's, insisted that she had never enjoyed a first night so much. She recalled the 'intermittent ripples of laughter, running all over the house, at the witty sayings Oscar put into the mouths of his characters'.[8] Perhaps the notoriously puritanical Scott was outraged by the audience's tacit approval of Mrs Erlynne's scandalous behaviour. His views on women, actresses in particular, unlike Oscar's, were utterly unsympathetic. Six years later, in 1898, Scott was forced into retirement after he gave an ill-considered interview to the evangelical periodical *Great Thoughts* during which he declared: 'It is really impossible for a woman to remain pure who adopts the stage as a profession'.[9]

Oscar's play was all about women. The critic with *The Sunday Times* proclaimed, 'The men are not conspicuous successes as characters, though they all talk interestingly and amusingly, except Lord Windermere'.[10] Central to his plot was Mrs Erlynne, a fallen woman who was blackmailing her son-in-law in a bid to gain readmittance into society. Although the fallen woman was a stock character on the Victorian stage, she was, as a general rule, required to be penitent or vulgar; she was never allowed to triumph; and she often paid for her transgressions with her life. Oscar's Margaret Erlynne bore scant resemblance to her peers. Rather than present a coarse or contrite woman, he invented a witty and humane adventuress who was, in accordance with his explicit stage directions, 'beautifully dressed and very dignified'. Here was a Victorian mother who had transgressed in the worst way possible by abandoning her child in infancy, but who had survived, thrived even, by means of her ingenuity. As such, she embodied the characteristics and behaviour of many of Oscar's woman friends, who set their own rules and, with great inventiveness, circumvented the strictures imposed by patriarchal Victorian society.

Oscar's compatriot George Bernard Shaw, who sat among the audience that night, admired *Lady Windermere's Fan* enormously and sought to emulate its style.* Also present was Henry James, another would-be playwright but someone who rarely had a kind word for Oscar. He deemed the play 'infantine' and of a 'primitive simplicity', a pronouncement that had all the characteristics of a fit of professional pique. Yet, even he could not ignore the obvious enjoyment of those seated around him, and he was forced to admit, albeit grudgingly:

> There is so much drollery – that is, "cheeky" paradoxical wit of dialogue, and the pit and gallery are so pleased at finding themselves clever enough to "catch on" to four or five of the ingenious – too ingenious – *mots* in the dozen, that it makes them feel quite *"décadent"* . . . and they enjoy the sensation as a change from the stodgy.[11]

---

* Oscar sent Shaw a copy of *Lady Windermere's Fan*, inscribed: 'Op. 1 of the Hibernian School, London '93'.

Although this was his fourth play, *Lady Windermere's Fan* was Oscar's first comedy and the first of his plays to be produced on the London stage. Yet, he had sufficient self-belief to shun Alexander's initial offer of £1,000 in favour of a share of the takings. Whether reckless or astute, his gamble paid off: the play was a resounding success and ran for five months in the St James's Theatre before touring the provinces and returning to the West End for a second successful run towards the end of 1892. During that first year alone, it netted Oscar a sum that could have been as high as £7,000,* and was boosted by the returns from a successful New York production. Although this would have funded a very comfortable lifestyle for Oscar and his family, including his impoverished mother, it was frittered away instead in a hedonistic blur of champagne, cigarette cases and a succession of sumptuous hotel suites and dining rooms.

At the end of that first performance, Oscar bounded on stage, scandalising all of London by holding a lit cigarette as he spoke. As smoking in the company of women was rarely tolerated, his detractors assumed that he was being deliberately provocative, but Louise Jopling insisted that he was suffering from 'sheer nervousness'.[12] Women, who were expected by men to feel insulted by his behaviour, were often the first to leap to Oscar's defence. In his buttonhole, he wore a peculiar blue-green hued carnation that found its match in a dozen or more displayed on the lapels of a coterie of young men seated among the audience. This odd bloom, which signalled a shift in Oscar's allegiances, was treated with great suspicion by Scott and others. His star may have been in the ascendency that night but the anonymous publication, less than three years later, of *The Green Carnation*, a scandalous lampoon, would signal a turn in the tide of public opinion against him.

Oscar's speech that night caused further controversy. Although the exact wording is disputed, George Alexander insisted that Oscar was arrogant in congratulating his audience for having the wit to appreciate his play. This was a misinterpreted joke in all probability. He was also careful to praise his cast. Most prominent among them was Marion Terry, who, at thirty-nine, was nearing the end of her second decade on the stage. Although she played leading roles in more than 125 plays during a career that spanned fifty years, the role of Mrs Erlynne was to become her most celebrated. The Terrys were theatre royalty but Marion had always

---

* This equates to more than £600,000 in today's terms, although some analysts, most notably Josephine Guy and Ian Small, believe the sum may be closer to half this amount (*Oscar Wilde's Profession*, pp. 107–11).

been overshadowed by her more famous older siblings: Ellen, a fixture at the Lyceum and a great friend of Oscar's; and Kate, who had retired by then and would become grandmother to Sir John Gielgud. The success of Mrs Erlynne was a huge boost to Marion's career, yet it was a role she very nearly missed out on.

Although Oscar collaborated closely with several actresses and campaigned vociferously to secure his preferred leading ladies, he did not always get his way. Towards the end of September 1891, he had written to theatre director Augustin Daly, and offered the part to Ada Rehan, the lead actress in Daly's New York-based company: 'I would sooner see her play the part of Mrs. Erlynne than any English-speaking actress we have, or French actress for that matter', he insisted.[13] Rehan, who Oscar described as, 'that brilliant and fascinating genius', had enjoyed enormous success on the stages of America and Europe, and was considered a worthy rival to the magnificent Sarah Bernhardt.[14] Born Delia Crehan in County Limerick, Ireland in 1857, her family had moved to Brooklyn when she was just a child. Her unconventional name was the result of a typographical error made early in her career, when she was billed as Ada C. Rehan. Adopting this as her stage name, she gained great renown as a Shakespearean actress, doing particularly well in his comedies.

When Daly turned Mrs Erlynne down on Rehan's behalf, he ensured that she missed out on the opportunity to play one of the most memorable roles in theatrical history. Yet, despite his flattering words, she had not been Oscar's first choice either. The woman who inspired the character of Margaret Erlynne but passed up on the opportunity of playing her was sitting in the theatre on that first night. Lillie Langtry, muse, celebrated beauty and, at Oscar's instigation, actress was always at the centre of any glitzy occasion, but this one had more resonance for her than most. In her memoir, *The Days I Knew*, Langtry described how:

> He [Oscar Wilde] called one afternoon, with an important air and a roll of manuscript, placed it on the table, pointed to it with a sweeping gesture, and said: "There is a play which I have written for you".[15]

When she asked which part was intended for her, Oscar replied: 'A woman with a grown-up illegitimate daughter'. Lillie, in her late thirties, reacted with incredulity: 'My Dear Oscar', she remonstrated, 'am I old enough to have a grown-up daughter of any description?' Although she insisted that he put his manuscript away for twenty years, Oscar went ahead, and incorporated her rejection into his plot by having Mrs Erlynne declare:

Besides, my dear Windermere, how on earth could I pose as a mother with a grown-up daughter? Margaret is twenty-one, and I have never admitted that I am more than twenty-nine, or thirty at the most. Twenty-nine when there are pink shades, thirty when there are not.[16]

We can tell a lot about Oscar and any man perhaps, by examining the women he befriended. Throughout his life he gravitated towards outsiders who contravened the rules, and as more restrictions were placed on them, many of his friends were unconventional women. As Mrs Allonby says in *A Woman of No Importance*, 'There are far more things forbidden to us [women] than are forbidden to them [men].' Jersey-born Lillie and Dublin-born Oscar, two outsiders in London, had been firm friends ever since they met at the studio of the artist Frank Miles. Oscar, aged twenty-two, was a brilliant undergraduate at Magdalen College, Oxford, while Lillie, one year older almost to the day, had escaped the stifling confines of Jersey society by marrying Edward Langtry, an outwardly well-to-do, widowed Irish landowner, within six weeks of meeting him. Both were determined to defy the invisible conventions that marked them as outsiders. On reaching London, Lillie had abandoned her husband to his first love, alcohol, and made her way by means of her extraordinary beauty. Her timing was perfect: the technology that had transformed the printing industry allowed Miles to reproduce his portraits of her in the pages of newspapers and magazines, making her iconic.

Although Oscar was sexually attracted to beautiful young men for much, probably all, of his adult life, he was fascinated by beautiful young women too. He had a tendency to idealise their beauty, to be intimidated by it even, and he regarded Lillie's beauty as 'a form of genius'. His description of her lovely face is characteristically florid:

> Pure Greek it is, with the grave low forehead, the exquisitely arched brow; the noble chiselling of the mouth, shaped as if it were the mouthpiece of an instrument of music; the supreme and splendid curve of the cheek; the augustly pillared throat which bears it all: it is Greek, because the lines which compose it are so definite and so strong, and yet so exquisitely harmonised that the effect is one of simple loveliness purely: Greek, because its essence and its quality, as is the quality of music and of architecture, is that of beauty based on absolutely mathematical laws.[17]

It is often assumed that Oscar Wilde used the adjective 'Greek' to refer to male beauty or homosexual love. Clearly, this was not always the case.

Tall, broad-hipped and full-bosomed, with a luminescent complexion and golden-brown hair, Lillie was so beautiful, and had such mysterious origins, that she was allowed to bypass convention and gain entry into the most exclusive social circles in London. Oscar, who won similar passage by means of his wit, was a fixture at her side. Jilted by another beautiful young woman just two years earlier, he was on the rebound and it was widely speculated in the press, and, more credibly, by his biographer and friend Vincent O'Sullivan, that Lillie and he were lovers. This seems unlikely. Although she admired 'the splendour of his great, eager eyes', Lillie was not attracted by Oscar's appearance. What drew her to him was his 'remarkably fascinating and compelling personality'. Of this, she recalled:

> . . . there was about him an enthusiasm singularly captivating. He had one of the most alluring voices that I have ever listened to, round and soft, and full of variety and expression, and the cleverness of his remarks received added value from his manner of delivering them.[18]

When Oscar set up home with Frank Miles in 1879, Lillie and he became inseparable. Laura Troubridge, who at one time believed herself 'awfully in love' with Oscar, described his sitting room as if it was a shrine: 'a mass of white lilies, photos of Mrs. Langtry, peacock feather screens and coloured pots, pictures of various merit'.[19] Lillie lent Oscar the portrait that Edward Poynter had painted of her, and he displayed it on an easel at one end of his room, like an altar. His devotion was canny. As she was the most talked-about woman in London, he, as her escort, became one of the most talked-about men.

Oscar fêted the women he admired with flowers and sonnets written in their honour. For years, Lillie bore the brunt of his attentions. To her bemusement, she would spot him wandering the streets of her fashionable Park Lane neighbourhood; she imagined he was 'probably investing me with every quality I never possessed'.[20] He called to see her almost every day, often presenting her with a solitary amaryllis or Jersey Lily, which he would purchase in the Covent Garden flower market before walking the length of Piccadilly to her Park Lane home.* Such aesthetic behaviour attracted the attention of the librettist W. S. Gilbert, who incorporated it into *Patience*, a comic opera devised with his partner, composer Arthur Sullivan:

---

* Oscar later claimed, 'the difficult thing to achieve was to make people believe that I had done it', yet Lillie is adamant that he did present her with flowers (*The Days I Knew*, p. 82).

> Though the Philistines may jostle
> You will rank as an apostle
>   In the high aesthetic band
> If you walk down Piccadilly
> With a poppy or a lily
>   In your medieval hand

Oscar promised to write sonnets to Lillie until she was ninety. He became consumed with the task of composing a poem in her honour, and produced 'The New Helen', which was published in the society newspaper, *The World*. In all, she inspired half a dozen sonnets, including the florid 'Roses and Rue (To L.L.)'. His was a very public courtship. Naturally, all this adoration attracted the attention of the acerbic writers at *Punch*, who lampooned him mercilessly. He may have hoped for this outcome. In a fanciful review of Lillie as Lady Macbeth, *Punch* imagined that her performance:

> . . . sent a thrill of excitement through the audience, and provoked an impromptu sonnet from the trembling lips of Mr. Oscar Wilde, who fainted with ecstasy, and was carried out by the attendants.[21]

There was a serious side to their relationship. William Corbet le Breton, the enlightened Dean of Jersey, had allowed his only daughter to take lessons with her six brothers and Lillie was proficient in Latin, Greek, mathematics, German, French, music and art. She was exceptionally bright and eager to learn, and she found in Oscar a 'kind tutor' who had just taken a double first at Oxford. Like his mother, he firmly believed that women could, and should, be educated. They took to attending Sir Charles Newton's lectures on Greek antiquities at King's College, where they were greeted each morning by the cheers of their fellow students. When Oscar introduced Lillie to John Ruskin, then Slade Professor of Fine Art at Oxford, for the first time in their friendship she saw him adopt an unfamiliar attitude of 'extreme reverence and humility'.[22] She was one of the few who were privy to his true, and not in any way trivial, nature.

Over time, Oscar's increasingly outlandish adulation became tiresome to Lillie, prompting her to conclude, astutely, that: 'although Wilde had a keen sense of the ridiculous, he sometimes unconsciously bordered thereon himself'.[23] This observation followed his insistence on sleeping on her doorstep one evening while she was out, causing a drunken Edward Langtry to: 'put an end to his poetic dreams by tripping over him'.[24] At times Lillie could be hurtful. One evening, while seated in her box in the theatre, she noticed a commotion in the stalls and observed Oscar being led away in tears by Frank Miles; he had been stung by her latest 'frank remark' and couldn't stand to see her there.

Like most of Oscar's women friends, Lillie had many admirers and her marital status proved no deterrent to the men who fêted her. The most illustrious of these was Bertie, Prince of Wales and eldest son of Queen Victoria, the man destined to be crowned Edward VII. He sidestepped his marriage to Princess Alexandra of Denmark to embark on a very public and unusually exclusive affair with Lillie, which endured for an unprecedented three years. Of course, this royal connection gave Oscar access to the uppermost echelons of British society, a remarkable opportunity for an ambitious young Dubliner whose mother had once campaigned for revolution against the Crown.

Although Lillie held Bertie's attention for longer than most women, once his patronage was withdrawn she found herself trapped in poverty and a loveless marriage with her reputation in tatters and creditors besieging her home. Painfully aware that she needed an occupation, she asked admirers to propose something suitable. Artist James McNeill Whistler suggested she might paint and Frank Miles, a keen gardener, proposed horticulture, prompting Oscar to protest that this would 'compel the Lily to tramp the fields in muddy boots'.[25] Oscar, who understood celebrity better than anyone, insisted that Lillie belonged on the stage and introduced her to Henrietta Hodson, an influential retired actress and theatre manager, known to him as 'Little Hettie'.[26]

Legend had it that Hodson, another deeply unconventional woman friend of Oscar's, was born amidst the sawdust of the orchestra pit at the Bower Saloon in Lambeth. Her mother, an actress and singer, was back on stage the following night. Hodson had fled an abusive marriage by the time she met Oscar, and was living in some style as the self-professed 'concubine' of the radical MP and newspaper magnate, Henry Du Pré Labouchère. By coincidence, it was 'Labby' who tabled the Criminal Law Amendment Act of 1885, known as the Labouchère Amendment, which made sexual relations between men, in private as well as in public, a criminal offence in Great Britain. This legislation was used to prosecute Oscar in 1895.

Hodson agreed to train Lillie and arranged to appear opposite her in a charity performance of a one-act, two-hander comedy called *A Fair Encounter* on the tiny stage of the Town Hall in Twickenham. Poor Lillie stumbled through her first performance and swore that it would also be her last. She had reckoned without the determination of the indomitable Henrietta, who signed her up to play Kate Hardcastle in a charity mat-inee performance of Goldsmith's *She Stoops to Conquer* in the Haymarket Theatre. Hodson was no fool: like Oscar, she realised that Lillie's popu-larity would ensure a packed theatre. Most audience members queued for hours outside the pit and gallery doors on a wintery afternoon in mid-December 1881. The critic in *The Times* confirmed that the house overflowed with rank, fashion, and celebrity, among them the Prince and Princess of Wales, and mentioned 'the enthusiastic applause which greeted Mrs. Langtry on her entrance'.[27] A more brutal assessment of her proficiency as an actress may have been encapsulated in this popular quip of the time: 'What is the difference between Madame Modjeska* and Lillie Langtry? The one is a Pole, and the other a Stick.'[28]

As ever, Lillie had influential male admirers. Essayist Abraham Hay-ward, commissioned by *The Times* to review her performance, gushed:

> The oldest playgoers, who had seen half a dozen Miss Hardcastles, were astonished at the ease with which she glided into the part, the accuracy of the conception, and the felicity of the execution throughout.

He concluded:

> As it was understood that her success or failure in this performance was to decide whether she would or would not adopt the stage as a profession, it was confidently assumed that the die was cast, and speculations are already afloat as to the next part she would play.[29]

Lillie, to her credit, embraced her new career with enthusiasm and professionalism. Although her celebrity status ensured she would always draw an audience, she persuaded François-Joseph Regnier, veteran of the Comédie-Française, Professor at the Conservatoire and the leading drama coach of the day, to take her on exclusively for three months. Her greatest success was achieved in North America, where she was aided by Oscar and completed thirteen lucrative tours, investing some of her newfound wealth in wineries and racing stables. In February 1890, Lillie returned to London to take over the management of the St James's Theatre for a season. Dogged by ill-health during her tenure, she took to calling it her 'unlucky theatre'. She was succeeded in 1881 by George Alexander.

---

* Helena Modjeska was a celebrated Polish actress and also a great friend to Oscar Wilde.

Lillie was an inspired choice for the role of Mrs Erlynne, as her notoriety would generate huge publicity and her presence on stage would ensure full houses at every performance. She also had the perfect look and reputation to play a woman described in the second act as: 'an *édition de luxe* of a wicked French novel, meant specially for the English market'. Ironically, given her stated reason for rejecting the role, she was also the mother of a rarely acknowledged daughter. In a letter to an unknown correspondent, Oscar disclosed the inspiration for *Lady Windermere's Fan*:

> The psychological idea that suggested to me the play is this. A woman who has had a child, but never known the passion of maternity (there are such women), suddenly sees the child she has abandoned falling over a precipice.[30]

Lillie hid her illicit pregnancy during the latter half of 1890, and spent the final weeks of her confinement on the island of Jersey. Although it was rumoured that the Prince of Wales's private physician was in attendance when her daughter, Jeanne-Marie, was born in Paris on 8 March 1881, Bertie was not the father of Lillie's baby. After they parted, Lillie had become involved with Arthur Jones, an old friend from Jersey. She also embarked on a consolatory affair with Prince Louis of Battenberg, and she allowed him to believe that he was Jeanne-Marie's father. Although he played no part in her life, Louis agreed to provide a settlement for the young girl, who was raised by her grandmother and encouraged to believe that she was the daughter of one of the six Langtry boys. She called Lillie '*ma tante*' until she was fourteen years old.

It was not uncommon in Victorian England for women with means to hide their children. Actresses, as working women, were considered little removed from prostitutes and judged accordingly: Ellen Terry gave her two children, born into a loving and stable, although not marital, relationship, a false surname; it was widely assumed that the happily married Mrs Pat Campbell lived a debauched lifestyle similar to Paula Tanqueray, a character she played; and only Sarah Bernhardt, a Frenchwoman, took pride in introducing her son as Maurice Bernhardt. Ironically, this expectation that actresses would behave badly gave them a measure of freedom not afforded to other women, who were held rigidly to the double standard.

Although she felt unable to acknowledge her daughter publically, Lillie entrusted her secret to a small circle of close friends, and Oscar, one of her closest confidantes, must have known about Jeanne-Marie. Lillie may not have had 'a grown-up daughter', but she was unquestionably a clandestine mother. Perhaps Oscar was too hard on her. He was intrigued by the notion of a woman who had no interest in her child, and had his Mrs Erlynne play no part in her daughter's upbringing. Yet, Lillie did support Jeanne-Marie and had some involvement in her life. Her motivation for hiding her daughter had more to do with the consequences of being discovered, both by a judgemental public and by her estranged husband, Edward, who could make life very difficult for her.

Perhaps she should have been pleased that Oscar made Mrs Erlynne heroic. Since his 'bad mother' was permitted to pursue the life she desired without suffering the dire consequences that should have been her due, his play was profoundly subversive: 'I have lived childless – I want to live childless still', she declares. Yet, he was pragmatic enough to ensure that she did so overseas. The lines that are most condemnatory of the hypocritical rules considered nonsensical by Oscar but which women were expected to adhere to at that time, are delivered by Margaret Erlynne when she mocks her son-in-law:

> I suppose, Windermere, you would like me to retire into a convent, or become a hospital nurse, or something of that kind, as people do in silly modern novels. That is stupid of you, Arthur; in real life we don't do such things – not as long as we have any good looks left, at any rate. No – what consoles one nowadays is not repentance, but pleasure. Repentance is quite out of date. And besides, if a woman really repents, she has to go to a bad dressmaker, otherwise no one believes in her. And nothing in the world would induce me to do that. No, I am going to pass entirely out of your two lives. My coming into them has been a mistake – I discovered that last night.

The version of Margaret Erlynne that appeared onstage in the St James's Theatre that first night was a less forthright version of the character outlined in earlier drafts, yet she remained shocking nonetheless.[31] In *Lady Windermere's Fan*, Oscar called into question a fundamental tenet of Victorian morality, that motherhood was a woman's highest calling, by having Margaret Erlynne say of the twenty-one-year-old daughter she had abandoned as a baby: 'She's grown quite pretty. The last time I saw her – twenty years ago, she was a fright in flannel. Positive fright, I assure you'. When Windermere reminds her that she was once the 'young innocent-looking girl with beautiful dark hair' in the miniature treasured by his wife, her disdainful response is: 'Dark hair and an innocent expression were the fashion then, Windermere!' She justifies her decision to be true to herself by declaring:

There are moments when one has to choose between living one's own life, fully, entirely, completely – or dragging out some false, shallow, degrading existence that the world in its hypocrisy demands.

That sentiment, more than any other, would appear to encapsulate Oscar's feelings at that time.

Most shocking of all is the assertion, in the very last line of the play, made by an unwitting daughter to describe her mother, who is black-mailing her husband and who, up until then, she had treated as a social pariah, that she is 'a very good woman'. This statement is a response to Mrs Erlynne's risky and selfless intervention, which prevents Lady Windermere from leaving a safe and stable marriage, and losing her position in society as a result. Mrs Erlynne is wiser and wittier than any other character in the play, and she alone enjoys perfect insight into all that has unfolded. She has had to work tirelessly and employ all of her considerable ingenuity in order to earn her readmittence into society and, even at that, she is obliged to live overseas. It is clear to her that her daughter, Lady Windermere, also the mother of a young child, lacks the capacity to do the same: 'You don't know what it is', she warns her, 'to fall into the pit, to be despised, mocked, abandoned, sneered at – to be an outcast! . . . one pays for one's sins, and then one pays again, and all one's life one pays'. These chilling and prophetic words foreshadowed Oscar's own isolation. Mrs Erlynne's actions have a transforming effect on her daughter, turning her from a strict moralist into a far more humane woman who learns that a single transgression is not indicative of a bad character, and that a sinner can be noble too. Their actions promote solidarity among women, something that was all too often lacking in Victorian society.

Although Oscar wrote Mrs Erlynne incredibly sympathetically, the strong bond that once existed between Lillie and he was damaged irreparably. Perhaps this was because he had betrayed her trust or perhaps they had simply grown apart. In *The Days I Knew*, published three decades later, while admitting that Oscar had once been brilliant, Lillie was damning in her summation:

> It seemed to me, however, that he gradually grew less spontaneous and more laboured in his conversation as he became the fashion, which was not to be wondered at when he was counted on to be the life of every after-noon tea, and was expected to supply a bon mot between every mouthful at dinner.[32]

Lillie acknowledged Jeanne-Marie after Edward Langtry's death, but allowed her to believe that Edward had been her father. Although they had lived separately for years, she had provided him with an allowance on the understanding that he would keep his distance. Over time, he fell deeper into drunkenness until, in October 1897, he was discovered wandering 'bruised and dazed' in the vicinity of Crewe railway station, having returned from Dublin by steamer. Judged to be demented, he was committed to the Asylum for the Insane in Chester, where he died nine days later. Jeanne-Marie was eighteen and about to be married before she discovered her father's 'true' identity, and it was not Lillie who told her but the waspish-tongued Margot Asquith. She felt horribly betrayed and her relationship with her mother, always fractured, was never repaired.

This was not Oscar's experience of motherhood. His wife was devoted to their sons and his relationship with his own mother, Lady Jane Wilde, was one of deep love, mutual admiration and profound respect. He was proud of her considerable intellect and appreciative of her wit. Through her example he understood that women could be just as creative, intelligent and resourceful as men. More pertinent perhaps was his admiration for her absolute devotion to his father and her willingness to accommodate all of his foibles and indiscretions. The touching inscription Oscar wrote in the copy of *Lady Windermere's Fan* he presented to his mother reads: 'To my dear wonderful mother with all my love, Oscar Wilde '93'. When she had heard that the provisional title of his play was 'A Good Woman', she wrote immediately to express her disapproval: 'I do not like it– "A Good Woman". It is mawkish. No one cares for a good woman. "A Noble Woman" would be better'.[33]

Jane Wilde was a very noble woman indeed: a poet, an essayist, an accomplished linguist, a campaigner for liberty and for women's rights, a wit, a beauty, and a very loving wife and mother. The poet William Butler Yeats, who knew her well, said of her:

> When one listens to her and remembers that Sir William Wilde was in his day a famous raconteur, one finds it no way wonderful that Oscar Wilde should be the most finished talker of our time.[34]

Oscar claimed that she 'knew life as a whole'.[35] She had a profound influence on his writing, and on his life. In order to understand this one must look back to Ireland in the 1830s, when Jane Francesca Elgee was agitating for revolution in the politically turbulent city of Dublin.

Chapter 2

THE PRECOCIOUS MISS ELGEE

She is quite a genius, and thoroughly aware of it.
SIR WILLIAM ROWAN HAMILTON of his friend Jane Wilde[1]

This could of course be said of any mother and her son but, truly, without Jane there would be no Oscar as we know him. Since time began, society has expressed a fear that too much motherly love and protection may make a son less manly, while not enough may make him cold. Jane Wilde loved her children dearly and demonstrably. She left her mark by means of the force of her personality and the influence she brought to bear on every aspect of their lives. Through her wit, intelligence and innate sense of social justice she gifted them an incomparable role model. Yet, through her supreme self-belief, her worship of genius above all else, and her indomitable faith in their superiority, she may have set both up for a fall. She was wonderful but she was deeply unconventional and she lived in an age when conformity, particularly for women, was insisted upon.

Throughout her life, Jane Francesca Agnez Elgee* was in the habit of deducting several years from her age, a practice adopted by her son Oscar, who damaged his credibility by lying about his age under oath during the libel action he took against John Sholto Douglas, 9th *Marquess of Queensberry* in 1895.[2] When asserting a tenuous claim to a share in the estate of her first cousin Sir Robert John le Mesurier McClure, discoverer of the Northwest Passage,† Jane insisted that, at the time of her birth, it had been neither fashionable nor compulsory to record the arrival of Ireland's newest citizens.[3] During the census of 1891, she recorded her

---

* This is how she signed herself in the Cavers Manse visitors' book on 24 August 1847.
† It seems Robert McClure and his widowed mother, Jane, lived with his grandfather Rev. John Elgee in Wexford until he was four years old. His mother had married, given birth and been widowed, all by the age of eighteen. Jane Wilde's bid was unsuccessful. She received a letter from her cousin, solicitor Richard Waddy Elgee, refuting her claim and confirming that the estate had been divided equally between seventeen claimants.

age as sixty-eight at her last birthday, and, if pressed, she would admit, reluctantly, that she had been born in 1826, although this seemed unlikely, since her father, Charles Elgee, had died two years earlier. Most biographers accept as accurate her application for a grant from the Royal Literary Fund, when she gave her date of birth as 27 December 1821. Her request for £100 met with the approval of the trustees.[4]

What is clear is that Jane could not always be relied upon to be truthful. In one of her wilder flights of fancy, she claimed Elgee was a corruption of the sixteenth-century Italian surname Algiati. By insisting that Algiati was a version of Alighieri, she argued an unconvincing connection to Dante Alighieri, author of *The Divine Comedy*. In her correspondence with Henry Wadsworth Longfellow, translator of Dante's works, she signed herself 'Francesca Speranza Wilde', possibly to sustain the illusion of exotic, Italianate origins. Her connection with the great American poet began when she read an extract from 'The White Czar', and asked an acquaintance in Boston to send her a copy. Instead, she received both the poem and an 'interesting letter' from Longfellow himself.[5] In 1877, when *The Philadelphia Press* published 'Ave Caesar', a poem Jane wrote to mark Longfellow's seventieth birthday, it lauded her work as 'worthy of the theme' and a 'general and generous tribute to the genius of our great poet'.[6] Jane was celebrated long before Oscar.

Although she, like he, felt entitled to move in the most illustrious circles, any connection with Dante seems highly improbable; her true origins were quite mundane. Her great-grandfather Charles Elgee, a bricklayer from County Durham, arrived in the town of Dundalk, in County Louth, with his brother William, a carpenter, during the Irish building boom of the 1730s. Both prospered.[*] Charles and his wife, Alice, a local woman, had eight children and their youngest son, John, the sole surviving boy of three born to them, attended Trinity College, Dublin, where he was awarded a scholarship. Afterwards, he entered the church and was posted to Wexford where he married Jane Waddy in December 1782. Jane's father, Charles, the first child of seven, was born to them in 1783.

John Elgee, Rector of Wexford by then, almost lost his life during the rising of 1798, when his home was occupied by a bloodthirsty band of local pikemen. Although many Protestant clergymen and their families

---

* William was commissioned to build the County Court House in Dundalk and is believed to have laid out Market Square at the same time; it is overlooked by Elgee Buildings to this day.

were murdered at that time, the Elgee family was spared; otherwise there would never have been an Oscar Wilde. Local historians attributed this act of mercy to the gratitude of a former prisoner to whom Elgee had shown kindness in his role as inspector of the local gaol.[7]

Jane's version of events was as follows:

> On the day the rebels entered Wexford, the rector Archdeacon Elgee, my grandfather, assembled a few of his parishioners in the church to partake of the sacrament together, knowing that a dreadful death awaited them. On his return, the rebels were already forcing their way into his house; they seized him, and the pikes were already at his breast, when a man stepped forth and told of some great act of kindness which the Archdeacon had shown his family.
>
> In an instant the feeling changed, and the leader gave orders that the Archdeacon and all that belonged to him should be held safe from harm. A rebel guard was set over his house and not a single act of violence was permitted.
>
> But that same evening all the leading gentlemen of the town were dragged from their houses and piked by the rebels upon Wexford Bridge.[8]

Rector Elgee, widely admired, was appointed Mayor of Wexford in 1802 and elevated to Archdeacon of Leighlin in 1804. Jane was little more than a baby when he died in 1823. A tribute in the *Waterford Mirror* lamented the passing of a man who had 'died universally regretted – as he had lived beloved by all his parishioners'.[9]

On 23 December 1809, Jane's father, Charles, who practiced as a solicitor from premises at 8 Essex Bridge in Dublin, married the beautiful Sarah Kingsbury in the Church of St Iberius on North Main Street, Wexford. Sarah came from a prosperous Dublin family. Her grandfather, Dr Thomas Kingsbury, a former President of the Royal College of Physicians, was a close friend to Dean Jonathan Swift and was said to have been privy to the great man's last lucid conversation when he ministered to him during his final illness. Sarah's father, also Thomas, was Vicar of Kildare and held the secular post of Commissioner of Bankruptcy. Her only brother, yet another Thomas, was Archdeacon of Killala in County Mayo. Sarah's oldest sister, Elizabeth, married Sir Charles Montague Ormsby, MP for Carlow from 1801 to 1806. As Ormsby was awarded a baronetcy in 1812, the couple's two sons — Jane's first cousins — became baronets in succession.

The extent of Jane's rebellious nature can be measured by the distance she moved from her entrenched family values. The Kingsbury family was staunchly protestant and strongly supportive of the Act of Union,* which proved disastrous for Ireland and for the city of Dublin in particular. With the benefit of hindsight, Jane wrote:

> After the Union, the palaces of the nobles were left desolate; wealth, spirit, enterprise, all the brilliancy of social and intellectual life vanished from the capital; the various trades died out one by one; literature became extinct; the publishing trade, once so vigorous and flourishing, almost entirely disappeared; the currents of thought and energy set to London, and have continued to flow there ever since, draining the life-blood of Ireland to fill the veins of England, and all that makes a nation great and strong and self-respecting was annihilated.[10]

Sarah had another sister, Henrietta, who appears to have been more like Jane. An acclaimed singer who trained with Angelica Catalini, the leading soprano of the day, she married her childhood sweetheart Charles Maturin, cleric, playwright and gothic novelist. Maturin seemed tremendously proud of his beautiful, talented wife and, although money was often scarce, their marriage was an exceptionally happy and eccentric one. When Sir Thomas Charles Morgan, whose novelist wife, Sydney Owenson shared a publisher with Maturin, handed the couple £50 to see them through a particularly challenging time, they used it to throw a lavish party, receiving their guests while seated on an 'old theatrical property throne under a canopy of crimson velvet'.[11] Maturin was successful but he lost what fortune he had when he stood surety for a relative who went bankrupt. He died in 1824, aged just forty-four, leaving Henrietta with few resources and four young children to care for. Although Jane scarcely knew him, she admired Maturin enormously and displayed a bust of him in her home at 1 Merrion Square. She passed this admiration on to Oscar: traces of Maturin's *Melmoth the Wanderer* are evident in *The Picture of Dorian Gray*, and he adopted the pseudonym Sebastian Melmoth towards the end of his life.

Sarah Kingsbury's marriage was a turbulent affair and the early years, during which three of her four children were born,† were characterised by regular changes of address. Charles experienced financial difficulties and a deed registered on 11 November 1814, granting him £130 from his

---

* The Act, which came into effect on 1 January 1801, centralised administrative power in Westminster.
† They were Emily Thomasine (1811), John Kingsbury (1812) and Frances, who died in infancy (1815).

wife's inheritance to discharge his debts, contained an ominous clause in which he agreed not to touch his wife's assets should they decide to separate. This was necessary, since until the passing of the Married Women's Property Act 1882, English law defined a wife as subordinate to her husband and stripped her of her legal identity. Jane was born towards the end of this unstable marriage, and evidence suggests that the family was living in County Wexford at the time.[12] The circumstances of Charles Elgee's early death, scarcely eighteen months later, are shrouded in mystery. The last known record of him is an obituary published in the *Freeman's Journal* on 4 February 1825:

> On the 13th August last, at Bangalore, in the East Indies, Charles Elgee, Esq., eldest son of the late venerable Archdeacon Elgee, of Wexford.[13]

It is not known why Charles travelled to India, although he may have had 'some connection with the East-India Company'.[14]

The effect on Jane of growing up in a household without a father can only be imagined, but it must have coloured her opinion of marriage and family life. A strong and supremely confident woman, she was to show an extraordinary level of devotion to her own husband, accommodating his many foibles, including infidelity. This was the model of a happy marriage – and it undoubtedly was happy – that Oscar grew up with. Little wonder he wished for something similar from his own. It is telling that, when asked what the distinguishing characteristic of a wife should be, he quipped, 'devotion to her husband'.[15]

As Jane rarely spoke about her childhood and never about her father, the whereabouts of Sarah and her three surviving children after 1822 are unclear. They may have been living in Wexford and Sarah would appear to have taken charge of their education.* In 1828, when Jane's brother, John Kingsbury Elgee entered Trinity College, Dublin, aged just fifteen, he wrote 'Wexford' in the column reserved for 'place of birth/residence'.[16] He left the university without taking his degree on account of 'domestic difficulties'. Immediately afterwards, he married Dubliner Matilda Duff, who was ten years his senior and their daughter, Eliza, was born when her father was just eighteen.[17] All three left for Louisiana the following year, where John became a prominent member of the legal profession, and a

---

* An obituary for John Kingsbury Elgee's son, Charles Le Doux Elgee, contained in the *Report of the Secretary, Class of 1856, Harvard* (Boston, Geo. C. Rand & Avery, 1865, p. 16) reported: 'John was educated in his early youth by his mother, until, at the age of fifteen, he entered the University of Dublin.

key player on the Confederate side of the civil war.[18] He died a wealthy man.[*]

By 1843 Jane and her mother were living as tenants above a wax and tallow chandlers shop at 34 Leeson Street. At one point, Emily's husband Captain Samuel Warren of the 65th Regiment,[†] suggested to his wife that her mother and sister Jane, who he called 'the rebel', might come and live with them in England, but they remained in Dublin.[19] Emily disapproved of Jane's nationalist leanings, a situation that Oscar and his mother joked about in early letters; both pretended not to mind when they were disapproved of, he more so than she.[20] Although she was bright and eager to learn, Jane's education was haphazard and she was largely left to her own devices. She had little option: Trinity College, Dublin, which accepted her brother, did not admit its first woman student until 1904. In 1895, the board of the university, under increasing pressure to accommodate women students, warned:

> If a female had once passed the gate, it would be practically impossible to watch what buildings or what chambers she might enter, or how long she might remain there.[21]

Jane tried to compensate for the deficiencies in the system by educating herself. She confirmed this in an interview she gave to *Hearth and Home Magazine* towards the end of her life:

> I was always very fond of study, and of books. My favourite study was languages. I succeeded in mastering ten of the European languages. Till my eighteenth year I never wrote anything. All my time was given to study.[22]

---

* John Kingsbury Elgee died in 1864 and left behind a considerable fortune. While he made provision for his sister Emily and his old Nurse Bolger, who lived in Wexford, he left nothing for Jane. There may have been nothing sinister in this. Emily was widowed while Jane was married to a prominent and successful man. She wore mourning dress for him, even though she hated black, considering it, 'unlovely and unbecoming to everyone' (*Social Studies*, Ward & Downey 1893, p. 114).

† Emily Elgee's late husband was Captain Samuel Warren, of the 65th Regiment and they spent much of his army career overseas. He was appointed Deputy Quartermaster General of Jamaica in 1842, and three of their four children were born in what was then the British West Indies. Emily survived her husband by more than two decades and died in Brighton on 9 November 1881. Although Jane was living in London at the time, the sisters had little to do with each other.

It is extraordinary to think that the woman who would one day be described as 'the most ardent and hot-headed of nationalists' demonstrated little interest in politics in her youth and described herself as 'quite indifferent to the national movement'.[23] Later, she admitted: 'Nationality was certainly the first awakener of any mental power of genius within me, and the strongest sentiments of my intellectual life'. She qualified this by stating, 'but the present state of Irish affairs requires the strong guiding hand of men, there is no place anymore for the more passionate aspirations of a woman's nature'.[24] This was characteristic of Jane's unique brand of proto-feminism. Surely, she was aware of the desperate and steadily worsening plight of the many thousands of Irish tenant farmers exploited by absentee landlords who cared only for profit and had no interest in reform.

Daniel O'Connell, the 'Great Liberator', in his seventies by then, pinned his fading hopes on an alliance with the Whig party. Several of his followers, Protestant and Catholic, frustrated by the lack of reform, became convinced that the key to autonomy was the fostering of a proud, non-sectarian sense of nationhood amongst Ireland's beleaguered population. In 1842, three members of this 'Young Ireland' movement founded *The Nation*, a weekly newspaper promoting Irish history and culture. They were: Thomas Osborne Davis, the Cork-born Protestant son of a British Army surgeon, and a graduate of Trinity College, Dublin; John Blake Dillon, a Catholic barrister from County Mayo; and Charles Gavan Duffy, a Catholic journalist and the son of a shopkeeper from County Monaghan. Duffy, the most experienced, was appointed editor.

A century later, historian T. F. O'Sullivan wrote of *The Nation*:

> There has never been published in this, or any other country, a journal, which was imbued with higher ideals of nationality, which attracted such a brilliant band of writers in prose and verse, which inspired such widespread enthusiasm, or which exercised a greater influence over all classes of its readers, which after a time included every section of the community.[25]

Contributions were invited from sympathetic readers, and the most eye-catching of these came from Jane Elgee, who was in her early twenties by then. Although the impetus for Jane's decision to join the ranks of the Young Irelanders remains unclear, it is often attributed to her reaction to the death of Thomas Davis, aged thirty, from scarlet fever. Regarded by many as the most talented and passionate of the Young Irelanders, his loss was a terrible blow to the movement.

When the poet W. B. Yeats delivered a speech marking the centenary of Davis's birth on 20 November 1914, he included an account, which he claimed came directly from Jane, of how she had happened upon Davis's funeral procession in September 1845.[26] Impressed that a poet with such high ideals could provoke this outpouring of adulation and grief, she decided to embrace his cause. Oscar recounted a similar version during a lecture he delivered to the Irish Diaspora in San Francisco in 1882, although he had his mother watching Davis's funeral from the window of her home, which was impossible, since it didn't pass that way; he never let the facts stand in the way of a dramatic story.[27] Jane claimed her interest was piqued when she read a monthly shilling volume from *The Library of Ireland*,* a sister publication to *The Nation* and the brainchild of Davis, who she admired as, 'an incarnation of passionate genius – the most powerful of the poets, the most brilliant of the essayists'.[28]

Davis's message of reconciliation between Protestant and Catholic and his advocacy of a non-secular education for all appealed to Jane, since she too believed that a lack of education and an overreliance on religion was keeping the peasantry down: 'The world above is a reality to the Irish peasant,' she wrote:

> No people have more intense faith in the unseen. It is their religious temperament, so childlike in its simplicity and trust, that alone makes their life of privation endurable, and enables them to meet all sorrows, even death itself, with the pathetic fatalism expressed in the phrase so often heard from peasant lips, "It was the will of God."[29]

Awakened to her country's tragic history, she discovered that this newfound passion had unlocked her creativity: 'Once I had caught the national spirit, all the literature of Irish wrongs and sufferings had an enthralling interest for me,' she declared, 'then it was that I discovered that I could write poetry.'[30]

The first poem from the pen of 'Speranza'† was 'The Holy War', translated from a German original and published in *The Nation* on 21 February 1846. Jane signed the accompanying letter 'John Fanshaw Ellis',

---

* The book in question is believed to have been *The Spirit of the Nation (1845)*, a collection of ballads and songs composed by contributors to *The Nation*.

† The Italian word for hope, and described by Jane as her 'nom de guerre, or rather nom de vers'. Her motto was 'Fidanza, Speranza, Costanza', or Faith, Hope, Constancy.

a pseudonym adopted to conceal her activities from her unsympathetic family; she may also have assumed, with good reason, that a male contributor would be looked upon more favourably. Impressed with his fiery new contributor, Duffy posted a message in the 'answers to correspondents' section, asking that 'he' make himself known at the headquarters of the newspaper at 4 D'Olier Street; this was impossible of course. Jane described how her true identity was revealed:

> One day my uncle came into my room and found *The Nation* on my table. Then he accused me of contributing to it, declaring the while that such a seditious paper was fit only for the fire. The secret being out in my own family there was no longer much motive for concealment, and I gave my editor permission to call upon me.[31]

In his memoir *Four Years of Irish History 1845–1849*, Duffy recalled being introduced to '. . . a tall girl . . . whose stately carriage and figure, flashing brown eyes, and features cast in an heroic mould, seemed fit for the genius of poetry, or the spirit of revolution'.[32] Recognising in Jane, 'the spirit of Irish liberty embodied in a stately and beautiful woman', he became convinced that her reputation would one day rival that of Elizabeth Barrett Browning, a poet Oscar would also compare her to.[33] Jane, in turn, admired Duffy as:

> A man of the highest culture, of exquisite literary taste, and a clear and powerful writer, both in prose and verse, he was eminently fitted for guide and counsellor to all the young fiery intellects that composed his staff, while his winning manners and earnest sympathy with all that was noble and beautiful in literature and art gained their admiration and love.[34]

Although she maintained the pseudonyms Speranza and John Fanshaw Ellis, and wrote occasionally as 'Albanus', or simply 'A', Duffy knew Jane as 'Francesca J. Elgee'. He realised that her 'little scented notes, sealed with wax of a delicate hue and dainty device, represented a substantial force in Irish politics, the vehement will of a woman of genius'.[35] She had no other outlet but her pen: Irish women under 30 were not eligible to vote until equal suffrage was granted in 1922, when the Irish Free State was established. As it happens, the first female MP elected to Westminster was Jane's compatriot Countess Constance Markievicz in 1918, although she did not take her seat.

Jane's correspondence with Duffy could be playful, flirtatious even. On one occasion, she teased that she would 'embitter' his 'existence' by making him read a new poem but invited him to: '. . . illuminate your paper, or your cigar with it, which you please'.[36]

Duffy was not alone in his admiration for Jane. When Alexander Martin Sullivan took over at *The Nation* in 1855, he described her as:

> Young, beautiful, highly educated, endowed with rarest gifts of intellect, her personal attractions, her cultivated mind, her originality and force of character, made her a central figure in Dublin society.[37]

Although Jane's early poems were translations of suitably rousing verse from the original Russian, Turkish, Spanish, German, Italian and Portuguese, she soon gained the confidence to write poetry of her own. In 1847, she found a catastrophe to write about: Ireland's rich soil yielded an abundance of high-quality grain, meat and dairy products, and land-owners sold the bulk of their produce overseas. When the price of grain became artificially inflated during the campaigns against the French, it was designated a cash crop for export. At the same time, the Irish popula-tion was growing inexorably, from 5 million in 1800 to in excess of 8 mil-lion by 1841. The teeming families that farmed thousands of subdivided smallholdings, half of them covering less than five acres, were required to survive on the potato crop alone. When the blight that ravaged America in 1842 crossed the Atlantic in the years that followed, the subsistence farmers of Ireland were hardest hit. Harsh governance and the laissez-faire trading policies adopted in Westminster exacerbated the problem, leading to famine in one of the most fertile countries in the world.

Jane's words had a galvanizing effect: 'a nation is arising from her long and ghastly swoon', she declared.[38] In 'The Lament', she gave voice to the Young Irelanders' criticism of the increasingly ineffectual Daniel O'Connell: 'gone from us . . . dead to us . . . he whom we worshipped', she wrote. In 'The Voice of the Poor', she railed against the horrors of famine, writing, 'before us die our brothers of starvation'; 'The Famine Year' condemned the arrival of 'stately ships to bear our food away'; 'The Exodus' lamented the 'million a decade' forced to flee their homeland. The most popular of Jane's compositions was 'The Brothers', a rousing ballad eulogising Henry and John Sheares, one a lawyer, the other a bar-rister, both United Irishmen hanged for their part in the rising of 1798. In tone and theme it shares much with her son's 'Ballad of Reading Gaol', and it was taken up by the street balladeers of Dublin.

Snow lay deep when the famine reached its height in February 1847, and a typhus epidemic raged uncontrollably. The non-interventionist policies adopted by the newly installed Whig government were proving disastrous, and the soup kitchens and relief works set up to help the starving population were woefully inadequate. As the country headed inexorably towards insurrection, Jane's contributions became increasingly provocative. Her poem, 'The Enigma', described how the living envied the dead as Ireland's abundance was 'taken to pander a foreigner's pride'. She lamented the loss of 'the young men, and strong men,' who 'starve and die, for want of bread in their own rich land'.

When the offices of *The Nation* were raided in July 1848, Charles Gavan Duffy was arrested and charged under the new Treason-Felony Act for publishing a newspaper article advocating the repeal of the Act of Union, a crime that carried the penalty of transportation. While he was in prison awaiting trial, he entrusted editorship of *The Nation* to his sister-in-law, Margaret Callan, aided by Jane. On 22 July *The Nation* carried Jane's inflammatory poem, 'The Challenge to Ireland'. The following week, she wrote an unattributed leader titled 'Jacta Alea Est';* it was an unmistakable call-to-arms:

> O! for a hundred thousand muskets, glittering brightly in the light of Heaven, and the monumental barricades stretching across each of our noble streets made desolate by England . . .

As if this were not sufficiently treasonous, she beseeched:

> Is there one man that thinks that Ireland has not been sufficiently insulted, has not been sufficiently degraded in her honour and her rights, to justify her now in fiercely turning on her oppressor?

Duffy, languishing in his cell, deemed 'Jacta Alea Est' a rallying call so strong and unequivocal that it could have been issued, 'from the headquarters of the national army'.[39] The authorities reacted by destroying every copy they could seize and suppressing *The Nation* on the grounds of sedition.

When the Habeas Corpus Act was suspended, facilitating the arrest and detention of anyone suspected of plotting an uprising, the Young Irelanders, hopelessly ill-prepared, decided to act. They were not alone: 1848 was a year of revolutions. Shots rang out across Europe, starting with Sicily and spreading to Naples, before convulsing Paris, Vienna, Berlin, Prague, Budapest and Munich. William Smith O'Brien, a Harrow- and Cambridge- educated landowner from County Limerick, and a former

---

* The Die is Cast.

Westminster MP, headed the group that saw the only significant action in Ireland. He took to the roads, preaching revolution and gathering followers. By the time he reached Tipperary, he had 6,000 men, each one armed with a makeshift weapon, but they slunk back home once they realised that he couldn't feed them. Barely four-dozen remained when they encountered a unit of the Royal Irish Constabulary in the village of Ballingarry, in County Tipperary, on 30 July 1848. The constables took refuge in the home of Margaret McCormack, a widowed mother whose four young children were held hostage inside. A skirmish erupted but was quashed within hours and the whole affair earned the ignoble title, 'The Battle of the Widow McCormack's Cabbage Patch'.* The revolution lasted for little more than a week: '. . . Ballingarry killed us all. I have never laughed joyously since', Jane wrote.[40]

Afterwards, the British government flooded Ireland with thousands of additional troops. Decades later, when the crisis had passed and she could afford to be more flippant, although no less cutting, Jane described, with Swiftian satire, how:

> Fifty thousand soldiers were recently required in our little Ireland, only a hundred miles broad, to guard the granaries of the rich from the thin hands of the poor; and every potato was watched by a policeman, and every turnip by a dragoon, and no pig could go to market without an escort of cavalry.[41]

When Duffy was charged with the publication of 'Jacta Alea Est', Jane felt compelled to intervene. Various colourful accounts describe how she stood in the public gallery of the courtroom as the charge was read out and identified herself as the author.[42] The official trial report contradicts this. Isaac Butt QC, representing Duffy, informed the court that he could prove if required that this treasonous article had been written 'by one of the fairer sex,' adding that she was 'not perhaps a very formidable opponent to the whole military power of Great Britain'.[43] The charge was hastily dropped.† Jane enjoyed the notoriety: 'I think this piece of Heroism will make a good scene when I write my Life,' she quipped, but she was despondent at 'our grand Revolution ending in shielding itself with a lady's name'.[44] When Duffy revived *The Nation* in September 1848,

---

* Smith O'Brien's death sentence was commuted to transportation to Van Diemen's Land
† Duffy was tried six times in all, with each trial collapsing. He was released in April 1849.

Jane wrote a poem to mark the occasion, but she had lost her fire and so had he.[45]

As the Young Ireland movement disintegrated, Jane was left disillusioned. Her horror at the treatment of its leaders gives great insight into the high esteem in which she held these Irish intellectuals, men comparable in many ways to her son Oscar:

Yet these singers and scholars, these brilliant young orators and writers, who showed to what height Irish genius might rise if trained and guided, with their sublime ideal of nationhood and heroic means of action, were deemed more dangerous by England than even the assassin's knife; for enlightenment means independence.[46]

Decades later, when Oscar, with Jane's encouragement, employed his skills of oratory in the battle for his own freedom, he was as unsuccessful in the face of officialdom as they had been.

Her revolution over, Jane swapped sedition for literature, which she feared was 'fast dying out in Ireland', although, when it was suggested to her that a page of *The Nation* might be devoted to 'feminine contributions', her rapier response was: 'it probably would be the only page left unread'. She had strong views on such segregation: 'I know of no writing intended particularly for ladies that ever did them any good,' she exclaimed, 'I myself always shunned books and papers of this one-sided nature'. Throughout her life, Jane was bitter in her condemnation of the neglect of women: 'no one puts faith in the opinion of women', she wrote, '& justly, for from our education it is impossible we could possess all the requisites for political teachers'.[47]

Eager to find an outlet for her powerful intellect, Jane accepted a commission to translate *Sidonia von Bork* (1848), Wilhelm Meinhold's tale of the witchcraft trials of a seventeenth-century Pomeranian aristocrat. Her English version, *Sidonia the Sorceress*, published in 1849, gained cult status among the Pre-Raphaelites and inspired Edward Burne-Jones to paint twin portraits of Sidonia and her sister Clara. In 1893, William Morris's Kelmscott Press reprinted Jane's translation in a beautiful edition. Oscar's acceptance by this group had much to do with the high status afforded to his mother as translator of one of their key texts.

Although Jane followed up with a translation of Alphonse de Lamartine's *Pictures from the First French Revolution* (1850), she remained dissatisfied: 'Writing for money is a very dull thing compared to writing for a Revolution,' she told John Hilson, a Scottish friend, adding, 'I am

longing to light up another'.[48] Hilson was an important figure in her life.*
Although they met only once and for a very short time, their correspondence spanned three decades, and the letters she sent him were warm,
frank and often flirtatious. One gives great insight into her typical day:

> I rise at ten or often eleven, glide down to breakfast which mama has all
> arranged for me, find letters, papers, notes on the table awaiting me, some-
> times a Scotch postmark, very welcome that. Breakfast over, I plunge into
> my ink-bottle. Silence and solitude reign in the drawing room till 2 o'clock,
> for everyone knows I admit no visitor before that hour. It strikes – Up go
> books and papers, a general clearance of the table of all literary activities
> and I vanish to my chamber to dress. At three I descend, but visitors call
> at that hour, knowing I am visible. From that till five the day is utterly
> wasted, either with visitors, or visiting or shopping or some promenad-
> ing, complete idling, in fact, for I can never write effectively unless in the
> unceintured comfort of a Peignoir. We dine between five and six, after
> which I have the whole evening to myself. Mama takes a siesta till tea at
> eight o'clock. I read or write in my room, descend to tea, the eternal pen
> again or book until eleven o'clock when mama departs to rest – I to my
> room where the midnight lamp is seen burning by observant neighbours
> until three. In fact I have never the least inclination to lie down at night or
> to rise in the morning.[49]

She favoured rainy days, when she was left to her own devices.

Introspective by nature, Jane suffered from periods of debilitating low-
ness, describing these times as:

> Black, bleak and unutterably desolate, isolation, gloom, a horrible sense of
> loneliness, a despairing as if all the world were standing in sunlight, I alone
> condemned to darkness.[50]

She hated her 'idle life of ladyhood', and resented the 'vapid lives'
imposed on women.[51] Yet she believed that she was unique: 'the ladies of
Dublin care more for one valse with a moustached dragoon than for all
the literature of Europe put together', she complained.[52] Her own brand
of proto-feminist thinking is nowhere more evident than in an article she

---

* Hilson was a young Scottish writer and partner in a woollen tweed
manufacturing business. Jane began corresponding with him after she met him
in Scotland whilst visiting her second cousin Jean Renwick, whose father had
emigrated to Wexford. His identity was uncovered by Jean Muir as described in
'Speranza' & 'Gurth', *The Wildean* 21 July 2002.

wrote for *The Nation* in April 1850 on the role of women. Harnessing her finest revolutionary rhetoric, she implored the 'redundant female population' who led lives of 'vacuity, inanity, vanity, absurdity and idleness', to 'combine amongst themselves to organize some noble vocation that would make them independent of commercial marriage', and she raged:

> Women truly need much to be done for them. At present they have neither dignity nor position. All avenues to wealth and rank are closed to them. The state takes no notice of their existence except to injure them by its laws.[53]

Little wonder novelist William Carleton, a man who admired the 'great ocean of her soul', described Jane as 'the most extraordinary prodigy of a female that this country, or perhaps any other, has ever produced'.[54] Her musings on gender may have influenced Oscar too. In his Oxford notebooks, he made observations about the erosion of traditional gender roles: '[m]anliness has become quite effeminate', he wrote, 'Only women are manly nowadays'.[55]

Fortunately, Jane had an aptitude for reinventing herself: 'How many lives we live in life!' she exclaimed.[56] Embracing her celebrity status, she threw herself into the social whirl of balls and theatre that characterised mid-century Dublin life. Fashion dictated an abundance of flounces and frills, with bright colours, elaborate headdresses and long trailing ribbons; Jane embraced this melange and never gave it up. She was uncharacteristically and inaccurately modest about her own appearance, and valued brains over looks. 'Beauty is the grand characteristic of the Dublin Belles', she wrote, 'so in that department I leave them undisturbed in possession of their domain and am contented with undisputed sovereignty in mine'.[57]

Yet, she remained dissatisfied: 'I should like to rage through life,' she told John Hilson, 'this orthodox creeping is too tame for me – ah, this wild ambitious nature of mine'.[58] At twenty-eight, when she ought to have been looking for a husband, Jane showed little interest in marriage and decried an education system that prepared girls for 'husband worship' alone.[59] She realised she would struggle to find a worthy mate: '. . . in love I like to feel myself a slave', she told John Hilson, 'the difficulty is to find anyone capable of ruling me. I love them when I feel their power'.[60] Literary men attracted her, particularly those who admired her in turn. When she wrote a glowing review of *The Beauties of the Boyne, and its Tributary, the Blackwater* for *The Nation* in September 1849, it would not have escaped her notice that this book included a quotation from 'Ruins', a poem by Speranza. The 'accomplished author' was Dr William Wilde.[61]

Chapter 3

TAMING SPERANZA

Had she married a man of inferior mind he would have dwindled down into insignificance or their struggle for superiority would have been terrific.
    JOHN ELGEE, writing about his niece Jane[1]

Shortly after eight o'clock on the morning of Wednesday, 12 November 1851, a carriage brought Dr William Wilde and Jane's uncle John Elgee to the door of 34 Leeson Street, the home she had shared with her mother, recently deceased, for the past eight years. To the men's surprise, Jane was ready to leave, allowing them to reach St Peter's on Aungier Street,* her parish church, in time for a nine o'clock wedding. The modest ceremony that joined 'William R. Wilde Esq., F.R.C.S.' and 'Jane Francesca' was conducted by the groom's older brother, Reverend John M. Wilde. For the occasion, Jane had exchanged her mourning clothes for a 'very rich dress of Limerick lace' with matching veil worn under a head wreath of white flowers, but she was back in black by eleven o'clock that same morning.

Both bride and groom were well known in the capital, and their dozens of acquaintances would surely have delighted in witnessing the sealing of such a dynamic alliance, but a lavish wedding would have been inappropriate on account of Sarah's death. Describing the day to the bride's estranged sister, Emily, Elgee hinted that the couple had married a day earlier than expected and confirmed: 'nobody were present save our own party and the old hangers on of the church'. Perhaps they desired an auspicious start to their married life. An old folk rhyme beloved of Victorian brides advised: 'Wed on Wednesday, happy match'. Theirs was certainly happy, but it did not lack turbulence.

After a celebratory breakfast at the Glebe house, Elgee waved the newlyweds off on their short journey to the coastal village of Kingstown, now Dun Laoghaire, where they caught the steamer to Holyhead. Judging by his letter to Emily, he was determined to improve relations between

---

* This was the church where her literary uncle by marriage, Charles Maturin, served as Anglican Curate for the last eighteen years of his life.

the sisters: 'I don't want to see open war between you and them', he cautioned. Acknowledging that 'love of self' was a prominent feature of Jane's flamboyant character, he countered by insisting that she possessed, 'some heart' and, 'good impulses'. It reassured him that she chose for her husband a man she clearly liked and respected. 'Had she married a man of inferior mind he would have dwindled down into insignificance or their struggle for superiority would have been terrific', he warned.

William Wilde was an exceptional man and Jane would not have been content with anyone lesser. Three years earlier, she had told her friend John Hilson, 'My soul needs to worship; it seems the fulfilment of my being'.[2] Now, she described her impressive new husband to him:

> . . . he is a celebrity – a man eminent in his profession, of acute intellect and much learning, the best conversationalist in our metropolis, and author of many books, literary and scientific.[3]

The third son of a country doctor, William had followed his father into the medical profession rather than join his two older brothers in the church. He excelled at his training, rounding off his apprenticeship with a year of midwifery at the Rotunda Hospital, where he achieved the highest pass in the final examination. William's mentor, the eminent surgeon Dr Robert Graves, suggested that he fund further study overseas by accepting the post of personal physician to a tubercular Scottish merchant who planned to embark on a nine-month-long voyage around the Mediterranean. Afterwards, William published *The Narrative of a Voyage to Madeira, Tenerife, and Along the Shores of the Mediterranean*, a colourful and commercially successful account of his experiences.[4]

Letters of introduction supplied by his friend Maria Edgeworth, a prolific and respected writer, and an honorary member of the Royal Irish Academy, gave William access to the highest intellectual circles in Europe.* Having completed his medical training in London, Vienna, Munich, Prague, Dresden and Heidelberg, he returned to Dublin and operated a clinic from his home at 15 Westland Row; he also converted a disused stable into a dispensary for the treatment of eye and ear complaints afflicting the grateful poor of the city. In 1841, William was appointed Medical Commissioner for the Irish census, an onerous role that required a comprehensive audit of

---

* This was unusual for a woman. Edgeworth, however, was a key advisor to William Rowan Hamilton, President of the RIA, who was, in turn, a great friend to Jane Wilde.

the incidence of sickness and disease across the island. Three years later, he established St Mark's Hospital and Dispensary for Diseases of the Eye and Ear, the first hospital in Ireland to combine treatment of the eye and ear, and the first in the British Isles to teach aural surgery. He also co-founded and edited the highly respected *Dublin Quarterly Journal of Medical Science*. William Wilde combined medical eminence with a scholarly interest in the folk traditions of Ireland. He wrote books and papers on a wide variety of subjects: medical, ethnological, archaeological and historical.

At thirty-six, William was a worldly man who had fathered three children, each one acknowledged and supported by him. His son, Henry Wilson was thirteen at the time of his father's wedding and was commonly passed off as his nephew. His daughters, Emily, aged four, and her infant sister Mary lived under the care of his brother Ralph, Church of Ireland Rector at Drumsnat in County Monaghan. Although the identity of the mother, or mothers, of these children was never disclosed, a mysterious black-veiled woman was wont to appear at times of crisis and John Butler Yeats, who knew the Wilde family well, told his son William that the girls' mother kept a 'small black oak shop' in Dublin.[5] As public attitudes towards unmarried mothers were censorious, women often concealed their illegitimate children.

In Jane Elgee, William had found a worthy partner who was described by those who knew her as 'extremely attractive in appearance and brilliant in conversation'.[6] Poet Denis Florence McCarthy considered her 'gifted', but, 'terrible and beautiful as an Amazon'.[7] Statuesque at almost six feet tall, she towered over her slightly built husband, but their intellects were well matched if their appearances were not. Both were gifted linguists: while Jane spoke several European languages and was well respected as a translator of literary works, William acted as Secretary of Foreign Correspondence for the Royal Irish Academy. They shared a keen interest in ethnology and a love for their country, recording together and separately the folklore, customs and traditions of Ireland. William used the opportunity of the census to collect firsthand accounts from peasant families. In her introduction to his *Memoir of Gabriel Béranger*, which she completed after his death, Jane admired the way her husband, 'the *Docteur Mor* (the great Doctor as they called him)', had 'brought back joy and hope to many households' by treating the ailments of the poor in exchange for a story or an artefact.[8]

Although less overtly political than his wife, William abhorred the inequalities that persisted in Irish society and railed against the: 'unjust economy which the English Exchequer has ever pursued towards

Ireland'.[9] In his role as Medical Commissioner for the Irish census of 1841, and, later, as Assistant Commissioner for the census of 1851, he witnessed first-hand the devastation that had been wrought by the famine. Like Jane, he berated the landlords and governors of Ireland for failing to improve the lot of her citizens and despaired at the tide of emigration that had taken the most able-bodied overseas. As a medical practitioner, he felt personally affronted by the scourge of unchecked disease, which filled hospitals beyond their capacity. It was his contention that the root of this hardship lay in the plantations of the sixteenth and seventeenth centuries when 'The "mere Irish" were driven like wolves into the wilds and fastnesses of Donegal and Connaught, without their condition being one iota improved in two centuries'.[10]

Jane, raised by her mother alone, had oddly subjugated notions of marriage, even for an era when married women were categorised in common law as 'feme covert' to emphasise their subordination: '. . . my great soul is prisoned within a <u>woman's</u> <u>destiny</u>' she cried: 'Nothing interests me beyond the desire to make him [William] happy — for this I could kill myself'.[11] In this, she was strangely dichotomous and it is noteworthy that, while Oscar enjoyed the company of women who were strong, intelligent, forthright and arresting in appearance, he chose as his wife a woman with all of those characteristics who also pledged her life to him: 'I worship you my hero and my god!', she wrote, choosing language that is strikingly similar to that used by her mother-in-law.[12]

After they were married, William and Jane moved into his old bachelor home at 21 Westland Row in the heart of Dublin. A popular duo, they were welcomed into society and Jane was not in the least bit intimidated in any company. In *Reminiscences*, Dublin-born novelist and poet Katharine Tynan, who would later befriend Oscar and his wife, Constance, described an occasion when her father, Andrew Cullen Tynan, a livestock farmer and enthusiastic nationalist who admired Jane greatly, spotted her, 'fighting her way, like any man . . . into some banquet or other'. He admitted ruefully that he 'still loved her verse though she had disappointed him'.[13]

The most glittering events were held in Dublin Castle, an imposing seat of power that Jane had advocated be surrounded by barricades and burned to the ground. She found this highly amusing: 'I went to the last Drawing Room at the castle and Lord Aberdeen smiled very archly as he bent to kiss my cheek,' she told John Hilson. 'I smiled too and thought of *Jacta Alea Est*'.[14] Although he too could be tremendously sociable, William was consumed by his medical practice and the mammoth task of completing his census report. During what little spare time remained, he compiled *Irish Popular Superstitions*, which he dedicated 'to Speranza'. Jane was occupied too. Her translation of Alexandre Dumas Père's *The Glacier Land* appeared in 1852, and she began work on a revised translation from the original Latin of *Heaven and Hell*, Emanuel Swedenborg's intricate imagining of the afterlife. Her critical review of the 'personal narrative' of the ship's surgeon who accompanied her intrepid cousin Robert John le Mesurier McClure appeared in the *Dublin University Magazine* and she reviewed 'The Dramas of *Calderón*' for the same publication.

William and Jane's first child, William Charles Kingsbury Wills Wilde arrived on 26 September 1852, six weeks short of his parent's first wedding anniversary. Jane was caught completely unawares by the intensity of her emotions: 'What an enchanting richness and fullness these young give to one's life', she exclaimed. 'It is like the return of a second youth. Hope, Energy, Purpose, all awake again with a nobler object than ever'. Gazing down at her infant son, she wondered, 'How is it I am enthralled by these tiny hands? Was there a woman's nature in me after all?'[15]

She had great ambitions for Willie, who was 'twined round all the fibres' of her heart, and she decided to 'rear him a Hero perhaps and President of the future Irish Republic'.[16] Motherhood forced Jane to re-evaluate all that had once interested her: 'Well, well', she mused, 'after all talk of Politics, Patriots, poetry, love, literature, intellect, nothing fills the heart like a wee, wee child'.[17] But domesticity alone could never fulfill her and her great spirit remained unbowed: 'I have not fulfilled my destiny yet', she declared: 'Gruel and the nursery cannot end me'.[18]

The death of William's mentor and friend, Robert Graves, in March 1853, threw him into crisis. Not only had this brilliant man overseen his young student's medical training, he had also treated him successfully for severe asthma and debilitating bouts of typhoid fever. Overworked, exhausted and beset by grief, William grew increasingly morose, prompting Jane to lament that, although he was so brilliant in society, he had:

> . . . a strange, nervous, hypochondriacal home nature which the world never sees – only I and often it makes me miserable, for I do not know how to deal with fantastic evils, though I could bear up grandly against a real calamity.[19]

When she asked what might make him happy, 'he answers death'. Although deeply concerned, Jane was willing to accommodate William's 'wayward, turbulent and terrible temperament of genius'.[20] She believed that men as brilliant as her husband, and, in time, her son, were 'masses of emotional force, alternations of violent impulses and silent despair'.[21] Her calling, she believed, was to calm his soul:

For the woman that stands beside the man of genius in life much is demanded. She is the angel of his destiny, and accountable to the world for the treasure committed to her care – the peace and serenity of his soul.[22]

Diversion arrived in the shape of baby Oscar Fingal O'Flahertie Wills Wilde, born on 16 October 1854. Now, Jane was:

. . . bound heart and soul to the home hearth by the tiny hands of little Willie and as if these sweet hands were not enough, behold me – me, Speranza – also rocking a cradle . . . in which lies my second son.[23]

Although Oscar was 'large and fine and handsome and healthy', his brilliant mother grew increasingly morose. She became preoccupied with the worrisome news reaching Dublin from Crimea, where bloody warfare and rampant disease were taking the lives of thousands of young men. She said of her boys: 'If I can but make them wise and good it seems to me that is all can be done in this brief moment-life of ours'.[24] Writing had lost its joy, merely serving to remind her of her lost intellect: 'I look back on the past as into a former existence', she told John Hilson, 'and wonder at my own self that then was'.[25] Barely a month after Oscar's arrival, she wrote: 'Life has such infinite capacities of woe'.[26] It is entirely possible that she was suffering from mild post-partum depression; she exhibited many of the symptoms.

Soon afterwards, Jane found consolation in the deep, rewarding friendship she forged with physicist, astronomer and mathematician Sir William Rowan Hamilton. By coincidence, her husband formed a new friendship too, one that ended in disaster and disgrace ten years later. Hamilton, an extraordinarily brilliant man whose reputation for genius spanned the globe, was appointed Professor of Astronomy and Royal Astronomer of Ireland as an undergraduate at Trinity College, Dublin. He developed his groundbreaking theory of quaternions more than a decade before he met Jane. A true polymath and an accomplished poet, he had twice been awarded the Vice-Chancellor's Prize for English verse and enjoyed the friendship of Samuel Taylor Coleridge and William Wordsworth. Although Wordsworth admired Hamilton's poetry, he counseled:

You send me showers of verses, which I receive with much pleasure, as do we all; yet have we fears that this employment may seduce you from the path of Science, which you seem destined to tread with so much honour to yourself and profit to others.[27]

Hamilton met Jane at a dinner party hosted by Colonel Thomas Larcom, Under-Secretary for Ireland, and his wife Georgina on 13 April 1855. As William and he were members of the Royal Irish Academy, he was asked to hand Jane in to dinner. To his astonishment, after practically no introduction, this 'very odd and original lady' asked if he would be godfather to her 'young pagan'. He was further taken aback to learn that this child was to be given a 'long baptismal name, or string of names, the two first of which are Oscar and Fingal!'[28] Although he declined, Jane bore no grudge, and endeared herself by expressing admiration for poetry composed by his late sister. The next time they met, he presented her with an inscribed copy of Eliza Hamilton's *Poems*.[29]

Over lunch at Dunsink Observatory, Hamilton's home, Jane informed him that Oscar had been baptised the previous day and they drank a toast to his health. Afterwards, he gave her a tour of his atmospheric house, which Eliza had believed was haunted; Jane expressed a hope that this was true. Yet, although she liked and admired her host, she could not hide her resentment at the wealth his eminence had secured: 'Let a woman be as clever as she may, there is no prize like this for *her*!' she declared.[30] Hamilton's letters to Jane demonstrate a great regard for her intellect. He felt free to discuss any topic with her and included quotations in Latin and Greek, which he acknowledged need not be translated. He admired her noble nature and regarded her as an 'entirely truthful person'.[31] His long, rambling letters could be quite flirtatious: in one, he called her, 'a very remarkable, a very interesting, and (if I could be forgiven for adding it) a very lovable person'. Yet, he kept his distance and congratulated her on 'being so happily married'.[32]

The characteristics Hamilton admired in Jane were not generally prized in Victorian women. He described her as 'almost amusingly fearless and original and averse', and he admired her declaration that she liked to 'make a sensation'.[33] Although their politics were at variance, this formed no barrier to their friendship. His heart still 'throbbed with sympathy, for the great British Empire', but he argued that this had the advantage of allowing him to understand Jane better, since they shared the experience of sympathising with a whole nation.[34]

Jane introduced Hamilton to fresh experiences and recommended that he read Hawthorne's *The Scarlet Letter* five years before it was published in

London on the basis that it had cost her three nights sleep. Oscar invoked this same novel when writing *A Woman of No Importance*. When Jane sent Hamilton her sixteen-stanza poem *Shadows from Life* he praised it as 'wonderfully beautiful', but suggested several changes, which she made. He shared it with poet Aubrey de Vere, who declared:

> She certainly must be a woman of real poetic genius to have written anything so beautiful and also so full of power and grace as the poem you showed me.

De Vere urged: 'for the sake both of poetry and Old Ireland you must do all you can to make her go on writing, and publish a volume soon'.[35] Hamilton invited both friends to a 'Feast of Poets', but warned Jane not to allow de Vere to convert her to Catholicism, which she found fascinating.[36] Jane admired the Roman Catholic Church, which 'so well understands the working of the innermost wheels of our complex human nature'. In contrast, she thought of Protestantism as 'stern, cold and logical', traits she cared little for.[37]

Such delights distracted Jane from her troubles at home, where William's condition was not improving. During the summer of 1855, he fell desperately ill and seemed unable to rest: 'I look with terror on all that can ruffle the calm happiness of the home life', Jane wrote.[38] The only thing that comforted him was his deep affinity for the West of Ireland. In 1853, William had leased nine acres of remote land in Illaunroe on the shores of Lough Fee, where he built a modest hunting lodge that allowed him to retreat from the world. As his health deteriorated, the whole family decamped there for a fortnight, but Jane struggled in that 'grand, desolate and bleak' place, and the sight of roofless cabins whose former occupants had died, or fled as a consequence of famine, left her feeling 'sick with helpless despair and rage'.[39]

One consolation of William's brilliance was the financial security it brought. Returning from Connemara, they swapped the modesty of 21 Westland Row for the opulence of 1 Merrion Square North, a sizable corner house in one of the city's most fashionable districts. Jane described her new home as having 'fine rooms and the best situation in Dublin'.[40] Alongside the expanding Wilde family, the house could accommodate six domestic servants, a German governess and a French bonne:* both William and Jane were keen to foster proficiency for languages in their

* A French nursemaid or maidservant.

children. Their home was also a place of business for William: the third floor contained a set of consulting rooms, connected by a back staircase to his study, a sanctuary where he retired to write in peace.

The rest of the house was Jane's domain. Flower-decked balconies overlooked the great expanse of Merrion Square and she filled her rooms with imposing walnut and mahogany furniture, laid colourful Turkish carpets underfoot and covered the walls with rich oil paintings, many of them portraits of their more illustrious acquaintances. The first floor dining room was used for Saturday supper parties that lasted from 6.30 p.m. till 11 p.m. and were attended by a dozen 'clever and learned men', who discussed 'all the current topics & literature & science of the day'.[41] One guest, William Smith O'Brien, leader of the failed revolution of 1848, insisted on referring to himself as 'the convict'. Jane always preferred the company of men: 'As a rule I cannot stand girls or women,' she told Henriette Corkran, a rare female friend, 'they are so flimsy, frivolous, feeble in purpose — they so seldom achieve anything'.[42]

Corkran provides one of the best descriptions of Jane:

A very tall woman – she looked over six feet high – she wore that day a long crimson silk gown which swept the floor. Her skirt was voluminous; underneath there must have been two crinolines, for when she walked there was a peculiar swelling movement like that of a vessel at sea, the sails filled with wind. Over the crimson were flounces of Limerick lace, and round what had once been a waist, an Oriental scarf, embroidered with gold, was twisted. Her long, massive, handsome face was plastered with white powder; over the blue-black glossy hair was a gilt crown of laurels. Her throat was bare, so were her arms, but they were covered with quaint jewellery.[43]

When the daughter Jane had apparently longed for arrived on 2 April 1857, her family was complete. Some nonsense is talked, even now, about how Jane put Oscar in dresses because she would have preferred him to be a girl. Inevitably, this leads to further nonsense about the effect this had on his sexuality. In fact, Isola was just two-and-a-half years younger than Oscar and the smocks he wore as an infant were commonplace, particularly in Ireland, where a belief persisted that, while the fairies might steal a boy child, these mythical and malevolent creatures would have no interest in a girl. Everyone doted on Isola Francesca Emily Wilde. Jane called her 'the pet of the house', adding: 'She has fine eyes & promises to have a most acute intellect – these two gifts are enough for any woman'.[44] At last, Jane seemed content. Her recipe for family harmony, which Oscar embraced with gusto, is very revealing and highly unorthodox:

> The best chance, perhaps, of domestic felicity is when all the family are bohemians, and all clever, and all enjoy thoroughly the erratic, impulsive, reckless life of work and glory, indifferent to everything save the intense moments of popular applause.[45]

Shortly after Isola arrived, Jane formed an extremely significant friendship with a progressive young Swedish woman named Charlotte 'Lotten' von Kraemer. Then, as now, Scandinavians took a more enlightened approach to gender equality and Jane's admiration demonstrates how far ahead of her time she was. It must be remembered that many Victorian women were complicit in their subjugation, propping up male-dominated institutions that kept them down and shunning women who objected.

As Lotten suffered from a painful and debilitating ailment of the ear, triggered by a bout of scarlet fever in adolescence, she had been advised to consult Dr William Wilde, one of Europe's leading aural specialists. She and her father, Baron Robert Fredrik von Kraemer, Governor of Uppsala, arrived at lunchtime one Sunday in July 1857. They were surprised to learn, by means of a wink and a nod that the lady of the house was not yet up. Instead, they were shown into William's study. He arrived, holding one 'unruly little boy' by the hand and carrying a smaller boy in his arms. This was Oscar, not yet three, with 'curly brown hair and large dreamy eyes'. Lotten was moved by the warm affection William showed towards his sons.[46]

Hospitable as ever, William invited these visitors to return for dinner. In the meantime, he volunteered his wife to take them on a tour of Dublin, which she did with great good humour. Willie and Oscar were present that evening, a highly unusual practice in a Victorian household and one that was to continue when Oscar had sons of his own. William stroked little Oscar's cheek and sent him to fetch a book, while Jane prevailed upon Baron von Kraemer to teach her the rudiments of Swedish. Lotten admired her 'soulful and captivating vivacity', recognising that the fire in her glance betrayed her past as a revolutionary poet. She was struck by the affability of the occasion and the exceptionally congenial bond that existed between husband and wife.

Lotten and Jane had much in common. During her lifetime, Lotten was a published poet, essayist, and editor of *Var Tid* (Our Time), a magazine of modern culture. She also endowed a scholarship enabling female medical students to attend Uppsala University; she founded *Samfundet De Nio* (the Nine Society), a prestigious and progressive Swedish literary society; and she provided vital finance to the Country Association for Women's Suffrage. Although early correspondence was taken up with medical advice passed on by William, much of it involving the application of leeches, Lotten and Jane were soon discussing topics of mutual interest: literature, culture and the position of women in society. It impressed Jane that:

> Clever and intellectual women, also, in Sweden hold a much higher position in society than their literary sisters in England. They are honoured and made much of, and treated with considerable distinction, solely from belonging to the peerage of intellect. Whereas in England wealth, with the ponderous routine of life that wealth entails, seems to be the chief measure of merit and the highest standard of perfection in social circles.[47]

Ever the linguist, she attempted to master Swedish but the lack of a tutor obliged her to struggle alone with the aid of a dictionary. Although she managed a few letters, she never mastered the language: 'Even this endeavour [learning Swedish] I have given up with all other literary employment since the cares of a household have come on me', she told Lotten.[48] One ambition Jane did not abandon was that of instilling a love for literature in her children; she was successful in this. While Willie enjoyed Tennyson's epic ballad, *Lady Clare*, and Longfellow's *Hiawatha*, Oscar remembered Walt Whitman's recently published collection, *Leaves of Grass* (1855) being read to him. He mentioned this when he met its author in New Jersey in 1882. Once Willie turned six, Jane hired an English governess, an arrangement that allowed her to travel with William: 'without this, we're apt to fossilize in married state' she declared.[49] During the autumn of 1859, they toured Scandinavia. Jane said of Stockholm, 'I will never enjoy any place again so much'.[50] She was less taken with Germany, concluding, erroneously as it happened, that people 'who live on beer and cheese, are not, and never can be, politically dangerous'.[51]

Years later, Jane organised her journals into *Driftwood from Scandinavia*, a moderately successful travel book in which she expressed her admiration for the elevated status of women in Swedish society. Through Lotten, Jane met Rosalie Olivecrona, a pioneer of the Swedish women's rights movement and co-founder of *Tidskrift för Hemmet* (Journal for the Home), a campaigning feminist publication 'devoted to general literature and the advancement of women politically and intellectually'. What impressed

Jane about Rosalie was that, although she held 'a very important place in the highest circles of Stockholm society', she remained 'with all her learning, a most attractive and elegant woman in style, look, and manner'.[52]

Although Jane told Lotten that she had 'little time for writing or even for thought,' she managed to complete all three volumes – 1,446 pages – of *The First Temptation; Or, "Eritis Sicut Deus": A Philosophical Romance [by W. Canz]. Translated from the German by Mrs. W. R. Wilde.*[53] Her skills as a translator were lauded, but this odd and controversial book received mixed reviews, although one damning assessment was motivated by revenge, as would become apparent. Jane enjoyed her status as a public figure and began one very revealing letter to Lotten: 'When my correspondence is collected and published after my death . . .' Yet, the incompatibility of literary and family life concerned her: 'After all writing is a fatal gift for a woman', she told Lotten, who was childless, 'I would be a much better wife, mother, & head of a household if I never touched a pen. I feel this so strongly that I shall never encourage my daughter to authorship'.[54] Such misplaced guilt remains familiar to her contemporary counterparts.

When Jane learned that her Swedish friends hosted regular literary receptions, she decided to establish 'weekly conversazione' in order to 'agglomerate together all the thinking minds of Dublin'.[55] The *Athenaeum* described 1 Merrion Square as 'the first, and for a long time the only, bohemian house in Dublin', but expressed concern that Jane had gathered together all those 'whom prudish Dublin had hitherto kept carefully apart'.[56] *The Irish Times* attributed her success to an absence of snobbery, 'so fatal to social gatherings in Ireland'.[57] Delighted with her initiative, Jane became determined to live up to her maxim; one Oscar adapted and made his own. 'It is monotony that kills, not excitement,' she wrote:

> Dull people fail in the will to live, and so they soon lose their hold on life. Excellent good women, who give up society and devote themselves exclusively to home and homely duties, grow old so soon.[58]

As was her wont, she invited mostly men and those few women she admired: novelist Rosa Mulholland Gilbert, and literary sisters Alice and Henriette Corkran. Gilbert remembered Jane: 'dressed in long flowing robes of Irish poplin and Limerick lace . . . adorned with gold chains and brooches modelled on the ancient ornaments of Erin's early queens'. She considered Jane to be 'of a kindly nature, and warm and sincere in her friendships,' adding, 'she had a commendable desire to make her house a social centre for all who were engaged in intellectual pursuits, or interested in literature or the arts'.[59] Henriette Corkran thought her 'an odd mixture of nonsense, with a sprinkling of genius', and declared that 'her talk was like fireworks – brilliant, whimsical and flashy'.[60] In time, Oscar's conversation would also be likened to fireworks.

Domestic matters dominated by May 1862. The children all had whooping cough and the family spent a few miserable weeks in Connemara. As Willie's illness lingered throughout the summer, Jane took the children to the seaside resort of Bray, where William owned four adjoining houses on the seafront. Oscar was poorly by Christmas and spent five weeks in bed with fever. They returned to Bray in April, this time accompanied by a new Swiss governess. Jane was concerned about Willie, who was almost eleven and very clever but excessively high-spirited: 'tho' he obeys me, [he] will scarcely obey a governess,' she told Lotten, 'I feel it would be a risk to leave him'.[61] She saw great promise in Oscar: 'Willie is alright,' she told the poet George Henry Moore, 'but as for Oscar, he will turn out something wonderful'.[62]

In January 1864, William was knighted in recognition of his services to the medical profession and his key role in compiling census statistics. Without hesitation, Jane became Lady Wilde. In February, she sent Willie, aged twelve, and Oscar, who was only nine, to Portora Royal School in Enniskillen, a prestigious boarding school by Irish standards, located 100 miles north of Dublin. This move coincided with a revival of her literary fortunes and the publication of *Poems* by Speranza, which she dedicated 'to Willie and Oscar':

> I made them indeed, speak plain the word COUNTRY. I taught them, no doubt, that a country's a thing men should die for at need![63]

Her slim volume was well received; *The Dublin Review* paid tribute to the 'extraordinary influence' her poems had 'on all the intellectual and political activities of Young Ireland'.[64] Such contentment was fleeting and the year that started with such promise closed with public humiliation. The roots of this turmoil stretched back to before Oscar's birth, when Dr William Wilde began treating an attractive young woman for a hearing complaint.

Chapter 4

LOST SISTERS AND AN
EARLIER LIBEL TRIAL

Alas! I was entering into the shadow which now will never more
be lifted.
LADY JANE WILDE[1]

Stability or the lack of it in adolescence shapes the adult that emerges.
Trauma experienced during our formative years has a profound impact
on our character and the way in which we conduct the remainder of our
lives. Between the ages of ten and seventeen, Oscar Wilde experienced
periods of extreme turbulence and a bereavement that would affect him
for the rest of his life.

As 1864 drew to a close, Jane was shaken out of her newfound contentment in a very public fashion, although trouble, in the guise of Mary
Josephine Travers, had been brewing for more than a decade by then. It
all began on the afternoon of Saturday 22 July 1854, when a dark-haired,
willowy young woman, aged nineteen, turned up at William Wilde's surgery on Westmoreland Street accompanied by her mother. She brought
with her a letter from Dr William Stokes, a friend to both families, confirming that she had problems with her hearing. Mary was the oldest
daughter of Dr Robert Travers, Professor of Medical Jurisprudence in
Trinity College, Dublin, Physician to the South Dublin Cholera Hospital
and Assistant Keeper of Archbishop Marsh's Library, the first public
library in Ireland. A taciturn and bookish man, he was well respected but
not particularly well liked and he treated his daughter coldly.

William took Mary on as his patient, and waived his fee in consideration of her being the daughter of a fellow physician. Over the course
of a series of weekly appointments, doctor and patient grew close and
Mary disclosed the miserable details of her fractured family life. Her parents had separated some time earlier and her father, a remote man who
allowed his work to absorb him, made little time for his five children.
To make matters worse, Mary was barely on speaking terms with her
mother and she missed the company of her two older brothers, who had

left for Australia. She craved male attention, which William was happy to provide.

After her treatment, they kept up their weekly meetings and William took what he insisted was a paternal interest in this young woman who was less than half his age. Perhaps this was true at the outset. Mary, with her father's agreement, corrected some of William's manuscripts and in return, he oversaw her informal education by recommending books that might engage or improve her. Before long they were exchanging letters, an interchange described by him as a 'paternal discourse', although she saw more in it: 'An intimacy arose between us', she declared.[2]

Jane, never a jealous woman, seemed oblivious to this burgeoning relationship whatever its nature. She was pregnant with Oscar when Mary Travers first met her husband. Afterwards, she was preoccupied with a toddler and a newborn baby, and she struggled to cope with the diminishment of her literary life. Jane was introduced to Mary when the family moved to 1 Merrion Square, where a bevy of domestic servants lightened her load. From then on, she included her in family outings, inviting her to attend a pantomime with the Wilde children and to join them for a festive dinner on Christmas Day 1861. William was consorting openly with Mary by then. He presented her with a season ticket for the Dublin Exhibition and they attended several events together, sometimes accompanied by Jane, more often, not. When the Senate of Queen's University sat in Dublin Castle to confer degrees for the first time, Mary was there at William's invitation. Afterwards, Mary said he told her Jane had followed them in her carriage, although this seems utterly uncharacteristic and we only have Mary's word for it.

When William asked Mary the time, she confessed she had pawned her watch and he realised that she was kept short of money. Like most women of her class and standing, she had little opportunity to earn an independent income. Her reliance on his good offices deepened after he took to loaning her small sums of money, which she attempted to repay out of her modest dress allowance of £4 a quarter. Their relationship changed, with William taking an inappropriate interest in her appearance, commenting on her bonnets and offering to buy her dresses: 'It is terrible weather; get warm clothes and pam-jams* and a warm muff', he counselled.[3] She did purchase 'a dress and tickets for a Masonic ball' out of money he loaned her, a very compromising development.[4]

* Reported in the newspapers as 'a slang term for a lady's drawers'.

The first hint of trouble emerged in February 1862. By her own account, Mary was alone with William in his study when he embraced her, refusing to release her until she called him by his first name. Afterwards, he pleaded: 'Forgive, I am miserable. Do see me'.[5] When Oscar, aged eight, fell dangerously ill, his father attributed his recovery to an intimate dream in which Mary nursed his little boy back to health.[6] When Mary spoke of joining her brothers in Australia, William encouraged her and paid for her passage; it seems both were looking for a way out. Although she made the crossing to Liverpool in April, Mary returned several days later, protesting that there had been confusion over her berth. Weeks later, she sailed again, but returned once more, complaining variously of seasickness and a newfound reluctance to leave her native city.

Although Jane was an exceptionally tolerant wife, her patience with this highly-strung interloper was wearing dangerously thin and the two clashed several times that summer. On the first occasion, Jane interrupted William and Mary in his study. Pinching her rival's cheek with a little more force than could be described as playful, she demanded: 'Where do you want to take my husband now?' Sometime later, Jane invited a 'very particular friend' to come up to her bedroom and was horrified when Mary burst in alongside her. She made light of the incident: 'I expressed my surprise, she said, 'Miss Travers appeared to have taken great offence . . . I don't think she dined at our house afterwards'.[7] Mary's resentment increased when she arrived to take the Wilde children to the Chapel Royal at Dublin Castle only to discover that Jane had left without her: 'We were not friends since the quarrel about the church', Jane admitted.[8]

These slights, real or perceived, infuriated Mary and she took her grievances to William: 'I have come to the conclusion that both you and Mrs. Wilde are of the one mind with regard to me', she raged, 'and that is to see which one will insult me most'. She felt beholden to William and assured him that he had treated her as she 'strictly deserved', but she insisted that, when it came to Jane, she was 'not obliged to gulp down her insults'. She closed a letter demanding the return of a photograph William had allegedly snatched from her by declaring, 'you will not be troubled by me again'.[9] William must have shown this highly indignant communication to Jane, since it was she, assuming the role of his protector, who returned the photograph. By then, relations between the women were damaged beyond repair.

Whether she was motivated by revenge or whether she was the victim of an outrageous assault, Mary's account of an incident that unfolded on 14 October 1862, is deeply disturbing. While she was alone with William in his consulting room, with several patients waiting in the corridor outside, he asked if he might examine a burn on her neck, which she had sustained in childhood. When she acquiesced, he used the opportunity, she said, to press his hands against her neck until she lost consciousness, and then he raped her. Once she came round, he pressed wine on her and encouraged her to rest upstairs until she felt well enough to leave. Afterwards, he showered her with letters of apology and explanation, several of which she left unopened. He bought her a dress, which she refused to accept even when he tore the one she was wearing in a crude effort to persuade her. Mary did not report the incident at the time, but the unsubstantiated allegation emerged in a packed courtroom two years later.

During the days that followed, William was dismayed by Mary's altered demeanour: 'Love and hatred – bright smiles, joy and cheerfulness – gloom, sorrow and pain,' he wrote after seeing her laugh with friends before scowling as he approached.[10] He seemed fearful and urged: 'Do keep quiet, dear, for a while, and think what is best to be done. I am utterly sleepless. I feel for you but you don't feel for me'.[11] Certain she was bent on revenge, he seemed resigned to his fate:

> That you have done everything you say I have no doubt. The measure of revenge will and must be filled up. What this new cause is I cannot tell – I am unconscious. It must, however, be borne. Sooner or later, the revenge must come I see. What you want to be done I cannot guess; pray state it.[12]

William's letters grew increasingly frantic: 'There is madness in your eyes' he wrote, 'I cannot sleep at night thinking of you. I am convinced you will explode some time'.[13]

On Sunday 25 January 1863, in the wake of a ferocious argument, Mary stormed out of William's study in a distressed state. She returned clutching a two-ounce bottle of laudanum, which, to his absolute consternation, she drank in his presence. Although he became highly agitated, insisting that she planned to frame him for poisoning her, he had the presence of mind to write a prescription for zinc emetic, and to follow her to a local apothecary in order to ensure that she took it.[14] Afterwards, he insisted she explain the incident away as an accident and advised her to stay with friends, which she did. That summer, Mary's despair turned to anger. Addressing William as a 'spiteful old lunatic', she continued:

Since you want to do something for me please cut my corn that you did not half do before. I'll keep your nose to the grinding-stone while your wife is away, and when she returns I'll see her so you had better not make a fool of me this time.[15]

Mary's behaviour became increasingly vindictive. She took petty revenge by pouring a pungent mixture of garlic and water onto William's handkerchief and into the soap trays in his surgery, and she wrote unkind reviews of Jane's translation of *Eritis Sicut Deus* for *The Commercial Journal* and *The Weekly Advertiser*. In July, William fled to the West of Ireland to oversee the building of a new villa on 170 acres at Moytura, near Cong in County Mayo, which he was financing with £2,500 he had borrowed from Jane's marriage settlement. While Jane was in Bray with their children, she received a chilling notice by post:

July 21, suddenly, at the residence of her father, Williamstown. Mary Josephine, eldest daughter of Robert Travers MD, MRCSI.

Discerning what she believed to be a crude drawing of a coffin beneath this obvious forgery, she grew fearful of the harm that Mary might be capable of inflicting.

In mid-August 1863, when the Wildes were back in Merrion Square, Mary called and sent up her card. Jane sent it straight back down and refused to see her. Rather than retreat with dignity, Mary perched on the marble-topped table in the hall and glared up the stairway, remaining there for two hours until Jane was obliged to descend as a carriage had pulled up for her. Although she attempted to walk past her tormentor without comment, she had to pull one of her sons away when Mary engaged him in conversation.[16] Afterwards, William 'blazed' at Mary and she vowed that his 'abusive language' would not pass unnoticed.[17] Jane's determination to close ranks against this interloper provided a striking example of spousal solidarity and set a high bar for future daughters-in-law. Willie, Oscar and Isola must have been utterly perplexed by this turn of events since, until recently, Mary had been a close family friend.

From then on, Mary focussed much of her attention on Jane; in some ways, her tormenting behaviour paralleled that of the Marquess of Queensberry decades later. In a desperate bid to attract her attention, she sent Jane a copy of one of William's more incriminating letters but Jane sent it back with an imperious note stating she did not take the least interest in the subject. This snub provoked Mary into taking up her pen and writing a scurrilous pamphlet: *Florence Boyle Price, or a Warning* by 'Speranza', a cautionary tale featured the repellent 'Dr. Quilp', a thinly disguised William Wilde, who used chloroform to disable poor, defenceless Florence in order to rape her. Mrs Quilp, 'an odd sort of undomesticated woman', who 'spent the greater portion of her life in bed', refused to entertain Florence's grievance: 'It is sad to think', wrote Mary, 'that in this the nineteenth century a lady must not venture into a physician's study without a bodyguard'.

Mary had 1,000 copies printed up and circulated: 'We were deluged with them by post, by being dropped into the letterbox by friends to whom they had been sent', Jane testified, adding, 'this continued all through November, December, January, February and for several months'.[18] When challenged about her use of the name 'Speranza', Mary insisted: 'Mrs. Wilde, in one of her letters, had said that she had no objection, if I had a fancy to the name, to allow me to continue it', adding, 'that letter is in the hands of my solicitor'. It was never produced.[19]

After William was knighted, Mary stepped up her campaign, dropping scurrilous doggerel through the letterbox of 1 Merrion Square and arranging for more to be published in the *Dublin Weekly Advertiser*, much of it signed 'Speranza'. She fabricated a correspondence in the letters pages between 'Aurora Floyd' and Speranza, arguing for the punishment of errant knights. At the same time, she badgered William for money, on one occasion asking him to bring it to her home, where it seems she had some notion of arranging for a servant to record their conversation. William refused: 'To gratify your revenge for some fancied slight, you have endeavoured to injure your best friend and laboured to annoy others by every means in your power', he complained. He offered her some advice: 'Do not let yourself be altogether guided by personal revenge, or the printer's devil, who has been too frequently at your elbow, and at your behest of late'.[20] Naturally, this warning merely served to enrage her further.

On 27 April 1864, William and Jane arrived at the Metropolitan Hall in Abbey Street, where he was to deliver, 'Ireland, Past and Present; the Land and the People', one in a series of prestigious lectures commissioned by the Young Men's Christian Association. As they stepped down from their carriage, Jane heard shouts of 'Sir William Wilde's Letter', and noticed five newsboys carrying placards emblazoned with the words, 'Sir William Wilde & Speranza'. One rang a bell to attract attention. They were selling copies of *Florence Boyle Price* at a penny each, but this new version had a flysheet printed with passages from William's letters to Mary and a statement that read:

> This pamphlet contains, in the form of a tale, an altered, curtailed but by no means exaggerated account of Mr. (now Sir) W. R. Wilde's conduct.[21]

Although a friend attempted to grab as many as he could, several dozen were sold on the night.

Mary, who was watching from a cab nearby, had orchestrated the whole fiasco. She fuelled further interest by persuading the editor of *Saunders Newsletter* to publish a letter signed 'Inquirer', speculating as to the cause of the ruckus and pointing out: 'The pamphlet is six months in circulation and its accuracy has not been questioned'. Desperate to understand her motives, William sent her a terse and formal letter:

> Miss Travers, What is it you want by the publication of a parcel of stupid letters? Please state it.[22]

Thoroughly rattled, Jane left for Bray with Isola, but Mary followed them and arranged for her pamphlets to be sold in the town. The first newsboy who called at Jane's door was coaxed into admitting that 'a lady' had put him up to it. When a second newsboy called, little Isola, aged just seven, asked her mother what on earth was going on. This was provocation beyond endurance. Since the boy refused to sell her the four pamphlets he had, Jane held onto one and seized the placard he carried as well. This rash act left the way clear for Mary to take out a summons in the Bray Petty Sessions Court, charging Jane with theft and threatening behaviour towards a servant of hers. Meanwhile, Jane wrote a strongly worded letter to Robert Travers:

> Sir – You may not be aware of the disreputable conduct of your daughter at Bray, where she consorts with all the low newspaper boys in the place, employing them to disseminate offensive placards in which she makes it appear that she has had an intrigue with Sir William Wilde. If she chooses to disgrace herself that is not my affair; but as her object in insulting me is the hope of extorting money, for which she has several times applied to Sir William Wilde, with threats of more annoyance if not given, I think it right to inform you that no threat or additional insult shall ever extort money for her from our hands. The wages of disgrace she has so loosely treated for and demanded shall never be given her.[23]
>
> Jane F. Wilde

When Mary discovered Jane's letter in an unlocked cabinet three weeks later, she realised its value and handed it to her solicitor Robert H. Irvine, who promptly served a writ on Jane, seeking £2,000 in damages for a libel.[24] Under a now discarded principle of law that held a husband responsible for his wife's torts, William was joined in the action. They could have settled matters quietly, although that might not have prevented Mary from resuming her harassment.

When the case opened in Dublin's Four Courts on Monday, 12 December 1864, both plaintiff and defendant were expertly and expensively represented: Isaac Butt QC and Serjeant Richard Armstrong QC led for Mary Travers, while the Wildes retained the services of Serjeant Edward Sullivan, future Lord Chancellor of Ireland, and Michael Morris, later Lord Chief Justice. Butt was well known to Jane. Not only had he successfully defended Charles Gavan Duffy in 1848, he also featured in a mischievous letter from John Butler Yeats to his son William, alleging: 'When she was Miss Elgee, Mrs. Butt found her with her husband when the circumstances were not doubtful'.[25]

All of Ireland was riveted by the case; *The Irish Times* claimed that it 'shook society in Dublin like a thunderclap'. Newspapers carrying lengthy reports were so highly prized that it is said a thriving market for second-hand copies emerged. When the prosecution opened to a packed courtroom, Serjeant Armstrong castigated Jane's letter as a libel that reflected badly on the 'character and chastity' of his client. He treated the alleged rape as a matter of fact, declaring of Mary: 'She went in a maid. But out a maid she never departed', a poor paraphrasing of Ophelia's Song in Shakespeare's *Hamlet*.[26] When Armstrong interpreted Jane's references to Mary consorting with newsboys and demanding the wages of disgrace as clear accusations of prostitution, she denied this, pointing out that the boys in question were only 'ten or twelve years old'.

The defence pleaded no libel, a denial of defamation, a denial of publication and a claim of justification. Serjeant Sullivan countered that Mary Travers was an acquaintance of Lady Wilde's who:

> took umbrage at some supposed slights which she thought her ladyship had put upon her, and from that time forward she conceived the desire of insulting and annoying her, by various ways and means . . .[27]

He portrayed Mary's relationship with William as a sentimental friendship, a kindly older man taking a benevolent interest in a young woman who was neglected by her own father. Although she adopted a façade of indifference, he spoke of the anguish and the sleepless nights that Jane had suffered. He was at pains to expose the many discrepancies in Mary's account of the alleged rape. It seemed utterly implausible to him that a 'violated woman' would not disclose this outrage for two years, but would continue to consort with the perpetrator. Without a trace of irony, Sullivan told the male prosecution team, male judge and twelve men who made up the jury that in this case, where one woman was pitted against another:

> We cannot, as it were, put our minds into the minds of women. We cannot transform our muscular mode of thinking, as it were, into the delicate feelings and mode of thinking of women.[28]

Summing up, Lord Chief Justice Monahan poured scorn on Travers' account of the rape, insisting that, had it been the subject of a criminal prosecution, it would have been thrown out without hesitation. He need not have done so. Whether she was lying or not, she was not on trial and nor was William.

Isaac Butt contended William's interest in Mary had been innocuous at first but, after they became emotionally involved, rather than admit the truth, William left his wife open to a charge of libel. His description of Jane as 'an Irish Lady of genius and intellect' was greeted with warm applause.[29] The public gallery erupted when she took the stand. Butt adopted a less sympathetic approach when questioning her, portraying her as a pitiless wife who dismissed the genuine grievances of a vulnerable young woman injured by her husband. Jane remained calm and dignified throughout. As Oscar would shield Bosie,[*] she shielded William, assuring the court that she considered him innocent of all wrongdoing and gave him her full support. Unflappable as ever, she provoked laughter by describing a letter received from Mary in August 1863: 'She wrote to me explaining why she died', she declared.[30] At times her eloquence and composure in the dock foreshadowed that of her son decades later.

The jury took less than two hours to find for Travers, but they humiliated her by awarding her a paltry one farthing in damages. Costs amounting to far more than the £2,000 originally sought were allocated to the Wildes; they had salvaged their reputations, but at a very high price. What mattered was that popular opinion was with them. Describing her as 'high, pure and spotless', the *Morning News* declared that no verdict could 'dim the purity

---

* A corruption of 'Boysie', a childhood term of endearment given to Lord Alfred Douglas by his mother.

and brightness of her name, or weaken the esteem in which she is held by her countrymen'.[31] Jane felt vindicated: 'All Dublin has called on us to offer their sympathy', she told Rosalie Olivecrona, adding 'our enemy has been signally defeated in her efforts to injure us'; this from a woman who had lost a libel case.[32] William fared less well. The medical profession backed him for the most part, but he felt jaded by the strain of having private matters aired for all to hear. Although he had been under no obligation to take the stand, Butt had made much of his refusal: 'If her [Mary's] story is not true why did Sir William Wilde not come to contradict it?' he asked:

> Will you convict her while the man who asks you to believe she is perjured shrinks from coming in here and pledging his oath to which he asks twelve Irish gentlemen to pledge theirs?[33]

Jane attempted to deflect attention by portraying herself as the sole target of Mary's ire, assuring Rosalie Olivecrona:

> The simple solution to the affair is this – This Miss Travers is half mad – all her family are mad too – She was very destitute and haunted our house to borrow money etc. We were very kind to her as we pitied her — but suddenly she took a dislike to me amounting to hatred — and to endeavour to ruin my peace of mind commenced a series of anonymous attacks.[34]

This strong sense of justification in the face of defeat instilled in her a belief that one should defend one's good character in the face of provocation, no matter what was at stake. In time, she would offer this catastrophic advice to her younger son. Although Oscar was at Portora during the trial, his Christmas holidays coincided with its aftermath and it would have been impossible to avoid the furore. Also, one of his schoolmates, Edward Sullivan, was the son of Serjeant Sullivan. He must have heard some of the details and he would certainly have witnessed his mother's apparent delight at a verdict that had gone against her; how confusing that must have been for a young boy.

The press called Mary Travers 'wayward' and condemned her behaviour as, 'scandalous', 'unwomanly', 'vulgar' and 'degrading'. She was not done yet. In June 1865, she sued *Saunders Newsletter* for implying that she had perjured herself; this time the jury took less than half an hour to decide against her. The remainder of her life was solitary and undistinguished. When her father died in 1888, she sought financial aid from the Royal College of Physicians on the grounds that she had been wholly dependent on his income. When she was refused, she and her younger sister Emily applied for admittance to Kingston College, a charitable institution for impoverished gentlefolk located in Mitchelstown, County Cork. Without a husband to support her, she had no alternative, and what man would take on a woman who had been so roundly vilified in victory. Mary Travers died in Kingston College in 1919, aged 83.

The whole episode was irritating and expensive, but seemed soon forgotten by Jane, who was preoccupied with the possibility of a new uprising, this time orchestrated by the republican Fenian Movement. As Lady Jane Wilde, she was less supportive: 'I am not a Fenian and I disapprove highly of their prospects', she declared:

> . . . it is decidedly a democratic movement – & the gentry and aristocracy will suffer much from them – their object is to form a <u>Republic</u>. Heaven keep me from a Fenian Republic![35]

She had no concerns for William or herself, 'both national favourites'. Although revolution was on her mind, a more personal tragedy was to befall her. In February 1867, little Isola, who had been ill with fever but appeared to be recovering well, was sent to stay with her aunt Margaret Noble, William's sister and wife of the Reverend William Noble, at the Glebe at Edgeworthstown in County Longford. On 23 February, two months short of her tenth birthday, Isola's health took a dramatic turn for the worse. William and Jane reached her bedside as quickly as they could, but she died within hours. Jane was devastated by the loss of this, 'most lovable, hope-giving child'.* Describing Isola as 'the radiant angel of our home – and so bright and strong and joyous', she spoke of an evil foreboding she had experienced for months beforehand, a susceptibility to superstitious dread that was inherited by Oscar too. Jane told Lotten: '. . . a sadness is on me for life, a bitter sorrow that never can be healed'.[36] She took consolation in her sons and assured John Hilson:

> I have a belief that God will leave them to me for it seems to me as if I could bear no more sorrow and live.[37]

Poor Oscar was shattered. The doctor who attended Isola during her final days, described her as 'the most gifted and lovable child', and remembered her twelve-year-old brother as:

---

* This dreadful tragedy hit William equally hard. He erected a monument to his lovely, lost daughter in the grounds of his beloved Moytura, and retreated there as often as he could.

An affectionate, gentle, retiring, dreamy boy whose lonely and inscrutable grief found its outward expression in long and frequent visits to his sister's grave in the village cemetery.[38]

Years later, a friend[*] recalled that,

when he spoke, as he often did, of his sister who was dead, his wondrous eyes softened. "She was like a golden ray of sunshine dancing about our home".[39]

After he died, among his meagre possessions, friends found a beautiful, hand-decorated envelope containing a few golden strands and labeled 'My Isola's Hair'.[40] Perhaps his most lasting testament to her is his beautiful 'Requiescat':

> Tread lightly, she is near
> Under the snow,
> Speak gently, she can hear
> The daisies grow.
>
> All her bright golden hair
> Tarnished with rust,
> She that was young and fair
> Fallen to dust.
>
> Lily-like, white as snow,
> She hardly knew
> She was a woman, so,
> Sweetly she grew.
>
> Coffin-board, heavy stone
> Lie on her breast,
> I vex my heart alone,
> She is at rest.
>
> Peace, Peace, she cannot hear
> Lyre or sonnet,
> All my life's buried here,
> Heap earth upon it[†]

When William Butler Yeats asked for Oscar's permission to include 'Requiescat' in an anthology of Irish verse, he replied: 'I don't know that

[*] Robert Sherard.
[†] The first four lines of 'Requiescat' are inscribed on the replacement tombstone that was erected for Isola in St John's graveyard in 2013.

I think 'Requiescat' very typical of my work'.[41] Yeats used it anyway and it was hailed as 'the brightest gem in this collection'.[42]

Although Jane had lost her only daughter, William still had Emily and Mary. He took an interest in their welfare, but probably never introduced them to their half-siblings, who may not have been aware of their existence. On Halloween night, 31 October 1871, less than five years after Isola's death, Emily and Mary attended a ball at Drumaconnor House in County Monaghan. Towards the end of the evening, Andrew Nicholl Reid, their host, invited Emily to take a last turn around the floor. As they waltzed past an open fireplace, Emily's crinoline dress brushed against the embers and caught alight. When Mary rushed to her sister's aid, she managed to set her own dress on fire in the attempt.

Eyewitness reports suggest that Reid wrapped his coat around Emily and attempted to extinguish the flames by rolling her on the ground outside. It seems Mary was left to fend for herself.[43] Describing the incident in a letter to his son William, several decades later, John Butler Yeats cited a Mrs Hime, a friend who was present that night and had noted the 'prettiness' of both young women:

> After Mrs. Hime had left, one of the girls had gone too close to the fire. . . with the result that she was instantly in flames . . . both girls died.[44]

As is evidenced by the dates recorded in the brief notice that appeared in the *Northern Standard* on 25 November 1871, their suffering was agonising and prolonged:

DIED
At Drumaconnor, on the 8th inst., Mary Wilde
At Drumaconnor, on the 21st inst., Emma [sic] Wilde

Entries in the Coroner's Inquisition Book for County Monaghan suggest that this incident was the subject of two separate enquiries.[45] The first examined the circumstances of Mary's death, referring to her throughout as 'Miss Wylie', and her father as 'Sir Willm Wylie of Dublin'. Although this may have been a simple spelling mistake, it is perhaps more likely to have been a deliberate attempt to protect William's good name. Certainly, the report refers to a letter from him requesting that no inquest be held:

> doing so, might be of fatal consequence to deceased's sister, who is dangerously ill from severe burns caused to her while endeavouring to extinguish the burning clothes of her sister.[46]

Confirming the details of Mary's death, the coroner concluded that everything possible had been done to save her. Poor Emily lingered for almost a fortnight more and a second investigation determined that no inquest was required since both had died accidentally and no intervention would have prevented this. Mary and Emily Wilde were buried in the graveyard of St Molua's church in Drumnat, County Monaghan. The headstone erected to commemorate them read:

> In memory of
> 2 loving and beloved sisters
> Emily Wilde aged 24
> And
> Mary Wilde aged 22
> who lost their lives by accident
> in this parish in Novr 1871
> They were lovely and pleasant in
> their lives and in their death they
> were not divided.
> (II Samuel Chap. I, v 23)*

William was dreadfully upset by the loss of his daughters: Mrs Hime insisted that his 'groans could be heard by people outside the house'.[47] Oscar may not have known his half-sisters but, as he was living at home in Merrion Square when the incident had occurred, he must have observed the decline in his father. Mrs Hime's suggestion that the girls' mother was with them when they died was supported by local rumour. Anecdotal evidence suggests that, for 20 years afterwards, an enigmatic 'lady in black' travelled from Dublin to Monaghan by train, before taking a carriage to Drumsnatt cemetery, where she would stand silently by their graveside. When the churchwarden queried her relationship to the tragic young women, she replied that they had been very dear to her.[48] Although the identity of this veiled woman was never discovered, she was almost certainly the same 'woman dressed in black and closely veiled' who arrived at William's bedside five years later when he lay dying.

---

* When the original inscription became illegible, a replacement was erected in 2010 by the Oscar Wilde Society and Drumsnatt Parish Church.

Chapter 5

'THE SWEETEST YEARS'

She thinks I never loved her, thinks I forget. My God how
could I!
    OSCAR WILDE of Florence Balcombe[1]

On 10 October 1871, one week short of his seventeenth birthday, and
three weeks before the dreadful accident befell his half-sisters, Oscar
Wilde entered the tranquil environs of Trinity College, Dublin as an
undergraduate. As his family home was less than ten minutes stroll from
campus, it made sense to move back in with William and Jane for his
first year.* During his second year, he shared a cramped and dingy suite
of rooms at 18 Botany Bay with his brother Willie, who was in his final
year.† Oscar took to displaying an eternally unfinished landscape in oils
on an easel he placed in the centre of their sitting room. On the rare
occasions when visitors were admitted, Sir Edward Sullivan remembered:
'He [Oscar] would invariably refer to it, telling one in his humorously
unconvincing way that "he had just put in the butterfly"', a reference to
Whistler of course.[2]

    Willie, a stellar student, paved the way for his younger brother by win-
ning accolades that included a gold medal in ethics and logic and a medal
for oratory and composition. An enthusiastic member of 'The Phil', the
university's legendary Philosophical Society, he was admired as a persuasive and entertaining debater. He also contributed to *Kottabos*, a miscellany of Greek, Latin and English poetry composed by undergraduates
and alumni; one of his poems was titled, 'Salome'. Although Willie was
a hard act to follow, Oscar, who arrived with a Royal School Scholarship
from Portora, rose to the challenge admirably, amassing an even more
impressive array of prizes and contributing six poems to *Kottabos*; he even
surpassed Willie's W.C.K.W. by writing as O.F.O'F.W.W.[3]

---

* An entry in the Register of Chambers, November 1871 indicates that he was
allocated rooms.
† This residence block, overlooking what had been the college vegetable garden,
was named for its unruly occupants, who were deemed suitable for deportation
to the British penal colony of the same name.

Sir William Wilde's eminence, combined with Lady Jane Wilde's heroic standing and flair for entertaining, ensured that Oscar was well acquainted with the university's leading scholars, most of whom were regular attendees at his mother's Saturday *conversazione*. Prominent among them was the Reverend John Pentland Mahaffy, Trinity's newly appointed Professor of Ancient History, a man renowned as a sparkling conversationalist with an acerbic wit. Jane credited Mahaffy with giving 'the first noble impulse' to her brilliant son's intellect.[4] Recognizing Oscar's rare potential, Mahaffy recruited him to assist with the completion of his scholarly *Social Life in Greece from Homer to Menander*, which was published in 1874. In his preface to the first edition, Mahaffy acknowledged that his young student had 'made improvements and corrections all through the book', but he dropped this nod from later versions. Gone too was his controversial but enlightened acknowledgement of instances of homosexual love between an older and a younger Greek man.

Oscar found a second mentor in Robert Yelverton Tyrrell, founding editor of *Kottabos* and, at twenty-six, a startlingly youthful Professor of Latin. He blossomed under the guidance of these brilliant scholars, displaying an exceptional talent as a classicist and coming 'first of the firsts' among the intake of 1871. In his second year, Oscar was granted a Foundation Scholarship, an honour reserved for students of outstanding ability. His crowning achievement came in his final year, when he was awarded the prestigious Berkeley Gold Medal for Greek for an essay examining August Meineke's *Fragmenta Comicorum Graecorum*. Jane was immensely proud. When D. J. O'Donoghue compiled a biographical note for his *Irish Poetry of the Nineteenth Century*, she insisted he mention that both her boys were gold medalists.[5] Although Oscar valued his Berkeley medal, necessity obliged him to leave it with various pawnbrokers throughout his life; after his death, a ticket to reclaim it was found among his few possessions.[6]

As expected, Oscar's academic ambitions didn't end at the gates of Trinity College, Dublin. Rather than take his third year exams, he answered an advertisement in the *Oxford University Gazette* publicizing two five-year classical Demyships at Magdalen College, each awarded by exam and each worth £95 a year.* On learning that his young protégé had achieved first place, Mahaffy supposedly quipped: 'Go to Oxford, my dear Oscar: we are all much too clever for you over here'.[7] Master and

* A Demyship is a form of scholarship peculiar to Oxford University.

pupil maintained a close association during the years that followed, and they explored the antiquities of Italy and Greece together, but Mahaffy, unlike Tyrrell, distanced himself from Oscar after his conviction, refusing to sign a petition of support and insisting: 'We no longer speak, Sir, of Mr. Oscar Wilde'.[8] In time, he admitted Oscar had been 'a delightful man to talk to on matters of scholarship', as 'his views were always so fresh and unconventional'.[9]

On 17 October 1874, the day after his twentieth birthday, Oscar took up his place at Magdalen College, Oxford, where he read *Literae Humaniores*.* There, he honed the aesthetic sensibilities that had emerged at Trinity, developing a deep admiration for beauty and a lasting penchant for blue china. Although he was always conspicuous, he toned down his attire and modified his speech in an effort to blend in with his peers: 'My Irish accent was one of the many things I forgot at Oxford', he claimed.[10] The various distractions on hand led to an uncharacteristically mediocre performance during his first term; he failed Responsions and was one of only ten men during his whole time at Magdalen to be put into the *Not Commended* category.[11] Yet, he soon lived up to his dazzling potential.

Genial and amusing, Oscar formed friendships with ease. Two particular pals were Reginald 'Kitten' Harding and William 'Bouncer' Ward, who had the rooms above him. Ward introduced Oscar, nicknamed Hoskey, to David Hunter Blair, or 'Dunsky', enthusing:

> Why, he is a demy who hails from Trinity College, Dublin, where he got medals and things. A most interesting chap: I'll get him to come up here and meet you. You ought to hear him talk![12]

Hunter Blair included a lovely description of Oscar and a tribute to Jane in his memoirs:

> . . . the large features lit up by intelligence, sparkling eyes, and broad cheerful smile; altogether an attractive personality, enhanced by his extraordinary conversational abilities. One could not know him, even slightly, without realising that he had brilliant gifts, inherited from a father of exceptional mental powers, and a mother – "Speranza" of the Irish Nation – not less remarkable in a quite different way.[13]

He described the Wildes as 'an interesting and delightful family circle, into which I felt it an honour and a pleasure to be admitted'.[14]

* Oxford University's undergraduate course in Classics.

Oscar spent much of the summer of 1875 touring Italy with Mahaffy.
The latter part of his second year in Oxford was marred by tragedy. Sir
William Wilde's health had been failing for months, keeping Jane 'in con-
stant anxiety about him'. She confided in Rosalie Olivecrona:

> He is low & languid – scarcely eats & seldom goes out . . . he seems fading
> away before our eyes – & has grown so pale & wan & thin & low-spirited,
> that I too have fallen like an unstrung instrument and no poet-music can
> be struck from my heart.[15]

As William's end approached, his wife and sons kept vigil by his side.
Bedridden and barely conscious, he took great comfort from Jane's devotion and slipped away peacefully on 19 April 1876, with his hand clasped
in hers. Oscar's admiration for his mother, always strong, was never
deeper than when he witnessed her magnanimity at his father's deathbed:
'She was a wonderful woman,' he declared, 'and such a feeling as vulgar
jealousy could take no hold on her. She was well aware of my father's
constant infidelities, but simply ignored them'.[16] The act that prompted
this outpouring of admiration was extraordinarily selfless. During the last
days of her husband's life, Jane permitted a woman, dressed in black and
closely veiled, to sit at his bedside for hours at a time. She never spoke
nor lifted her veil to acknowledge Jane, Willie or Oscar, and they did not
acknowledge her.

Oscar believed that Jane's generosity allowed William to die 'with his
heart full of gratitude and affection for her'.

> Not one woman in a thousand would have tolerated her presence, but my
> mother allowed it, because she knew that my father loved this woman and
> felt that it must be a joy and a comfort to have her there by his dying bed.[17]

One wonders if he expected this level of devotion from his own wife.
Perhaps he desired the 'unconditional, unequal love of a wife for her husband' described by his Lord Goring in *An Ideal Husband*: 'women are not
meant to judge us, but to forgive us when we need forgiveness', Goring
insists. Elements of Oscar's behaviour towards his own wife suggest that
he may have believed this too.

Although Jane was willing to share her grief, she alone bore the consequences of William's poor financial management: 'the loss is one that
plunges our life into darkness,' she lamented, 'I feel like one shipwrecked.
A wife feels the position more fatally than all others – a broken, desolate
life, a changed fortune'. Her sorrow was tinged with fear: 'while my eyes are

blinded with tears, my brain, alas, is filled with many sad, bewildering cares and anxieties for the future', she confessed.[18] The damaging inequality that made wives utterly financial dependent on their husbands led to great hardship when these men died without making sufficient provision for their wives, as was the case with Jane. Nerve-jangling financial uncertainty compounded her emotional loss. Unbeknownst to Jane, whose permission was not required, William had taken out crippling mortgages on various properties, including the family home at 1 Merrion Square. She would have been homeless had Henry Wilson, her husband's eldest son, not bought the roof over her head and allowed her to stay. Secure in her home, Jane completed William's last book and included a glowing eulogy to him.[19]

At this time, Oscar found consolation in a new relationship with a lovely young woman. Sometime that summer, he paid a visit to the Balcombe family at 1 Marino Crescent on the north side of Dublin. It is not clear how he knew them as they had only recently arrived in the city. On New Year's Eve 1875, after a glittering military career[*] spanning four decades, Lieutenant-Colonel James Balcombe resigned his commission and accepted the post of Secretary to the Commissioners of Clontarf Township Office.[20] While serving as Quartermaster with the 57th regiment during the harsh winter of 1854, he had been commended for his efficiency in bringing up supplies to the beleaguered men waging the Crimean campaign. His bravery during the battles of Balaclava, Inkerman and Sebastopol earned him both the Crimean War Medal with Clasps, and the Turkish War Medal. He ended his military career in his native Ireland, serving with the Royal South Down Militia.[21]

Oscar's interest was in seventeen-year-old Florence, the fourth of six daughters born to Balcombe and his wife Phillippa Anne, née Marshall; they also had two sons.[†] When the 57th Regiment left for India on 11 May 1858, Phillippa, who was seven months pregnant, had taken her children to Cornwall where she had family connections. An army wife was expected to raise her children alone. As a consequence, Florence Ann Lemon Balcombe was born in Falmouth on 17 July 1858, while her father was stationed in Bombay. Given his involvement in the Crimean campaign, she may well have been named for Florence Nightingale; the Lemon came from her grandfather, Lemon William Marshall.

---

[*] He had enlisted as a private in 1835.
[†] She is often referred to as their third daughter, but they had a daughter who died in infancy.

By the time Oscar escorted Florence to the afternoon service at St Patrick's Cathedral on 6 August 1876, she had grown into a strikingly beautiful young woman, tall at 5'8", with soulful grey-blue eyes and lustrous chestnut hair. Oscar was besotted and gushed to 'Kitten' Harding:

> I am just going out to bring an exquisitely pretty girl to afternoon service in the Cathedral. She is just seventeen with the most perfectly beautiful face I ever saw and not a sixpence of money. I will show you her photograph when I see you next.[22]

Florence's beauty was remarked upon constantly. Her son Noel testified that she remained beautiful into her seventies and remembered men standing on their seats to get a glimpse of her when she went to the theatre. Society magazine *The Era* described her as 'one of the most brilliant constellations at the first Drawing-Room of the Dublin season', confirming that she was 'the most lovely lady present . . . beautifully and artistically dressed'.[23] Prime Minister William Ewart Gladstone referred to her simply as, 'the beauty', while George du Maurier, cartoonist grandfather of Daphne, deemed her one of the three most beautiful women* he had ever seen.[24]

Yet there was far more to Florence than beauty alone. Perhaps it was her reputation for being witty and talkative that appealed to Oscar. As well as her loveliness, *The Era* noted her 'intellectual features' and 'intelligence', characteristics rarely mentioned in the few biographical sketches that exist.[25] It is telling that the often acerbic Horace Wyndham described her as 'a charming woman and brim full of Irish wit and impulsiveness'.[26] Her niece Dr Eleanor Knott, a renowned early Irish scholar and academic, remembered her as 'a wonderful letter-writer . . . always crisp & gay – often sardonic; never dull'.[27] She was clever and tenacious, and devoted the last two decades of her long life to the astute management of her financial affairs, demonstrating a steely determination coupled with excellent business acumen. Her surviving letters reveal a strong and confident woman, keen to assert her rights: 'To hell with these annoyances!!' she exclaimed in one.[28]

Shortly after Oscar took Florence to church, he left to spend time at Moytura House with another new friend, the artist Frank Miles. Theirs was a deep friendship, some say more than that, and they shared a house in London after Oscar came down from Oxford.[29] In May, Oscar worked

* The other two were, 'Mrs. Stillman and Mrs. John Hare'.

hard on an essay that combined a review of 'The Women of Homer', a chapter from John Addington Symonds's newly published *Studies of the Greek Poets*, with his own views on the heroines of Homer's epics. It is telling that he chose this topic: women occupy a place of honour in Homer's works, and he elevated them in an era when they were expected to do little more than bear children and pleasure men. Homer, like Oscar, realised that a wise and clever woman could use her ingenuity to rule her husband and her house. A brilliant classicist, Oscar also admired Sappho, who retold Homer's epics in her poetry and wrote of love for both sexes. Although he wrote more than eight thousand words, he never completed his essay.[*]

Returning to Dublin, Oscar presented Florence with 'View from Moytura House', a rather amateurish watercolour inscribed, 'for Florrie'; his delicate pencil sketch of her is far more successful. She displayed the little landscape 'that poor O painted for me' until the end of her life, telling her sister Philippa, 'Oscar's little watercolour creates much envy in the breasts of the Oscar cult'.[30] The affection between the couple deepened: 'Believe me ever yours', she wrote, and she invited him to visit her at home to read aloud a poem he had written for her.[31] When asked his favourite name for a girl, Oscar answered 'Florence'.[32] On Christmas Morning 1876, six months into their relationship, he gave her a delicate gold cross with his name engraved on it, an act that is interpreted as a prelude to an engagement.

As Oscar was at Oxford University, the lovers saw little of each other. In Greece with Mahaffy during the Easter break of 1877, he received a card from Florence, assuring him he was in her thoughts; he was touched by her warm wishes, sent 'over so many miles of land and sea'.[33] Swapping the antique splendour of Greece for Dublin, he found 'Florrie more lovely than ever'.[34] Little wonder poet Denis Florence McCarthy described Oscar at that time as having 'so much amiable enthusiasm about everything that is good and beautiful'.[35] Yet, his ardour appears to have waned as the months went by. Perhaps chaste worship from afar suited his temperament and tastes better than the mundanity of a conventional courtship. Pleading ill-health, he spent four days of the Easter break of 1878 at the Royal Bath Hotel in Bournemouth. A letter to 'My dear Florrie',

[*] It was finished on his behalf: *Oscar Wilde: The Women of Homer*, edited by Thomas Wright and Donald Mead, was published by the Oscar Wilde Society in November 2008.

signed 'Ever yours, Oscar', assured her he was missing her but disclosed the presence of 'a delightful friend (a *new* friend)', whose identity or gender was not disclosed.[36]

Meanwhile, Florence was stranded in Dublin and worried for her future. As a beautiful young woman of slender means and little education, her best hope of future security was to marry well. Although she was very fond of Oscar, he was always away and she had attracted the attention of another brilliant young Dubliner, a man who appeared to have better prospects. Bram Stoker knew the Wilde family well. A decade older than Florence and seven years Oscar's senior, he too was an alumnus of Trinity College, Dublin. As an undergraduate, he had accepted a full-time post as a clerk in the Registrar of Petty Sessions in Dublin Castle, but his new responsibilities did not prevent him from participating fully in college life: he was Auditor of the Historical Society, President of the Philosophical Society, and Chairman of the University Foot-Races Committee, a post held previously by Isaac Butt. Despite his strong build, Oscar demonstrated little interest in sport. Bram, who was bedridden in childhood, showed tremendous athletic prowess as an adult. Tall and powerfully built, he was a running and walking champion, an accomplished weightlifter, and a strong swimmer. He excelled at gymnastics and played rugby for the Trinity College first team. Beyond the playing fields, he earned a certificate in oratory and silver medals in aesthetics, composition and history. He graduated with a B.A. in 1870, and added an extramural M.A. in 1875.

Although they were not close friends, Bram had nominated Oscar for membership of 'The Phil'. He was far friendlier with Willie and surviving letters between them are warm and affectionate. He was acquainted with William and Jane too. A history enthusiast, Bram often took refuge in William's study during Jane's "Conversazione", to listen to tales of exploration and adventure. William Wilde was a keen Egyptologist and was instrumental in the decision to relocate one of Cleopatra's needles to the banks of the Thames.[37] His discovery of the mummified remains of a dwarf is believed to have informed Bram's novel *The Jewel of the Seven Stars* (1903).

Bram's formidable mother, Charlotte shared a philanthropic mission with William Wilde, since both addressed the neglect of 'deaf mutes' in Ireland. On 13 May 1863, Charlotte Stoker had read a paper *On the Necessity of a State Provision for the Education of the Deaf and Dumb* to the Statistical and Social Inquiry Society of Ireland, one of few Irish organisations that encouraged women, as associate members, to present papers, and debate social issues on equal terms with men. William, a founding member of the society, contributed to the discussion and supported Charlotte's contention with facts and figures from his census report. Like Jane, Charlotte advocated better access to education for women, although she did not extend this sentiment to her own daughters.

Bram's friendship with Jane Wilde lasted until the end of her life. A letter from his father is testament to its strength: 'I suppose you dined with Lady Wilde as usual', he asked.[38] Both were fascinated by Irish folklore and elements of the supernatural stories she collected in *Ancient Legends, Mystic Charms & Superstitions of Ireland*, published ten years before *Dracula*, find their echo in his most celebrated novel and in other work too. Bram was certainly aware of Jane's observation: '. . . in the Transylvanian legends and superstitions . . . many will be found identical with the Irish'. Particularly significant, she argued, was the shared belief that: 'the dead are only in a trance; they can hear everything but can make no sign'.[39] Her descriptions of horned witches who drew blood from victims as they slept must have informed his 'weird sisters', three female vampires who fed on the blood of men. While she told tales of men who assumed the shape of wolves and monstrous, soul-devouring hounds, his best loved book reverberates with the howling of wolves, and his Dracula assumes the shape of 'an immense dog'. Jane Wilde, it seems, had as great an influence on *Dracula* as many more widely acknowledged sources.

Bram Stoker's first book was *The Duties of Clerks of Petty Sessions in Ireland*. His future as a civil servant looked secure, but his abiding passion since childhood was for the theatre. In May 1870, he saw Henry Irving play Digby Grant in the comedy *Two Roses* at Dublin's Theatre Royal. Keen to discover if the critics shared his high opinion of this production, he bought the Irish newspapers the following day, but found not a single review. Proactive as ever, his response was to volunteer as an unpaid theatre reviewer for the *Dublin Evening Mail*. His exceptionally flattering review of Irving's *Hamlet* at the Theatre Royal prompted the actor to invite Bram to supper in his suite in the Shelbourne Hotel: 'Soul had looked into soul!', Bram wrote, 'From that hour began a friendship as profound, as close, as lasting as can be between two men'.[40]

In December 1878, when Irving took over as Actor/Manager at the Lyceum Theatre in London, he persuaded Bram to leave his secure civil service job and become Acting Manager. He was, in the words of his newest employee: 'mightily surprised when he found that I had a wife – *the* wife

– with me'.[41] It's not certain when or where Florence Balcombe met Bram Stoker, perhaps they were introduced by the Wildes.* Whatever the circumstances, matters between them had progressed quickly. When Oscar arrived in Dublin in September 1878, he learned, not from Florence, that she was engaged to be married to Bram. He had been complacent and now he felt crushed.

Announcing his intention to return to England, 'probably for good', Oscar asked Florence to return the little gold cross he had given her. He undertook to carry it with him at all times as a memento of 'two sweet years – the sweetest of all the years of my youth'.[42] With great melodrama, he declared: 'I at least cannot be indifferent to your welfare: the currents of our lives flowed too long beside one another for that'.[43] Although Florence's reply does not survive, she suggested they meet in Harcourt Street, which caused Oscar great distress as he was only willing to meet 'Florence', no longer 'Florrie', at her mother's house in Clontarf where they first met.† Promising to return her letters, he enclosed a 'scrap' he had carried with him for eighteen months – almost certainly the Easter card he received in Greece – 'how strange and out of tune it all reads now', he grieved.[44] Oscar's final letter in this exchange adopted an angry tone and he expressed disappointment that Florence had interpreted his suggestion as a desire for a clandestine meeting: 'after all, I find you know me very little,' he exclaimed.[45]

Florence Balcombe married Bram Stoker in St Ann's Church on Dawson Street on 4 December 1878, twelve months earlier than planned so that they could move to London as man and wife.[46] Florence, aged nineteen, is classified as a minor on her marriage certificate. It is distinctly odd that she gave her address as 16 Harcourt Street, rather than her family home in Clontarf. There has never been any suggestion of a falling out with her family and Bram was executor of her mother's will. Over the years, a pervasive notion that their marriage was not successful has persisted. The evidence cited most often in support of this theory is the fact that they only had one child, Noel Stoker, born on New Year's Eve,

* By coincidence, Bram had lived in Marino Crescent too, but had left long before the Balcombe family arrived and he did not meet Florence there as many believe.
† Street directories of the time list Bram as sometimes resident at 16 Harcourt Street, an address he shared with his older brother Thornley, an eminent surgeon. Three of the Stoker brothers, Thornley, Richard and George, all of them doctors, were registered to a practice at 16 Harcourt Street.

1879. There could have been any number of reasons for this. Certainly, Noel's daughter, Ann, was adamant that Bram was absolutely devoted to Florence.[*]

Renowned for his kindness, his keen sense of humour and his endless repertoire of amusing stories, Bram made an excellent companion. Although consumed with Irving and his work at the Lyceum, he made no apology for this and was happy for Florence to have friends of her own. She entertained lavishly, enjoyed regular shopping trips to Paris, and was escorted around London by the librettist W. S. Gilbert, who admired her hugely and could be very flirtatious: 'My wife sends her love & I would if I dared', he wrote.[47] Bram, in turn, enjoyed friendships with several women, including Jane Wilde. He was particularly fond of actress Ellen Terry, who called him 'Ma', and he developed a close and lasting friendship with soprano and actress Genevieve Ward. An exceptionally kind man, he once sent a fourteen-page letter of advice to Helen Barry, who took up acting aged thirty-two after the marriage she contracted, aged fifteen and heavily pregnant, was finally dissolved.

Bram was an intensely private man who left little account of his innermost thoughts, but it seems clear from what evidence remains that he loved Florence dearly. When he toured America with Irving, he complained of the loneliness of being away from his wife, and he always invited her along. Florence, who loved adventure, did join him once, but the week-long voyage terrified her. She had been shipwrecked with Noel when he was just seven years old and spent twelve hours drifting in a flimsy lifeboat before it washed up at Fécamp in Normandy; Florence wrote an article for the *Dublin Evening News* and the Stoker family made an annual pilgrimage to Fécamp to commemorate the rescue. She never lost her fear of sea travel and was horrified when the Titanic sank in 1912, a week before Bram's death.[48]

The Stoker family holidayed together regularly. In Scotland, a Mrs. Cruickshank, proprietor of the Kilmarnock Arms, said of them:

> He was one of the nicest men I ever knew . . . A big, cheery, handsome Irishman; and his wife was the most beautiful woman I ever set eyes on.[49]

During the summer of 1890, they spent three memorable weeks in the seaside town of Whitby in East Yorkshire, where much of Dracula is set.

[*] In conversation with Bram Stoker's biographer Paul Murray, for his excellent *From the Shadow of Dracula: A Life of Bram Stoker* (Jonathan Cape, 2004).

There, they were invited to tea by the novelist Violet Hunt, who, by her own account, had been on the receiving end of a proposal of marriage from Oscar by then: 'Bram is a dear and Mrs. is so pretty and kind', she wrote.[50]

Florence and Bram enjoyed a strong working partnership. Informing her mother that she was taking singing lessons, Florence admitted: 'It's the only amusement I indulge in as there's so much I do now for Bram'.[51] Towards the end of his life, Bram's health failed and Florence nursed him without complaint: 'It is harder on poor Florence (who has been an angel) than on me', he told his brother Thornley. 'She had to do all the book-keeping and find the money to live on – God only knows how she man-aged'.[52] Bram's great friend, novelist and playwright Hall Caine, wrote admiringly of Florence's devotion, declaring: 'If his was the genius of friendship, hers must have been the genius of love'.[53]

Had Florence, who was always so level-headed, married Oscar, her sister Philippa argued fancifully, he never would have suffered as he did. She was certainly tenacious in the protection of Bram's literary legacy. After his death in 1912, she published a posthumous collection of short stories, which included 'Dracula's Guest', a lost chapter from *Dracula*. In her introduction, she wrote:

> A few months before the lamented death of my husband — I might say even as the shadow of death was over him — he planned three series of short stories for publication, and the present volume is one of them . . . Had my husband lived longer, he might have seen fit to revise this work, which is mainly from the earlier years of his strenuous life. But, as fate has entrusted to me the issuing of it, I consider it fitting and proper to let it go forth practically as it was left by him.[54]

Florence was resolute in asserting her rights to *Dracula*, her chief source of income. When she discovered, by way of an anonymous letter, that Prana Films, a German company was showing *Nosferatu*, an unauthorised version of *Dracula*, she acted immediately. Lacking resources, she joined the Society of Authors and, through this organisation, demanded and was granted £5,000 in royalties along with an undertaking that every copy of *Nosferatu* would be destroyed.[*] In October 1928, when she read an article in *Today's Cinema* claiming, inaccurately, that Universal Studios

---

[*] Florence prevailed after a torturous three-year battle, although several copies of *Nosferatu* have resurfaced since.

had bought the rights, she took the fight to Hollywood and prevented the studios from profiting at her expense.

Oscar overcame his pique and re-established good relations with Florence and Bram. He attended her Sunday gatherings and joined the Beefsteak Club at the Lyceum, a lively backstage dining club revived by Bram. Both Bram and Florence attended the premiere of *Lady Windermere's Fan*, and Oscar presented 'My Dear Florence' with inscribed copies of *The Happy Prince and Other Stories* and *Salomé*. Yet, his strong romantic feelings for Florence lasted for more than two years. When she played a vestal virgin in Tennyson's *The Cup* at the Lyceum Theatre on 3 January 1881, Oscar sent two crowns of flowers to his friend Ellen Terry, who was playing the lead, accompanied by this revealing note:

> Will you accept one of them, whichever you think will suit you best. The other – don't think me treacherous, Nellie – but the other please give to Florrie from yourself. I should like to think that she was wearing something of mine the first night she comes on the stage, that anything of mine should touch her. Of course if you think – but you won't think she will suspect? How could she? She thinks I never loved her, thinks I forget. My God how could I![55]

Perhaps the most poignant legacy of their relationship is the poetry Florence inspired. Oscar's companion poems, 'Her Voice' and 'My Voice', are interpreted as a dialogue between them; although each takes a different perspective, both speak with regret.[56] Lines in 'Her Voice' suggest an engagement:

> It was here I trow
> I made that vow
> Swore that two lives should be like one

The woman declares, 'It shall be, I said, for eternity 'Twixt you and me!' But she disappoints her lover, declaring bluntly, 'those times are over and done, Love's web is spun'. She offers consolation with the line, 'I have my beauty, — you your Art'. In 'My Voice', the man's response is terse and sorrowful; he is distressed that his lover can so easily swap their dreamlike world for dull reality.[57]

In 'Silentium Amoris',[*] the narrator has lost his lover 'to some lips of sweeter melody', and is left 'to nurse the barren memory of unkissed

---

* The Silence of Love.

kisses, and songs never sung'. He admits that her beauty, the 'resplendent sun' to his 'pallid moon', has inhibited him from expressing his love forcefully enough and she has left him as a result.[58] In 'Quia Multum Amavi',* Oscar uses Catholic imagery† to compare his sense of wonder 'When first my smitten eyes beat full on thee' to the awe experienced by a priest at the moment of transubstantiation, insisting that his emotions are the stronger. Although the narrator laments his loss, he admits, 'I am most glad I loved thee'. In 'Flower of Love', Oscar compares their love to that of Dante and Beatrice. He accepts the blame for its failure, but assures her, 'Yet I am not sorry that I loved you'.

Their relationship may have inspired Bram too. In *The Snake's Pass*, which contains a reference to a 'Docther Wilde', his Arthur Severn is hopeful that Norah Joyce, a beautiful peasant girl, will rescind her promise to marry his rival Dick Sutherland, and that Sutherland will accept this with good grace. His short story 'Greater Love', which was published posthumously by Florence, centres on two friends in love with the same girl. An undated journal entry describes a chilling story he was thinking of writing:

> Seaport. Two sailors love girl – one marries her, other swears revenge. Husband goes out to sea soon after marriage & on return after some days sees in grey light of morning his young wife crucified on the great cross which stands at end of pier.[59]

Although Oscar was hurt by Florence's rejection, he recovered sufficiently to propose marriage to at least two women before meeting Constance Lloyd, the woman who became his wife.

---

* Because I Have Loved Too Much.
† Both demonstrated an interest in Roman Catholicism – he had a lifelong flirtation and a deathbed conversion, while she converted in her mid-forties.

Chapter 6

'TEA AND BEAUTIES'

With women he succeeded a great deal better than with men.
LORD ALFRED DOUGLAS on Oscar Wilde[1]

Although his relationships with men, Lord Alfred Douglas in particular, are well documented, Florence Balcombe was not the only woman to excite Oscar's youthful ardour. During the summer of 1875,[*] he received an indignant letter from one Dublin matron, reproaching him for kissing her daughter at every opportunity. Having found them in a compromising clinch, she felt compelled to write:

> Dear Oscar, I was very much pained the last time I was at your house when I went into the drawing room and saw Fidelia sitting upon your knee. Young as she is, she ought to have (and I told her) the instinctive delicacy that would have shrunk from it – but oh! Oscar, the thing was neither right, nor manly, nor gentlemanlike in you.[2]

Perhaps this was on his mind when he had his Lady Bracknell walk in on young Jack Worthing, down on bended knee before her daughter Gwendolyn: 'Mr. Worthing! Rise, sir, from this semi-recumbent posture. It is most indecorous', she exclaimed.

October brought a more encouraging letter from Edith J. Kingsford, who hinted that her parents would welcome a proposal of marriage to their ward Eva, an orphaned cousin of his.[3] Oscar was not as keen as she supposed. In June 1876, his flirtatious behaviour towards 'Bouncer' Ward's sister Gertrude[†] during a picnic lunch for undergraduates and their families provoked intense speculation, particularly when he admitted he thought her 'very charming indeed'.[4] The following month, Oscar spent a week at Bingham Rectory as the guest of Frank Miles, and wrote admiringly of his friend's talented mother, Mary, and artistic sisters: Eleanor,

---

* Ellmann says 1875 but others suggest this letter was dated 1876 or 1877.
† Two years later, almost to the day, Gertrude, aged twenty-one, married Reverend Harris Fleming St. John, who was more than two decades her senior.

Sybilla, Clara and Agatha. He thought the girls 'all very pretty indeed', and admitted that his heart was 'torn in sunder with admiration for them all', although one in particular, it's not clear who, was 'quite lovely'.[5]

Although women could not matriculate or take degrees at Oxford University until 1920, Oscar became friendly with several who moved in the same intellectual circles, albeit through their connection to prominent men.* One was Marian Fitzgerald Willets, stepdaughter of James Legge, the university's first Professor of Chinese. At her request, Oscar sent her *The Irish Monthly*, which contained a poem of his, and later a reproduction of 'Hope', a Burne-Jones watercolour depicting this theological virtue as a beautiful woman; he admired it, he said, for its 'humanity and sympathy'. Marian was the object of worshipful glances from Oscar's friend Bertram Hunt who had seen her on a train but had no idea how to make her acquaintance. When he happened upon her, standing on a towpath and chatting with Oscar, he persuaded his friend to invite her to one of his tea parties; they were married shortly afterwards.

Oscar's enchanting get-togethers were hugely popular. On Sunday evenings after commons, he entertained friends in his well-appointed and exquisitely decorated rooms, considered the finest in Oxford. One guest recalled: 'The panelled walls were thickly hung with old engravings – chiefly engravings of the fair sex artistically clad as nature clad them'; further evidence of Oscar's youthful admiration for the female form, at least in the abstract.[6] These convivial gatherings were best described by Oscar's friend, David Hunter Blair:

> On the table smoked two brimming bowls of gin-and-whisky punch; and long churchwarden pipes, with a brand of choice tobacco, were provided for the guests. The meetings were gay and hilarious – not uproarious; and no one that I saw was ever the worse for the punch. There was generally music.[7]

Afterwards, Hunter Blair and 'Bouncer' Ward would huddle around the fire, while Oscar led the talk, 'pouring out a flood of paradoxes,

---

* From 1866, women could obtain special permission to attend lectures given by their relatives or friends. A statute passed in 1875 introduced special higher examinations for women set at approximately the level of undergraduate preliminary and final examinations but with no degree attached. Activism on the part of the Association for Promoting the Higher Education of Women (AEW) led to the establishment of colleges for women from 1879; these were not given full collegiate status until 1959.

untenable propositions, quaint comments on men and things'. Not once did 'a coarse or unseemly word fall from his lips'.[8]

One regular tea party attendee was novelist Margaret Louisa Woods, daughter of George Granville Bradley, who was Master of University College. Afterwards, she would share any salacious details with her friend and fellow novelist Rhoda Broughton, who was not welcome to attend.[9] According to Woods, Rhoda absolutely loathed Oscar and he in turn felt intimidated by her. They met when she and her widowed sister Eleanor arrived in Oxford during Oscar's final year, at the suggestion of the poet Matthew Arnold. At thirty-eight she was considerably older than Oscar and had earned notoriety by writing six scandalous novels. The gossip she gleaned from Woods went into her eighth.

Although Rhoda was born in North Wales, her Irish roots stretched deep. Her late mother, Jane Bennett, had grown up at 18 Merrion Square. In 1856, the Bennett parents let their home to gothic novelist Joseph Sheridan le Fanu and his wife, Susanna, Jane's sister. Le Fanu was well acquainted with William and Jane Wilde, who lived a few doors up. After Suzanna fell into despair and died in mysterious circumstances that were never discussed, Rhoda remained close to her uncle, who encouraged her literary ambitions. On a rainy Sunday afternoon in 1867, as Rhoda struggled through a tedious novel, 'the spirit moved her to write'.[10] She tossed her dreary book aside and scribbled furiously for six weeks, producing *Not Wisely but Too Well*, the lurid tale of young Kate Chester, who stops just short of an adulterous affair with the self-regarding Dare Stamer; it was rumoured to be semi-autobiographical.

Le Fanu serialised it in the *Dublin University Magazine*, which he edited at the time, and persuaded Rhoda to send it to publisher George Bentley & Sons; Bentley turned it down after his editorial reader Geraldine Jewsbury declared it 'The most thoroughly sensual tale I have read in English for a long time'. This was exactly what readers wanted. When *Not Wisely but Too Well* was brought out by the more audacious Tinsley Brothers, it became the first in a string of hugely controversial bestsellers. Three years later, the circulating libraries lifted their ban on her books and Rhoda's popularity soared. Yet, she published anonymously until 1872, and most readers assumed she was a man. One unwitting reviewer for the *Athenaeum* declared:

> That the author is not a young woman, but a man, who, in the present story, shows himself destitute of refinement of thought or feeling and

ignorant of all that women either are or ought to be, is evident on every page.[11]

Exuberant and ferociously independent, with a well-deserved reputation as a waspish wit, Rhoda divided opinion. Oscar's friend James Rennell Rodd observed that she had 'a great heart but a caustic tongue'.[12] Among her supporters were Matthew Arnold, Robert Browning, Thomas Hardy and Henry James, who shared her apparently irrational dislike of Oscar. The Reverend Charles Dodgson, known to us as Lewis Carroll, refused to attend a dinner with her as he 'greatly disapproved' of her novels. Anthony Trollope admired her, but despaired at how she 'made her ladies do and say things which ladies would not do and say'.

> They throw themselves at men's heads, and when they are not accepted only think how they may throw themselves again. Miss Broughton is still so young that I hope she may live to overcome her fault in this direction.[13]

Rhoda insisted she was merely responding to market forces: 'since the public like it hot and strong, I am not the person to disoblige them', she declared.[14] Somerset Maugham sympathised and had a character in his short story "The Round Dozen" observe:

> I remember Miss Broughton telling me once that when she was young people said her books were fast and when she was old they said they were slow, and it was very hard since she had written exactly the same sort of book for forty years.[15]

It's difficult to fathom the animosity that crackled between Oscar and Rhoda as they had much in common: both were blessed with witty and persuasive personalities; both eschewed the narrowly prescribed gender roles imposed by a judgemental Victorian society; and both courted controversy by tackling taboos in their writing. Besides, Oscar was not easily intimidated by anyone. Whatever the reason, he stopped inviting Rhoda to tea and she took this exclusion to heart. Her good friend Ethel Arnold, niece of Matthew and a pioneering journalist in her own right, claimed Rhoda was referring to Oscar when she carped:

> I can't forget those early years of my life, when those from whom I had every right and reason to expect kindness and hospitality showed me nothing but cold incivility. I resent it still, and I shall resent it until my dying day.[16]

Oscar was reportedly furious when Rhoda caricatured him in *Second Thoughts* as 'long pale poet' Francis Chaloner, who carries a, 'lotus lily in one pale hand'. Leaving no room for doubt, she furnished Chaloner's room with a great white lily in a large blue vase that stood alongside easels supporting, 'various pictures in different stages of finish'. It seems she barely knew him, since she made Chaloner egotistical and humourless. Oscar was understandably wary and Margaret Woods recalled:

> The last time I met Oscar Wilde was at a private view of the Royal Academy; he then said that he had lately come across Rhoda Broughton and found her tongue as bitter as ever.[17]

He took his revenge by reviewing Broughton's *Betty's Visions* for the *Pall Mall Gazette* in October 1886: 'No one can ever say of her that she has tried to separate flippancy from fiction', he wrote, 'whatever harsh criticisms may be passed on the construction of her sentences, she at least possesses that one touch of vulgarity that makes the whole world kin'. He closed by declaring, 'In Philistia lies Miss Broughton's true sphere and to Philistia she should return'.[18] Of course, he may have simply disliked her novel, but his words give an insight into how, for all his apparent poise, Oscar was rattled by those who showed him disdain: he could certainly harbor a grudge.

Oscar got on wonderfully well with most women. As Lord Alfred Douglas said, with uncharacteristic accuracy, women loved him, 'because, although he was expected to talk brilliantly, he really did a great deal of listening'.[19] He also inspired characters that were far more sympathetic than Chaloner and the first of these was 'Claude Davenant', a garrulous aesthete with exquisite sensibilities and glorious banter. Oscar knew Davenant's creator as 'my friend Miss Fletcher (the author of *The Nile Novel)*'.[20] In 1876, Julia Constance Fletcher, aged eighteen, an American-born author living in Venice, published the highly regarded *A Nile Novel, or Kismet* under her pseudonym, George Fleming. Months later, she bumped into Oscar, who was in Rome with 'Bouncer' Ward and David Hunter-Blair.

Oscar found Julia fascinating, particularly when he heard rumours of her brief but tempestuous affair with Byron's grandson, Lord Lovelace. There were whispers of a broken engagement, followed by desperate but futile attempts to retrieve letters and keepsakes that had belonged to his grandfather.[21] As they rode together through the pastoral beauty of the Campagna, Julia took the opportunity to study Oscar. Weeks later, she wrote him into *Mirage*, the sentimental tale of 'Constance Varley', a perceptive and urbane young American who encounters 'Claude Davenant' while riding through Syria and Palestine. Varley likens Davenant to a portrait by Holbein: 'pale, large-featured', with unconventionally long hair: 'He spoke like a man who has made a study of expression. He listened like one accustomed to speak', she observed.[22] Although Constance rejects Claude for a more conventional suitor, she does so with regret. Fletcher dedicated *Mirage* to Walter Pater, hero of the Aesthetic movement and a fellow at Brasenose College, admired by both Oscar and she.

Perhaps Julia was one of the attractions that led Oscar to return late for the start of the new term at Magdalen.* He begged Bouncer Ward to supply her address '*immediately*', as he had promised to send her some of Pater's articles.[23] Her reply delighted him and he told Bouncer that she 'writes as cleverly as she talks', adding, 'I am much attracted by her in every way'.[24] Julia's arrival in Oxford the following summer coincided with one of Oscar's greatest literary successes. On 10 June 1878, he was announced as the winner of the prestigious Newdigate Prize for his poem, 'Ravenna'. Her letter, dated 12 June, confirms her arrival later that week and congratulates him on his success; she signed off with an affectionate 'Dudu'.[25]

Oscar's telegram to Jane elicited a wildly enthusiastic response addressed, 'To The Olympic Victor':

> Oh, Gloria, Gloria! Thank you a million times for the telegram – It is the first pleasant throb of joy I have had this year – How I long to read the poem – Well, after all, we have a genius. That is something. Attorneys can't take that away.
>
> Oh, I do hope you will have some joy in your heart – You have got honour and recognition – and this at only 22 is a grand thing. I am proud of you – & I am happier than I can tell – This gives you a certainty of success in the future. You can now trust your own intellect & know what it can do – I should so like to see the smile on your face now – Ever & ever. With joy & pride,
>
> Your Loving Mother[26]

A congratulatory notice in *The Nation* hailed the triumph of 'Mr. Oscar Wilde, son of our national poetess, "Speranza,"', and trumpeted:

---

* He had informed the college authorities, but was rusticated and fined £47, which was returned the following year in recognition of his academic achievements.

We heartily congratulate our young countryman on his distinguished success, and we congratulate also his gifted mother on an event of which she has such good reason to feel proud.[27]

In Ireland and much of America too, Oscar was, first and foremost, Speranza's son.

When Oscar read 'Ravenna' at Encaenia* on 26 June 1878, he was 'listened to with rapt attention and frequently applauded'.[28] He dedicated the published version:

TO MY FRIEND
GEORGE FLEMING,
AUTHOR OF "THE NILE NOVEL," AND "MIRAGE"

Their friendship endured. A decade later, as editor of *The Woman's World*, Oscar serialised Julia's novel, *The Truth about Clement Ker*. In 1894, he attended the first night of *Mrs. Lessingham*, a dramatic exploration of female solidarity Julia staged in collaboration with pioneering actress Elizabeth Robins, who was also a friend of his.

Julia outlived Oscar by almost four decades. She never married and devoted the latter half of her life to the care of her ailing mother. When war broke out in 1914, she worked tirelessly as a volunteer nurse in the military hospitals of Venice. Her wartime service to her adopted nation earned her the Croce de Guerra, the Campaign Ribbon with two stars, the medal for epidemics, the Duke of Aosta's medal of the Tirza Armata, and the silver medal of military merit. An obituary in *The Times* of 11 July 1938, lamented the loss of 'her brilliant personality and exceedingly witty talk'.[29]

As the summer of 1878 drew to a close, Oscar met another intelligent and progressive young woman, fifteen-year-old Helena Sickert, daughter of the artist Oswald Sickert and his wife, Eleanor Louisa. Helena, whom Oscar christened 'Miss Nellie' was struck by his unfailing 'joyousness', and wrote: 'I have never known any grown person who laughed so wholeheartedly and who made such mellow music of it'.[30] Oscar encouraged Helena's love of poetry, and recited 'Ravenna' to her as they sat beneath the gnarled and fragrant apple trees at her home in Neuville near Dieppe. He invented 'poetical nonsense of exactly the right blend' for her little brothers, Oswald, aged seven, and Leo, aged five, before

* The ceremony at which the University of Oxford awards honorary degrees and commemorates its benefactors.

joining the rough and tumble of their games, as he would one day with his own two sons.[31]

When the Sickerts moved to London, Oscar was a welcome visitor who 'poured out the riches of his talk' for hours at a time. He gave Helena a copy of the *Selected Poems* of Matthew Arnold, inscribed to 'Nellie Sickert, from her friend Oscar Wilde'; he had taken the trouble to mark his favourites.[32] Years later, she conjured up those delightful days in her memoir, *I Have Been Young*:

> When I try to recapture the enchantment I see the big indolent figure, lounging in an easy chair, his face alive with delight in what he was saying, pouring out stories and descriptions whose extravagance piled up and up till they toppled over in a wave of laughter . . . I can't remember any of his countless witty sayings, but his laughter I shall hear till I die. His extravaganzas had no end, his invention was inexhaustible, and everything he said was full of joy and energy.[33]

Oscar introduced Helena to Jane, and she realised immediately that he loved his mother dearly. She was mortified when Jane drew her to the window, pushed her hair back from her face and declared 'in a deep dramatic voice', 'A highly intellectual countenance! I shall hear of you in the literary world', a declaration reminiscent of Lady Bracknell's seeing 'social possibilities' in Cecily's profile in *The Importance of Being Earnest*.[34] She was not wrong.

As a schoolgirl, Helena Sickert honed her burgeoning feminism by reading John Stuart Mill's *The Subjugation of Women*. The unease she expressed at the limited role offered to women damaged her relationship with her parents and her father refused to pay her fees to Girton College, Cambridge. Fortunately, she won a partial scholarship and her godmother paid the balance. Helena was particularly disappointed in her mother: 'A boy might be a person but not a girl', she complained:

> This was the ineradicable root of our differences. All my brothers had rights as persons; not I. Till I married [aged twenty-four], she never, in her heart, conceded me personal rights.[35]

While Helena was an undergraduate, Oscar commissioned her first piece of journalism, an article for *The Woman's World*. As her degree in Moral Science allowed her to lecture in psychology and economics, Oscar christened her 'The Economist'. Later, she became a longstanding contributor to the liberal newspaper *The Manchester Guardian*, which supported the campaign for women's suffrage. She also published a series of progressive books under her married name, Helena Swanwick.

Over time, Helena became convinced that the campaigns for peace and for women's rights were inextricably linked. A founding member and first president of the Women's International League for Peace and Freedom, she was also on the executive of the National Union of Women's Suffrage Societies. A Labour Party activist, she was twice appointed substitute-delegate to the League of Nations during the interwar years. A vociferous opponent of the punitive terms of the Treaty of Versailles, she warned that they would lead inevitably to fresh hostilities. She was right. Her grief at the death of her husband,* combined with debilitating health problems of her own and a growing disillusionment with international affairs, fed into feelings of utter despair. On 16 November 1939, shortly after the outbreak of World War II, the extraordinary Helena Swanwick, aged seventy-five, took an overdose of Veronal and ended her life.

She left us her remarkable autobiography, *I Have Been Young*, in which she declared 'What I saw of Oscar was all good'. She remembered how: 'His friendly eyes, his full warm voice, his cordial laughter brought sunshine'. Her most touching vignette describes him comforting her mother, maddened by grief after the sudden death of her husband:

> One afternoon Oscar called: I told him of her desperate state, and he said he must see her. She stubbornly refused, and I went back to him to say I could not prevail on her. "But she must see me," he replied. "She must. Tell her I shall stay here till she does." Back I went, and for a few minutes my mother sat, crying and wringing her hands, and saying "I can't. Send him away." Then she rose and went into the room where he was waiting, crying as she went. I saw Oscar take both her hands and draw her to a chair, beside which he set his own; then I left them alone. He stayed a long time, and before he went I heard my mother laughing.[36]

In November 1878, when Oscar went down from Oxford with an impressive double first in Literae Humaniores ('Greats'), those who knew him best were not at all surprised: 'He liked to pose as a dilettante trifling with his books', wrote David Hunter Blair, 'but I knew of his hours of assiduous and laborious reading, often into the small hours of the morning after our pleasant symposia in his rooms'.[37] Although he would have welcomed a fellowship, none was forthcoming; he might have made

---

* Mathematician Frederick Swanwick died in 1934.

an exceptionally fine academic and later admitted, 'I often think with some regret of my Oxford days and wish I had not left Parnassus for Piccadilly'.[38] Styling himself, 'A Professor of aesthetics, and a Critic of Art', he headed for London, where he had much to do 'looking for lodgings and making literary friends.[39]

After he applied for a reader's ticket to the British Museum Library, he encountered a group of intelligent and progressive women with whom he would collaborate when editing *The Woman's World*. These insurgents included brilliant essayist, poet and novelist Amy Levy; pioneering trade unionist Clementina Black, cofounder of the Women's Trade Union Association; 'new woman' novelists, Ella Hepworth Dixon and Olive Schreiner; and scholarly poet A. Mary F. Robinson. Another regular was Violet Paget, a transgender woman who wrote as Vernon Lee and developed progressive theories of aestheticism based on the work of Walter Pater. In a letter to her mother, Lee complained that '. . . the only two creatures who seemed to have heard of me as a writer were Wm. Rossetti & Oscar Wilde!'[40] Born in France and brought up on the continent, she was an outsider like 'wonderful' Oscar: 'a good half of his absurdities are mere laughing at people,' she declared, adding astutely: 'The English don't see that'.[41] Yet Lee had little time for any cult of the individual and she satirised Oscar in *Miss Brown*, as Posthlethwaite,[*] a voluble talker who wore, 'a Japanese lily bobbing out of the button-hole of his ancestral dress-coat'.[42]

Beyond the rarefied confines of the British Museum reading room, Oscar's entry into high society was eased by Constance, Duchess of Westminster, beautiful and vivacious sister of his rather louche friend Ronald Gower. Oscar called Constance 'my divine friend' and thought her 'the most fascinating, Circe-like, brilliant woman I have ever met in England: something too charming'.[43] In 1880, their friendship was cut tragically short when Constance died, aged just forty-six, of Bright's disease, a condition of the kidneys. Oscar was sharing two floors of 13 Salisbury Street with Frank Miles by then. This Dickensian establishment was kept by a Miss Merritt, who installed her aged parents on the ground-floor and let the top floor to an elderly, eccentric doctor named Turner. She rented a cramped ground floor study to General Sir John Bisset, and he allowed his fourteen-year-old nephew, Harry Marillier, who was at school at nearby Christ's Hospital, to study there.

---

[*] A nod to George du Maurier's *Punch* character of the same name.

Young Marillier remembered Oscar as:

> . . . a remarkable young man of beautiful appearance, gorgeously but fancifully arrayed, and more like the incarnation of Apollo than an ordinary human being.[44]

When Oscar offered to help him with his Greek studies in exchange for cups of coffee, Marillier gained access to his white-panelled sitting room and noted the graffiti left by celebrities who called to see Oscar and Frank; one entire panel, just below the ceiling, was taken up with 'Sarah Bernhardt' scrawled in outsized letters with a thick carpenter's pencil.* Prominent too was Poynter's portrait of Lillie Langtry, its sumptuous umber and scarlet tones lending warmth to the room. Lillie, a frequent visitor, described 13 Salisbury Street as 'a very ghostly mansion, with antique staircases, twisting passages, broken down furniture, and dim corners'; Oscar preferred to think of it as 'untidy and romantic'.[45]

Frank Miles's status as artist-in-chief at *Life* magazine attracted the most beautiful women in London to their modest home. These 'Professional Beauties' or P.B.s owed their existence to the emerging cult of celebrity, manifest in photographic reproductions and glossy illustrated periodicals that sold by the thousands. Prominent among them were: Lillie Langtry; Georgiana, Lady Dudley; Daisy, Countess of Warwick, who inspired the song 'Bicycle built for two'; Jennie, Lady Randolph Churchill; and 'Patsy' Cornwallis-West. These women bore no resemblance to impoverished artist's models, characterised by Oscar as:

> . . . a pretty girl, from about twelve to twenty-five years of age, who knows nothing about art, cares less, and is merely anxious to earn seven or eight shillings a day without much trouble.[46]

The P.B.s required no payment for their posing; to be sought after was reward enough. Artists clamoured to paint or sketch them, while canny milliners and couturiers plied them with their latest creations, confident that once a P.B. wore it, other women would want it. Reproductions of their portraits were displayed prominently in the windows of fashionable emporia and hung in middle-class homes, while the originals were snapped up by wealthy patrons of the arts, aristocrats and even royals. It was said that when Queen Victoria's youngest son, Prince Leopold hung

---

* Oscar told Bouncer Ward that Sarah Bernhardt had 'tried to see how high she could jump and write her name'.

Frank Miles' pen-and-ink sketch of Lillie in his bedchamber, his mother had it removed. Society hostesses vied to entice the professional beauties to their receptions so they could scrawl on their invitations: '*Do come, the P.B.s will be there*'; before long, they were adding '*O.W.*' too.[47]

Oscar's home was at the forefront of a movement that marked the collapse of the demarcation between artist, celebrity and aristocrat. As well as P.B.s, regular and illustrious callers included Queen Victoria's daughter Princess Louise and her brother Prince Leopold, and actors Sarah Bernhardt and Ellen Terry. Miles's reputation was enhanced in December 1879, when the Royal Academy awarded him the Turner Silver Medal for his landscape painting of the Welsh coastline, an irony that may have prompted Oscar to include a fitting but surely apocryphal anecdote in 'London Models', an article he wrote for *English Illustrated Magazine*:

> "What do you sit for?" said a young artist to a model who had sent him in her card . . . "Oh, for anything you like, sir," said the girl, "landscape if necessary!"[48]

On Christmas Eve 1879, Oscar and Frank hosted a tea party to showcase the prize-winning painting. Helena Sickert was invited; so too were Lillie Langtry and Constance Gladys, the woman to whom Oscar would dedicate *A Woman of No Importance*. These lively parties, dubbed 'Tea and Beauties' became regular events and Laura Troubridge, whose cousin Cressie was at Magdalen with Oscar, thought them 'great fun'. She remembered 'lots of vague "intense" men, such duffers, who amused us awfully'. When Laura met Oscar, she recorded in her diary that she: 'fell awfully in love with him, thought him quite delightful'.[49] In fact it was he who had engineered the meeting in return for introducing Cressie to Sarah Bernhardt. He admired the talented Troubridge sisters and his poem, *Wasted Days*,* was inspired by a tile painting of a young boy done by Laura's sister Violet. However, in years to come, Laura would take against Oscar, and her husband would play a sinister role in his life.

Another regular at Thames House was artist Louise Jopling, one of the first women admitted to the Royal Society of British Artists and a confidante of Whistler and Millais, both of whom painted major portraits

---

* The full title is *Wasted Days (from a picture painted by Miss V.T.)*. The poem first appeared in *Kottabos* in 1877. The original opens with the line, 'a fair, slim boy not made for this world's pain', but Oscar changed this to, 'a lily-girl', made several additional changes and renamed it 'Madonna Mia' before including it in *Poems* (1881).

of her. Oscar and she moved in the same circles: Ellen Terry and Lillie Langtry both sat for her. She met Oscar when he was asked to take her into tea at a musical afternoon given by Lady Lindsay. She adored his sparkling wit and admired him for never deploying it maliciously. In *Twenty Years of My Life*, she recorded: 'He had an extravagant and enthusiastic way of talking sense and nonsense that was most fascinating'.[50] Later, Oscar invited her to tea with Lillie Langtry and Polish actress Helena Modjeska, and presented each with a lily as she left.

In her mid-thirties and married for a second time, Louise had escaped an abusive marriage, contracted when she was just seventeen. Although terrified of losing custody of her children, she obtained both a judicial separation and a barring order, obliging her to provide for her family by exhibiting and giving lessons. As the Married Women's Property Act was not passed until 1882, her spurned husband threatened to seize her paintings, as was his right. Little wonder she grew increasingly disillusioned with the male-dominated art world: 'I hate being a woman,' she raged, 'women never do anything'.[51] Her essay, 'On the Education of the Artistic Faculty', argued persuasively for women to be educated on equal terms with men. Oscar admired her hugely, and took to arriving unannounced at her Chelsea home. On one occasion, she answered a tapping on the door of her studio to find him standing outside with a large snake coiled around his neck; he assured her that the poison sacs had been removed.

Oscar had many women friends but Jane was keen to see him married, preferably to an heiress. One likely candidate was Violet Hunt, daughter of Pre-Raphaelite landscape painter Alfred William Hunt and his wife, Margaret, bestselling novelist and translator of the stories of the Brothers Grimm. When Letitia Scott, wife of Margaret's art tutor, William Bell Scott, invited Margaret to come and meet 'a wonderful young Irishman just up from Oxford', she brought seventeen-year-old Violet along. Oscar flirted outrageously with Violet: 'Beautiful women like you hold the fortunes of the world in your hands to make or mar', he told her, adding conspiratorially: 'We will rule the world – you and I – you with your looks and I with my wits'.[52] Little wonder she was, 'a little in love' with him.[53]

Violet was bright, vivacious and very beautiful. At thirteen, she was writing poetry for *Century Magazine*. Ellen Terry described her as 'out of Botticelli by Burne-Jones', while Oscar considered her, 'the sweetest Violet in England'.[54] In her memoir, *The Flurried Years* (1926), she insisted she had 'as nearly as possible escaped the honour of being Mrs. Wilde'.[55]

I believe that Oscar was really in love with me – for the moment and perhaps more than a moment for Alice Corkran told me quite seriously that he had said to her quite seriously, "Now, shall I go to Mr. Hunt and ask him to give me little Violet?"[56]

Oscar called on the Hunts almost every Sunday for two years. When he went to America, Violet sought Jane out, hoping for news of her son: 'Lady Wilde sits there in an old white ball dress, in which she must have graced the soirees of Dublin a great many years ago', she wrote; she was not as sweet as she looked. When Oscar returned with his hair freshly coiffed and curled, Violet decided he was 'not nearly so nice'.

Although she adored the company of men, and described life as 'a succession of affairs,' Violet Hunt never married. She would 'snub eligibles on principle', preferring married men since 'no one could imagine that I wanted to catch them'.[57] She could be terrifying: 'I rather liked her,' D. H. Lawrence admitted, adding: 'She's such a real assassin'.[58] Her many conquests included H. G. Wells and Somerset Maugham, but her most enduring love was for Ford Madox Ford, who, at thirty-six, was eleven years her junior when they embarked on their lengthy affair. Violet's once good opinion of Oscar may have been tainted by Ford's dismissal of his writing as 'derivative and of no importance', although he did acknowledge 'as a scholar he was worthy of the greatest respect'.[59]

In later years, Violet remembered Oscar as:

. . . a slightly stuttering, slightly lisping, long-limbed boy, sitting in the big armchair at Tor Villa, where we lived then, tossing the long black lock on his forehead that America swept away, and talking – talking . . .[60]

Oscar always encouraged Violet to write and, in time, she enjoyed an enviable reputation as a novelist, biographer and hostess of a thriving literary salon. Her interest in furthering the cause of women is reflected in the themes of her seventeen novels, the first of which, *The Maiden's Progress,* was published in 1894. She joined the Women Writers' Suffrage League in 1908, the year she helped Ford establish *The English Review.* Although she never published her memoir *My Oscar,* she did fictionalise him as fickle suitor Philip Wynyard in her semi-autobiographical novel *Their Lives* (1916).

Violet Hunt was not the only prospective Mrs. Oscar Wilde. When Oscar's good friend Leonard Montefiore died in America of 'acute rheumatism', aged just twenty-six, Oscar comforted his sister Charlotte, writing:

when a friend dies those who are left become very close to one another, just as when an oak falls in the forest the other trees reach out and join branches over the vacant place.[61]

Decades later, Charlotte told her son-in-law that Oscar had proposed to her but she turned him down because she did not love him. She claimed to have destroyed the note he sent in response: 'Charlotte, I am so sorry about your decision. With your money and my brain we could have gone so far'.[62] Their friendship survived nonetheless.*

* Charlotte had an impetuous streak. On the morning of 12 September 1894, she left her Portman Square home, assuring her family that she was heading to Baker Street Bazaar to make some 'trifling purchases'. Instead, she went to the District Registrar's Office in nearby Marylebone Road, where she married Lewis M'Iver, of the Indian Civil Service. Her husband was elected to parliament the following year, and she became Lady Charlotte when he was created a baronet in 1896.

Chapter 7

'How Different an Actress Is!'

> Why didn't you tell me that the only thing worth loving is an
> actress?
>> DORIAN GRAY to Lord Henry Wotton in *The Picture of*
>> *Dorian Gray*

In June 1877, Oscar wrote to 'Kitten' Harding from Dublin, expressing
his sorrow at the unexpected death of a cousin. This 'cousin' was his half-
brother, Dr Henry Wilson, whose death, which Oscar attributed to a chill
caught while out riding, came as a dreadful shock to the family. Just four
days earlier, Oscar had attended a dinner party hosted by Wilson and he
had seemed in perfect health. He had fallen ill that evening and he died
of pneumonia on 13 June, despite the best efforts of six colleagues, who
remained with him during his final days. He was thirty-nine years old and
had never married. Describing him as 'under the guardianship of his relative Sir William Wilde', an obituary in the *Dublin Journal of Medical Science*
eulogised him as a learned and popular man with a 'kindly and cheerful
manner' and a 'genial nature'.[1]

Willie and Oscar were chief mourners at Wilson's funeral and fully
expected to be the main beneficiaries of his will. Instead, he bequeathed
£8,000, subject to a life interest granted to two unnamed female relatives, to St Mark's Ophthalmic Hospital, where he had worked alongside his father before succeeding him as senior surgeon. Willie inherited
1 Merrion Square and a sum of £2,000, which allowed him to remain
there with Jane. Oscar received just £100 and Wilson's half share in
Illanroe, both carrying the proviso that he refrain from converting to
Roman Catholicism for at least five years. As this modest sum scarcely
dented the debts he had incurred at Oxford, he was obliged to sell the four
houses in Bray left to him by his father. A misunderstanding resulted in
these properties being offered to two buyers at once and, although Oscar
won the consequential lawsuit, the expenses he incurred, compounded by
an outstanding mortgage, put the London lifestyle he desired far beyond
his means.

By then, Willie, described by Jane as 'a brilliant fine-souled young man of infinite promise', had returned from studying law at the Middle Temple and planned to practice at the Irish bar.[2] As legal briefs were hard to come by, his uncertain income, combined with sporadic rent from Moytura and the tiny sum Jane could earn with her pen, fell woefully short of their needs. When their combined efforts to find an heiress for Willie to marry proved fruitless, they were obliged to sell 1 Merrion Square and join Oscar in London. Hearing that the bailiffs had arrived, a good friend of Jane's rushed over to offer moral support. When she was directed upstairs by a tearful servant, she discovered the dispossessed mistress of the house reclining on the drawing room couch, declaiming passages from *The Prometheus Vinctus of Aeschylus*.[3] Much of Jane's bravado was a façade and others who knew her remembered her looking gaunt and tired at this time.

By the time he left for London, Willie had given up on the law and turned his hand to journalism instead, a volte-face that had his mother's full and enthusiastic support. Both saw lucrative opportunities in Fleet Street for a 'delightful, brilliant, genial Irishman'.[4] He had not abandoned the notion of marrying well. Although he possessed no fortune, Willie was an attractive prospect as a husband, described by one contemporary as:

> . . . a tall, well-made fellow of thirty or thereabouts with an expressive talking face, lit up with a pair of deep blue laughing eyes. He had any amount of physical vivacity, and told a good story with immense verve . . .[5]

When Willie bumped into Ethel Smyth, the teenage daughter of a major general in the Royal Artillery during the crossing to Holyhead, he used the opportunity to deploy his charm. The two had spent the previous day playing lawn tennis in Bray and had, by her account, 'discussed poetry, the arts, and more particularly philosophy, in remoter parts of the garden'.[6] They got on famously after Willie showed great good humour in taking a nasty bout of seasickness on Ethel's part in his stride, so much so that, when he proposed to her during the train journey from Holyhead to Euston, she accepted with alacrity. Their engagement lasted for all of three weeks and Willie graciously allowed Ethel to keep the Claddagh* ring he bought her, but she lost it a year or two later 'while separating two dogs who were fighting in deep snow in the heather'.[7] In old age, Dame Ethel Smyth OBE, celebrated composer, author, lesbian and campaigner

---

* A traditional Irish ring representing love, loyalty, and friendship, symbolised by two clasped hands.

for women's suffrage, confessed: 'I was no more in love with [Willie] than I was with the engine-driver!'[8]

Jane arrived in London on 7 May 1879, and stayed at 13 Salisbury Street with Oscar until the house Willie found on unfashionable Ovington Square in Chelsea was ready for them. She embraced her new home with characteristic enthusiasm, describing London as, 'the focus of light, progress and intellect'.[9] Although still a celebrity in Ireland, she was approaching her sixtieth birthday by then and her eccentric appearance and record of vociferous opposition to British rule were likely to count against her. It is to her great credit that she established herself as a regular contributor to the *Pall Mall Gazette*, the *Burlington Magazine* and *Queen*, as well as writing occasionally for the *Lady's Pictorial*, the *St. James's Magazine* and *Tinsley's Magazine*.

Willie enjoyed even more success. A witty and talented writer, he soon earned a reputation as an excellent literary and drama critic and was appointed leader writer for *The Daily Telegraph* within a year. In his memoir, *Pitcher in Paradise*, Willie's contemporary Arthur M. Binstead called him 'the personification of good nature and irresponsibility'.[10] He recounted Willie's amusing description of his typical working day, which began when he popped into his editor's office at noon to suggest an idea for a feature; 'the anniversary of the penny postage stamp' for instance. Then:

> I bow myself out. I may then eat a few oysters and drink half a bottle of Chablis at Sweeting's, or, alternatively, partake of a light lunch . . . I then stroll towards the Park. I bow to the fashionables. I am seen along incomparable Piccadilly. It is grand. But meantime I am thinking only of that penny postage stamp.[11]

Afterwards, Willie would repair to his club to spend two hours scribbling furiously before dispatching his leader to *The Daily Telegraph* offices and heading out, arm in arm with a friend, to enjoy:

> . . . that paradise of cigar-ashes, bottles, corks, ballet, and those countless circumstances of gaiety and relaxation, known only to those who are indwellers in the magic circles of London's literary Bohemia.[12]

Jane had few friends in London and her social life revolved around Oscar, who was happy to introduce her into his circle: 'Oscar brought Lady Wilde to see me', wrote Louise Jopling, 'and I shall never forget the proud and devoted tone of his voice as he said, "My mother"'.[13] When Jopling paid a return visit, she was surprised to find Jane's house in darkness while the sun blazed outside. Jane was also present at the Christmas

Eve party held in honour of Frank Miles's Turner Medal, and she took tea regularly with Oscar's more outré actress friends, no doubt feeling completely at home among them.

Oscar recognised that actresses were afforded more freedom than other women and he wrote exceptionally strong and enduring characters for them to play. Women like Sarah Bernhardt, Ellen Terry and their peers influenced fashion, grew independently wealthy, occupied managerial roles in the theatre, and enjoyed a degree of latitude in their personal lives. An enthusiastic theatregoer, Oscar's arrival in London coincided with the halcyon days of the West End. By 1894, residents of Greater London had access to more than forty theatres, most of them clustered along a few bright streets in the centre of the city. An ambitious slum clearance project led to the construction of Shaftsbury Avenue, a broad diagonal that cut through the teeming, and often squalid, districts of St Giles and Soho. With half a dozen new theatres scattered along it, this shimmering thoroughfare became the beating heart of London's theatreland.

There was something for everyone: from rarefied opera at Covent Garden; to the lighter fare offered by W. S. Gilbert and Arthur Sullivan at the newly built Savoy; and the immensely popular variety shows staged in London's many music halls. The majestic Henry Irving, aided by Oscar's old rival Bram Stoker, presided over the Lyceum on Wellington Street, where he offered high-end classic drama and Shakespearean revivals. Irving's leading lady, the magnificent Ellen Terry, was described by Oscar as 'the kindest-hearted, sweetest, loveliest of women'.[14] He sent her a photograph inscribed, 'for dear wonderful Ellen'. She in turn declared:

> The most remarkable men I have known were, without a doubt, Whistler and Oscar Wilde . . . there was something about both of them more instantaneously individual and audacious than it is possible to describe.[15]

Ellen, in her early thirties when she met Oscar, had packed more into three decades than most women manage in a lifetime.

In her autobiography, *The Story of My Life*, Ellen described her first memory; being locked into the attic of a theatrical lodging house in Glasgow while her father, mother and older sister Kate appeared onstage in a theatre nearby. She was born in a near identical boarding house in Coventry on 27 February 1847,* and spent her youth traipsing from one temporary home to the next. When a fire broke out in one, Ellen's mother,

---

* Although Terry insisted she was born in 1848, her birth certificate is dated 1847.

comic actress Sarah Ballard, rushed off stage to rescue her young children before carrying on with the next act as if nothing had happened.

Before she turned ten, Ellen had joined her parents on stage. At fourteen, she became a member of the Theatre Royal Company in Bristol, where one of her fellow actors was Henrietta Hodson, the woman who would one day tutor Lillie Langtry. On 20 February 1864, a week short of her seventeenth birthday, she walked off stage at the Haymarket Theatre in London during a run of Tom Taylor's hugely popular farce, *The American Cousin** in order to marry painter George Frederick Watts, aged forty-seven. Her new husband introduced her to several influential men, among them William Ewart Gladstone, Benjamin Disraeli, Robert Browning and Alfred Tennyson, but Ellen preferred playing 'Indians and Knights of the Round Table' with Tennyson's sons, Hallam and Lionel, to sitting indoors listening to their eminent father.[16] After ten disastrous months, Ellen's family and friends arranged a discreet separation, although she described the ending of her marriage as 'a natural, almost inevitable, catastrophe'.[17]

In 1868, Ellen turned her back on the theatre for a second time to set up home in rural Hertfordshire with progressive architect and designer Edward Godwin, who remodelled two houses on Tite Street that were home to Oscar. Ellen was twenty to Edward's forty-four and, as her marriage to Watts had never been annulled, they gave their children, Edith and Edward, the surname Craig in order to conceal their illegitimacy. Financial necessity drove her back onto the stage in 1874. She separated from Godwin shortly afterwards, but they remained on good terms. The major turning point in her career came four years later, when she joined Henry Irving's company at the Lyceum. On 27 June 1879, Oscar was mesmerised by her magnificent portrayal of Queen Henrietta Maria, wife of the titular monarch in *Charles I*.

Perhaps he was keen to acknowledge her genius. Perhaps he relished the prospect of forming an association with one of the most famous women in London; the truth most likely combines the two. Whatever the reason, Oscar was moved to write a sonnet in Ellen's honour. He included 'Queen Henrietta Maria (Charles I, act iii)' in a letter declaring his 'loyal admiration' for her talent: 'No actress has ever affected me as you have', he wrote, 'I do not think you will ever have a more sincere and impassioned admirer than I am'.[18] This sonnet, published in *The World* on 16 July 1879, began:

* This is the play that was being performed when Abraham Lincoln was assassinated.

> In the lone tent, waiting for victory,
> She stands with eyes marred by the mists of pain,
> Like some wan lily overdrenched with rain;

Ellen felt proud that her performance inspired this 'lovely sonnet'. In her memoir, she wrote:

> That phrase 'wan lily' represented perfectly what I had tried to convey, not only in this part, but in Ophelia. I hope I thanked Oscar enough at the time. Now he is dead and I cannot thank him any more . . . I had so much bad poetry written to me that these lovely sonnets from a real poet should have given me the greater pleasure.[19]

He was not done: when she appeared in *The Merchant of Venice*, Oscar wrote 'Portia' as a tribute to her beauty.[20] His sonnet 'Camma' commemorated her portrayal of Tennyson's Priestess of Artemis in *The Cup*, the play that featured Florence Balcombe in a tiny part. She in turn admired his 'very beautiful' eyes. They became close friends.

Oscar included all three sonnets to Ellen in *Poems*, published in 1881 at his own expense.* This exquisite little volume, printed on Dutch hand-made paper and bound in parchment vellum with gilt prune blossoms drawn by Oscar himself, contained sixty-one poems, half of them new, the other half published earlier in various journals and magazines. The reviews were decidedly mixed. Describing *Poems* as, 'neither good nor bad', the *Saturday Review* accused Oscar of lacking 'literary sincerity', concluding: 'This book is not without traces of cleverness, but it is marred everywhere by imitation, insincerity, and bad taste'.[21] A marginally more favourable review in the *Athenaeum* accused him of 'artificiality and insincerity', and decided that his poems had 'no element of endurance'.[22]

Predictably, the most damning judgement was delivered by *Punch*. Describing *Poems* as, 'a volume of echoes', the anonymous reviewer asserted: 'There is a certain amount of originality about the binding, but that is more than can be said for the inside of the volume', and quipped:

> Aesthete of aesthetes
> What's in a name?

---

* Its publisher, David Bogue, went into liquidation in August 1882. In 1892 Matthews and Lane took the sheets of Bogue's fifth edition, put in a substitute title page and a limitation page, and had Charles Ricketts design the endpapers and binding for the most beautiful of Wilde's books.

The poet is Wilde
But his poetry is tame.[23]

The decision by the editor of *Time* magazine to carry a mocking caricature of Oscar accompanied by six stanzas of "The New Helen" by 'Oscuro Mild' seems odd since two years earlier that same magazine had published the original sonnet, dedicated to Lillie Langtry.[24] In a rare act of appreciation, *Century Illustrated Monthly Magazine* acknowledged Oscar as, 'the son of a clever authoress of excellent family in Dublin', and admired in particular his 'Ave Imperatrix', which 'outweighs a hundred cartoons of "Punch"'.[25]

The harshest rejection came from his alma mater. Although the secretary of the Oxford Union had requested a copy of *Poems* for the society's library, several members objected on the grounds that Oscar's poems were merely poor imitations of greater works. When the full membership was balloted, a decision to reject *Poems* was carried by 188 votes to 180. In response, Oscar expressed the hope that no other poet or writer would be subjected to 'the coarse impertinence of having a work officially rejected which had been no less officially sought for'.[26] His pride was not the only casualty. When the Reverend Robert Henry William Miles, with the backing of his wife, wrote to express displeasure at his son Frank's continued association with the author of a poem as licentious as 'Charmides', Oscar lost his home too.

In the wake of such criticism, he was appreciative of the support he received from his woman friends. Thanking Violet Hunt for describing his poems as 'beautiful', he declared:

> In an age like this when Slander, and Ridicule, and Envy walk quite unashamed among us, and when any attempt to produce serious beautiful work is greeted with a very tornado of lies and evil-speaking, it is a wonderful joy, a wonderful spur for ambition and work, to receive any such encouragement and appreciation as your letter brought me, and I thank you for it again and again.[27]

Oscar understood better than anyone that the opinion of the critics was of little consequence compared to his growing celebrity and the sanction of beloved figures like Ellen Terry, Lillie Langtry and others. Their public enthusiasm helped ensure that three runs of 250 copies each sold out within the first year.*

---

* Roberts Brothers of Boston brought out an American edition to coincide with his visit.

Oscar inscribed Lillie's copy of *Poems*, 'To Helen formerly of Troy, now of London'. Her extraordinary beauty was widely admired: 'I saw Mrs Langtry in evening dress for the first time,' wrote Ellen Terry, 'and for the first time I realised how beautiful she was. Her neck and shoulders kept me so busy looking that I could neither talk nor listen'.[28] Ellen shared Oscar's opinion that Lillie's extraordinary notoriety would guarantee success on the stage. She wrote:

> That most lovely and exquisite creature, Mrs. Langtry, could not go out anywhere, at the dawn of the 'eighties, without a crowd collecting to look at her! It was no rare thing to see the crowd, to ask its cause, to receive the answer, "Mrs. Langtry!" and to look in vain for the object of the crowd's admiring curiosity.[29]

Oscar was celebrated too, so much so that when Polish actress Helena Modjeska arrived in London to star in *Heartsease** at the Court Theatre, she reportedly asked:

> What has he done, this young man that one meets him everywhere? Oh yes he talks well, but what has he done? He has written nothing, he does not sing or paint or act – he does nothing but talk. I do not understand'.[30]

Helena was a veteran of the stage. Born into a talented family in Krakow in 1840, at twenty, she joined a company of strolling players managed by Gustave Modrzejewski. She married Modrzejewski and had two children with him, before discovering that their marriage was bigamous since he had a wife who was very much alive. She left him when their daughter died in 1865, and took their son with her to Krakow. There she married Karol Bozenta Chlapowski, editor of the liberal nationalist newspaper *Kraj* and their home became the focus of Krakow's dissident, artistic and literary milieu. In 1876, the couple's political activities obliged them flee to California, where Chlapowski established an experimental and idealistic Polish colony. After it failed spectacularly, leaving them penniless, Helena was obliged to resume her career. Although she had been a principle actress at the Polish National Theatre, she needed to learn English to secure major roles; she achieved this in a matter of months by practising the language between performances for six or seven hours every day.

In London, Helena reported delightedly: 'My success surpassed all my expectations; everyone here seems to think it quite extraordinary, and my

---

* The English title chosen for Dumas' *La Dame aux Camelia*, performed in 1880.

manager has already numerous projects concerning my future'.[31] The Prince of Wales came to her dressing room and she shared a stage with Jane's great friend Genevieve Ward at a party given in his honour. Despite press reports to the contrary, there was surprisingly little professional jealousy among leading actresses and the two women got on famously. At supper that evening, Helena was seated near Lillie Langtry and noted her extraordinary beauty, admiring in particular her 'perfect neck and shoulders'. When Lillie came backstage during a performance of *Romeo and Juliet*, Helena joined the ranks of those encouraging her to act. Sarah Bernhardt, described by Helena as 'the wonderful creature', sent her supposed rival a bouquet of white camellias, assuring her that she was moved to tears by her performance. When Ellen Terry came to her dressing room, Helena declared: 'Whoever has met Ellen Terry knows that she is irresistible, and I liked her from the first'.[32]

Offstage, Helena was embraced by fashionable society and she received an invitation to Lady Jeune's unmissable 'five o'clocks'; as Oscar once quipped, 'there were three inevitables – death, quarter-day and Lady Jeune's parties'.* She may have impressed Arthur Conan Doyle too, since she is thought to have inspired his intrepid Irene Adler. Keen to befriend this newfound star, Oscar invited her to tea. Her instinct was to refuse, since she thought it unwise to visit a young man unaccompanied, but she relented once he assured her that Lillie Langtry and Louise Jopling would be there too. They became good friends and collaborated on 'Sen Artysty; or the Artist's Dream by Madame Helena Modjeska (translated from the Polish by Oscar Wilde)', which appeared in the Christmas 1880 edition of *The Green Room*. 'If there is any beauty in this poem,' Oscar enthused, 'it is the work of the subtle imagination and passionate artistic nature of Mme Modjeska. I myself am but a pipe through which her tones full of sweetness have flown'.[33] They considered adapting Verdi's opera, *Luisa Miller*, but the project came to nothing.[34]

Oscar had long expressed a desire to write for Sarah Bernhardt, who was the most celebrated actress in the world. He thought of casting her as Elizabeth I, declaring: 'She would look wonderful in monstrous dresses covered with peacocks and pearls!'[35] His devotion to Bernhardt dated back to the day she arrived in Folkestone with the *Comédie-Française* in May

---

* Lady Jeune, Susan Mary Elizabeth Stanley, a leading society hostess, would collaborate with Oscar in the compilation of a list of contributors for *The Woman's World*. Quarter-days were the four days each year on which servants were hired, school terms started, and rents were due.

1879, when Oscar was there to greet her. The description of how he spread lilies at her feet is often repeated, but Bernhardt's own version of events is at variance and suggests he was reacting with characteristic humour to an unkind remark made at her expense:

> One of my comrades who was just near, and with whom I was not a favourite, said to me in a spiteful tone:
>
> "They'll make you a carpet of flowers soon."
>
> "Here is one!" exclaimed a young man, throwing an armful of lilies on the ground in front of me.
>
> I stopped short, rather confused, not daring to walk on these white flowers, but the crowd pressing on behind compelled me to advance, and the poor lilies had to be trodden under foot.[36]

This less obsequious account tallies with James Rennell Rodd's assessment of his friend: 'He had undoubtedly a keen perception of beauty, almost overshadowed by his tremendous sense of humour'. Rennell Rodd, who knew Oscar well, believed he was 'much too brilliant to take seriously the movement that had grown up around him'. Describing Oscar's laugh as 'genuine, spontaneous and infectious', he insisted:

> No-one was more ready than he was at that time to accept the laugh against himself, and no one could be more generous in acknowledging the qualities and gifts of his friends.[37]

Sarah's first impressions of Oscar do not suggest an effete or sycophantic man:

> His head was above all the other heads; he had luminous eyes and long hair, and looked like a German student. He was an English poet [sic], though, and one of the greatest of the century, a poet who was a genius, but who was, alas! later tortured and finally vanquished by madness. It was Oscar Wilde.[38]

When Oscar saw Sarah play *Phedre* at the Gaiety Theatre on 2 June 1879, he declared her 'the most splendid creation I ever witnessed'.[39] Almost a decade later, he wrote, 'it was not until I heard Sarah Bernhardt in *Phèdre* that I absolutely realised the sweetness of the music of Racine'.[40] Her brilliance prompted a sonnet: 'How vain and dull this common world must seem to such a one as thou', it began.[*] As ever, his admiration bordered on

---

[*] It was published in *The World* in June 1879 as, 'To Sarah Bernhardt', and reprinted in *Poems* as '*Phèdre*'.

obsession; he took to dragging Lillie around the British Museum in search of Roman antiquities that bore an aquiline likeness to 'the Divine Sarah'.* She didn't mind. Although the press portrayed them as rivals, Sarah and she were friends, and the renowned actress had endorsed the young pretender.

Although Oscar's life was full of glamorous women, he was an egalitarian at heart. Artist Charles Ricketts, who remembered his 'irrepressible inward gaiety', described how: 'Kindliness and the desire to please gave charm to his face'.[41] Rennell Rodd told a wonderful story, which began with an uncommonly high tide and disastrous flooding in the down-at-heel district of Lambeth. When Oscar and he turned up to offer assistance, the former spent several hours in the miserable tenement home of an 'old bed-ridden Irishwoman':

> . . . cheering her with his merry humour and assisting her with little necessaries for which, as he said, she had more than compensated him by praying that "the Lord would give him a bed in glory".[42]

This strong sense of empathy fed into his emerging and unique socialist sympathies: 'What is needed is Individualism', Oscar argued:

> If the Socialism is Authoritarian; if there are Governments armed with economic power as they are now with political power; if, in a word, we are to have Industrial Tyrannies, then the last state of man will be worse than the first'.[43]

These sentiments, combined with Jane's staunch nationalism, surely informed his first play, *Vera; or, the Nihilists*, published in 1880. Although nihilism was a common theme at the time, few writers portrayed it in a favourable light. By choosing the struggle against Russian imperialism as his theme, Oscar must have been nodding towards its British equivalent and the impact this had on his native Ireland.

Although displaying few conspicuously nationalist leanings when consorting with the elite of English society, Oscar was prone to the occasional patriotic outburst if the audience was receptive. Lecturing in San Francisco in 1882, he declared:

> . . . with the coming of the English, art in Ireland came to an end and it had no existence for over seven hundred years. I am glad it has not, for art could not live and flourish under a tyrant.

* According to Langtry, Bernhardt had been christened 'Divine Sarah' when she played the Queen in Victor Hugo's *Ruy Blas*.

More radical still was his contention: 'The Saxon took our lands from us and left them desolate. We took their language and added new beauty to it'.[44] Ten years later, when *Salomé* was rejected, he declared: 'I am not English. I am Irish, which is quite another thing'.[45] And from his jail cell, he reminded Lord Alfred Douglas of 'the ruin that your race has brought on mine'.[46]

Before Jane left Dublin, she had allowed Speranza one final outing. Her pamphlet, *The American Irish*, whipped up nationalist sentiment and revived her long-cherished dream of independence for her homeland. Oscar sent a copy to James Knowles, founding editor of literary magazine *The Nineteenth Century*: 'I don't think that age has dimmed the fire and enthusiasm of that pen which set the young Irelanders in a blaze,' he declared. He ended with a characteristically lovely sentiment: 'I should like so much to have the privilege of introducing you to my mother – all brilliant people should cross each other's cycles, like some of the nicest planets'.[47]

No one understood better than Oscar the influence an idealistic young woman could bring to bear on a fight for freedom, and his tale of a corrupt, self-interested elite ruling over an oppressed peasantry brings to mind the famine-stricken Ireland of his mother's youth. The plot of *Vera* centres on an insurgent cell led by the beautiful and principled Vera Sabouroff. In true melodramatic fashion, she falls desperately in love with her comrade Alexis, a sympathetic medical student, only to discover that he is the reforming son of the despotic Czar. Rather than assassinate Alexis, Vera plunges her dagger into her own breast to obtain the bloody proof demanded by her comrades, insisting that she is dying, not for love, but to save Russia. Although Oscar changed the year to 1800 and relocated the action to Moscow, it is widely believed that *Vera* was inspired by twenty-two-year-old Vera Zasulich, who attempted to assassinate General Fyodor Fyodorovich Trepov, Governor of St Petersburg on 24 January 1878.[48]

Zasulich had much in common with Jane Elgee. The educated daughter of a minor nobleman who died when she was three years old, she joined a group of insurgents in her late teens and her keen intelligence, facilitated by the nihilist commitment to gender equality, propelled her to leadership. On that day in January, she joined a queue of petitioners seeking an audience with Trepov, produced a pistol from under her cloak and shot him with the intention of killing him; he survived but was seriously wounded. Afterwards, Vera waited calmly to be arrested. Although she admitted her guilt without hesitation, a sympathetic jury acquitted her.

The international press, which displayed scant sympathy for nihilists, condemned her actions and her acquittal. An editorial in *The Times* declared that 'We could have understood the trial if it had happened in Dublin'.[49] In contrast, the *Dublin University Magazine*, which counted Jane and Oscar among its contributors, carried a long and enthusiastic article praising her patriotic actions and condemning her mistreatment.*

Zasulich fled into exile, and turned her back on terrorism in order to pursue a socialist agenda. A staunch and idealistic feminist, she wrote:

> In the 1870's women ceased to be exceptional phenomena. Ordinary women – an entire network of such women – attained a good fortune rarely achieved in history: the possibility of acting in the capacity not of aspiring wives and mothers, but in total independence as the equals of men in all social and political activity. And however great were the sufferings that the government vengefully inflicted upon them for their actions, they did not envy anyone. They were very happy.[50]

This was not the experience of women living in patriarchal Victorian England, where gender norms were rigidly enforced.

Oscar sent a copy of *Vera* to Ellen Terry, beautifully bound in dark red leather with her name embossed in gold on the binding. He inscribed it, 'from her sincere admirer the author', and wrote: 'Perhaps some day I shall be fortunate enough to write something worthy of your playing'.[51] Although she was flattered, she turned *Vera* down, obliging him to look elsewhere. Tapping into his mother's contacts, Oscar approached Genevieve Ward, one of the most popular women on the London stage, who admired Jane as 'a poet of high repute'.[52] Oscar may have hoped that *Vera* would resonate with Ward who, aged nineteen, had married and almost immediately parted from Count Constantine de Guerbel, an unscrupulous Russian nobleman. It did not.

Eventually, *Vera* was accepted by an up-and-coming young actress named Fanny Bernard-Beere, who had made her debut at the Opéra Comique four years earlier. Her enthusiasm may have been sparked by the success Sarah Bernhardt enjoyed playing Princess Fédora Romanoff, a part written for her by Victorien Sardou, in his nihilist play, *Fédora*.† 'Bernie' and Oscar enjoyed a long association, personal and professional.

---

* 'Vjera Sassulitch [sic]and Constitutional Aspirations in Russia' is in *The Dublin University Magazine*, Volume I January to June, 1878, pp. 652–64.
† The soft felt hat Bernhardt wore became fashionable and took its name from her character.

In 1893, when she played Mrs Arbuthnot in *A Woman of No Importance*, she told an interviewer from *The Sketch*:

> Mr Oscar Wilde is a delightful author . . . it is very delightful dealing with a man of real intellect, who both knows what he wants and understands in a moment what is wanted.[53]

Although no record exists of a licence being issued for *Vera*, Oscar did arrange and pay for a single daytime performance in the Adelphi Theatre on Saturday 17 December 1881: 'I suppose everyone will be Russian to see it', declared a commentator in *Fun*, 'will it be quite too utterly *Botticellian*, I wonder?'[54] He never got the chance to find out. On 30 November 1881, a notice, possibly written by Willie, appeared in *The World*. It read: 'Considering the present state of political feeling in England, Mr. Oscar Wilde has decided on postponing, for a time, the production of his drama *Vera*'.[55] Three days later, *Bell's Life in London and Sporting Chronicle* provided the following information:

> Mr. Wilde has admitted his play to a committee of literary persons, who have advised him to keep it from the stage. The work, composed about four years ago, abounds in revolutionary sentiments, which it is thought might stand in the way of its success with loyal British audiences.[56]

The New York Times suggested that the cancellation was prompted by diplomatic communications from the Russian government to Lord Granville, Secretary of State for Foreign Affairs.[57] It was even rumoured that the Prince of Wales had intervened. The assassination of Czar Alexander II on 13 March 1881 made a Czarina of his Danish sister-in-law, who was married to the new Czar Alexander III.

Feelings were running high: Johan Most, editor of anarchic journal *Freiheit* was jailed for eighteen months for writing approvingly of the assassination. To compound matters, American President James Garfield, who had been shot by a former supporter in July, died of his injuries on 19 September 1881. Oscar's nationality can't have helped. A Fenian dynamite campaign, orchestrated from New York by Jeremiah O'Donovan Rossa of the Irish Republican Brotherhood, was terrorising the citizens of British cities at the time, and bombs had exploded or been diffused in Manchester, Chester, Liverpool and London. Little wonder the authorities were reluctant to facilitate the staging of what Oscar described as, 'my first attack on Tyranny'.[58] Undaunted, he declared his intention of taking *Vera* to America, where he believed he would find 'more freedom'. It was not the last time his attempts to stage a play in London would be thwarted.

Chapter 8

'THE PARADISE FOR WOMEN'

The American Woman is by far the most important element in
the social machinery of the States.
LADY JANE WILDE in *Social Studies*[1]

On Christmas Eve 1881, the passenger liner SS *Arizona* steamed out of
Liverpool on her way to New York. Included on her passenger manifest
was 'passenger number 114, Oscar Wilde, gentleman'. Aged twenty-seven
at the time and known primarily as an aesthetic man-about-town, and
author of a rather poorly received collection of poetry, Oscar reportedly
credited the suggestion that he tour America to Sarah Bernhardt.[2] Fifteen
months earlier, following her second tempestuous departure from the
Comédie-Française, 'La Divine Sarah' had crossed the Atlantic with her
own touring company, and reaped the rewards of some excellent pre-tour
publicity to become an overnight sensation.

Newspapers reported her every move. Their fashion pages carried
meticulous accounts of her clothing, jewellery and accessories, and her
adoring public clamoured for merchandise that might lend them even the
tiniest whiff of Bernhardt glamour: themed postcards, perfume, candy,
eyeglasses and even cigars were snapped up. Although she insisted on
performing in her native French, captivated audiences tossed aside their
English translations in order to give her their full attention. Sarah revelled
in the adulation, declaring: 'I adore this country, in which woman reigns,
and reigns so absolutely'.[3] Her first tour was such an unmitigated success
that it led to eight more.

Sarah may have suggested it, but Oscar's tour came about at the
invitation and expense of the impresario Richard D'Oyly Carte, who
engaged him to deliver a series of lectures on aestheticism, intended to
tie in with an American run of Gilbert and Sullivan's operetta *Patience*,
which satirised the Aesthetic movement.[4] Although it is often reported
that Oscar alone was parodied as 'Reginald Bunthorne', a foppish man
who craved the attention of women, this character was a pastiche of
several leading aesthetes, and Oscar may also have inspired Bunthorne's

poetic rival, 'Archibald Grosvenor', who was tall, attractive and impeccably dressed.

Encouraged by the popularity of *Patience*, which enjoyed a longer run than the ultimately more enduring *H.M.S Pinafore*, D'Oyly Carte had taken it to New York the previous September, but American audiences, unfamiliar with the 'Bunthornes' that populated London's social scene, simply didn't get it. The Wilde solution was suggested by one enterprising woman, and largely implemented by another. A third, Jane Wilde, insisted that although *Patience* was 'meant to satirise the cultus of beauty' it 'actually gained proselytes to the aesthetic[sic] movement'.[5]

Much of the planning for Oscar's tour was undertaken by Helen Lenoir, D'Oyly Carte's secretary at the time and later his second wife. The woman who instigated the endeavour was acknowledged, more than two decades later, by Colonel W. F. Morse, D'Oyly Carte's agent in New York:

> One afternoon in September, 1891, a lady – well known in English and American Newspaper circles as a writer upon the current society topics of the day on both sides of the water – suggested that perhaps Mr. Wilde would consent to give a series of lectures in this country [America]. At once a cable was sent.[6]

That 'lady' was the formidable Mrs Frank Leslie, newspaper magnate and proprietor of a publishing empire that included the popular and pioneering *Frank Leslie's Illustrated Newspaper*. Born Miriam Florence Folline in New Orleans on 5 June 1836, in 1880 she had taken on and turned around her late husband's ailing publishing company, stamping her seal of authority on the enterprise by changing her name by deed poll to 'Frank Leslie', the name assumed by him when he established the business.* As she had inherited insurmountable debts, her creditors were circling and the whole enterprise would have foundered but for the intervention of Eliza Jane Smith, a wealthy widow and former housemaid who advanced Miriam a loan of $50,000 to be repaid over five years; it was returned within five months.

An accomplished linguist and frequent visitor to London for the season, Miriam attended Jane's Saturday salons and attempted to emulate them with 'Thursdays' of her own. She was described by Jane as 'the most important and successful journalist in the States'. Jane elaborated:

---

* Frank Leslie was born Henry Carter in Ipswich, England.

She owns and edits many journals, and writes with bright vivacity on the social subjects of the day, yet always evinces a high and good purpose; and, with her many gifts, her brilliant powers of conversation in all the leading tongues of Europe, her splendid residence and immense income, nobly earned and nobly spent, Mrs. Frank Leslie may be considered the leader and head of the intellectual circles of New York.[7]

Miriam's connection to the Wilde family, which began with Oscar's tour, strengthened in 1891, when she took Willie as her fourth husband, a disastrous alliance, as will become apparent.

Transatlantic tours were a well-established phenomenon by 1882, and could be very lucrative for all concerned. In return for introducing the tropes of the Aesthetic movement to the new world, Oscar was promised one third of the net receipts, a welcome boost to the bank balance of an impoverished poet with exquisite taste. Like Sarah, Oscar made sure to publicise his arrival well in advance and brought dozens of letters of introduction, many addressed to powerful women. He realised that:

The remarkable intellectual progress of that country [America] is very largely due to the efforts of American women, who edit many of the most powerful magazines and newspapers, take part in the discussion of every question of public interest, and exercise an important influence upon the growth and tendencies of literature and art.[8]

By the time the *Arizona* reached New York harbour, late on the afternoon of 2 January 1882, interest in Oscar was at fever pitch. As she lay at anchor off Staten Island, waiting to clear quarantine, several members of the New York press corps braved choppy waters to interview him. Determined not to disappoint, Oscar stepped out of the captain's quarters wearing a full-length, fur-trimmed, olive green coat over a shirt with a wide, Byronic collar, a sky-blue necktie and a pair of patent leather boots. Upon his head was perched what the *New York World* described as a 'smoking-cap or turban', beneath which flowed waves of dark brown hair.[9]

Of course, this costume was part of his pose, devised to signal his impeccable aesthetic credentials and his strong sense of individualism. Oscar had a unique sense of style and favoured men's fashions from 'the second part of the seventeenth century', but his strongest views were reserved for women's clothing, which he regarded not only as ugly but ridiculously restrictive and impractical as well.[10] In time, he would become a staunch advocate of the Rational Dress Movement, supporting that organisation's assertion that forcing women to wear unhealthy clothing in which they could hardly breathe and had limited mobility was all part of the subjugation process. As Oscar would put it:

> From the sixteenth century to our own day there is hardly any form of torture that has not been inflicted on girls and endured by women, in obedience to the dictates of an unreasonable and monstrous Fashion.[11]

Oscar eschewed gendered clothing, activities and occupations, arguing that, in time: 'dress of the two sexes will be assimilated as similarity of costume always follows similarity of pursuits'. He showed remarkable prescience in asserting the probability that: 'dress of the twentieth century will emphasise distinctions of occupation, not distinctions of sex'.[12]

A reporter for *The Sun*, a politically conservative American broadsheet, recorded Oscar's observations of his voyage and reported that he drawled:

> By the by, do you know, I was very much disappointed in the Atlantic Ocean; it was very tame. I expected to have it roar about and be beautiful in its storms.[13]

This statement made headlines around the world, exactly as Oscar intended, and provoked a response in the letters page of British periodical *Truth*, purporting to have come from the Atlantic itself and expressing a reciprocal disappointment in Oscar Wilde.[14]

With a week to fill before his first lecture, Oscar set about attending the many receptions and luncheons held in his honour, since securing the approval of New York's most prominent society women was essential to the success of the whole enterprise. He also paid a visit to the Union Square studio of celebrity photographer Napoleon Sarony. Naturally, Sarah had been there first and had received $1,500 for allowing herself to be photographed reclining on Sarony's 'fainting couch', although he recouped his investment and more besides by licensing the sale of thousands of postcard prints. Oscar posed in the costume he planned to wear for his lectures: a velvet jacket and vest, silk knee breeches and stockings, and slippers adorned with grosgrain bows. Rather than something of his own invention, this eye-catching get-up was the costume worn by members of Oxford's Masonic Apollo Lodge.

On 5 January, Oscar attended an afternoon reception held in his honour by travel correspondent Augustus Allen Hayes Jr and his wife Emily. *The New York Times* reported that 'a line of private conveyances with liveried coachmen filled the street, and invited guests were constantly arriving or departing'. In the midst of this throng stood Oscar, perfectly at ease and dressed in plain black with not a hint of a sunflower as 'the ladies clustered about him, and seemed greatly interested in what he had to say'.[15] That day, he was introduced to the incorrigible Jane Tunis Poultney Bigelow, an important figure in the New York literary scene and a woman who made it her business to cultivate the leading writers of the day.* Bigelow's correspondence with Wilkie Collins spanned two decades, and she had developed an interest in Charles Dickens that bordered on an obsession. On one occasion, she was alleged to have knocked unconscious an elderly widow who had the temerity to visit him at his hotel. She took to Oscar immediately.

On the eve of Oscar's first lecture, he attended three significant gatherings: The first was a dinner held in his honour at the Gramercy Park home of Jane Bigelow. In return, he presented her with a copy of his poem 'To M.B.J.', inscribed, 'for my friend, Mrs. Bigelow'. She was thrilled, and invited him to come and stay in her summer home in West Point that summer. At 9.30, he headed for the magnificent 5th Avenue mansion of Marietta Paran Stevens, who he had met at the Hayes's reception. A widowed philanthropist, art collector and society patron, Mrs Paran Stevens was described by *The New York Times* as an 'impulsive woman, never hesitating to give full expression of her opinions about everybody and everything uppermost in her mind'. Her lavish gatherings were legendary and her influence was all-pervasive: 'No woman in New York society was better known than Mrs. Paran Stevens', *The New York Times* declared, adding, 'she was equally well known in Paris, London, Berlin and Vienna'. Paying tribute to her influence, the same writer asserted that 'probably no woman in New York has launched a greater number of ambitious young men and women into the social maelstrom'.[16] Among them was Oscar Wilde.

Oscar's final engagement that evening was a reception hosted by English-born Jane Cunningham Croly in honour of author Louisa May Alcott, who was nearing the end of her career and her life. Croly, better known by her pen name 'Jennie June', was an exceptionally useful supporter to cultivate. Credited with pioneering and syndicating the 'woman's

---

* At one time, Jane's husband, John Bigelow, co-editor and co-owner of the *New York Evening Post*, was Ambassador to Paris, but she was considered a liability, since she apparently slapped the Prince of Wales on the back and allowed her servants to sit in the German imperial box at the opera. Many believed that Bigelow lost out on the coveted post as American minister to London because of his wife's undiplomatic behaviour.

column', she ran the women's department at the *New York World* for ten years and was chief staff writer at *Mme. Demorest's Mirror of Fashions*, later renamed *Demorest's Monthly Magazine*. As 'Jennie June', she wrote 'Gossip with and for Women' for the *New York Dispatch* and 'Parlour and Sidewalk Gossip' for *Noah's Sunday Times*. The sole breadwinner in her family, she juggled the responsibilities of motherhood and journalism by spending mornings at home before heading into the office at noon and working steadily until after midnight. Sunday nights were reserved for entertaining New York's intellectual and artistic elite.

A passionate believer in networking for women, Croly founded the Women's Parliament in 1856. She responded to the exclusion of women journalists, herself included, from an honorary dinner organised for Charles Dickens by the New York Press Club by founding Sorosis, America's first professional woman's club. She also established the General Federation of Women's Clubs, and the New York Women's Press Club. The elite members of her own New York Women's Club campaigned for education, improved working conditions and better healthcare for women. An uncompromising realist, she once wrote:

> Girls are none the worse for being a little wild, a little startling to very proper norms, and much less likely, in that case, to spend their time gasping over sentimental novels, and imagining that every whiskered specimen they see is their hero.[17]

It was after eleven o'clock by the time Oscar arrived and immediately he 'drew off part of the crowd which had formed around Miss Alcott'.[18] The following day, Monday 9 January, Jane Croly and many of her guests from the previous evening paid a dollar each to hear him lecture on 'The English Renaissance' to a packed Chickering Hall. By five o'clock, the event was sold out and enterprising touts were offering a handful of tickets for twice their face value.[19] Inside the hall, the throng, reported to be pretty evenly divided by gender, took up every available seat and several people stood in the aisles in defiance of New York City fire regulations.

Oscar was uncharacteristically nervous. Two days earlier, he had confided in Elizabeth Lewis, wife of his solicitor, Sir George Lewis and a close friend: '. . . if I am not a success on Monday I shall be very wretched'.[20] At 8.30, he appeared onstage and delivered, in a 'well-modulated voice', what was, in the opinion of Henry Collins Brown, founder of the Museum of the City of New York, an 'excellent scholarly address on Aestheticism, enlivened with shafts of humour'.[21] Helen Potter, the elocutionist and costumed impersonator, took careful note of Oscar's attire and speech patterns, recording that he spoke 'very deliberately' in a voice that was 'clear, easy and not forced'.[22] Afterwards, the crowd 'applauded the poet generously'.[23] Surprised that 'the address struck a loftier note than was expected', Brown realised that:

> Instead of being the posturing idiot the Press made him out to be, [Wilde] was justly admitted to be possessed of much wit, much culture and on the whole a decidedly worth-while person.[24]

A jubilant Oscar described his audience as 'larger and more wonderful than even Dickens had', and insisted the lionising he received was 'worse than that given to Sarah Bernhardt'.[25] That night, he attended a reception hosted in his honour at the opulent 5th Avenue home of Mrs John Mack, where the *New York Herald* noted that 'scores upon scores of beautiful and elegantly dressed ladies crowded each other in their effort to grasp his hand'.[26] There too were Jane Croly, Louisa May Alcott, Jane Bigelow and Kate Field. Actress, journalist and campaigner for woman's rights, Field was nothing short of legendary; the *New York Tribune* described her as 'one of the best known women in America', while the *Chicago Tribune* called her 'the most unique woman the present century has produced'.[27]

A popular lecturer and prolific travel writer, Field wrote for several prestigious newspapers including the *Chicago Times-Herald*, the *New York Tribune* and *The Boston Post*. She was the inspiration for Henrietta Stackpole, Henry James's crusading feminist journalist in *The Portrait of a Lady*. Extraordinarily well connected, she had hosted such luminaries as Charles Dickens, Robert Browning, Elizabeth Barrett Browning, George Eliot, Anthony Trollope, and Mark Twain. Although she knew Dickens well and had covered his final American tour for the *New York Tribune*, Field too was barred from the Press Club dinner that honoured him, a snub that prompted her to assist Jane Croly in founding Sorosis.

Oscar brought a letter of introduction to Field from actor and voice coach Hermann Vezin, a mutual friend. Two days after his first lecture, she hosted a luncheon for him at the headquarters of her Cooperative Dress Association, an organisation she founded in order to provide equitable employment and affordable clothing to women and children. At Oscar's request, Field invited poet, critic and essayist Edmund Clarence Stedman, writing: 'Wilde is clever and wants to meet artists only'. Stedman declined, telling Thomas Bailey Aldrich, editor of *The Atlantic Monthly*:

This Philistine town [New York] is making a fool of itself over Oscar Wilde, who is lecturing on Art Subjects, appearing in public in an extraordinary dress – a loose shirt with a turn-down collar, a flowing tie of uncommon shade, velvet coat, knee breeches – and often he is seen in public carrying a lily, or a sunflower, in his hand. He has brought hundreds of letters of introduction.[28]

Stedman had also turned down an invitation to the Croly's, and had been furious when Laura, his wife, attended alone, since several newspapers reported that he had accompanied her.[29]

The *New York Daily Graphic* ridiculed Oscar's visit to the Cooperative Dress Association, claiming he had been 'measured for his petticoats' and presented with 'a pair of gilt-edged corsets' by shareholders who adopted 'poses of aesthetic adoration'.[30] In response, Kate Field sent a strongly worded letter to the editor of *The Boston Journal* praising Oscar's stellar academic credentials and condemning the American press for its snide coverage of his tour, pointing out that it was they who looked foolish rather than Oscar. She wrote, 'Knee-Breeches – Why Not?' for the *Philadelphia Illustrated Weekly*, in defence of his choice of costume.

Before leaving New York, Oscar attended a gathering hosted by prominent writer and socialite Anne Charlotte Lynch Botta, whose father, revolutionary Dubliner Patrick Lynch, had been imprisoned then deported from Ireland after the rising of 1798. In many ways, Lynch Botta was Jane Wilde's New York equivalent. Her literary salon was attended by every major poet, artist and musician of the day including Thackeray, Trollope and Poe, who read *The Raven* for the first time at one of her gatherings. Although she too was a published poet, friends said of her:

It was not so much what Mrs. Botta did for literature with her own pen, as what she helped others to do, that will make her name a part of the literary history of the country.[31]

Her endorsement was invaluable.

On 16 January, the eve of his departure, Oscar dined with Marietta Paran Stevens one last time before paying a final visit to Jane Bigelow. As a consequence, he overslept the next morning and missed breakfast before embarking on a gruelling tour encompassing 140 lectures in cities and towns scattered along a 1,500 mile route that criss-crossed America and Canada. That evening, he lectured on the English Renaissance to 1,500 appreciative Philadelphians, who rewarded him with two encores.

One audience member, Elizabeth Robins, admitted to having felt 'no particular excitement' at the prospect of hearing Oscar and expressed 'impatience with his pose'. Afterwards, she conceded that he had been 'amusing' and 'refreshingly enthusiastic'.[32]

Robins' opinion grew even warmer when Oscar took to calling on her uncle, art educationalist Charles Godfrey Leland. In the relaxed surroundings of the Broad Street boarding house where Leland was staying, Oscar introduced the unworldly Robins to art, specifically the work of James McNeill Whistler, who he described as the greatest artist living. His enthusiasm was infectious. Two years later, Robins married the artist Joseph Pennell and accepted a travel writing commission from *Century Magazine* to document their cycling journeys across Europe. When the couple settled in London, Robins Pennell established a popular salon and earned a reputation as an influential columnist, biographer and art critic. She never lost her passion for Whistler and co-authored, with her husband, several authoritative books on his life and work.[33]

In Washington, Oscar was championed by Mary Robeson, wife of a New Jersey congressman, who stirred up controversy by taking him to a series of prestigious diplomatic and social events. Robeson's largesse irritated Henry James, who never had a good word to say about Oscar, but he excused her on the grounds that she was 'fifty years old and fundamentally coarse'.[34] When Robeson brought Oscar to a meeting of the Washington Literary Society at the home of the vivacious Frances Hodgson Burnett, he endeared himself to his hostess by informing her that John Ruskin considered her a 'true artist' and had read everything she wrote.[35] Oscar looked resplendent that evening in full Aesthetic costume of velvet jacket and knee breeches, and it seems likely that the flowing curls and velvet suits with lace collars that Hodgson Burnett adopted for her real life sons, Lionel and Vivien, and her fictional *Little Lord Fauntleroy*, published four years later, were influenced by his flamboyant attire.[*]

Oscar was popular with American women and his lectures often attracted a predominantly female audience. Everywhere he went, groups of excited young women turned up just to catch a glimpse of this exotic young man and Washington was no exception. A group of girls clustered outside his room in the Arlington Hotel, peering in and giggling every time his door was opened.[36] He did not find universal favour among the

---

* Ann Thwaite speculates this may have been the case in her biography *Waiting for the Party: the Life of Frances Hodgson Burnett* (London, Secker & Warburg, 1974).

women of Washington though. When society hostess Marian 'Clover' Hooper Adams, wife of Henry Adams and muse of Henry James, spotted him sauntering down Pennsylvania Avenue with 'long hair, dressed in stockings and tights, a brown plush tunic, a big yellow sunflower pinned above his heart, a queer cap on his head', she declared him a 'noodle'.[37] She made no secret of her distaste: 'We are urged to meet Oscar Wilde tonight at the Lorings', she wrote, 'I tartly remarked "that fools don't amuse me" when a courteous refusal was unheeded'.[38] Adams begged her friend Henry James not to call on her with Oscar in tow and was delighted when he assured her that he too considered 'Hosscar' Wilde, 'a fatuous fool and a tenth-rate cad'.[39] This was a pity: Adams would have made a useful ally, since her Pennsylvania Avenue home, which stood directly opposite the White House, attracted many literary giants of the day.

In nearby Baltimore, Oscar addressed 'quite a large turnout of ladies', who braved inclement weather to hear him.[40] On to Boston, where social activist Julia Ward Howe* learned from her nephew that the young poet was keen to meet her and graciously invited Oscar to lunch the next day, obliging her daughter Maud to hastily assemble both food and guests while she attended church. On her return, Ward Howe was greeted by an animated Maud, who declared, 'Oscar is coming!'[41] Both were very taken with him and Ward Howe noted in her diary that she found Oscar 'delightful, simple, sincere, and very clever'.[42] Included among the dozen or so guests Maud had assembled was art collector and philanthropist Isabella Stewart Gardner, one of America's foremost female patrons of the arts. Although her close friend Henry James had warned her that this young Irishman was 'repulsive and fatuous' she ignored this and graciously accepted an autographed photograph.[43] In time Gardner would be celebrated for her sensitivity towards and complete acceptance of young gay men, who formed a bright and cultured circle around her. Her enlightened attitude was informed by the tragedy of one of her nephews, who took his own life in response to his unrequited love for another man.

Two days later, Ward Howe joined the audience at the Boston Music Hall, and witnessed Oscar's aesthetic style being parodied by a group of sixty Harvard students who arrived late, occupied the two front rows of the auditorium, and disrupted proceedings by clapping wildly every time he paused to take a sip of water. She recognised one of these upstarts as

---

* Julia Ward Howe is best remembered perhaps as the composer of the 'Battle Hymn of the Republic' (1861).

her grandnephew Winthrop Chanler. Oscar had been forewarned and took the sting out of their juvenile antics by arriving onstage wearing perfectly ordinary evening clothes. The *Boston Evening Transcript* commended him for his dignity in the face of such provocation and their critic reported: 'a lady near us said "How mortified I should be if a son of mine were amongst them!"'.[44]

Afterwards, Ward Howe hosted a party for Oscar: 'We all think him a man with genuine enthusiasm and with much talent', she wrote.[45] Her very public approval provoked the ire of abolitionist and advocate for woman's suffrage Thomas Wentworth Higginson, who criticised her for 'entertaining this pornographic poet in her home' in an article he wrote for the *Woman's Journal*.[46] Undaunted, Ward Howe responded with a letter to the *Boston Evening Transcript* assuring Wentworth Higginson that she would associate with whomsoever she pleased and asserting: 'Mr Wilde is a young man in whom many excellent people have found much to like'.[47] Oscar sent her a note of thanks: 'Your letter is noble and beautiful,' he wrote, 'I have only just seen it, and shall not forget ever the chivalrous and pure-minded woman who wrote it'.[48]

Before leaving Boston, Oscar met with Henry Wadsworth Longfellow, onetime correspondent of his mother's. The aged poet said of the youthful pretender, 'Whatever he may be in public, in private he is a very agreeable young man'.[49] He also found time to visit nearby Niagara Falls. Although he admired the attraction, he detested the yellow oilskins that visitors were obliged to wear but conceded that it was:

> a consolation to know, however, that such an artist as Madame Bernhardt has not only worn that yellow, ugly dress, but has been photographed in it.[50]

Once again, Sarah had been there first.

As his tour progressed, Oscar sensed a waning enthusiasm for his scholarly 'English Renaissance' lecture, which borrowed heavily from Pater, Ruskin and Morris. He simplified it, and wrote a second, 'The House Beautiful', for cities where he was scheduled to appear more than once. This new lecture, intended to appeal primarily to women and described by the *Chicago Tribune* as 'his views on interior and exterior house decoration', drew on the work of the scholar and artist Mary Eliza Haweis, who advocated rational dress and had exhibited at the Royal Academy.[51] In it, he credited women with 'natural art instincts which men usually acquire only after long special training and study,' insisting, 'it may be the mission of the women of this country to revive decorative art into honest, healthy life'. Moreover, he asserted, 'there has been no good decorative work done in any age, or in any country where women have not occupied a high social position'.[52]

Although Oscar met with a mixed reception in Chicago, he did secure the approval of the 'remarkable' Elizabeth Jaeger, 'beautiful and witty' second wife of prominent Chicago businessman Horatio Odell Stone, and recognised as an 'undisputed social leader'. Her afternoon reception for Oscar was proclaimed her 'most renowned entertainment' by the *Chicago Tribune,* which reported that the many women who attended found Oscar 'perfectly charming'.[53] Lecturing in Louisville, Oscar spoke of his admiration for John Keats and cited 'Answer to a sonnet by J. H. Reynolds'. Afterwards, 'a lady of middle-age, with a sweet gentle manner and a most musical voice' approached him to thank him for his kind words. She was Emma Keats Speed, niece of the poet, and she invited him to spend a delightful afternoon at her home, 'pouring over torn yellow leaves and faded scraps of paper'.[54] Shortly afterwards, in an act of overwhelming generosity, she sent Oscar the original manuscript of 'Answer to a sonnet by J. H. Reynolds', prompting him to write, 'What you have given me is more golden than gold, more precious than any treasure this great country could yield me'.[55]

In Fort Wayne, Indiana, Oscar bumped into Genevieve Ward. Although Ward considered Jane Wilde charming and highly accomplished, she was more measured in her assessment of Oscar, describing him as 'the young poet, whose verses are, at this time of writing, provoking both trenchant criticism and recognition on both sides of the Atlantic'. In her opinion, 'he was always very nice until he got this absurd aesthetic notion in his head'.[56] Oscar benefitted hugely from the high standing his mother enjoyed among influential sections of the American public and press. Much of the coverage of his tour mentioned his relationship to her and the *Times of Philadelphia* described him as 'not an Englishman but the son of Lady Wilde, whose patriotic Irish lyrics in the Dublin Nation thirty years ago attracted great attention'.[57] Oscar carried a photograph of Jane wherever he went and sent her newspaper cuttings, and very welcome cheques. She in turn wrote every week to assure him he had not been forgotten: 'You are still the talk of London,' she wrote. 'The cab men ask if I am anything to Oscar Wilde. The milkman has bought your picture! & in fact nothing seems <u>celebrated</u> in London but you'.[58]

On a rainy St. Patrick's Day in St. Paul, Minnesota, a Father Shanley pronounced himself 'pleased to announce the presence with them of a son of one of Ireland's noblest daughters'. In San Francisco, where Oscar lectured on 'Irish Poets and Poetry of the Nineteenth Century', he finished with two of Jane's longer poems, 'The Brothers' and 'Courage', which he read 'with much effect and feeling and was heartily applauded therefore'.[59] Oscar was warm in his appreciation, declaring:

> Of the quality of Speranza's poem perhaps I should not speak – for criticism is disarmed before love – but I am content to abide by the verdict of the nation which has so welcomed her genius . . .[60]

He would like to have read more, but finished by saying: 'it is enough for me to have once had the privilege of speaking about my mother to the race she loves so well'.[61] In an interview with journalist Mary Watson, he admitted that 'his mother, of whom he is very proud, inspired him with the desire to become a poet'.[62]

In San Francisco, Oscar was entertained by Bella Strong, stepdaughter of Robert Louis Stevenson, who hosted a party in his honour in the studio of her artist husband, Joe. Bella thought Oscar 'very impressive', adding:

> He was charming. His enthusiasm, his frank sincerity, dispelled at once any constraint we may have felt at meeting such a distinguished stranger. We didn't know that we were listening to one who was acknowledged to be the wittiest man in London. We were exhilarated by his talk, gay, quick, delightfully cordial and almost affectionately friendly.[63]

It was a memorable occasion: 'When he left we all felt we had met a truly great man', Bella decided.

Oscar traversed North America as the months rolled by, garnering a mixed reception along the way. Some towns simply weren't ready for him and, often, it was the men who shunned and ridiculed him while he was fêted by their sisters, mothers, wives and daughters. In June, he stayed in the summer house of Julia Ward Howe in Newport, Rhode Island, prompting newspaper reports that he had become engaged to Maud. Although she admitted he talked amazingly well, her mother was adamant that they were entirely unsuited. In July, Oscar accompanied Ward Howe's brother, Sam Ward, to the Long Island resort of Long Beach where they spent a day on the beach with Alice Pike Barney and her six-year-old daughter, Natalie. When Alice injured her leg, Oscar gallantly carried her up the beach and they got talking. Although hugely talented, Alice's ambitions to study art were opposed by her boorish husband,

Albert Clifford Barney, a hard-drinking man with a habit of infidelity. With Oscar's encouragement, she took art lessons in Paris and was later admitted to the Society of Washington Artists.[64] Little Natalie remembered Oscar scooping her up onto his knee to tell her 'a wonderful tale'.[65] In adulthood, she ran a vibrant salon in Paris and enjoyed dalliances with two women closely connected with him: his niece, Dolly Wilde, and Olive Custance, the woman who married Lord Alfred Douglas.

Reaching Saratoga as September drew to a close, Oscar was mobbed by a crowd of eager young women who followed him into the billiard room of his hotel. Seeking refuge in the bar, he thought of asking 'what'll you have, ladies?', but realised that, had he done so, 'all the country would have said I had insulted the ladies at Saratoga'.[66] When he returned to New York at the end of ten gruelling months, the social whirl continued with a dinner organised to introduce him to twenty of the brightest and most beautiful women from New York and Boston. A young Anna, Comtesse de Brémont claims to have been present; although she is believed to have exaggerated her connection to the Wildes and cannot always be relied upon.* She described Oscar enthroned on a high-backed chair wearing his knee britches, black silk stockings, and shoes with glittering buckles, a sunflower pushed through the lapel of his black velvet coat, and said he delighted his audience by declaring 'the American woman is the most decorated and decorative object that I have seen in America', an assertion that triggered enthusiastic applause and a shower of red rose petals.

Oscar's return to New York coincided with the arrival of Lillie Langtry, who was embarking on her first American tour. He had quipped that he would 'rather have discovered Mrs. Langtry than have discovered America'. Now he set about persuading his influential new friends to entertain her, and informed the press that he had 'not the slightest doubt of her dramatic genius'.[67] He even accompanied her to Sarony's studio for publicity shots. When Abbey's Park Theatre burnt down on the evening of what was to have been Lillie's debut, Oscar was there to comfort her; while they watched the flames engulf the building, it is reported that he remarked 'it is a beautiful fire'.[68]

When the *New York World* commissioned Oscar to review Lillie's first outing as Hester Glazebrook in romantic comedy, *An Unequal Match,* he praised her beauty and her costumes but refrained from critiquing her

---

* An American-born singer, novelist, poet and journalist who had started life as plain Anna Dunphy but gained a title by marrying Count Leon de Brémont.

acting. The less reticent critic at the *New York Dramatic Mirror* declared: 'No one was so absurd as to imagine she would prove a mistress of dramatic art', concluding: '[S]he is not and perhaps never will be an actress of genuine worth'.[69] *The New York Times* described her performance as 'strained and awkward', and decided, erroneously, that her popularity would 'pass away quickly'.[70] The *Chicago Daily News* focused on her relationship with Oscar, reporting that he was 'head over heels in love' with Lillie: 'Ever since Mrs. Langtry's arrival, Wilde has clung to her skirts'.

Oscar sailed out of New York on the SS *Bothnia* on 27 December 1882. Throughout his tour, his progress had been facilitated by prominent and influential society women. He spoke highly of them in turn, declaring, 'American women are bright, clever, and wonderfully cosmopolitan'.[71] He was greatly affected by the experience and recorded his observations in playful letters to, among others, Fanny Bernard Beere and Helena Sickert; both of whom defended him in the face of critical coverage in the English press. Although Oscar would never tour America again, he returned eight months later to oversee the Broadway debut of *Vera*. By then he was deeply involved with the woman he would marry.

Chapter 9

THE REVOLUTIONARY
AND THE DUCHESS

Mr Wilde has entrusted his play to an inferior actress.
THE PILOT

In September 1880, at the suggestion of his friend and fellow Dubliner
Dion Boucicault,* Oscar sent a copy of *Vera* to the much-admired
Canadian-born actress Clara Morris. Paying tribute to her 'genius', he
expressed his hope that she might accept his play:

> On account of its avowedly republican sentiments I have not been able
> to get permission to have it brought out here, but with you there is more
> freedom . . .[1]

Boucicault, an accomplished actor, prolific playwright and hugely successful theatre manager, had already given Oscar his opinion: 'You have
dramatic powers but have not shaped your subject perfectly before beginning it', he offered, and he urged Oscar to convert his stilted dialogue into
'action' rather than 'discussion'.[2]

A contemporary of William and Jane Wilde, Boucicault had always
been welcome at 1 Merrion Square.[3] For decades, he had divided his
time between London and New York, delighting audiences with his
repertoire of original plays and adaptations of the work of others. He
improved the lot of fellow playwrights by leading a campaign for the
introduction of American copyright laws for original drama; legislation
Oscar would one day rely on to secure his claim to *Vera*. Boucicault took
a keen interest in *Vera* and *The New York Times* reported him as having
produced the aborted London staging, planned for the Adelphi Theatre
on 17 December 1881. In 1882, three weeks into his grueling schedule,
Oscar met Boucicault in Boston and shared concerns he had raised with
D'Oyly Carte's New York agent, Colonel Morse: 'Six lectures a week for
three weeks seem to me enormous', he complained, 'I do not know if I

---

* Pronounced 'Boo-see-ko'.

can stand it . . . However, I will do my best – and if I feel Titan-like will do *matinées*'.[4]

The strain of touring was visible and Boucicault expressed alarm to their mutual friend Elizabeth Lewis: 'He [Oscar] has been much distressed; and came here last night looking worn and thin', he wrote, adding:

> Oscar is helpless, because he is not a practical man of business, so when I advised him to throw over [D'Oyly] Carte, and offered to see him through financially if he did so, he felt afraid. I offered him a thousand pounds or two if he required it, but he says he will play out his contract to April . . . There is a future for him here, but he wants management.[5]

In an amusing postscript, Boucicault suggested that, as well as securing better management, Oscar needed to 'reduce his hair and take his legs out of the last century'.

Since there was little likelihood of the inflammatory *Vera* being staged in London, Oscar used the opportunity of his trip to America to find a champion for his first play. As the sole female character and focus of all the drama, the eponymous nihilist was an exceptionally strong role for any woman to play, but Oscar had no reputation as a playwright and would need to convince an iconic actress to take a chance on him. As if *Vera* were not controversial enough, he ended up collaborating with a woman notorious for her performances in the dock as much as on the stage. The results were disastrous.

Sarah Bernhardt had advised Oscar of 'two things in America worth seeing – one was Clara Morris's acting, and the other was some dreadful method of killing pigs in Chicago'; he was keen to see the former but managed to avoid the latter.[6] Sarah may have seen something of herself in her North American counterpart. They were frequently likened and Clara was dubbed 'Queen of Melodrama' in tribute to her unfailing ability to move her audience to tears. On seeing Clara play Camille, a part more closely associated with herself, Sarah declared with characteristic generosity: 'My God this woman is not acting; she is suffering'.[7] Her admiration was shared by Helena Modjeska, who described Clara as: 'A born actress, genuine, admirable, spontaneous, and powerful in her tragic moments, tender and gentle in the touching scenes, and always true to nature'.[8]

Six years older than Oscar, Clara had endured a childhood significantly less stable than his: 'I came to a house where Trouble and Poverty had preceded me,' she wrote, 'and, worse than both these put together – treachery'.[9] By her own account, Clara was the product of a bigamous relationship and was taken to America by her mother once her father's duplicity was exposed. As they had few resources, acting offered her a route out of abject poverty. Aged twenty-two, she joined Augustin Daly's company and enthralled audiences and critics with her portrayal of tragic Anne Sylvester in Wilkie Collins's *Man and Wife*. In the words of theatre historian George C. D. Odell she 'became at once a new sensation'.[10] By 1882, Clara was at the height of her powers. Persuading her to play *Vera* would represent a major coup.

Clara met Oscar at the reception Jane Croly hosted for Louisa May Alcott in New York in January 1882. Several newspapers reported that she had been invited at his request and the *Argonaut* insisted her choice of outfit, 'a dress of white brocade satin, cut low in the neck, profusely trimmed with pearl and crystal beads', had been dictated by Oscar.[11] Just before Oscar arrived, Clara had stepped out of the crush and 'thrown herself into an armchair in the anti-room to "get a breath of fresh air"'.[12] Eyewitnesses reported that she took fright and fled as soon as she saw him, but she was persuaded back. Oscar clasped her hand in both of his, a habit he shared with Jane. According to the *Cincinnati Enquirer*, he declared: 'I am nobody but M'lle Sarah Bernhardt is an authority; she has told me how greatly she admired your acting'.[13]

Both attended Kate Field's lunch and Oscar used the opportunity to extract a promise from Clara that she would consider playing the lead in *Vera*. Later that week, he watched her perform as Mercy Merrick in Wilkie Collins' *The New Magdalen*. Hailing her as 'a veritable genius', he enthused:

> Miss Morris is the greatest actress I ever saw, if it be fair to form an opinion of her from her rendition of this one role . . . We have no such powerfully intense actress in England. She is a great artist, in my sense of the word, because all she does, all she says, in the matter of the doing and of the saying, constantly evoke the imagination to supplement it. That is what I mean by art.[14]

Although a sceptical American press dismissed this histrionic assessment as a cynical attempt to generate some early publicity for his play, Oscar was sincere in his appreciation of imagination as superior to reality and art as grander than life.

Three weeks later, in early February 1882, Clara Morris turned *Vera* down. She refused to reconsider, even when D'Oyly Carte intervened at Oscar's behest. As she had just been announced for Bathsheba Everdene in a stage adaptation of Thomas Hardy's novel *Far From the Madding Crowd*, Colonel Morse saved face by attributing her decision to unfortunate timing, but her objection may have been more principled. In a diary entry dated 2 July 1881, Clara had expressed revulsion at the attack on President James A. Garfield, a man she had met in childhood. The following day, she sent a message of support to his wife: 'Of course, hundreds are at hand to render all great services for the patient,' she wrote, 'but if I can aid in even the most trivial way, command me I entreat you'.[15] She would hardly be keen to play a would-be assassin.

Equally pertinent, perhaps, were the concerns she expressed about *A Nihilist Princess*, a novel written by the socialist and feminist author Marie Louise Gagneur. Published in 1880 as *Les Vierges Russes* and translated into English in 1881, this melodramatic novel, like *Vera*, portrays nihilism as heroic. The cross-dressing Princess Wanda Kryloff, daughter of a powerful prince, joins a nihilist cell and uses her extraordinary beauty and royal connections to undermine authoritarian Russian rule. In time, she discovers that her supposedly deceased mother is a member of this revolutionary movement too. Gagneur, a feminist activist who campaigned for reform of the divorce laws in her native France, allowed her women to participate fully in revolutionary action; she even quoted Vera Zasulich in her preface. When Oscar learned Clara was 'afraid of it', he asked D'Oyly Carte to assure her that *A Nihilist Princess* was 'a sham, and empty of all dramatic matter'.[16]

Once Clara turned *Vera* down, Oscar huffed that she could be *'difficile'*. He half-heartedly pursued a couple of lesser-known American actresses before shifting his attention to his second play, a five-act blank verse tragedy he would call *The Duchess of Padua*.* Two days after arriving in New York, he had watched Mary Anderson, known to the American public as 'Our Mary', play Juliet in Shakespeare's *Romeo and Juliet*; his lukewarm appraisal was reported in *The New York Times*. That autumn, as he neared the end of his tour, Oscar requested a meeting with Mary to discuss a potential collaboration prompted by a scheme put to him by innovative actor-dramatist James Morrison Steele MacKaye, who planned to open a spectacular new theatre at the intersection of 33rd Street and Broadway. If Oscar could secure a crowd-pulling actress, Steele MacKaye was willing to open with *The Duchess of Padua*, and stage *Vera* at a later date. Anderson, at the pinnacle of a glittering fifteen-year career and poised to make her London debut, seemed a perfect fit: 'I think I have so conceived it that we shall simultaneously become immortal in one night!', Oscar gushed.[17]

* He had the first thought of calling it *The Duchess of Florence* in 1880.

It seems clear that Oscar desired a highly collaborative relationship. Letters exchanged with Mary give fascinating insights into his approach as a dramatist: 'I cannot write the scenario till I see you and talk to you,' he told her: 'All good plays are a combination of the dream of a poet and that practical knowledge of the actor . . .'[18] Hyperbole flowed from his pen as he assured Mary that she ranked 'with the great actresses of the earth'. Such flattery proved irresistible. When they met on 11 September 1882, at the luxurious Fifth Avenue Hotel in Manhattan, Oscar presented Mary with a beautifully bound edition of *Poems*, inscribed 'from a poet to a poem',[*] an accolade he reached for on a number of occasions.[19]

In return for an advance of \$5,000 and a royalty payable after each performance, Oscar offered Mary and her overbearing stepfather turned business manager Dr Hamilton Griffin, a man Oscar described a 'padded horror', exclusive rights to his play.[20] Although Mary had first refusal, Oscar told her he had received a, 'very large offer' from actor-impresario Lawrence Barrett; subsequent events indicate that this was indeed the case.[21] Mary was intrigued, but she saw room to negotiate with this untested young playwright. In early October, Oscar complained to Steele MacKaye: 'No news from the Anderson – from the Griffin none'.[22] Days later, he received provisional agreement, contingent on his postponing the production for twelve months and opening in Booth's Theatre rather than Steele MacKaye's proposed new venue. This seems an odd choice, since Edwin Booth, actor brother of the notorious John Wilkes Booth, assassin of Abraham Lincoln, had sold his theatre by then and the new owners had announced, with great fanfare, their plans to convert it into a dry goods store. Weeks before the proposed opening of *The Duchess of Padua*, Booth's Theatre closed with a benefit performance of *Romeo and Juliet* starring Oscar's great friend Helena Modjeska.

Although negotiations appeared to be proceeding smoothly, Oscar made the fatal mistake of underestimating Mary. At times his obsequiousness was risible: insisting on the importance of securing a worthy leading man, he fawned:

> A mediocrity acting with a woman of such noble presence as you are dwindles and shrivels into a mere nothing, and becomes no better than a doublet and hose filled with sawdust.[23]

---

[*] The novelist Coulson Kernahan saw at least two identical dedications.

This was disingenuous. In a letter to Steele MacKaye, Oscar described Mary as 'simple and nice'; she may have been nice but she was far from simple.[24] In *Some Victorian Women: Good, Bad and Indifferent*, Irish illustrator Harry Furniss described her as 'a clever businesswoman', who would direct rehearsals of the plays in which she appeared until the early hours of the morning. He also remarked on her 'delightful personality'.[25]

Once Mary and the Griffin persuaded Oscar to waive his author's royalty, the way was clear for both parties to sign a contract. Under its terms, Oscar agreed to write:

> . . . a first class Five act tragedy to be completed on or before March 1st 1883 – Said tragedy to be the property of Miss Mary Anderson and her heirs forever.[26]

In return, he would receive $5,000 as requested, although just $1,000 would be paid up front with the balance falling due if, and only if, Mary approved his completed manuscript. Flushed with success, Oscar sent Mary a copy of *Vera*: '*Vera* charms me', she assured him, 'it is very mournful. I think I would like to play the part'.[27] She never did but *Vera* had a new champion by then.

By October 1882, Steele MacKaye had abandoned his plans and thrown himself into the task of securing a deal for *Vera* instead. He approached Marie Prescott, a highly ambitious yet deeply controversial actress with a talent for attracting the attention of the press in a manner that was not always to her advantage. Like Clara Morris, Prescott's decision to tread the boards was born out of necessity. At eighteen, the Kentucky-born actress-to-be had shared a modest home with her husband, her mother and her two younger siblings. Her father had been committed to the Eastern State Lunatic Asylum, which he never left. Marie gave birth to three sons during the first five years of her marriage, although one died in infancy. When her husband left during the sixth year, she gave music lessons to support her extended family. Acting seemed a better option.

In 1877, Marie made her acting debut playing Lady Macbeth in the Grand Opera House in Cincinnati. By coincidence, the appreciative crowd was still raving about the brilliant 'Juliet' they had been given, months earlier, by her fellow 'Kentuckian', Mary Anderson.* Although

---

* Although Mary was born in California, when she was a child her father was killed in the American Civil War and her mother had remarried and moved with her to Kentucky.

hailed as 'promising', Marie's burgeoning career was jeopardised by Ernest Harvier, a spurned lover and former manager who leaked damaging allegations concerning the legitimacy of her sons to the press. As a result, she was obliged to own up to her failed marriage, a circumstance considered marginally more acceptable than unmarried motherhood. Shortly afterwards, Marie joined Dion Boucicault's company at Booth's Theatre, but their collaboration was short-lived and she struggled to maintain harmonious relationships with her fellow thespians.

In the weeks leading up to her first meeting with Oscar, Marie Prescott was embroiled in a sensational and widely reported libel case she had taken against the American News Company for distributing a gossip sheet that questioned her decency and chastity. These grubby pieces had been written anonymously by Harvier, who harassed her for years. Marie was in the habit of seeking redress in the courts, but she must have cut a lonely figure as the only woman in a packed courtroom in which intimate details of her private life were laid bare.

Initially, Marie prevailed and was awarded damages of $12,500, but the judgement was reversed on appeal and the most damaging consequence was her uneasy relationship with the hostile American press. An editorial in the *National Police Gazette*[*] illustrates this:

> Marie Prescott let her ambition run away with her in many respects and she gave herself away unreservedly in enlisting help to boost her up the rocky steps of dramatic fame. Like the whole crowd of silly, stage-struck women she was prepared to go to any extreme to gain prominence and notoriety as an artiste and was willing to allow the gossips the greatest latitude in construing her erratic conduct if only her artistic end might be attained.[28]

The author of this damning piece went on to describe Marie as 'fresh' and 'free and easy' with her favours: 'It's a dirty code of morals that prevails on the stage,' he declared. 'The sacrifice of self-respect that an actress finds necessary at the outset proves it'. American actresses, it seems, were treated with the same derision as many of their English counterparts.

Oscar and Steele MacKaye met Marie for breakfast at fashionable Delmonico's[†] on Sunday 12 November 1882, at her invitation. They

---

[*] This lurid yet hugely popular magazine was ostensibly concerned with matters of interest to the police. This gave its contributors an excuse to cover all manner of murders, crimes and scandals. It was immensely influential.

[†] An opulent restaurant with Moorish decor and antique-filled rooms described

were joined by her recently acquired husband-manager, William Perzel.[*] Although Marie assured Oscar she was 'so anxious to succeed' with *Vera*, she warned him that the royalty he sought was 'exorbitant'.[29] As negotiations were entrusted to the ineffectual Perzel, Oscar sailed for England in December without securing a deal. The SS *Bothnia* had hardly docked when he received a letter on paper headed, 'Marie Prescott, Tragedienne', informing him that she had taken over from Perzel: 'I am a splendid business woman (although I hate to be)', she assured him.[30]

Marie's letters to Oscar were disarmingly frank and she had a tendency to talk up her own popularity while undermining his. In one instance, she chastised him for revealing the plot of *Vera* to the press while swearing her to secrecy. In a shrewd pitting of apprentice against mentor, Marie offered Oscar an advance of $1,000 with an additional $50 per performance, which she assured him was twice the sum commanded by Dion Boucicault at the height of his success. She also promised to spend as much as $20,000 staging a Broadway run. In return, she requested the exclusive right to play Vera: 'I am sure of its success therefore I am willing to spend a great deal of money on it', she declared.[31] She was true to her word.

Before a contract was signed, Marie Prescott placed notices in several New York newspapers announcing that she was to star in 'the greatest play of the era'. A firm believer in the power of publicity, her philosophy was: 'The actor or actress who starts in to win fame by merit alone has a "mighty long road"'. Speaking from bitter experience, she declared: 'poverty is usually the better half of modesty'.[32] Oscar was far more circumspect: '. . . no amount of advertising will make a bad play succeed, if it is not a good play well acted', he counselled.[33] Marie was ebullient when he accepted her terms: 'I have given up some brilliant offers to go out with Vera', she told him, 'and I am confident I have done the best thing for myself'.[34]

By then, Oscar was in Paris working on *The Duchess of Padua*. He had used Mary Anderson's advance to secure a suite of rooms on the second floor of the Hotel Voltaire, overlooking the Seine, where he had stayed with Jane and Willie. Among the dozens of letters of introduction he brought to ease his way into the vibrant Parisian literary and artistic

---

by Oscar as one of 'the two most remarkable bits of scenery in the States'; the other was 'the Yosemite Valley' ('Dinners and Dishes', *Pall Mall Gazette*, Vol. XLI, No. 6236, March 7, 1885, p. 5).

[*] Although Prescott always referred to Perzel as her husband, he disputed this. Several years later, when she attempted to sue him for divorce, no evidence of a marriage could be found.

community was one from Edward Burne-Jones to his muse and former lover, Maria Cassavetti Zambaco, a wealthy and beautiful woman of Greek heritage.[*] A talented sculptor, Zambaco had come to Paris to study with Rodin. In Paris, she formed a friendship with Sarah Bernhardt, also an accomplished sculptor and on her return to London, she rented a garden studio from Louise Jopling.

Oscar had long admired Zambaco's androgynous beauty and once described her as 'a tall, lithe woman, beautiful and subtle to look on, like a snake'.[35] Burne-Jones, who used her as a model for male and female figures, cast her as Nimuë, the Lady of the Lake in his *The Beguiling of Merlin*, one of Oscar's favourite paintings. She took pleasure in introducing her young admirer to Parisian society and it was at a dinner party she held in his honour that Oscar met Robert Sherard, great-grandson of William Wordsworth, who was estranged from his family and struggled to make a living as a writer. The two men got along exceptionally well and Oscar treated Sherard to dinner at the celebrated restaurant in the Hotel Foyot the following evening. Making light of the cost, he declared: 'we dine with the Duchess to-night'.[36]

As Oscar had every expectation that Mary Anderson would accept *The Duchess*, he saw no reason to economise. He worked hard on his play and Sherard saw evidence of his industry scattered all about his hotel room; 'a glance at these sheets showed that many of the lines had been written over and over again', he recalled.[37] Oscar dispatched his completed manuscript on 15 March 1883, and followed up with a long and exceptionally revealing letter outlining the approach he had taken to 'the masterpiece of all my literary work, the *chef-d'oeuvre* of my youth'.[38] Noteworthy, at this early stage, is his absolute conviction that an element of comedy was essential in even the darkest tragedy, since an audience would not weep unless first made to laugh.

Levity is scarce in *The Duchess of Padua*, but it features from time to time. So too does a strong condemnation of gender inequality. Oscar saw Beatrice, his duchess, as '*universal*', an 'incarnation of the lives of all women'.[39] He gave her some hard-hitting lines. Lamenting the inequality of marriage, she declared:

> Men when they woo us call us pretty children,
> Tell us we have not wit to make our lives,

---

[*] Burne-Jones was captivated by her, and they were rumoured to have entered a suicide pact at her insistence.

> And so they mar them for us. Did I say woo?
> We are their chattels, and their common slaves,

Beatrice evokes a monstrous portrait of a marriage characterised by poverty, drunkenness and domestic violence:

> I see when men love women
> They give them but a little of their lives
> But women when they love give everything;

Oscar assured Mary that writing *The Duchess* for her had been 'a task of pleasure, and a labour of love'.[40] When his heartfelt missive elicited no response, he followed up with a telegram. Within hours, he had Mary's devastating decision. Sherard witnessed his muted reaction:

> . . . he gave no sign of his disappointment. I can remember his tearing a little piece off the blue telegraph-form and rolling it up into a pellet and putting it into his mouth, as, by curious habit, he did with every paper or book that came into his hands. And all he said, as he passed the telegram over to me, was, "This, Robert, is rather tedious".[41]

Anderson was terse in her refusal: 'Neither of us can afford failure now,' she explained, 'and your Duchess in my hands would not succeed, as the part does not fit me'.[42] She was far more forthcoming in a letter to William Winter, drama editor of the *New York Tribune* and a great friend of hers: 'I have had a play from Oscar Wilde, which I shall decline,' she wrote, 'the situations and business are fine – but crime is its sole aspect – and I cannot deal with crime even in an artistic way, at least not yet'.[43] *The Duchess of Padua* is brutal and Oscar's letters indicate that Mary had asked for Beatrice to be more remorseful.

Guido, the young male protagonist, is determined to avenge his father's death by assassinating the despotic Duke of Padua. When he falls in love with Beatrice, he spares her abusive husband only to witness her murdering him instead. Appalled by Beatrice's crime, Guido rejects her, provoking her to pin the crime on him. Rather than implicate his lover, Guido assumes guilt and is sentenced to death. Beatrice is ashamed of her treachery but when she realises that she cannot save Guido, she drinks poison and dies in his arms. As the prison guards approach, Guido grabs her dagger and ends his life.

Mary Anderson was a 'thoroughly devout Catholic', who was unwavering in her faith.[44] In April 1884, she closed a hugely popular run of W. S.

Gilbert's *Comedy and Tragedy* in London's Lyceum Theatre by refusing to play a role written specifically for her during Holy Week.[45] Although she never spoke publicly of her failed collaboration with Oscar, she included one revealing detail in her autobiography: 'The number of plays submitted to artists is incredible,' she wrote; 'Generally they are absolutely unsuited to the person who is requested to read, and, if possible, produce them'.[46]

Oscar maintained good relations with Mary, congratulating her on her appearance as 'Juliet' on the London stage and including a flattering profile of her in *The Woman's World* when he was editor. Yet, in his anonymous review of her widely acclaimed dual performance as Perdita and Hermione in *The Winter's Tale* at the Lyceum in 1887, he declared: 'A certain artificial staginess has, up to this, marred to a certain degree most, if not all, of Miss Anderson's performances'.[47] Perhaps he held a grudge after all.

Although Oscar's funds had dwindled to nothing, he stayed on in Paris to see Sarah Bernhardt play the title role in Sardou's nihilist play, *Fédora*. Meanwhile, Marie Prescott was worked tirelessly on *Vera*, and had even resolved a looming copyright dispute.* Although she managed to persuade Oscar to rewrite Act II and part of Act IV in accordance with her detailed instructions, he refused to remove the comic epigrams he had given to Prince Paul, the most recognisably Wildean character in the play: '. . . you can produce tragic effects by introducing comedy,' he insisted; 'A laugh in an audience does not destroy terror, but, by relieving it, aids it'.[48] This is the clearest glimpse of the playwright he would one day become. Some of Marie's interventions were welcome. Oscar had given lines to five children, but she persuaded him to use just one, counselling: 'Children are very hard to procure for travelling'.[49]

In May 1883, Oscar returned to London with a head full of curls and an empty wallet. He stayed with Jane before taking furnished rooms, 'for single men of distinction', on nearby Charles Street. Frank Harris claimed that Jane had suggested Charles Street. She felt he should live at a suitably impressive address since she 'never doubted his ultimate triumph' and 'knew all his poems by heart'.[50] These lodgings were managed by a retired butler, and his wife, an excellent cook, both of whom were

* In April 1883, Frank Parker Hulette, managing editor of the *Evening Observer*, insisted that he had registered a copyright for *Vera*, a 'Russo-Parisian society drama in five acts'. Prescott applied to Washington for a copy of Oscar's copyright, countering that he had asserted his rights as early as October 1882.

devoted to their brilliant young tenant; they 'could not speak too highly of his cleverness, kindness and consideration' and overlooked his tardiness in settling his account.[51]

In London, Oscar renewed his acquaintance with a young woman he had met during the summer of 1881, when he and his mother had been invited to tea at the Devonshire Terrace home of Ada Swinburne-King, daughter of Mary Atkinson, an old Dublin neighbour of theirs.* That day, there had been a scheme afoot to introduce Oscar to Ada's considerably younger sister Ellena, but he was far more interested in Constance, Ada's strikingly pretty twenty-two-year-old daughter. As mother and daughter had a poor relationship, Constance lived with her grandfather John Horatio Lloyd and his daughter Emily at their imposing but inhospitable home at 100 Lancaster Gate.

Constance and Oscar seemed entirely comfortable in each other's company and it was clear that their relationship had survived separation and false reports of Oscar's engagement to Maud Howe, which had been telegraphed to several European newspapers: 'I can't help liking him,' Constance told her older brother, Otho, 'because when he's talking to me alone he's never a bit affected, and speaks naturally, excepting that he uses better language than most people'.[52] They parted once again when Oscar undertook a short lecture tour of England before sailing for New York to attend the opening night of *Vera*, scheduled to run for four weeks at the Union Square Theatre from 20 August 1883.[53] Many New Yorkers had not yet returned to the city but Marie Prescott had whipped up interest by publishing several of Oscar's letters.

He arrived, nine days before opening night, to a lukewarm reception. The reliably hostile *National Police Gazette* declared him a 'monstrous charlatan and humbug', and insisted *Vera* had been described as a 'masterpiece of rot', adding, 'Of all the ridiculous failures of the year, none will be so thorough, so complete, or so well deserved, as *Vera*'.[54] This was grossly unfair: *Vera* was not a bad play, but it was an unfortunate one and Oscar paid a high price for his sympathetic portrayal of nihilism and his association with the controversial Marie Prescott.

The theatre was full on opening night and the audience included several actors and theatre managers whose productions had not yet opened.

* Mary Atkinson, the widow of Captain John Atkinson, Receiver General of the Post Office, lived at 1 Ely Place, near Merrion Square in Dublin. At nineteen, her daughter Ada married Horace Lloyd, who died in 1874, when their daughter Constance was in her teens. Ada remarried four years later.

Most striking, however, was the profusion of fans flapping ineffectually in front of the faces of overheated patrons. New York was wilting under the intensity of an enervating heat wave and the *Spirit of the Times* likened the Union Square Theatre to 'the hottest room of a Turkish bath'.[55] These stifling conditions could not have contrasted more markedly with the play's setting: a frozen Russian winter that obliged cast members to don heavy brocade costumes, many of them fur-lined. While the audience struggled to cope with furnace-like heat, frozen peasants huddled around open fires onstage. It must have been impossible for overheated patrons to suspend their disbelief.

The play started well. There were calls for the author after the first act and Oscar stepped forward to bow his thanks after the second. Although one intensely sentimental scene between Vera and Alexis during the melodramatic last act was greeted with laughter, catcalls and kissing noises from the cheap seats, *Vera* was well received and Oscar's brief words of appreciation were applauded warmly.[56] Yet, Anna de Brémont, who was present that night, worried that Americans, who loved their actresses, might feel cheated by having been given only one. Echoing her concern, the *Spirit of the Times* insisted that only an inexperienced or very conceited dramatist would put his heroine on stage for five acts without a mother, a sister, a confidante, or even a maid, to keep her company.

Reviews for *Vera* were overwhelmingly disappointing. Describing it as 'an energetic tirade against tyrants and despots . . . full of long speeches in which the glory of liberty is eloquently described', *The New York Times* condemned the play as 'unreal, long-winded and wearisome'. Its critic warned:

> A dramatist . . . who puts a gang of Nihilists upon the stage, on the ground that they are interesting characters of the time and that their convictions make them dramatic, does so at his own peril.[57]

The *New York Herald* described *Vera* as 'long-drawn, dramatic rot, a series of disconnected essays and sickening rant, with a coarse and common kind of cleverness'. The critic attacked Oscar as 'not only a buffoon but a bore'. The *New York Tribune* insisted that his play was:

> . . . a fanciful, foolish, highly-peppered story of love, intrigue, and politics, invested with Russian accessories of fur and dark-lanterns, and overlaid with bantam gabble about freedom and the people. It was little better than fizzle.[58]

There were notable exceptions: the *New York Sun* hailed *Vera* as a masterpiece, while the *New York Mirror* called the play 'the noblest contribution to its literature that the stage has received in many years'. This latter publication whipped up controversy by claiming that a clique of theatre critics had conspired to crush *Vera,* declaring:

> It has been the pleasure of the newspapers and that portion of the public which revels in its ignorance and flaunts its vulgarity to assail Mr. Wilde with every manner of coarse, cheap and indecent indignity.

With uncanny foresight, this newspaper declared: 'It is not the first instance in history of the crucifixion of a good man on the cross of popular prejudice and disbelief'.[59]

Several critics placed the blame firmly with Marie Prescott. Insisting, 'if well acted, it would be a great success', the *Pilot* fuelled a rumour that Prescott had invited Oscar to play 'Alexis', by declaring:

> Mr. Wilde has entrusted his play to an inferior actress, who can only scold on the stage and off it. To save herself she is now trying to induce the author to appear in one of the characters. This would be great folly on his part. A young man can outlive even a bad play; but there are limits which may not be passed.[60]

In a spirited rebuttal, published by several newspaper editors, Marie Prescott cited the good opinion of 'prominent citizens' who had assured her that the critics' views diverged wildly from their own. Unfortunately, the damage was done. It didn't help that the father-in-law of the manager of Haverly's Fourteenth-Street Theatre had fallen ill during the performance and died of a heart attack on the pavement outside, prompting several wags to attribute his demise to the poor quality of the play.[61] One week after *Vera* opened, William Perzel was pushed forward to explain that, as his wife had lost $2,500 that week alone, was struggling to pay her company and could no longer afford to rent the theatre, she had 'yielded to dismal necessity' and was withdrawing the play.[62] Oscar said little. He returned to London and the predictable derision of *Punch,* which declared that his play, 'from all accounts, except the Poet's own, was "Vera bad"'.[63] The ill-fated *Vera* all but disappeared.*

Several years later, on 21 January 1891, 'A new Italian Love Tragedy' called *Guido Ferranti* opened at the Broadway Theatre in New York. A long

---

* Marie Prescott performed *Vera* in the Detroit Opera House on 28 and 29 December 1883, but reviews were poor and it was rarely seen again.

and largely positive review by William Winter[*] of the *New York Tribune* announced:

> The authorship of Guido Ferranti has not been disclosed. There need not have been any hesitation about it – for he is a practised writer and a good one. We recognise in this work a play that we had the pleasure of reading several years ago, in manuscript. It was then called The Duchess of Padua. The author of it is Oscar Wilde.[64]

Actor-manager Lawrence Barrett, who first expressed interest in 1882, had acquired *The Duchess* and, with Oscar's agreement, amended the title to shift the emphasis onto the male lead. Five weeks later, Barrett, aged fifty-three, fell ill on stage and died shortly afterwards. Mina K. Gale,[†] the actress who played Beatrice to Barrett's Guido, acquired the rights, but Oscar, desperate for money by then, insisted that she was limiting his royalties by performing it infrequently: 'This is of course extremely unjust to me', he raged.[65] Had he known, he could have taken consolation from the fact that he was on the cusp of enormous success with his fourth play, *Lady Windermere's Fan*.

[*] Winter turned against Oscar in time, refusing to review *The Importance of Being Earnest* and describing its author as, 'a person of slender talent and no lasting importance' (*New York Daily Tribune* 14 November 1905, p. 7).
[†] Mina Gale was managed by Mary Anderson's actor brother Joseph, who was married to Lawrence Barrett's daughter Gertrude. Joseph Anderson was also involved in negotiations with Augustin Daly and Ada Rehan for 'A Good Woman' aka *Lady Windermere's Fan*.

Chapter 10
Speranza's Saturdays

Her talk was like fireworks – brilliant, whimsical and flashy.
HENRIETTE CORKRAN on Lady Jane Wilde[1]

When Jane Wilde packed up what remained of her Dublin life and took the boat from Kingstown to Holyhead, she was sailing into an uncertain future, but William's profligacy had left her with little choice. After he died, she had lost all the comforts and privileges extended to the wife of an eminent man. Paradoxically, one consequence of the land wars that gripped Ireland as the century neared its end was that this once great champion of Irish freedom lost the paltry £200 she could claim from the annual rent paid by tenants on the Moytura estate. In a letter to her great friend Lotten van Kraemer, she lamented the 'very unquiet state' her country was in: 'people will refuse to pay rents and whoever enforces payment will be assuredly shot', she warned.[2]

Since becoming Lady Wilde, Jane had toned down her radical views. She must have realised that it would be unwise to revive them in London, a city where her dissident past might attract opprobrium. Yet, in 1878, before leaving Dublin, Jane, as Speranza, whipped up nationalist sentiment once more by producing *The American Irish*, an inflammatory pamphlet that warned of returning emigrants who would take up the struggle for freedom. In London, her enduring interest in Irish politics brought her to the Ladies' Gallery in the House of Commons for debates concerning the Irish question, and she expressed admiration for Charles Stewart Parnell, founder and leader of the Irish Parliamentary Party. Ironically, as a former president of the Irish National Land League, an organisation that strove to rid Ireland of absentee landlords, his agitation may have deprived her of a large part of her income. Yet, if Irish-born editor and publisher Frank Harris is to be believed, and often he is not, Jane hailed Parnell as 'the man of destiny,' who would 'strike off the fetters and free Ireland, and throne her as Queen among the nations'.[3]

Jane was unknown in London, but she remained hugely popular in her native country. When Dublin-based magazine *Lady of the House* held a competition to determine the greatest living Irishwoman, she secured 78 per cent of the vote.[4] Her friend Catherine Hamilton, author of *Notable Irish Women*, declared her a woman 'of a strong and pronounced individuality'. Remarking on how she 'always had an eye to theatrical effect', Hamilton praised Jane as: 'Warm-hearted, enthusiastic, romantic and generous'.[5] Henriette Corkran, a lifelong friend, paid tribute to her generosity:

> . . . in great adversity, she was brave, indeed heroic, and went through terrible ordeals; and though she felt the sharp pinch of poverty she was always ready to help those who were worse off than herself.[6]

During her first three years in London, Jane shared a modest suite of rented rooms at 1 Ovington Square in not-yet-fashionable Chelsea with her elder son, Willie, who gave every impression of being as devoted as Oscar and once refused to speak to an old school friend who had printed something unkind about her.[7] Regrettably, Willie had inherited the Wilde streak of extravagance and his costly lifestyle left little over when it came to paying household bills. Jane faced the prospect of taking up her pen to fund her modest lifestyle. Under no illusions as to how difficult this would be, she lamented that 'many a fine intellect amongst women lies buried under the desiccating social system like some grand statue of a god beneath the Libyan sands.' Yet, determined to fight on, she declared:

> The passionate pleadings of women for a due share of the rank and honours of the empire cannot always be stifled with the phrase:– 'Independent women, learned women, thinking women, are not liked; society only wants pretty, well-dressed women to attract and amuse.'[8]

Fortunately, the marketplace was shifting in Jane's favour. The public appetite for printed material was voracious and new titles were arriving on the newsstands every day. Within months of arriving in London, she was contributing wide-ranging and learned articles to the *Pall Mall Gazette*, *The Burlington Magazine*, *The Queen*, *The Lady's Pictorial*, *The St. James's Magazine*, and *Tinsley's Magazine*. With her powerful observational skills, sharp wit and access, through Oscar, to some of the most colourful characters in London, Jane would have made a brilliant social columnist, but she took a scholarly approach and was particular about the subjects she chose: 'I can't write', Catherine Hamilton overheard her saying, 'about such things as "Mrs. Green looked very well in black, and Mrs. Black looked very well in green"'.[9]

In 1884, publisher Richard Bentley paid Jane fifty guineas for *Driftwood from Scandinavia*, her first book since her collected poetry had appeared two decades earlier. The material for this light-hearted but well-informed travelogue was drawn from copious notes made during her trips with William. Written in her characteristically bright and chatty style, it includes fascinating geographical and historical detail, draws attention to all that she found admirable about the northernmost European nations, and pokes gentle fun at some of their inhabitants. It sold well, paving the way for a series of books published by Ward and Downey, a firm established by Jane's compatriot and fellow author Edmund Downey, who had a reputation for promoting the work of living Irish authors. In 1887, Ward and Downey published Jane's *Ancient Legends, Mystic Charms and Superstitions of Ireland*, a compendium of folk tales, several of them collected by her late husband. It was praised lavishly by W. B. Yeats, who referred to it liberally in his own *Fairy and Folk Tales of the Irish Peasantry*.[10]

In 1890, Ward and Downey brought out her *Ancient Cures, Charms and Usages of Ireland*, a companion book documenting the ancient art of folk healing. Jane followed up twelve months later with *Notes on Men, Women and Books*, a collection of previously published articles and reviews described by the *Spectator* as an assortment of 'disinterred essays', although their reviewer did concede that each one was 'entertaining', and 'worth reading'.[11] Jane's final book, *Social Studies*, published in 1893, was a collection of essays exploring, among other topics, her distinct take on feminism, comportment and clothing. Although *Social Studies* met with a mixed critical reception, it is a learned, humorous and eminently readable critique of life under the suffocating Victorian norms and values that Jane found almost intolerable.

Once her ebullience had returned, Jane decided to revive her Saturday salon and let it be known that she would be at home between 5 p.m. and 7 p.m. Visitors came in their droves: 'No more successful hostess than Lady Wilde could be found', wrote Catherine Hamilton, 'she managed to put people at their ease, and without talking too much herself, she drew out the best in others'.[12] In time, Jane's Saturdays proved so popular that she supplemented them with literary Wednesdays. Her guest list was always eclectic and it seems likely that Oscar captured the tone when he described the 'wonderful medley of people' that populated Lady Windermere's salon in 'Lord Arthur Savile's Crime':

Gorgeous peeresses chatted affably to violent Radicals, popular preachers brushed coat-tails with eminent sceptics, a perfect bevy of bishops kept following a stout prima-donna from room to room, on the staircase stood several Royal Academicians, disguised as artists, and it was said that at one time the supper-room was absolutely crammed with geniuses.[13]

Oscar's friends were welcome too; he told his pal Harold Boulton:

Any Saturday you are in London I hope you will call and see my mother who is always at home from five to seven on Saturday. She is always glad to see my friends, and usually some good literary and artistic people take tea with her.[14]

Also present on at least one occasion was Eleanor Marx, youngest daughter of Karl, who arrived in the company of her friend, feminist author and journalist Zadel Barnes Gustafson, who ran a literary salon of her own, to which she invited Oscar and Jane. According to her granddaughter Djuna Barnes, Gustafson admired Jane enormously. Eleanor too was drawn to Jane, but not to Oscar it seems: 'I have been asked to go this afternoon to a 'crush' at Lady Wilde's,' she told her sister Jenny Longuet:

She is the mother of that very limp and very nasty young man, Oscar Wilde, who has been making such a d.d. ass of himself in America. As the son has not yet returned and the mother is nice I may go – that is if I have time.[15]

Later, Marx was outraged by the unjust treatment meted out to Oscar and wrote an article defending his reputation. When no English newspaper would take it, she published it as 'Missive from England' in the Russian journal *Russkoye Bogatsvo*.[16]

Another prominent guest was Sir Charles Gavan Duffy, Jane's old partner in sedition and now a fully rehabilitated knight of the realm, who dropped in to see her on occasion. Although Jane was delighted to see faces from her past, the welcome she extended to young Dubliners who had not yet found their feet in London was just as warm. Mary Gilbert, a friend from Dublin, said that Jane told her that her Saturdays were 'full of poets, painters and "aesthetics", and the Irish, who fall upon her neck and weep'.[17] Jane's solicitous temperament persuaded at least one friend to believe that had she remained wealthy, she would have become a powerful patron of the arts and 'rescued many an unknown poet or writer from the oblivion and failure to which lack of means consigned their gifts'.[18] One impoverished young Irish writer who partook of the tea and cigarettes that were passed around freely at Jane's gatherings was George Bernard Shaw.* He recalled:

> Lady Wilde was nice to me in London during the desperate days between my arrival in 1876 and my first earning of an income by my pen in 1885.[19]

When W. B. Yeats persuaded novelist Katharine Tynan to write him a letter of introduction to Jane, he expressed the hope that he would find her 'as delightful as her book [*Ancient Legends, Mystic Charms and Superstitions of Ireland*] . . . as delightful as she certainly is unconventional'.[20] To Jane, he was 'my Irish poet' and, in time, he would call his great love and muse, Maud Gonne 'The New Speranza'.[21] Yeats, who thought the whole Wilde family 'very imaginative and learned', acknowledged that London had few better talkers than Jane.[22] Decades after Oscar's early death, he admitted 'of late years I have often explained Wilde to myself by his family history'.[23] He wrote of Jane that she 'longed always perhaps, though certainly amid much self-mockery, for some impossible splendour of character and circumstance'.

Katharine Tynan felt 'entirely grateful 'that Jane was 'very kind to an obscure Irish versifier'.[24] The first gathering she attended took place in the modest house on Park Street in Mayfair that Jane and Willie moved into towards the end of 1881. Although they had traded up to a more fashionable address, they had compromised on space and could barely manage the rent on 'a little house wedged in between another little house and a big public-house at the corner'. Katharine was greeted by Jane, who was decked out in 'a white dress like a Druid priestess, her grey hair hanging down her back'. The first thing that struck her was the gloom and she included a humorous anecdote in her memoir, *Twenty-Five Years Reminiscences*, describing how she stumbled in the direction Jane indicated until:

> A soft hand took mine and a soft voice spoke. "So fortunate," said the voice, "that no one could suspect dear Lady Wilde of being a practical joker! There really is a chair".[25]

Jane's blinds were down in defiance of the bright sunshine outside and the murk was punctured by the few feeble beams that radiated from a scattering of red-shaded tallow candles 'arranged so as to cast the limelight

---

* Frank Harris described one of Jane's gatherings: 'It was very dark and there were empty tea-cups and cigarette ends everywhere'.

on the prominent people, leaving the spectators in darkness'. In almost every account of Jane's life, it is assumed that vanity was her motivation for keeping her house in darkness so as to distract attention from her ravaged looks. Yet, Catherine Hamilton, among others, testified that her friend remained 'strikingly handsome' with 'glorious dark eyes' well into her sixties. According to Henriette Corkran, Jane told her that she simply detested 'the brutality of strong lights'.[26]

Certainly, Jane's own words support this. She told Oscar that she chose crimson wallpaper punctuated with gleaming golden stars in order to give her home 'a genial glow'.[27] In *Notes on Men, Women and Books*, she expressed approval for Sydney Smith's aphorism, 'light puts out conversation'. She also admired romantic poet Samuel Rogers for keeping his dining table in 'soft shadow' when most people would have 'a vulgar, blinding, flaring glare of gas pouring down upon the heads of the unfortunate, half-asphyxiated guests'.[28] Oscar's home would be admired as unconventionally bright and airy, yet it would seem that, on occasion, he shared his mother's appetite for gloom. French writer Jean-Joseph Renard remembered him begging one Parisian hostess to please close the shutters and light candles instead, as he could not stand the daylight.[29]

Although Jane aimed for a 'genial glow', the atmosphere at her Park Street home must have seemed oppressive to some. Pre-Raphaelite painter Herbert Gustav Schmalz, who was said to have clashed with Oscar when the latter accused him of leaving one of Jane's gatherings too early, remembered pastilles of compressed medicinal herbs smouldering on her mantelpiece, and curtain-draped mirrors hanging from ceiling to floor, making it difficult to discern where her room ended and where it began. On that first occasion she was invited, as Katharine Tynan's eyes adjusted to the gloom, she noticed that Jane's walls were crammed with photographs of Oscar in various poses; their subject arrived shortly afterwards. Although she had a sharp tongue and never hesitated to use it, Katharine declared that, on this and all other occasions, she found Oscar unfailingly 'pleasant, kind and interested', just like his mother.

That afternoon, the company was as varied as ever. One of the first people Katharine encountered was the actress May Fortescue, a member of the original cast of *Patience*. Born Emily Finney, the daughter of a Peckham coal merchant, May was prominent in the gossip columns since she had just announced her intention of using £10,000 awarded to her in a breach of promise action to establish her own theatre company. This was appropriately mischievous as she blamed Hugh McCalmont Cairns,

1st Earl Cairns, Lord Chancellor and a dour Ulsterman, for persuading Arthur William Cairns, Lord Garmoyle, his son and her erstwhile fiancé, to end their engagement on the grounds that he considered the theatre to be 'the ante-chamber of hell'. When Frank Harris, editor of the *Evening News* at the time, published May's account under the headline 'Beauty and the Peer', the circulation of his paper doubled.[30]

Also present that afternoon was Mary Potter, the daughter of an Irish clergyman and a second cousin of Lady Wilde.[31] As Oscar had inherited his mother's penchant for helping struggling performers, he persuaded her to reinvent herself as public reciter Romola Tynte. He also designed her costumes and wrote a letter of introduction to the impresario Major James Burton Pond[*] on her behalf. She also benefitted from a letter of introduction to leading theatre critic William Winter written for her by Ellen Terry. As a result, Potter enjoyed huge success in America, where she was hailed as 'the aesthetic cousin of the aesthetic Oscar Wilde'.[32] After she retired, Mary Potter became a prominent activist in the women's suffrage movement and addressed key meetings in England and America. Poet Gerard Manley Hopkins described her as 'a beautiful Sappho', an interesting observation since Oscar was a huge admirer of the original.[33] In 'English Poetesses', an article he wrote for *Queen*, Oscar called Sappho, whose poetry celebrated love for both men and women, 'the marvelous singer of Lesbos'. Comparing her to Elizabeth Barrett Browning, he described Sappho as 'undoubtedly a far more perfect and flawless artist'.[34]

When Anna de Brémont arrived in London in March 1886, she brought a letter of introduction to Jane, who was about to move to a rented house on Oakley Street in Chelsea. She was taken aback by the shabbiness of the soon-to-be abandoned house on Park Street, and described how she rapped on the door with a rusty knocker before being admitted by a dis-armingly informal Irish housemaid who guided her towards a shadowy drawing room illuminated with red-shaded candles; she insisted that, although the house was wanting, the welcome was not.[†]

Like just about everyone who met Jane, Anna was struck by the eccen-tricity of her costume:

* Pond was a fascinating character: an American Civil War hero turned hugely successful impresario and lecture manager. He had an impressive list of clients that included Mark Twain, Henry Morton Stanley and Winston Churchill.
† Although her description is supported by accounts given by others, Anna de Brémont's fanciful memoir, *Oscar Wilde and his Mother* (London, Everett & Co., 1914), is not entirely trustworthy.

The old-fashioned purple brocade gown, the towering headdress of velvet, the long gold earrings . . . the yellow fichu crossed on her breast and festooned with innumerable enormous brooches – the huge bracelets of turquoise and gold, the rings on every finger![35]

Yet, unlike her detractors, Anna admired Jane's ability to wear 'that ancient finery with a grace and dignity that robbed it of its grotesqueness'.[36] Oscar's friend Robert Sherard also 'saw nothing grotesque in Lady Wilde's attire'. What struck de Brémont most forcefully was Jane's supreme self-possession: 'Never before, nor since have I met a woman who was so absolutely sure of herself and of what she was', she wrote.

Soon afterwards, on a beautifully sunny summer afternoon, Anna de Brémont's cab turned into Oakley Street and she noticed a long line of hansoms and broughams outside number 146. As the front door swung wide and there was no servant to greet her, she followed the throng that elbowed its way upstairs.[37] Progress was made more difficult by Jane's insistence on holding her gatherings in an upstairs room of what Robert Sherard described as, 'a poor house, of the kind usually let out in furnished apartments'.[38]

Once they had negotiated the narrow stairway, guests were greeted by Jane or her garrulous elder son, Willie, who bore a striking resemblance to Oscar. Anna de Brémont describes how she lost her nerve and hovered on the threshold of the red-tinged semi-darkness until Jane called her by name and rose majestically, 'her headdress with its long white streamers and glittering jewels giving her quite a queenly air'. The gathering consisted of 'long-haired poets and short-haired novelists – smartly dressed Press women, and not a few richly gowned ladies of fashion'.[39] It was considered 'very intellectual' to be seen at Lady Wilde's crushes and a cacophony of accents competed to be heard: local Londoners vied with their Hibernian neighbours and a transatlantic twang would dominate at the height of the season when visiting Americans were drawn there by Oscar's popularity. Jane boasted: 'All London comes to me by way of King's Road . . . but the Americans come straight from the Atlantic steamers moored at Chelsea Bridge'.[40] Her reception for poet Oliver Wendell Holmes was said to have attracted the cream of literary London.

When Oscar arrived, as he generally did in those early days, the crowd would part, allowing him to bow over his mother's hand before taking up his favourite position by the chimneypiece, where he would strike an aesthetic pose. After a time, he would shake off his affectation in order to help his mother pass around the tea. In Anna's opinion, Oscar 'seemed to efface himself that his mother might display her brilliant wit and hold everyone by the charm of her conversation'.[41] Afterwards, she noticed, 'Lady Wilde was fairly sparkling with satisfaction'.[42] This impression was shared by Robert Sherard, who also believed that Oscar held back in order to let Jane shine. Although Sherard admired his friend's mother, he had been rather taken aback on an earlier occasion when Jane interrupted a conversation he was enjoying with Doctor Anna Kingsford* in order to present him with a bunch of narcissi; 'flowers for the poet', she exclaimed. It amused him greatly that *Whispers*, the volume that earned this adulation, was dedicated to Oscar but had been slated, quite rightly in Sherard's opinion, in a review Willie wrote for *Vanity Fair*.[43]

Jane's Oakley Street home was undoubtedly down at heel. Catherine Hamilton arrived one day to find the bell broken and the hall 'heaped with cloaks, waterproofs, and umbrellas'.[44] Although Jane could do little about her reduced circumstances, her guests noticed that she always took great care with her appearance. In an interview she gave to the *Kentish Mercury*, she declared: 'It's a woman's mission to adorn life, to impart beauty to the commonplace'.[45] Some ridiculed her eccentric dress and thickly-applied make-up, but many of the cruellest accounts were written with malice when Oscar's reputation was at its lowest ebb. True friends considered her magnificent, recognising that her choice of costume represented an extension of her eccentric and irrepressible personality.

Jane, like Oscar, refused to be enslaved to the 'frivolous mutations of fashion'.[46] Nevertheless, she put careful thought into what she wore: 'Humanity is distinguished from the ape by two things', she insisted, 'laughter and dress'; she took a keen interest in both.[47] A good portion of her *Social Studies* is given over to advice on the latter: 'nothing generates a morbid discontent like sombre, monotonous, ineffective costume', she counselled.[48] When deciding on colour, she adhered to strict rules of her own devising and, in characteristically forthright style, advised against the wearing of green, since 'tints of decomposing asparagus and cucumber do not suit the long, pale English face'.[49] She was uncompromising in her insistence that no woman should appear in the same dress twice, nor dress exactly like her peers, and proclaimed that:

---

* A campaigner for women's rights and one of the first women in Britain to earn a medical degree, Kingsford was the first president of the British Theosophical Society.

Uniformity of style is also equally depressing when all women look as if they were cut after the same paper pattern, and all interesting attractive distinctions of individuality are destroyed.[50]

Yet, as all Jane had available to her, for the most part, were the shabby relics of her Dublin wardrobe, she faced a challenge when putting her own rules into practice. Poverty obliged her to become increasingly inventive and she combined her few outdated garments in increasingly eccentric ways. With an artist's eye for detail, Herbert Schmalz described one of her costumes:

A low-cut, lavender-coloured silk dress over a crinoline, with a piece of crimson velvet about a foot deep round the skirt and a miniature, some six inches by four, pinned on her breast . . . her hair was dressed in ringlets, surmounted by a high headdress of lace, and hanging loosely around her waist was a Roman scarf which was bright green with stripes of scarlet, blue and yellow.[51]

Catherine Hamilton remembered her friend being

fantastically dressed in a trained black and white checked silk gown; from her head floated long white tulle streamers, mixed with ends of scarlet ribbons.[52]

Jane never skimped on accessories; Henriette Corkran recalled one occasion when she 'wore white kid gloves, held a scent bottle, a lace handkerchief and a fan'.[53]

Of course, there was far more to Lady Jane Wilde than eccentric clothing and high-spirited chat. She was daring and brave, and she refused to be trammelled by the narrow conventions of Victorian society. One contemporary of Oscar's insisted that she told him: 'There is one thing in the world worth living for, and that is sin'.[54] Her outspoken and progressive, albeit slightly erratic, views on the position of women in society were uncompromisingly frank and she injected much of the revolutionary fire she had harnessed in the pursuit of Irish nationalism into her arguments for gender equality. In 'The Bondage of Women', Jane expressed despair at the universal disregard shown for the intellect of women and the humiliation doled out to those who displayed traits of intelligence: 'For six thousand years,' she wrote, 'the history of women has been a mournful record of helpless resignation to social prejudice and legal tyranny'. She finished with an exceptionally powerful passage:

Genius never yet unsexed a woman, or learning or culture ever so extended; but the meanness of her ordinary social routine life, with all its petty duties and claims, and ritual of small observances, degrades and humiliates her, for it deprives her of all dignity, and leaves her without any meaning in God's great universe.[55]

In truth, Jane's approach to feminism was unorthodox and occasionally contradictory. She placed a strong emphasis on a wife's duty to show devotion to her husband, particularly if he was, like her own husband, a brilliant man. Early in her marriage, she wondered if she might have made a better wife and mother had she been less scholarly. Yet, she was enthusiastic about marriage reform that benefitted women. In 'A New Era in English and Irish Social Life', an essay she wrote for *Gentlewomen* in January 1883, Jane hailed the passing of the Married Women's Property Rights Act of 1882 as 'an important and remarkable epoch in the history of women'. Under its terms, women at last obtained a legal identity that permitted them to enter into contracts to buy or sell their own property. Jane expressed relief that a woman would no longer be required to enter marriage 'as a bonded slave, disenfranchised of all rights over her fortune'.[56] Yet she was bitterly aware that this progress came after millennia of neglect and cried:

> We have now traced the history of women from Paradise to the nineteenth century and have heard nothing through the long roll of the ages but the clank of their fetters.[57]

In an astute summation of the hurdles that held women back even while they were armed with these new rights, she explained:

> Women have been so long politically non-existent that they almost tremble to assert they have any rights apart from their husbands. They require much training in habits of self-assertion and self-reliance, and full knowledge of their newly acquired legal rights, in order that they may become worthy of the nobler life of freedom . . . which they are destined henceforth to occupy and adorn.[58]

Most noteworthy perhaps, given her haphazard upbringing, was her long and vociferous campaign for women to be granted greater access to formal education:

> It is impossible to believe that woman will be less attractive because educated, less tender and devoted because learned, less loving because she can

attain the high station, honour, dignity and wealth, which hitherto only marriage could confer, by her own unfettered intellect and genius.[59]

In 'Clever Women', an opinion piece written for *Queen* in April 1887, Jane argued for the establishment of an all-female university to mark Queen Victoria's Golden Jubilee. As older women of high intellect, herself included, would not be in a position to enter such a progressive institution, she insisted that they be awarded instead an Order of Merit granting them admittance to the male circles from which they were generally excluded.[60]

The constraints placed upon women by an overwhelmingly patriarchal society led Jane to express contradictory views that were, most likely, expressions of self-preservation:

> Women, especially, must beware of originality . . . There is always a coalition of society against it, for it is the daring self-assertion of the individual over the many, and calls down implacable revenge![61]

She could have replaced the word 'women' with the name of her younger son. Ultimately Jane, like Oscar, was a visionary idealist. When confronted with the inequities embedded in society, she often felt hopeful rather than despondent, believing that righteous thinking and courageous action would lead inevitably to change. Her optimism shines through in a passage from *Social Studies*:

> Now, for the first time in the history of the world, a path is opening to female intellect, energy and talent, and, henceforth, women, perhaps, may lead in the learned professions, take their part in home government, form ministries to organise the code of female rights, and claim the highest university honours in rivalry with men.[62]

In recognition of her clear-visioned devotion to gender equality, Jane was held in high regard by other women who campaigned for a more even-handed society. When prominent suffragist Florence Fenwick Miller invited her to join the Women's Franchise League, she explained: 'What we chiefly want is the influence of all women who think for themselves & feel for their sex'.[63]

Jane preferred the literary life, as evidenced by the drawing room of her Oakley Street home, which was 'crowded with books from floor to ceiling, and in many places along the floor'.[64] Many were newly published works pressed upon her by grateful poets, playwrights and novelists whose careers she had promoted. On each occasion, she would congratulate the author effusively before passing their precious offering around to be admired generally. Poets would be encouraged to read; Louise Chandler Moulton, a celebrated American poet who summered in London and spent the rest of the year in Boston, where she ran a well regarded literary salon of her own, obliged the gathering on at least one occasion.

Irish author and politician T. D. Sullivan recounted an amusing anecdote concerning a rare first edition of his poetry, which he had inscribed and presented to Jane. Sometime later, he came across that very book in a secondhand bookshop. He bought it, inscribed it a second time and presented it to Jane, drawing her attention to his first dedication. To her great credit, she found this highly amusing: 'and a very useful book it proved, my friend,' she quipped, 'for it served, like Caesar's dust, to fill up a hole in my purse'.[65] Although Jane prized these literary gifts, poverty obliged her to break up her precious library and sell its contents for whatever she could get. She was in dire straits as early as Christmas 1883, when Oscar returned from New York empty-handed and the rent from Moytura dried up completely. 'I have no receptions now,' she told Florence Stoker's elder sister Philippa Knott:

> I was too triste & low all the winter and I have no heart for anything, but I see a friend or so on [Saturdays] in the little study – The drawing rooms are turned into a lumber of books – that I meant to arrange, but time and courage failed me.[66]

Willie was next to useless and although Oscar helped where he could, he had little to spare before he found success in the 1890s. By then he was leading a hedonistic life and lavishing much of his income on a very demanding young man, prompting his mother to worry for his health and warn him to 'keep clear of suppers and late hours and champagne'.[67] As her debts mounted, Jane needed more money than could be generated by selling a book here and a book there. Sometime during 1886, she invited Walter Spencer, a local book dealer to inspect her bookshelves and make her an offer on any volume that took his fancy. Spencer remembered Jane welcoming him from a dais at the far end of the room like an enthroned queen. On that occasion, she readily accepted the £10 he offered her for 'a few good volumes'. From then on, he came by arrangement every fortnight.[68]

Jane's finances improved in 1888 when, with Oscar's help, she secured a grant of £100 from the Royal Literary Fund. She relied on his assistance again in 1890 when she applied for, and received, an annual Civil List pension of £70. Although this was granted in recognition of her late husband's contribution to statistical science and literature, Jane must have seen the irony in a former enemy of the state receiving succour from officialdom. Yet, her smiles were short-lived since the sum was inadequate and she resented the annual mandatory visits to verify that she was still alive.

Although she had little to live off, Jane kept up appearances as best she could. In the face of increasingly snide remarks, Catherine Hamilton spoke up for her friend, insisting that, since her welcome was unfailingly warm, any defects in her decor could surely be overlooked:

> What matter that the rooms were small, that the tea was overdrawn, or that there was a large hole in the red curtain that kept out the vulgar light of the day? . . . Here was a woman who understood the lost art of entertaining, and made her house a centre of light and leading.[69]

If Jane noticed any slights, she refused to acknowledge them. Anna de Brémont admired the way she 'possessed the supreme tact of appearing to ignore any *gaucherie* on the part of her guests,' adding, 'she had the admirable facility of appearing not to understand that which did not please her'.[70]

Early on, Jane realised that one solution to her indigence was for one or both of her sons to marry well. Although she kept a constant vigil for suitable candidates, not every young woman who attended her salon was invited to return. When one American singer exclaimed, 'Lady Wilde you remind me of my dear, old Grandmother,' Jane smiled politely but asked Anna de Brémont not to bring her again.[71] When de Brémont insisted that this woman was respectable, Jane countered: 'Never use that word here. It is only tradespeople who are respectable. We are above that'. She was always delighted to see Constance Lloyd and, when Oscar admitted the strength of his feelings for this lovely young woman, she relished the prospect of having her for a daughter-in-law.

Chapter 11

MARRIED LIFE

It is beautiful, it is fine, it is the noblest form of affection. There
is nothing unnatural about it.
    OSCAR WILDE on 'the love that dare not speak its name'[1]

Oscar Wilde is, quite correctly, held up as a gay icon who railed against
the ignorance and prejudice of those who would deny the authenticity
and appropriateness of love between two men. Yet, like every aspect of his
life, his sexuality is complex. It seems that from the early 1890s onward,
he was attracted exclusively to men, a realisation that his grandson Merlin
Holland senses came as a relief to him in many ways.[2] That said, there
is little doubt that his love for his wife, Constance, was genuine. Even
Lord Alfred Douglas, the love of Oscar's later life, believed that 'it was
a marriage of deep love and affection on both sides'.[3] Although society
was desperately intolerant and sodomy was classified as a crime, the 1885
Criminal Law Amendment Act outlawing gross indecency between men
was not passed until after he was married and he did not have as compelling a legal reason as many suppose to use his marriage as a smokescreen
for his true orientation. He is also unlikely to have married Constance for
her money, since she was far less wealthy than many suppose.

By 1883 the affection that had blossomed between Oscar and Constance
during the summer of 1881 had deepened into love. Although they saw
each other as much as possible, their courtship was curtailed by Oscar's regular absences. The failure of *Vera* obliged him to sign up for a lecture circuit
that took in a motley assortment of towns and cities scattered across the
British Isles. A flood of affectionate letters and telegrams passed between
them while he was away. Late in November 1883, Oscar travelled to Dublin
to deliver two afternoon lectures in the Gaiety Theatre. As Constance was
staying in the city with her Irish grandmother, Mama Mary,* at the time,

---

* This was the affectionate nickname given to Mary Atkinson (Moyle, p. 15).
Franny Moyle's *Constance: The Tragic and Scandalous Life of Mrs. Oscar Wilde* (John
Murray, 2012), a recent and exceptionally comprehensive study of Constance's
life, has informed much of the information relating to Constance.

he seized the opportunity to ask her the question that would change both their lives.

Although Constance found stability in her grandfather's home, she appears to have been treated more like a visitor than a resident. When the old man's health began to fail, his daughter, Constance's stern Aunt Emily, suggested that she move out for a time. She travelled to Dublin, taking with her the manuscript of *Vera*, which Oscar had asked her to read. Although Constance had 'no pretensions to being a critic', she admired *Vera* and could think of no reason for its failure bar poor acting or a lack of sympathy with its politics, but she echoed Dion Boucicault's criticism of Oscar's dialogue, describing it as 'slightly halting or strained'; astute observations on all counts.[4]

The letter in which she outlines these criticisms reveals key differences in her attitude: 'I hold that there is no perfect art without perfect morality,' she told Oscar, 'whilst you say that they are distinct and separate things'.[5] Constance warmed to the play: 'I have just read *Vera* through again and I really think it very fine,' she told her brother, Otho;

> Oscar says he wrote it to show that an abstract idea such as liberty could have quite as much power and be made quite as fine as the passion of love (or something of that sort).[6]

For Oscar, love and liberty were always intertwined.

When Oscar checked into the Shelbourne Hotel on 21 November, he was handed a note from Constance's cousins Stanhope and Eliza Hemphill, inviting him to visit Mary Atkinson's home that evening. Although Constance found Oscar as personable as ever, she thought him 'decidedly extra affected' and put this down to nerves.[7] Perhaps he was trying too hard to make a good impression. Next day, Constance, Stanhope and Eliza headed to the Gaiety Theatre to hear Oscar's take on 'The House Beautiful'. By now Constance's cousins were teasing her about her fascinating new friend. All three returned the following afternoon to hear his 'Personal Impressions of America', which included observations on 'the status, education, and training of women; their influence and their theories of dress'.[8]

Later that week, while they were alone in the drawing room of 1 Ely Place, Oscar asked Constance to marry him. She accepted with delight: 'Prepare yourself for an astounding piece of news!' she told Otho, 'I am engaged to Oscar Wilde and perfectly and insanely happy'.[9] Although her Dublin family was 'quite charmed' by her choice of beau, and Mama Mary declared her 'very lucky', Constance feared that the battle to convince the Lloyd family of Oscar's suitability would be hard-fought.[10] As she was counting on Otho's support, she must have been taken aback to receive his letter, which crossed with her own, expressing reservations about Oscar. This letter has not survived, but it prompted Constance to assure her brother and her fiancé that the past did not trouble her since she cared only for the future. Convinced of the depth of her commitment, Otho welcomed Oscar into the family: 'if Constance makes as good a wife as she has been a good sister to me your happiness is certain,' he assured Oscar, adding, 'she is staunch and true'.[11]

Oscar's lecturing commitments took him back to England and, early on the morning of his return, he woke Robert Sherard, who was staying at the same Charles Street lodgings; Sherard thought him 'much in love and very joyous'.[12] Oscar described Constance to his friend Thomas Waldo Story as 'quite young, very grave, and mystical, with wonderful eyes, and dark brown coils of hair,' adding: 'We are of course desperately in love'.[13] To Lillie Langtry, he wrote:

> I am going to be married to a beautiful young girl called Constance Lloyd, a grave, slight, violet-eyed little Artemis, with great coils of heavy brown hair which make her flower-like head droop like a flower, and wonderful ivory hands which draw music from the piano so sweet that the birds stop singing to listen to her.[14]

How similar this is to his description of poor, ill-fated Sibyl Vane in *The Picture of Dorian Gray*. She had 'a little, flowerlike face, a small Greek head with plaited coils of dark-brown hair'. Lillie's good opinion mattered a great deal to Oscar: 'I am so anxious for you to know and to like her', he beseeched. She was not at all surprised by this news, as he 'had often talked rapturously' about Constance.[15]

Not everyone wished them well. Violet Hunt was scathing and suggested that Oscar was after Constance's money, but with just £250 a year while her grandfather was alive, she was far less wealthy than Violet supposed. Louise Jopling claimed to have asked Oscar why he chose Constance and reported his reply: 'She scarcely ever speaks. I am always wondering what her thoughts are like'.[16] Although she is the only source, the sentiment is oddly reminiscent of the plot for Oscar's short story 'The Sphinx without a Secret', first published in 1887 as 'Lady Alroy'. Lord Murchison is attracted to the 'indefinable atmosphere of mystery' enveloping an enigmatic woman who speaks 'very little'. He is perplexed to discover that her 'secret' is mundane.

Constance Lloyd was far from mundane. An accomplished woman with a keen mind, she demonstrated a deep and abiding passion for Pre-Raphaelite and Aesthetic art and literature. She had a flair for languages and many of her favourite books were in French or Italian. She was musical and played the piano exceptionally well. Yet she could be painfully self-effacing: 'I have no beauty, no conversation, no small talk even to make me admired or liked', she told Otho.[17] While Jane built Oscar up, Ada seems to have undermined Constance at every turn. Her relationship with her father Horace, a barrister and *bon vivant* who was frequently absent from home, appears to have been warm, but he died when Constance was just sixteen.

Jane approved of the match and described Constance as: 'A very nice pretty sensible girl – well-connected and well brought up'.[18] Although far less flamboyant, she was, in some respects, a more understated version of what her mother-in-law had been: a beautiful young woman from a respectable Irish family, well-read, fluent in several languages and with strong proto-feminist sensibilities. She was also devoted to her husband: 'I am intensely pleased,' Jane assured Oscar; 'You have both been true and constant and a blessing will come on all true feeling'.[19] Yet, she recognised in Oscar the same core of genius that was present in his father and she realised that Constance's role would be a taxing one. In 'Genius and Marriage', Jane wrote:

> The daughters of men who wed with the sons of the gods, should have courage to face the lightnings and the thunders, if they dare to stand on the mountain height with an immortal husband. For such a man, and to insure his happiness, a woman should be ready to give her life with sublime self-immolation. At once an angel and a victim, sensitive to every chord of his nature, yet with a smile forever on the lip, no matter what anxieties may corrode the heart.[20]

Ambitious for Oscar, Jane saw Constance's role as a modest one: 'I would like you to have a small house in London and live the literary life,' she told her son, 'and teach Constance to correct proofs, and eventually go into parliament'.[21]

Ada Swinburne-King, who had never demonstrated much interest in her daughter's happiness, seemed pleased with the match: 'I think he & Constance are well suited to each other,' she assured Jane:

> Both are, as you say, young, gifted, & what is to my mind even more essential to the beginning of married life immensely attached to each other. I

have heard twice from Constance since the event & in each letter she says "she is so extremely happy".[22]

Fearing that the 'cold and practical' Lloyds might thwart her, Constance sent a note to Aunt Emily begging her not to oppose the match. Oscar had already written to John Horatio Lloyd. As they shared the distinction of a double first from Oxford and had always enjoyed each other's company, it came as a shock when the old man decided to withhold his consent. Oscar rushed to London to plead his case but Lloyd was far too ill to see him and it was left to Aunt Emily to outline what was required.

Far from opposing the match, her father was willing to put a modest marriage settlement in place once Oscar assured him that his finances were under control. Oscar agreed to defray his mounting debts by a modest £300,* leaving him more committed to the lecture circuit than ever; he confided in Lillie:

> it is horrid being so much away from her, but we telegraph to each other twice a day, and I rush back suddenly from the uttermost parts of the earth to see her for an hour, and do all the foolish things which wise lovers do.[23]

Constance too was unrestrained in her fervour:

> when I have you for my husband, I will hold you fast with chains of love & devotion, so that you shall never leave me, or love anyone as long as I can love & comfort . . .[24]

Constance's connection to Oscar thrust her into an unfamiliar limelight. Newspapers carried reports of their engagement, and audience and cast members alike stared with unconcealed curiosity when they attended the theatre. Artist James Whistler hosted a celebratory luncheon, which they shared with May Fortescue and her then-beau, Viscount Garmoyle. Constance commissioned her regular dressmaker, Adeline Nettleship, an innovative wielder of a needle with a workforce of thirty seamstresses, to create a wedding gown. It was the subject of intense public scrutiny and went on public display in March. Society magazine *Queen* described it as a:

---

* Oscar's debts amounted to approximately £1,500. Most of this sum had been borrowed from an American money lender. Lloyd deposited £5,000 of Constance's inheritance into a trust fund with the income accrued going to her. On 10 January 1884, Oscar and Constance witnessed a codicil to his will, ratifying this arrangement.

. . . rich creamy satin dress . . . of a delicate cowslip tint; the bodice, cut square and somewhat low in front, was finished with a high Medici collar; the ample sleeves were puffed; the skirt, made plain, was gathered by a silver girdle of beautiful workmanship, the gift of Mr. Oscar Wilde; the veil of saffron-coloured Indian silk gauze was embroidered with pearls and worn in Marie Stuart fashion; a thick wreath of myrtle leaves crowned her frizzed hair; the dress was ornamented with clusters of myrtle leaves; the large bouquet had as much green in it as white.[25]

Although they hoped to marry in April, the wedding was postponed until 29 May 1884, giving Oscar additional time to sort his finances. On the eve of his nuptials, he was invited to supper by Lady Elizabeth Lewis. In her memoir, Louise Jopling mentions that she 'gave him some good advice as to how a young husband should treat his wife'; she does not elaborate as to its nature.[26]

John Horatio Lloyd's uncertain health dictated that the wedding was an unexpectedly low-key event with admittance by invitation only, restricted to family and close friends. On the day, a sizable group of parishioners of St James's Church in Sussex Gardens protested against being kept outside and were admitted to sit alongside the wedding party. They and those who congregated outside must have been disappointed by the dearth of recognisable faces.[27] Oscar 'bore himself with calm dignity', depriving the gossip columnists of copy by wearing a perfectly ordinary blue morning frock-coat with grey trousers and 'a touch of pink in his neck tie'.[28] The ceremony was subdued, but bride and groom were jubilant. The *Lady's Pictorial* reported:

The newly-married pair, as they came down the long aisle arm-in-arm, looked as hundreds of newly-married people have looked before – the bridegroom happy and exultant; the bride with a tender flush on her face, and a happy hopeful light in her soft brown eyes.[29]

Jane, resplendent in grey satin, trimmed with a chenille fringe and topped off with a high crowned hat adorned with ostrich feathers, reportedly '"snatched" her new daughter to her heart with some effusion'.[30] Days later, she signed 'La Madre devotissima' at the bottom of the first of many warm letters to Constance. After a modest reception at Lancaster Gate, the newlyweds boarded the boat-train to Dover and travelled on to Paris: 'few married couples ever carried better wishes with them', gushed the *Aberdeen Evening Express*.[31]

Robert Sherard, back in Paris by then, described the couple's well-appointed three room suite in the Hotel Wagram on the Rue de Rivoli as 'full of flowers, youth and laughter'.[32] He thought Constance 'supremely happy', and described her as 'beautiful and gracious, kind-hearted, and devoted to her husband, for whose great cleverness she had the highest admiration'.[33] Oscar 'seemed then very much in love and said that marriage was a wonderful thing'.[34] Within minutes of leaving to revisit old Parisian haunts, Oscar stopped at a flower stall and organised for the loveliest blooms to be delivered to his wife. Sherard believed 'the union had every promise of being felicitous'.[35]

Constance held her first dinner party in Paris. One of her guests was the ebullient Henrietta Reubell, a wealthy and eccentric American of French descent who had hosted a breakfast for the couple. Artist William Rothenstein, who described Reubell as 'a great friend and admirer of Oscar Wilde, to whom she was constantly loyal,' left a wonderful description of this extraordinary woman:

> In face and figure she reminded me of Queen Elizabeth – if one can imagine an Elizabeth with an American accent and a high, shrill voice like a parrot's. All that was distinguished in French, English and American society came at one time or another to her apartment in the Avenue Gabriel; she was adept at bringing out the most entertaining qualities of the guests at her table.[36]

Reubell never doubted her own attractions even if others remained unconvinced. She was effusive in her praise of Constance's outfit and insisted she ask Adeline Nettleship to replicate it for her; Constance was certain this would horrify Oscar.

Mr and Mrs Wilde returned to London on 24 June 1884, after a thrilling fortnight in Paris, followed by a delightful week in Dieppe. Lloyd's largesse allowed them to take a six-year lease on 16 Tite Street and they had commissioned architect Edward Godwin to transform it into a suitably bohemian home. As it was far from complete, they spent two nights in the Brunswick Hotel while Constance dropped heavy hints in the direction of Aunt Emily before asking outright if they could stay at Lancaster Gate. Emily gave her grudging approval but her father was close to death, so they moved into Oscar's old Charles Street lodgings soon afterwards. Six weeks later, the old man lost his struggle and Constance's income almost trebled as a result.

When Oscar returned to the lecture circuit, Constance cast her practical eye over the chaos that had been allowed to reign in Tite Street. Oscar

had fired the builder engaged by Godwin and was being sued for non
-payment as a result. A second builder had run well over budget. Under
her supervision, their 'sweet little nest' was ready early in 1885.[37] The
light and airy melange of soft yellows, blues and whites contrasted starkly
with the dark hues favoured by their more conventional neighbours. Anna
de Brémont described their home as having 'an air of brightness and
luxury'.[38]

When Oscar glanced out of their window and saw Ellen Terry arriving at John Singer Sargent's Chelsea studio wearing her costume for
Lady Macbeth, a remarkable emerald gown that shimmered with the
iridescent wings of the jewel beetles sewn into it by Ada Nettleship, he
remarked:

> The street that on a wet and dreary morning has vouchsafed the vision
> of Lady Macbeth in full regalia magnificently seated in a four-wheeler
> can never again be as other streets: it must always be full of wonderful
> possibilities.[39]

Marriage gave Constance the independence she craved. Although she
was more retiring than her husband, she supported Oscar by entertaining influential women and men who helped advance his career. She also
developed interests beyond her hall door and her involvement with the
Rational Dress Society and the Chelsea Women's Liberal Association
demonstrated her commitment to women's issues. Like Oscar, Constance
had strong views on dress reform; she was recognised as an accomplished
public speaker on the topic. In 'Clothed in Our Right Minds', a lecture she addressed to the Rational Dress Society on 6 November 1888,
she advocated the wearing of divided skirts, insisting that, as God had
given women two legs, they should have the freedom to use them. She
broadened her argument to insist that women deserved a wider role in all
aspects of life.[40]

In 'Children's Dress in this Century', an article she wrote for *The
Woman's World*, which was edited by Oscar, Constance insisted: 'The
Rational Dress should be adopted by all mothers who wish their girls to
grow up healthy and happy'.[41] When she edited *The Rational Dress Society
Gazette*, she assumed responsibility for attracting new subscribers, growing
advertising, overseeing printing and managing accounts. She was perfectly
willing to wear the clothing she advocated and to have this reported by the
press. When Oscar and she manned a charity flower stall in support of
London's hospitals, Constance made a point of wearing a divided skirt.

Although Oscar encouraged Constance to dress in a freer and more flattering style, he is probably given too much credit for her choices. The novelist Marie Belloc Lowndes, who thought Constance strikingly pretty but timid, attributed her preference for simple dresses at home but eccentric outfits in public to Oscar's influence, but Vyvyan Holland insisted that, while his father certainly encouraged her, his mother designed clothes that reflected her devotion to the Pre-Raphaelites.[42]

Not everyone approved of Constance's style. When Beatrix Potter spotted them heading into the Fine Art Society, she described Oscar as a 'rather fine looking gentleman, but inclined to stoutness' and remarked that Constance was 'strangely dressed'.[43] At a ball given by the artist John Everett Millais, Potter noted that Constance had 'her front covered with great water-lilies'.[44] Laura Troubridge, who thought Constance 'shy and dull', had the couple to tea and described Constance's outfit as 'too hopeless'. Laura's fiancé, Adrian Hope, a distant relative of Constance's who would prove to be a malevolent influence in her life, insisted that she looked 'horrid' and sneered that she 'never opened her lips'.[45]

Those who scoffed were out of step. Constance was exceptionally beautiful and her unconventional outfits were widely admired. Praising the 'charming gown of dark crimson and gold brocade' she wore to the opening of *Twelfth Night* at the Lyceum, the *Lady's Pictorial* declared: 'her costume was altogether admirably suited to her picturesque and southern style of beauty'.[46] That same magazine also noted a 'very pretty and graceful gown' designed to complement a Lincoln green coat worn by Oscar.[47] Anna de Brémont's first impression of Constance was of:

> . . . a young woman arrayed in an exquisite Greek costume of cowslip yellow and apple leaf green. Her hair, a thick mass of ruddy brown, was wonderfully set off by the bands of yellow ribbon, supporting the knot of hair low on the nape of her neck, and crossing the wavy masses above the brow. The whole arrangement was exceedingly becoming to the youthful, almost boyish face with its clear colouring and full, dark eyes.[48]

Detecting 'an air of shy self-consciousness and restraint' about her, Anna took Constance for a timid actress who had been prevailed upon to perform and was amazed when Oscar introduced her as his wife.

One of those who believed that Oscar's love for Constance was genuine was Ada Leverson, who had no difficulty accepting his relationships with men: 'When he was first married, he was quite madly in love, and showed himself an unusually devoted husband', she wrote.[49] Certainly,

Oscar hated it when lecturing engagements took him away from home. In Edinburgh in December 1884, he composed an exceptionally tender letter to Constance:

> I feel your fingers in my hair, and your cheek brushing mine . . . The air is full of the music of your voice, my soul and body seem no longer mine, but mingled in some exquisite ecstasy with yours. I feel incomplete without you.[50]

He may not have realised it but Constance was three months pregnant by then.

Cyril Wilde arrived into the world at 10.45 a.m. on 5 June 1885. That day, his father wrote a lovely letter to Otho's wife Nellie, insisting that his 'amazing boy' knew him quite well already.[51] He told actor Norman Forbes Robertson that Cyril was 'wonderful', and encouraged him to get married '*at once!*'[52] Mercifully, he remained ignorant of Adrian Hope's mean-spirited declaration that he pitied the infant, and his by-now-wife, Laura's cruel speculation that Cyril would be 'swathed in artistic baby clothes – sage green bibs & tuckers . . . & peacock blue robes'.[53] Fatherhood awakened a new sense of responsibility in Oscar. Years earlier, he told Bouncer Ward that his paltry inheritance necessitated him 'doing some horrid work to earn bread'.[54] Now he applied unsuccessfully for a position as an inspector of schools before turning to journalism and securing regular commissions from the *Pall Mall Gazette*, and the *Dramatic Review*. He also wrote occasionally for the *Court and Society Review*, the *Nineteenth Century Magazine* and several others.

The *Dramatic Review* allowed Oscar a byline but the *Pall Mall Gazette* required reviewers to maintain their anonymity. An exception was made for Oscar's review of J. A. Froude's historical novel *The Two Chiefs of Dunboy*, allowing him to put his initials to criticisms of British government policy in Ireland:

> If in the last century she [England] tried to govern Ireland with an insolence that was intensified by race-hatred and religious prejudice, she has sought to rule her in this century with a stupidity that is aggravated by good intentions.[55]

Editor William Thomas Stead was sympathetic to the Irish question. A firm advocate for social justice, he was imprisoned in 1885 while working on 'The Maiden Tribute of Modern Babylon', a series of articles exposing the scourge of child prostitution. His campaign raised the age of consent but had the unintended consequence of prompting Henry Labouchère MP to draft a clause making gross indecency between men a criminal offence; the Criminal Law Amendment Act 1885 became known as 'the blackmailer's charter'. Oscar too had a campaigning agenda. His association with the *Pall Mall Gazette* commenced with a letter expressing strong opinions on the impracticality of women's dress.[56]

Keen to do more than raise a child and keep a fashionable home, Constance contributed articles on fashion and theatre to the *Ladies' Pictorial*. Her light, witty style undermines Louise Jopling's assertion that Oscar's friends found her humourless, although Jopling did concede that Constance's sense of humour was subtle rather than absent. She also thought of acting and played a minor role in a six-night run of John Todhunter's *Helena in Troas*, a play staged by Edward Godwin in May 1886. All proceeds went to The British School of Archaeology at Athens and Godwin cast amateurs, including Constance and Louise Jopling, alongside professional actors. Although careful not to mention his wife, Oscar gave a glowing account of the production in the *Dramatic Review*, commenting that Godwin gave his audience 'the most perfect exhibition of a Greek dramatic performance that has as yet been seen in this country'. Of Louise Jopling he wrote: 'Mrs. Jopling looked like a poem from the Pantheon'.[57] When Willie reviewed *Helena in Troas* for *Theatre* on 1 June 1896, he too was careful not to mention Constance.

Constance was three months pregnant when she made her acting debut and this pregnancy was far more debilitating than her first. The notoriously unreliable, but oft quoted, Frank Harris insisted that it triggered Oscar's waning interest in Constance. According to Harris, he could not bear to witness the metamorphoses of his 'beautiful girl, white and slim as a lily', into this 'heavy, shapeless, deformed' woman who dragged herself miserably around their house with a 'drawn blotched face and hideous body'. Harris contended that, although Oscar remained outwardly solicitous, he was confronting an uncomfortable reality: 'Desire is killed by maternity; passion buried in conception'.[58] Although Anna de Brémont insisted that Oscar and Constance were 'still fondly devoted to one another' after Cyril's birth, she too saw cracks emerging and observed that Constance's 'sincerity and devotion was her undoing'.

Vyvyan Oscar Beresford Wilde arrived into the world on an exceptionally foggy day in early November 1886. William Rothenstein observed that his parents 'seemed on affectionate terms' and was certain that Oscar 'delighted in his children', but he 'felt something wistful and a little sad about Mrs. Wilde'.[59] Perhaps the clearest indication that a facade was being constructed came from W. B. Yeats, who spent Christmas Day with the family in 1888 and wrote, with the benefit of hindsight:

> I remember thinking that the perfect harmony of his [Oscar's] life there, with his beautiful wife and his two young children, suggested some deliberate artistic composition.[60]

By all accounts, Cyril and Vyvyan Wilde were lovely, boisterous lads who enjoyed more freedom than many of their Victorian contemporaries. Eyewitness accounts confirm that both parents were indulgent and fond of them. Vyvyan's recollections of an exceptional and turbulent childhood demonstrate great warmth and a wryness that belies the tragedy that befell his family.* Both boys adored their father, who was kind-hearted and playful and perfectly happy to join in with nursery games, even if they involved getting down on all fours in order to play the part of a bear, a lion, a horse or whatever was required of him. He once spent an entire afternoon repairing a beloved wooden fort. Their boisterous games often spilled out into the beautiful dining room, where all three would dodge between the legs of the spindly white chairs before tumbling together in a tangle on the floor. When they grew tired, Oscar would tell them the most wonderful stories.[61]

Although it was Oscar who jeopardised and effectively abandoned his marriage, slight evidence suggests that Constance too had unconventional views. At a dinner party they hosted just before their first wedding anniversary, Adrian Hope expressed surprise at Constance's declaration that 'it should be free to either party to go off at the expiration of the first year'. When Oscar and he discussed the subject further, Hope reported that his host had declared a marriage should last '7 years only, to be renewed or not as either party saw fit'.[62] Laura's spiteful response on hearing this was:

> I dislike Constance Wilde for her remark . . . unless by the by it was a desperate attempt at originality. No wonder she has a sulky, dull face if those are the thoughts she has to talk with when she is alone.[63]

---

* *Son of Oscar Wilde* by Vyvyan Holland is a remarkable account of a fractured childhood, and gives unparalleled insights into a life that is perhaps more speculated about than any other. It contains a warm account of the time he and his brother had with their father, which lends added poignancy to the tragedy that they never saw him again after 1895.

Although Oscar described Laura to Adrian as, *'une femme de glace'*, he remained friendly towards her and insisted that she be given the commission to illustrate 'Le Jardin des Tuileries', a poem he contributed to *In a Good Cause*, an anthology sold in aid of the North Eastern Hospital for Children in 1885.[64] Laura availed of this opportunity to showcase her talent, but speculated that Oscar's *'Muse* was out of town' when he wrote his poem.[65] It hints at 'The Selfish Giant', which Oscar thought of asking Laura to illustrate before choosing Walter Crane.[*]

Although Constance had nothing approaching Oscar's talent, her maternal great-grandmother, Barbara Hare Hemphill, was a novelist of some note and she appears to have inherited some of her talent. A competent writer, she too published several stories for children and it is fascinating to read the joint review of their collections from *The Irish Times* of 2 February 1889:

> Mr and Mrs Wilde possess charming children of their own and they have utilised their acquaintance with the infant world in giving to it some delightful fairytales, which even the elders must appreciate. "The Happy Prince and Other Tales," illustrated by Walter Crane and Jacomb Hood, and published by David Nutt is one of the happiest works which Mr. Oscar Wilde has ever produced; whilst Mrs. Wilde's fairytales, also published recently and entitled "There Was Once," are a charming reproduction of the old stories, familiar to our childish days, which Nisbet [sic] has brought out.

The death of her beloved Mama Mary prompted Constance to compile *There Was Once – Grandma's Stories*, a beautifully illustrated collection of five traditional tales and four familiar rhymes. Publisher Ernest Nister also brought out *A Dandy Chair and Other Stories,* an illustrated collection of children's stories written by Constance Wilde, Edith Nesbit and Mary Louisa Molesworth. One story contributed by Constance was called 'The Little Swallow'. In 1887, *The Bairn's Annual of Old Fashioned Fairy Tales,* edited by Alice Corkran, sister of Jane's great friend Henriette, contained 'Was It a Dream' by Constance Wilde. Jane was also a contributor to this periodical. In 1892, Nister published *A Long Time Ago, favorite stories retold by*

* The last verse reads:

Ah! cruel tree! if I were you,
And children climbed me, for their sake
Though it be winter I would break
Into spring blossoms white and blue!

Mrs. Oscar Wilde & others, and *A Cosy Corner and Other Stories*, which included Constance's 'For Japan', which featured a little girl named Isola.*

Constance's serious nature led her into the world of politics. She joined the Chelsea branch of the Women's Liberal Association and campaigned to have Lady Margaret Sandhurst elected as Liberal candidate for Brixton to the London County Council. Although Sandhurst was successful, the courts supported a challenge from the man she had defeated and declared her election invalid. On 16 April 1888, Constance addressed a conference sponsored by the Women's Committee of the International Arbitration and Peace Association. The theme was 'By what methods can Women Best Promote the Cause of International Concorde' and Constance spoke on the importance of encouraging pacifist ideals at an early age: 'Children should be taught in their nursery to be against war', she counselled.[66]

She was an accomplished public speaker and her performance at the Women's Liberal Federation annual conference in 1889, when she discussed Home Rule for Ireland, was remarked upon by W. T. Stead in the *Pall Mall Gazette:*

> I was astonished and delighted to notice yesterday at the conference for the Women's Liberal Federation how very much Mrs. Oscar Wilde has improved in public speaking. She was always graceful and always charming, but there is now an earnestness and an ease about her which is the result of practice in platform speaking, and I shall not be surprised if in a few years Mrs. Wilde has become one of the most popular among "platform ladies".[67]

It may seem bizarre nowadays, but Constance, like many of her peers, including Yeats, took a keen interest in the occult. On 13 November 1888, she joined the Hermetic Order of the Golden Dawn, a society dedicated to the study of Rosicrucianism and ritual magic. She stood alongside Anna de Brémont while both were initiated into the order, wearing a black tunic with a cord wound three times around her waist, red shoes and a blindfold. The motto Constance chose was Qui Patitur Vincit (who endures wins). Anna evoked the day in rich detail:

> I felt her [Constance] tremble, and the hand that held mine was icy cold. Her voice faltered over the formula of admission that we recited together – a most formidable declaration, which threatened dire calamity to those who disclosed the secret studies or proceedings of the Order. My sense

---

* Constance's writing is covered comprehensively by Franny Moyle in *Constance: The Tragic and Scandalous Life of Mrs. Oscar Wilde* (London, John Murray, 2012).

of humour was secretly tried on that occasion, and I felt more inclined to laugh; although Constance Wilde's beautiful eyes were full of tears.[68]

Although Constance passed through every grade of the outer order during her first year, she did not continue beyond this point.

Constance also joined the Society for Psychical Research. When her interest turned to Christian Socialism, with its emphasis on charitable works and daily church attendance, she diverged significantly from Oscar, who had little interest in such humdrum piety and considered philanthropy not merely ineffectual but an insidious form of social control. The poor state of the couple's finances proved a further strain. By 1887 the expense of running a household requiring a cook, several housemaids, a footman and a children's nurse was proving an unsustainable drain on the couple's inadequate resources. Robert Sherard reported that one Tite Street neighbour was approached by Constance on several occasions when she needed to borrow money.[69] Oscar's income was sporadic and he was keen to find something more reliable. In April 1887, he accepted an interesting challenge that paid £6 per week.

Chapter 12

ENTERING THE WOMAN'S WORLD

The cultivation of separate sorts of virtues and separate ideals of
duty in men and women has led to the whole social fabric being
weaker and unhealthier than it need be.
OSCAR WILDE in 'Literary and Other Notes', *The Woman's
World*[1]

As a married man of thirty-two, with a young family to provide for and
exquisite tastes to gratify, Oscar found it impossible to fund the lifestyle
he desired out of the unreliable income earned from freelance journalism
and occasional lecturing. Without the contribution Constance made to
the family coffers, the six-year lease on their fashionable Tite Street home
would have been beyond them. They also struggled to repay £500 borrowed from Constance's brother Otho, who could ill-afford to be without
it.* In 1887, young Robbie Ross stayed for three months as a paying guest
while his mother travelled abroad. By then, the couple's pooled resources
had fallen distressingly short of their outgoings and they sought tenants for their lovely home.† Fortunately, in April 1887, Thomas Wemyss
Reid, newly appointed general manager of publishing house Cassell &
Company, offered Oscar an opportunity to earn a steady income.

Cassell's had launched *The Lady's World* in October 1886, in a bid to cap-
italise on an emerging market for magazines targeting women into which
forty-eight women's magazines were launched between 1880 and 1900.
Competition was fierce and, at a shilling an issue, *The Lady's World*, a high-
end, illustrated monthly, struggled to survive.[2] Reid believed that Oscar,
with his public profile and demonstrable interest in fashion, could help
address this. A bundle of back issues was dispatched for his consideration.

---

* In the summer of 1887, Otho left his wife Nellie and their two sons, and set up
home in Switzerland with her friend Mary Winter.
† Robert Baldwin Ross, a member of a prominent Canadian family, went on
to become a journalist, art critic and art dealer. At great personal risk, Ross was
openly homosexual and it is thought that Oscar's first homosexual relationship
was with him. They became lifelong friends and Ross was appointed executor of
Oscar's literary estate.

In a lengthy response, Oscar assured Reid that he would be 'very happy to join with you in the work of editing and to some extent reconstructing it'.[3]

Oscar considered *The Lady's World* to be 'too feminine and not sufficiently womanly'. In order to succeed, it needed to distance itself from rivals such as *Queen* and *The Lady's Pictorial*, publications that were preoccupied by 'mere millinery and trimmings'.[4] He was less diplomatic when he described it to poet Harriet Hamilton King as 'a very vulgar, trivial, and stupid production, with its silly gossip about silly people, and its social inanities'.[5] Rather than tweak the content and trust that the magazine would benefit from his celebrity, Oscar announced that he would transform it into 'the recognised organ for the expression of women's opinions on all subjects of literature, art, and modern life'.

Under his editorship, *The Lady's World* would become 'a magazine that men could read with pleasure, and consider it a privilege to contribute to'.[6] Oscar had a sophisticated understanding of gender as largely a set of rituals and expectations, and he shared his mother's opposition to gendered writing: 'artists have sex but art has none', he quipped.[7] A radical transformation would see *The Lady's World* 'take a wider range, as well as a high standpoint, and deal not merely with what women wear, but with what they think, and what they feel'.[8]

While negotiating his contract, Oscar enlisted the help of campaigning journalist and society hostess Mary Jeune, who thought him 'so delightfully clever, so brilliant!'[9] A regular and enthusiastic attendee at her glittering gatherings, he once assured her, 'the only place in London worth going to is your brilliant salon'.[10] Arthur Conan Doyle described Lady Jeune's 'famous luncheon parties' as 'quite one of the outstanding institutions of London'.[11] Her address book was unparalleled and together they compiled a list of potential contributors that included prominent social activists, literary luminaries and society women, among them two princesses. Oscar even invited Queen Victoria to contribute a poem and, although she declined, one of her ladies-in-waiting confirmed that she liked his magazine immensely. Her daughter Princess Christian of Schleswig-Holstein sent him 'Nursing as a Profession for Women', which she signed simply 'Helena'.

Under the terms of his contract, Oscar agreed to spend two mornings a week in the offices of Cassell & Company in return for a weekly salary of £6, which he negotiated to have backdated to 1 May in recognition of his having 'already devoted a great deal of time to devising the scheme, and having interviews with people of position and importance'. His zeal was palpable: 'I am resolved to throw myself into this thing,' he wrote, 'I grow very enthusiastic over our scheme'.[12] His first priority was to change the name. Although *The Lady's World* was 'quite applicable to the magazine in its present state', it would not do for a publication that aspired to be 'the organ of women of intellect, culture, and position'.[13]

Not only was *The Lady's World* 'extremely misleading', it also had, Oscar believed, 'a certain taint of vulgarity about it, that will always militate against the success of the new issue'. He became increasingly insistent in the face of Cassell's dogged resistance and warned his new employers that he was omitting the name of their publication from correspondence with potential contributors who took exception to it: his old friend Julia Constance Fletcher had objected 'in the strongest terms'; Annie Thackeray Ritchie, literary daughter of William Makepeace Thackeray, expressed reservations about any association with so 'vulgar' a magazine; and Lady Frances Verney, elder sister to Florence Nightingale, told him she had 'not the courage . . . to contribute to a magazine with such a title'.[14]

To strengthen his case, Oscar cited the example of *Every Girl's Magazine*, now *Atalanta*, which was attracting writers of the calibre of Robert Louis Stevenson, H. Rider Haggard, E. Nesbit, Frances Hodgson Burnett and Amy Levy. The name Oscar proposed, *The Woman's World*, was suggested to him by novelist and poet Dinah Craik, daughter of an eccentric Irishman and author of the exceptionally popular *John Halifax, Gentleman*. Oscar admired Craik enormously and planned to recruit her as a regular contributor and he was dismayed when she died of heart failure, aged sixty-one, just weeks before his first edition was due to appear. He eulogised her in his first editorial: 'She was very much interested in the scheme for the foundation of THE WOMAN'S WORLD,' he wrote, 'and promised to be one of its warmest supporters'.[15]

Anna de Brémont believed that 'society began to take Oscar Wilde seriously when he became editor of *The Woman's World*. The change of name was accompanied by a fresh cover design, which featured his name prominently with key contributors listed below. In a significant departure from convention, each article was attributed to its author by name. Oscar increased the page count from thirty-six to forty-eight and relegated fashion to the back, while promoting literature, art, travel and social studies. Gone entirely were 'Fashionable Marriages', 'Society Pleasures', 'Pastimes for Ladies' and 'Five o'clock Tea'. His own contribution took the form of 'Literary and Other Notes', a monthly round-up of books by women and a commentary on issues pertaining to their position in society.

The first edition appeared in November 1887 and signalled the editorial direction Oscar intended to take. 'The Position of Women', a lengthy article from Eveline, Countess of Portsmouth, welcomed amendments to marriage law designed to reform an institution that 'might and did very often represent to a wife a hopeless and bitter slavery'. Her condemnation of marriage echoed sentiments expressed by Oscar in *The Duchess of Padua* and she wrote:

The fruits of hard toil of the wife could be spent by the husband; her industry be devoured by his drunkenness. The inheritance of a woman could act as bait for the most contemptible of mankind.[16]

She hailed exercise and education as the key to emancipation, welcomed the solidarity that was emerging between women of different classes, and ended with a rallying cry:

May not the time be come when the strength of woman is imperative to make man stronger! – when it is necessary for him that she should be his fitting companion – loyal but not servile!

In 'Women in Germany' (August 1888), anarchist poet Louise S. Bevington declared: 'We are all creatures of circumstance and man's will or whim is women's chief circumstance the world over'.[17] In 'Woman and Democracy' (June 1888), feminist writer Julia Wedgewood, a niece of Charles Darwin and an advocate for universal suffrage, argued that 'obedience is no longer the ideal of marriage'.[18]

By necessity, *The Woman's World* was targeted at middle- and upper-class readers who could afford it, yet contributors strove to foster a sense of sisterhood that would transcend the class divide. In 'The Uses of the Drawing Room', social reformer and educationalist Henrietta Barnett issued a well-intentioned if naive rallying call encouraging readers to open their homes to the poor so they might experience lively conversation, improving music and good food.[19] And Mary Tabor praised the Working Ladies' Guild for its discreet channelling of fine sewing work to ladies who had fallen on hard times.[20]

Yet, such paternalism did not chime with Oscar's beliefs. Like Jane, he favoured the opening up of education and the professions to women as a means of improving their status, and he agreed entirely with Emily Faithfull, a member of the Society for Promoting the Employment of Women, when she wrote of the duty of teaching girls some trade, calling or profession. Several articles in *The Woman's World* drew attention to the blight of poverty afflicting women and children, and suggested solutions that went far beyond ineffectual charitable works.

In 'Something About Needlewomen' (May 1888), trade unionist Clementina Black, who had helped establish the Woman's Trade Union Association, highlighted the plight of impoverished needlewomen unable to earn a living wage from the piecework they were given. She encouraged them to combine into cooperatives.[21] In July 1888, in one of several features dealing with Irishwomen, Irish journalist Charlotte O'Connor Eccles drew attention to the alarming conditions endured by Dublin's women weavers, insisting that their poverty should be alleviated through education and training.[22]

When planning the editorial direction of *The Woman's World*, Oscar had written to Helena Sickert, a recent graduate of Girton College in Cambridge:

> The magazine will try to be representative of the thought and culture of the women of this century, and I am very anxious that those who have had university training, like yourself, should have an organ through which they can express their views on life and things.[23]

The first edition included a profile of 'The Oxford Ladies' Colleges', written by 'a member of one of them', feminist writer Janet Elizabeth Hogarth, who had been suggested by William Leonard Courtney, Oxford don, editor of *The Fortnightly Review* and the man who would become her husband.[24] Courtney contributed an article on 'The Women Benefactors of Oxford' (June 1888). Oscar also commissioned a profile of Alexandra College, Dublin from Lady Mary Catherine Ferguson. Alexandra College, established for the higher education of girls, had invited him to lecture on Ancient Greece a decade earlier.[25] Sickert's article, 'The Evolution of Economics' appeared in February 1889.

In 'Literary and Other Notes' (January 1888), Oscar praised *Women and Work*, a collection of essays by poet and philanthropist Emily Jane Pfeiffer. Describing this book as 'a most important contribution to the discussion of one of the great social problems of our day', he welcomed in particular her refutation of Professor George Romane's preposterous assertion that men and women should be 'mentally differentiated'. To illustrate his opposition to Romane, Oscar quoted Daniel Defoe: 'what has the woman done to forfeit the privilege of being taught!'[26] In December 1887, he took the opportunity to highlight the success of a Miss Story, the daughter of a Northern Irish clergyman, who had been awarded a literature scholarship by the Royal University in Ireland, remarking:

It is pleasant to be able to chronicle an item of Irish news that has nothing to do with the violence of party politics or party feeling, and that shows how worthy women are of that higher culture and education which has been so tardily, and in some instances, so grudgingly granted to them.[27]

Several articles encouraged those few, fortunate women who had benefitted from access to higher education to explore the opportunities that were opening up in the professions. Trade unionist and suffragist Edith Simcox, who had helped establish a women's shirt-making co-operative, contributed an article on, 'Elementary School Training as a Profession' (October 1888).[28] In 'Medicine as a Profession for Women', Mary A. Marshall MD pointed to the academic success achieved by the fifty-six women enrolled on the British Medical Register, arguing that 'the objection of mental incapability' was utterly invalid.[29]

Although Oscar insisted that his magazine had, 'no creed of its own, political, artistic, or theological', he was unequivocal in his support for the greater participation of women in politics.[30] Reviewing David Ritchie's *Darwinism and Politics*, he praised his rebuttal of Herbert Spencer's* contention that, should women be admitted to political life, they might do mischief by introducing the ethics of the family into affairs of state: 'If something is right in a family,' Oscar countered, 'it is difficult to see why it is, therefore, without any further reason, wrong in the state'. He argued that greater participation by women would lead to the 'moralisation of politics'. One sentence sums up his support for gender equality:

> The cultivation of separate sorts of virtues and separate ideals of duty in men and women has led to the whole social fabric being weaker and unhealthier than it need be.[31]

Oscar invited Millicent Garrett Fawcett, prominent suffragist and cofounder of Newnham College, Cambridge, to address the issue of women's suffrage. In Fawcett's opinion, the exclusion of women was, quite simply, morally reprehensible: 'Even felons were not excluded once their term of imprisonment was over; lunatics were joyfully admitted', she argued. It was her bold contention that by enfranchising women, a nation could put an end to war.[32] The most overtly political article in *The Woman's World* was 'On Woman's Work in Politics', the transcript of a speech delivered at Cambridge University by Lady Margaret Sandhurst while she

---

* British philosopher and sociologist who coined the expression 'survival of the fittest'.

was campaigning, with Constance Wilde's assistance, for election to the London County Council.

Several contributors to *The Woman's World* and many readers too, opposed the extension of the vote to women. Insisting that she cared little for women's suffrage, Dinah Craik told Oscar that she had 'given the widest berth to that set of women who are called, not unjustly, the Shrieking Sister-hood'.[33] Lucy M. J. Garnett, an immensely intelligent woman and an expert on the folklore and traditions of Balkan women, contributed the provocative 'Reasons for Opposing Women's Suffrage' (April 1889).[34] Her arguments were so gratuitously insulting, particularly to older women, that one suspects Oscar's motivation for publishing them was to elicit sympathy for the other side.

Garnett's contribution was out of step with the general tone. So too was 'Our Girl Workers' (February 1888), in which Theresa, Countess of Shrewsbury argued that women 'should be the guardian angel of the Englishman's hearth and home, instead of becoming his rival in the labour market, college and professions'. More typical was 'The Fallacy of the Superiority of Man' (December 1887), by Laura McLaren, founder of the Liberal Women's Suffrage Union, who knew Constance Wilde through their association with the International Arbitration and Peace Association. McLaren condemned those men who 'openly rejoice in superiority of all more definite qualities, mental and physical,' while allowing to women attributes considered of little value, such as 'physical charm or softness of heart or mental intuition or spiritual insight'. McLaren's rousing article threw down a gauntlet: 'If women are inferior in any point, let the world hear the evidence on which they are to be condemned'.[35] Such inflammatory language could have come from the pen of Jane Wilde. In 'The Fallacy of the Equality of Women', Lucy Garnett refuted McLaren's contention that women were 'jealously excluded' by men, and called instead for a recognition of difference rather than a measurement of superiority or inferiority, a debate that rages to this day.

With Oscar at the helm, fashion remained a key feature of *The Woman's World*, and he insisted that:

> Fashion is such an essential part of the mundus muliebris of our day, that it seems to me absolutely necessary that its growth, development, and phases should be duly chronicled.[36]

An unconventional approach saw the inclusion of 'Politics in Dress' (June 1889) by ethnographer Richard Heath. The following month,

Oscar chose John Singer Sargent's iconic painting of Ellen Terry as Lady Macbeth for the frontispiece. Sargent had suggested that Alice Comyns Carr, who had designed Terry's magnificent costume, should co-sign his painting. A prominent dress reformer and proponent of aesthetic fashion, Comyns Carr contributed 'A Lady of Fashion in 1750' (May 1889), an article extolling the accomplishments of influential women throughout history.[37]

A conventional round-up of latest fashions was supplemented with articles examining aesthetic design and rational dress. In his first 'Literary and Other Notes', Oscar castigated the:

> . . . absolute unsuitability of ordinary feminine attire to any sort of handicraft, or even to any occupation which necessitates a daily walk to business and back again in all kinds of weather.[38]

In 'A Monstrous Fashion', echoing the concerns of the Rational Dress Society, of which Constance was a prominent member, Oscar insisted: 'The health of a nation depends very much on its mode of dress'.[39] It was his contention that:

> From the Sixteenth Century to our own day there is hardly any form of torture that has not been inflicted on girls and endured by women, in obedience to the dictates of an unreasonable and monstrous Fashion.[40]

In his progressive opinion, restrictive clothing prevented women from taking their rightful place alongside men.

On the first page of his first edition, Oscar published 'The Woodland Gods' (November 1887) by the aristocratic Janey Sevilla Campbell,[*] a review of three cross-dressing dramas staged by her Pastoral Players at her home, Coombe House in Surrey. This article was illustrated with an image of Janey dressed as a young man to play Orlando in *As You Like It* and another of her dressed as Perigot embracing Amoret, played by Princess Hellen of Kappurthala, in Fletcher's *The Faithful Shepherdess*. In the *Dramatic Review*, Oscar described Janey's Orlando as 'really remarkable'. In a letter to James Whistler, he called her: 'the Moon-Lady, the Grey Lady, the beautiful wraith with her beryl eyes'.[41]

Several articles, including 'The Pictures of Sappho' (April 1888) by classical scholar Jane Ellen Harrison, challenged gender-based conventions in dress. A feature on fans as a feminine symbol pointed out that they

---

* More commonly referred to as Lady Archibald Campbell.

were originally carried by men as a sign of power, while one on gloves asked why men, once such decorative dressers, had become so 'sober'. In 'Women Wearers of Men's Clothes' (January 1889), Irish-born journalist Emily Crawford insisted that women who adopted masculine styles could accomplish 'heroic duties'.[42] Novelist Ella Hepworth Dixon applauded the 'semi-masculine and completely appropriate gear' adopted by women who rode. Oscar joined the debate, declaring it probable that, in time, 'the dress of the two sexes will be assimilated, as similarity of costume always follows similarity of pursuits'.[43]

Naturally, literature was a key focus of *The Woman's World*. One of Oscar's most rewarding tasks was the commissioning of new works of fiction from emerging and established women writers. The best article in the December 1887 issue, he told poet Louise Chandler Moulton, would be 'a story, one page long, by Amy Levy . . . a mere girl, but a girl of genius'.[44] Levy, a graduate of Newnham College, Cambridge, had sent the story unsolicited. Recognising 'a touch of genius' in it, Oscar called her writing 'as admirable as it is unique' and commissioned a second story, two poems, a profile of the poet Christina Rossetti, and 'Women and Club Life'.[45]

Levy was a member of 'A Men and Women's Club', a radical debating club. Hailed as a pioneer of lesbian writing, her own sexuality was never firmly established. She was hugely talented but desperately troubled and experienced debilitating bouts of depression exacerbated by failing physical health since her early youth. On 10 September 1889, two months short of her twenty-eighth birthday, Levy ended her life by inhaling charcoal fumes: 'the world must forgo the full fruition of her power', Oscar lamented in a heartfelt obituary.[46]

Oscar also championed radical feminist Olive Schreiner, a South African born writer, best known for her novel, *The Story of an African Farm*, who agitated for greater access to political life and an end to the sexual double standard. Schreiner was living in poverty in London's East End, a circumstance that prompted Oscar to write:

> Olive Schreiner . . . is staying in the East End because that is the only place where people do not wear masks upon their faces, but I have told her that I live in the West End because nothing in life interests me but the mask.[47]

Schreiner contributed two prose allegories to *The Woman's World*: 'The Lost', and 'A Dream of Wild Bees' and Oscar also published her poem 'Life's Gifts'.[48] She took to attending Jane's salon to meet him and her letters were full of warmth: 'I hope the world goes well with you in every way', she wrote.[49]

In 'Literary and Other Notes' Oscar gave 'special prominence to books written by women'.[50] Reviewing *A Village Tragedy* by his old friend from Oxford Margaret L. Woods, he compared her style to Fyodor Dostoyevsky and Guy de Maupassant. Praising Princess Christian of Schleswig-Holstein's translation of the memoirs of Wilhelmine, Margravine of Bayreuth, composer and older sister of Wilhelm the Great, he pointed out that Wilhelmine's 'influence on the intellectual development of her country' remained untold.[51] He promoted Aesthetic and new woman writers including poets E. Nesbit, A. Mary F. Robinson, Violet Fane, and the colourful and controversial Rosamund Marriot Watson, who wrote as Graham R. Tomson.*

Reviewing Tomson's collection *The Bird-Bride*, Oscar hailed her as 'one of our most artistic workers in poetry' and described her lines as 'little carved ivories of speech'.[52] He asked her to write 'Beauty from the Historical Point of View' (July 1888) and had her poem 'In Picardy' illustrated for the cover of the September 1889 edition. Tomson became editor of the Aesthetic magazine *Sylvia's Journal* in 1893, and it is clear that she learned much from her association with *The Woman's World*.

In his review of *Woman's Voices*, an anthology edited by Elizabeth Sharp, Oscar described young Edith Nesbit as 'a very pure and perfect artist'. He lauded her ambition to 'give poetic form to humanitarian dreams, and socialist aspirations'.[53] Nesbit had sent Oscar her collection *Lays and Legend* in 1886, and he had responded with an encouraging letter. He reviewed her collection *Leaves of Life* in *The Woman's World* and published three of her poems: 'Christmas Roses' (December 1888), 'The Soul to the Ideal' (July 1889) and 'Equal Love' (June 1890). The last of these advocated free love and Nesbit's own marriage to socialist Hubert Bland was open and tempestuous.

Oscar's review of *Woman's Voices* incurred his mother's wrath, since he failed to mention her ballad 'The Brothers'. In a stinging letter addressed to 'Dear Mr. Editor', she demanded to know why he had ignored: 'Me, who holds such an historic place in Irish literature?' Inviting him to 'come for a talk on Sunday evening', Jane warned: 'I have so little time left now – for I must certainly drown myself in a week or two – Life is quite too

---

* Nesbit and Watson also wrote for *The Yellow Book*, a literary periodical linked to aestheticism and decadence that gave prominence to women writers.

much trouble'.[54] Oscar redeemed himself somewhat by asking her to write 'Historic Women' and 'Irish Peasant Tales', and by publishing W. B. Yeats's flattering critique of her folklore collection.

Although he kept nepotism to a minimum, he did ask Constance to write 'Children's Dress in this Century' (July 1988), which was more radical than it sounds as it contained the sentiment:

> The greater number of children are undoubtedly dressed more simply, more rationally, more like human sentient beings, less like wooden dolls or dummies to wear the freaks or fancies dictated by dressmakers.[55]

A second article by Constance on 'Muffs' (February 1889), charted their history and depiction in works of art. Constance also introduced Oscar to several influential contributors, including Laura McLaren and Margaret Sandhurst. Laura Ormiston Chant, vice president of the Women's Liberal Federation, wrote 'The Gymnasium for Girls' while Viscountess Harberton, founder of the Rational Dress Society, contributed 'Mourning Clothes and Customs'. The earnest and scholarly Charlotte Carmichael Stopes, mother of Marie, who wrote several articles for the *Rational Dress Society Gazette*, complained to Constance when Oscar rejected an article of hers. In response, Constance assured her:

> I have nothing to do with the editing of the *Woman's World* and I did not know that my husband had returned manuscripts of yours. I know that he has enough for about two years hence, and his magazine being an illustrated magazine he requires illustrated articles more than anything else. I am sorry you should have been disappointed.[56]

Stopes, who went on to write *British Freewomen: Their Historical Privilege* (1894), a key text for first-wave British feminism, received several rejection letters from 'the Editor', explaining that her themes were too profound. Towards the end of Oscar's tenure and after he resigned his post, several articles of hers did appear'.[57]

Anna de Brémont declared that *The Woman's World* caused a 'flutter in the boudoirs of Mayfair and Belgravia'. Jane's Saturdays became thronged with would-be contributors. The press response was also positive: 'Mr Oscar Wilde has triumphed,' the *Nottingham Evening Post* declared; 'the first number of the "Woman's World" has already appeared, and has, I believe, been sold out'.[58] Praising Oscar for 'striking an original line', *The Times* hailed *The Woman's World* as 'gracefully got up . . . in every respect'.[59] Rival publication *Queen* praised the magazine's improved appearance and impressive array of contributors. The assessment of the *St James's Gazette* must have delighted Oscar:

> *The Woman's World* is a capital magazine for a married man to buy. He tells his wife he got it entirely for her sake; but he may always find some very good reading for himself.[60]

The Spectator declared: 'The change is undoubtedly one for the better, in the sense of the higher'.[61] Yet, three months later that same publication observed:

> Mr. Oscar Wilde has not yet realised his own ideal. His magazine is still too much one written by ladies for ladies, and not by women for women.[62]

The Irish Times declared that 'Mr. Oscar Wilde has fully justified the confidence reposed in him, the free hand given his genius by the proprietors', and described how, on the evening of the launch:

> There was not one in the West End to be had for love or money and impatient people could only get through the interval between Saturday and Monday by borrowing copies from friends.[63]

A later edition of *The Irish Times* described the articles in *The Woman's World* as 'extremely bright and useful'.[64] Perhaps the most significant reaction came from *The Englishwoman's Review*, the organ of the suffragist movement in Britain and the very epitome of Dinah Craik's 'Shrieking Sisterhood'. While refraining from praising *The Woman's World* overtly, it ran notices attracting the attention of readers to more progressive articles.

Early on, Oscar appeared to enjoy his mornings in the office. Every Tuesday and Thursday, he would walk the short distance from Tite Street to Slone Square tube station and take the Metropolitan District Railway to Charing Cross station.* Then, he would walk the length of the Strand, head down Fleet Street and turn left through an ancient archway into La Belle Sauvage. During the early months, he made an effort to be there by eleven o'clock. His presence caused quite a stir. One fellow employee, a friend of John Yeats', described Oscar as 'so indolent but such a genius'.[65] Arthur Fish, the young subeditor assigned to him, thought Oscar 'always well groomed but without any marked extravagances or eccentricities,' and added 'he was easily the best dressed man in the establishment'.[66]

---

* Now Embankment Station.

Oscar found Fish 'most reliable and intelligent'.[67] They grew close: 'I always think of you as one of my real friends,' Oscar wrote.[68]

After a while, Fish could tell:

> . . . by the sound of his [Oscar's] approach along the resounding corridor whether the necessary work to be done would be met cheerfully or postponed to a more congenial period.[69]

On a good day, there would be:

> . . . a smiling entrance, letters would be answered with epigrammatic brightness, there would be a cheery interval of talk when the work was accomplished, and the dull room would brighten under the influence of his great personality.[70]

Fish never doubted Oscar's commitment to *The Woman's World*, crediting him with securing 'a brilliant company of contributors which included the leaders of feminine thought and influence in every branch of work'.[71] In his opinion, the 'keynote' of the magazine was no less than 'the right of woman to equality of treatment with man'. Fish realised that 'some of the articles on women's work and their position in politics were far in advance of the thought of the day' and acknowledged that Oscar fought hard to ensure this:

> Sir Wemyss Reid, then General Manager of Cassell's, or John Williams the Chief Editor, would call in at our room and discuss them with Oscar Wilde, who would always express his entire sympathy with the views of the writers and reveal a liberality of thought with regard to the political aspirations of women that was undoubtedly sincere.[72]

Although Oscar grew disillusioned as early as October 1887, this was born of frustration rather than a lack of commitment: 'I am not allowed as free a hand as I would like', he told Helena Sickert.[73] This became his theme: 'The work of reconstruction was very difficult', he told William Sharp, 'as the *Lady's World* was a most vulgar trivial production, and the doctrine of heredity holds good in literature as in life'.[74]

In December 1887, Cassells objected to the 'too literary tendencies' of the magazine.[75] In October 1888, Oscar asked the board to authorise the purchase of a story from Frances Hodgson Burnett, but her name never appeared. Neither did four illustrated articles Oscar hoped to commission from French explorer and archaeologist Madame Jeanne Dieulafoy at sixteen guineas each. His disenchantment deepened when Cassell's refused to drop the price of *The Woman's World* to sixpence or seven pence in order to attract a wider readership. Arthur Fish recalled that: 'After a few months, his arrival became later and his departure earlier until at times his visit was little more than a call'.[76] 'Literary and Other Notes' disappeared after the fourth issue and he began to miss his deadlines after it was reinstated at Cassell's instance. By July 1889, Oscar was leaving notes for Fish: 'I have not been at all well and cannot get my notes done. Can you manage to put in something else?'[77]

Evidence of Oscar's disillusionment can be found in his declaration, in October 1888, that 'there are many things in which women are interested about which a man really cannot write'. He suggested that Cassells engage Florence Fenwick Miller to write, 'four pages of paragraphs on current topics every month'.[78] This suggestion was sound. Fenwick Miller's weekly 'Ladies Notes' in the *Illustrated London News* ran for more than three decades. A graduate of the Ladies School of Medicine, she had practiced briefly as a physician before reinventing herself as a campaigning journalist and lecturer on physiology, public health and the rights of women.

Fenwick Miller was a founding member of the Women's Franchise League and a member of the London Dialectical Society, which included some of London's most radical thinkers; she met her husband there and they debated topics that included birth control and cremation. An early advocate of birth control and a campaigner for enhanced rights for married women, her decision to keep her maiden name after her own marriage was roundly criticised. She shared a stage with Oscar when they addressed the Tyneside Sunday Lecture Society; he on 'Dress' and she on 'Our Puritan Forefathers'. A contributor to *The Woman's World*, she congratulated Oscar on the high standards he set for the magazine.[79] However, she did not replace him.

Fish described his boss as 'Pegasus in harness' and soon he was pulling against the reins.[80] It sounds trivial but one of the toughest challenges Oscar faced was Cassell's strict no smoking policy. Fish described a typical day towards the end of his tenure:

> He would sink with a sigh into his chair, carelessly glance at his letters, give a perfunctory look at proofs or make-up, ask "Is it necessary to settle anything to-day?" put on his hat, and, with a sad "Good-morning", depart again.[81]

In April 1889, Oscar informed the Board of Inland Revenue that he would be leaving Cassell & Co. in August. His last 'Literary and Other

Notes' appeared in June 1889 and by October his name was gone from the cover. After he left, *The Woman's World* reverted to its unadventurous roots and a renewed focus on fashion prompted *The Woman's Penny Paper* to scold: 'To dress is surely not considered the first or the only duty of women, even by their greatest enemies'. [82] The magazine was discontinued shortly afterwards.

During his two-year tenure, Oscar had not neglected his own work. Dozens of his poems, reviews, essays and stories were accepted by various periodicals and he published and promoted *The Happy Prince and Other Tales*, his first collection of stories. The break from Cassells heralded an exceptionally productive period that saw the publication of two more collections of short stories: *Lord Arthur Savile's Crime and Other Stories*, and *The House of Pomegranates*; *Intentions*, a collection of essays; and *The Picture of Dorian Gray*, his only novel. Oscar's time as editor of *The Woman's World* is often dismissed as an opportunity to earn a regular income, yet he achieved much in this role, facilitating the exploration of contentious issues faced by women and giving a platform to emerging women writers. While his sincerity and sympathy were never in doubt, his suitability to deal with the day-to-day challenges of bringing out a magazine on someone else's behalf was.

Chapter 13
STORIES FOR GIRLS

> . . . he had all the gifts necessary; an imposing presence, a pleas-
> ant voice, a control of language, charm, and an extraordinary
> tact in choosing subjects which would suit his listeners, and in
> judging his effects.
> VINCENT O'SULLIVAN on Oscar as a storyteller[1]

When Aimée Lowther was a child, she would rush home to write down
the wonderful stories that her friend Oscar told her. Years later, in 1912,
four of these stories were published in *The Mask: a Quarterly Journal of the
Art of the Theatre*. They were 'The Poet', 'The Actress', 'Simon of Cyrene'
and 'Jezebel'. Each one was captioned 'an unpublished story by Oscar
Wilde', and prefaced with the words:

> This story was told by Wilde to Miss Aimée Lowther when a child and
> written out by her. A few copies were privately printed but this is the first
> time it has been given to the public.[2]

Aimée was in her forties by then, and had enjoyed some success as a
playwright and amateur actress. The veracity of her claim was borne out
by a letter she received from Oscar in August 1899, asking her not to allow
the publication of 'the little poem in prose I call "The Poet"', as it was
due to 'appear next week in a Paris magazine above my own signature';
no such magazine has ever been identified.[3] Another of these stories, 'The
Actress' is thought to have been inspired by Ellen Terry; Edward Gordon
Craig, editor of *The Mask*, was her son, and Aimée, her close confidante.

Oscar loved Aimée: 'if you had been a boy you'd have wrecked my
life', he declared.[4] In return, she remained loyal to the end, and a visit
from her could lift his spirits even when he was at his lowest ebb: '. . . your
friendship is a blossom on the crown of thorns that my life has become',
he assured her.[5] A triolet he wrote describing her eyes was set to music by
her remarkable sister Toupie.*

---

* May 'Toupie' Lowther was an accomplished composer, an outstanding tennis
player and fencer, a keen motorist and a lesbian. During WWI, she organised an

> Your eyes are deep green pools
> In which the sun has gazed,
> And passing left a golden ray.[6]

Although Lowther's story is entirely plausible, confusion arose when Gabrielle Enthoven, a passionate collector of theatrical memorabilia, claimed that Oscar had told these stories to her. In 1948, she presented the British Library with a copy of *Echoes*, a limited edition, twelve-page pamphlet she had commissioned, which contained the four stories in question. Aimée Lowther owned a copy of *Echoes*, which she later gave to Oscar's younger son, Vyvyan, and the stories reproduced in *Echoes* and *The Mask* are almost word for word the same.[7]

Of course it is entirely possible that Oscar told his stories to both women. He was a born storyteller and his popularity was enhanced by his exceptionally melodious voice, described by Lord Alfred Douglas as 'golden'. Lillie Langtry declared: 'He had one of the most alluring voices that I have ever listened to, round and soft, and full of variety and expression'.[8] Frank Dyall, the actor who played Merriman in the first production of *The Importance of Being Earnest*, recalled it as being: '. . . of the brown velvet order – mellifluous, rounded, in a sense giving it a plummy quality, rather on the adenotic side, but practically pure cello, and very pleasing'.[9]

To add drama to a narrative, Oscar would modulate his voice from a whisper to a cry of triumph, losing himself in his stories to the extent that those present described him as seeming dazed by the effort of telling them. Yet his true power lay in the words he chose. W. B. Yeats said of him: 'I had never before heard a man talking in perfect sentences, as if he had written them all overnight with labour and yet all spontaneous'.[10] Oscar's friend Vincent O'Sullivan confirmed that he was 'spontaneous, no matter what hour of the day or night', adding: 'He did not try to enforce his moods; he gave the impression of adapting himself to the moods of others'.[11]

In *A Woman of No Importance*, Oscar had his Lord Illingworth say: 'A man who can dominate a London dinner-table can dominate the world'.[12] His own popularity prompted London's most fashionable hostesses to include 'to meet Oscar Wilde' on their invitations. One guest fortunate enough to be present at a lunch hosted by publisher and *bon vivant* Frank Harris, described how Oscar's musical voice and infectious laughter cut through

---

all-women team of ambulance drivers and was awarded the Croix de Guerre. Oscar's niece, Dolly Wilde, was one of her drivers.

the lively chatter, causing everyone present to fall silent in order to listen exclusively to him. In response, he filled the hours that followed with humorous anecdotes, embryonic plotlines for plays he was contemplating, macabre tales told in the style of Edgar Allan Poe, and his own distinctive take on the instructive bible stories that were popular at the time. Yet Harris insisted that Oscar never monopolised conversation; instead,

> he took the ball of talk wherever it happened to be at the moment and played with it so humorously that everyone was soon smiling delightedly.[13]

Harris published several of Oscar's 'Poems in Prose' in the *Fortnightly Review*, which he edited at the time. Yet he was convinced that they lost something in the transcribing. Robbie Ross, Oscar's great friend and literary executor, agreed that it was almost impossible to replicate the magic of the spoken version:

> To those who remember hearing them from Wilde's lips, there must always be a feeling of disappointment on reading them. He overloaded their ornament when he came to transcribe them, and some of his friends did not hesitate to make that criticism personally.[14]

The size of his audience was of no importance to Oscar, and he had the ability to spin a tale out of the most prosaic material. When young Harry Marillier was invited to lunch, Constance showed him her collection of moonstone jewelry while Oscar spun stories about the tiny people who inhabited every glowing gem.[15] There were those who believed that he could cure depression or ease pain simply by speaking to an afflicted person for five minutes. Some were moved despite themselves. Poet Ernest Dowson attested that Oscar 'has such a wonderful vitality and joie de vivre that after some hours of his society even a pessimist like myself is infected by it'.[16] Artist W. Graham Robertson, who considered Oscar 'A born *raconteur*', swore that he had cured him of a 'violent toothache' by telling stories 'so brilliantly that for an hour and a half on end I laughed without ceasing'.[17]

When Oscar asked Robertson to illustrate one of his stories, he shared with him the process of inventing it: 'I kept looking at the moon,' he wrote, 'and beseeching her to tell me a story. At last she did'.[18] Robertson shared the opinion that: 'When committed to paper, his [Oscar's] tales lost much of their charm'.[19] In *Time Was*, his autobiography, he transcribes one highly entertaining tale Oscar told him about his cantankerous 'Aunt Jane'. In order to reassert herself in society, this haughty old woman planned a glittering ball, but when no one arrived, she retired upstairs to die of shame. Later, it was discovered that she had forgotten to send out invitations.[20] Unless he too had a forgetful Aunt Jane, Evelyn Waugh appears to have drawn heavily on Oscar's story for his 'Bella Fleace Gave a Party', published in 1932; they are alike in almost every respect.

Although he was a very public raconteur, Oscar saved some of his best stories for home, remarking that it was the duty of every father to invent fairytales for his children. In his memoir, *Son of Oscar Wilde*, Vyvyan Holland wrote of a 'never-ending-supply' of fairy stories and tales of adventure, many of them inspired by the imaginings of Jules Verne, Robert Louis Stevenson and Rudyard Kipling; Oscar always was a literary magpie. Vyvyan recalled one particular bedtime story, reminiscent of 'The Elves and the Shoemaker', which described the helpful fairies who lived in the great bottles of coloured water found in the windows of chemist shops. They would dance about at night before making the pills that the chemist would dispense the next day.[21]

At least one of Oscar's stories recalled the West of Ireland, where the Wilde family had spent so much time. He kept his boys rapt with his description of the 'great melancholy carp' that lived in the deep waters of Lough Corrib, and refused to move off the bottom unless Oscar called them up with the ancient Irish songs taught to him by his father.[22] At times, he was moved to tears by his own ingenuity. His eyes glistened as he told them the story of 'The Selfish Giant'; when Cyril wondered why, Oscar replied that really beautiful things always made him cry.[23]

Thanks to Jane's foresight, Oscar spoke excellent, ponderous French in a 'slow musical tone'.[24] In Paris, he earned a reputation as 'the poet who tells fantastic tales' and his visit to that city in 1891 was described by *L'Echo de Paris* as 'le "great event" *des salons littéraires parisiens*'.[25] Young André Gide, who would win the Nobel Prize in Literature in 1947, met with Oscar every day of the three weeks he was in Paris and found him utterly captivating: 'the best of his writing is but a poor reflection of his brilliant conversations', he recalled.[26] After they parted, Gide felt unable to put pen to paper for several days. He finally made contact with poet Paul Valéry on Christmas Eve, 1891, and asked him to 'please forgive my silence: since Wilde, I hardly exist anymore'.[27] On one occasion, when Oscar dined at the home of Princess Ouroussoff, wife of the Russian ambassador to France, she declared: 'when he is speaking I see round his head a luminous aureole'.[28]

Oscar's would-be biographer, A. J. A. Symons (who never completed the documenting of his life), described him as 'thoroughly in accord with himself'; an entirely apt characterisation. Symons attributed Oscar's popularity to 'his constant good humour, lack of malice, tact in choice of subject, and almost telepathic sensitiveness to his listeners' moods'. This irresistible combination ensured that 'at scores of dinner tables he held listeners spellbound by witty improvisations'.[29] Such was Oscar's prolificacy that only a tiny fraction of the stories he told made it into print, and he would commit a story to paper only if the reaction of his audience merited it. Fortunately this was the case with *The Happy Prince*, one of his best-loved tales, which he told first to a rapturous gathering of Cambridge undergraduates in November 1885. It became the title story in his first collection, *The Happy Prince and Other Tales*, which appeared in May 1888 while Oscar was editing *The Woman's World*.

Oscar seemed unsure how to pitch his first collection. Reviewers were confused too: the *Athenaeum* reviewed *The Happy Prince and Other Tales* under the heading 'Books for the Young', while in *The Times*, Alexander Galt Ross (older brother of Robbie), argued that it would appeal to a wider readership. When Oscar sent a copy to William Gladstone, leader of the opposition and champion of Home Rule for Ireland, he described his tales as 'really meant for children'.[30] He told poet George Herbert Kersley they were:

> . . . studies in prose, put for Romance's sake into a fanciful form: meant partly for children, and partly for those who have kept the childlike faculties of wonder and joy, and who find in simplicity a subtle strangeness.[31]

Six months later, in a letter to American poet and novelist Amelie Rives Chanler, he insisted that his stories were 'not for children, but for childlike people from eighteen to eighty!' Denigrating them as 'slight and fanciful', he described his impetus as 'an attempt to mirror modern life in a form remote from reality – to deal with modern problems in a mode that is ideal and not imitative'.[32] Without doubt, Oscar's stories explored profound themes and their meaning and significance have been examined rigorously elsewhere, but it is worth examining aspects that pertain to his attitude towards and relationship with the women he knew.[*]

The Happy Prince bears a slight resemblance to *The Little Lame Prince* by Dinah Mulock Craik, who suggested the new title for *The Woman's World*;

---

[*] Two excellent examples are *Oscar Wilde's Fairy Tales: Origins and Contexts* by Dr Anne Markey (Irish Academic Press, 2011) and *The Fairy Tales of Oscar Wilde* by Dr Jarlath Killeen (Ashgate Publishing, 2007).

her young protagonist uses a magic travelling cloak to gaze down at the 'wretchedness' that lay 'close behind the grandeur' in his kingdom. Although it was written long before Oscar met Lord Alfred Douglas, passages in 'The Happy Prince' appear to indicate the direction in which his thoughts were turning. A swallow falls in love with a beautiful reed on account of her slender waist. When she refuses to travel with him, he takes up with a statue of a golden prince instead; 'she has no conversation', says the swallow of the reed. The swallow and his prince gaze down on a town blighted with the same poverty, unemployment and exploitation Oscar saw on his own doorstep. Victorian London suffered from more than its fair share of 'all the ugliness and all the misery', which Oscar recognised as the by-product of an unequal society.

Much of this suffering was targeted by altruistic women who contributed to *The Woman's World* and Oscar echoes their concerns in his descriptions of the charity children discouraged from dreaming by their Mathematical Master, the destitute seamstress with her 'coarse, red hands, all pricked by the needle', and the worthless bureaucrats who issued an order forbidding birds to die at the feet of the golden statue.[33] His inclusion of the impoverished match-girl must surely represent a nod to the 1,400 women and girls who had gone on strike at the Bryant and May match factory in 1888; they refused to work until their appalling conditions and inadequate wages were improved. That year, *The Woman's World* contributor Clementina Black, Secretary of the Women's Trade Union League, secured the first successful equal pay resolution at Trades Union Congress by carrying the motion unanimously:

> That, in the opinion of this congress it is desirable in the interests both of men and women that in trades where women do the same work as men they shall receive the same wages.[34]

Oscar supported such tangible action, yet he believed that the charitable work engaged in by some of his women friends was 'admirable though misdirected' and did nothing to tackle the underlying causes of deprivation: '. . . this is not a solution: it is an aggravation of the difficulty', he wrote in *The Soul of Man under Socialism*. He advocated reform: 'The proper aim,' he argued, 'is to try and reconstruct society on such a basis that poverty will be impossible'.[35] While his kind-hearted statue, aided by the swallow, gives away his ruby, his twin sapphires and his gold-leaf coating, his altruism helps a tiny few and his kindness makes no lasting difference to the lives of the citizens below. In time, the swallow loses his life by staying too long in the wintery city and the statue is melted down. They receive no earthly gratitude. Recompense awaits them in heaven.

The poverty, inequality and exploitation described in 'The Devoted Friend' are more extreme. A wealthy miller feigns friendship with Little Hans in order to take everything he owns, including his life. When the miller accepts Hans's meagre crops yet refuses him credit on the grounds that it would ruin him, an adult reader might be reminded of the laissez-faire policies adopted by a Whig government in famine-stricken Ireland. The miller's callous behaviour in calling Hans lazy when, clearly, he is exhausted and hungry, typifies the attitude Jane Wilde castigated in her poetry four decades earlier. Surely she is embodied in the unconventional mother duck who teaches her children to see life from a different perspective by standing on their heads. A keen advocate of marriage, mother duck declares: 'I can never look at a confirmed bachelor without the tears coming into my eyes'.[36] Jane may also have inspired the mother in 'The Remarkable Rocket',* who was 'the most celebrated Catherine Wheel of her day'.[37]

Twin themes of charity and self-sacrifice loom large in 'The Nightingale and the Rose'. Believing that nothing matters but true love, a nightingale impales herself on the thorn of a barren rosebush in order to force a perfect red bloom for a student to give to the girl he desires. But the girl rejects the rose because it doesn't match her outfit, and the student throws it away. Neither deserves the nightingale's futile sacrifice. Then again, neither asked for or was even aware of it. In a letter to author Thomas Hutchinson, Oscar characterised his student as 'a rather shallow young man, and almost as bad as the girl he thinks he loves'. Both, he explained, were 'like most of us, unworthy of Romance'. Oscar saved his admiration for the nightingale, 'the true lover, if there is one'. In time, he too would jeopardise everything in pursuit of what he saw as pure love, losing the devotion of his wife in the process. Such insights are precious. In the same letter, he wrote:

I like to fancy that there may be many meanings in the tale, for in writing it, and the others, I did not start with an idea and clothe it in form, but

---

* Her son, a pompous and self-regarding rocket, whose vanity occludes any self-awareness, is thought to resemble Oscar's erstwhile friend, James Whistler, who painted 'Nocturne in Black and Gold: The Falling Rocket' and sued John Ruskin for a review in *Fors Clavigera VII*.

1 Lillie Langtry by Edward John Poynter
(Jersey Heritage Collections). This is the
painting displayed by Oscar in the sitting
room of 13 Salisbury Street

2 Watercolour portrait of Lady Jane
Wilde by Bernard Mulrenin, painted for
the Royal Hibernian Academy Exhibition
of 1864 (Merlin Holland Picture Archive)

3 Envelope containing strands of Isola Wilde's hair, with the inscription
'My Isola's Hair'. Found among Oscar Wilde's possessions when he died
(Merlin Holland Picture Archive)

4 Sketch of Florence Balcombe by Oscar Wilde
(Merlin Holland Picture Archive)

5 Watercolour of *View from Moytura House* painted in 1876 by Oscar Wilde and presented by him to Florence Balcombe (Merlin Holland Picture Archive)

6 Cartoon from *Time* magazine, April 1880. Oscar with Ellen Terry (L) and Sarah Bernhardt (R)

7 Lillie Langtry and Sarah Bernhardt

8 Helena Modjeska

9 Constance Lloyd before her marriage to Oscar Wilde (Merlin Holland Picture Archive)

10 Warner Brothers Trade Card – Oscar Wilde looks on as a cherub presents a corset (Oscar Wilde Society)

11 Love letter from Oscar Wilde to his wife Constance, written on 16 December 1884, shortly after their marriage (Merlin Holland Picture Archive)

12 Ellen Terry as Lady Macbeth by John Singer Sargent 1889 (Tate London)

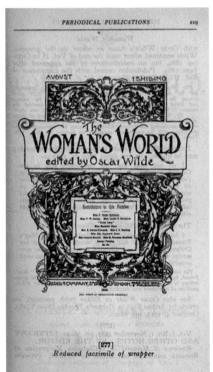

13 Cover of *The Woman's World*

14 Ouida

15 Sarah Bernhardt (Folger
Shakespeare Library)

16 *Salomé Dancing
before Herod* by Gustave
Moreau, 1876, is
included in the
Armand Hammer
Collection, Gift of the
Armand Hammer
Foundation, Hammer
Museum, Los Angeles

17 Photograph taken at the home of Jean and Walter Palmer in 1892 (Merlin Holland Picture Archive). Louise Jopling is beside Oscar Wilde, and Jean Palmer is in the front row. The third woman has been identified as Marie Evelyn Meredith (daughter of George Meredith, who is in the front row)

18 Lady Jane Wilde in old age (Merlin Holland Picture Archive)

19 Constance's grave in Genoa (photograph used with the permission of Outi Määttänen-Bourke/G is for Genoa)

20 Maud Allan as Salome

21 Dolly Wilde dressed as Oscar Wilde (Joan Schenkar)

began with a form, and strove to make it beautiful enough to have many secrets, and many answers.[38]

The Happy Prince and Other Tales was well reviewed and sold well too. Oscar sent copies to several friends, including 'Dear Florrie' Stoker. A charmed Ellen Terry wrote to say:

> They are quite beautiful, dear Oscar, and I thank you for them from the best bit of my heart . . . I should like to read one of them someday to NICE people – or even NOT nice people, and MAKE 'em nice.[39]

Unfortunately, Oscar's plans for Ellen to undertake a series of public readings never came to fruition.

In July 1891, Ettie Grenville opened a package containing a photograph of Oscar and a copy of *Lord Arthur Savile's Crime and Other Stories*, which, he told her, was a 'little book that contains a story, two stories in fact, that I told you at Taplow'.[40] Ettie's 'Saturday to Monday' parties at her Buckinghamshire home on the banks of the Thames were nothing short of legendary and only the most brilliant talkers were invited. Oscar's dazzling conversation charmed his hostess and her guests; as Ettie too was charismatic and brilliant, their admiration was mutual.

All four stories in *Lord Arthur Savile's Crime* had been published elsewhere: 'The Canterville Ghost' was serialised in the February and March 1887 editions of *The Court and Society Review*; that same magazine serialised 'Lord Arthur Savile's Crime' in May 1887; *The World* published 'The Sphinx without a Secret' as 'Lady Alroy' that same month, followed by 'The Model Millionaire' in June. Although the title story pokes fun at the Victorian penchant for consulting fortune tellers, Oscar embraced this activity with enthusiasm. He was devoted in particular to Mrs Robinson, a fashionable palmist said to have told him: 'I see a very brilliant life for you up to a certain point. Then I see a wall. Beyond the wall I see nothing'.[41]

In 'The Canterville Ghost', the Otis family occupies a house believed to be haunted. Their sensitive, fifteen-year-old daughter, Virginia, a girl who transcends death and communicates with the spirit world, has long been associated with Oscar's tragic sister, Isola.* In 'The Sphinx without a Secret', a woman's magnetism depends entirely on the air of mystery

---

* In *Wildean* 14 (Jan 1999), Michael Seeney suggests that Virginia Otis was based on Elsie Palmer, daughter of a wealthy American from Colorado who moved his family to England. She sat for John Singer Sargent and became a peripheral member of the Bloomsbury set.

she cultivates. In 'The Model Millionaire', Hughie Erskine, who was 'as popular with men as he was with women', is entirely dependent on an old aunt for his living. When an act of generosity is rewarded many times over, he is able to marry the woman he loves.

Ettie Grenville, along with many of her friends, was a member of the 'Souls', an aristocratic clique who prided themselves on being exceptionally well informed about art and literature. Margot Tennant, who distanced herself somewhat from the other Souls after her marriage to Herbert Asquith in 1894, claimed that the group's accidental origin was the death of her sister Laura Lyttelton, aged just twenty-three, eight days after the birth of her first child.[42] This unexpected tragedy traumatised Laura's family and friends, and they retreated into mourning; in time they grew to enjoy this exclusivity.

According to Ettie, the Souls got their name in the summer of 1888, when Lord Charles Beresford remarked: 'You all sit and talk about each other's souls — I shall call you the "Souls"'.[43] Although Oscar was never admitted to their ranks, he was welcome at their gatherings. Poet Wilfrid Scawen Blunt declared:

> The fine society of London and especially the "Souls" ran after him because they knew he could always amuse them, and the pretty women all allowed him great familiarities . . .[44]

Oscar dedicated his third collection, *A House of Pomegranates*, to Constance, but he used each tale to pay homage to four powerful society women, two of them 'Souls'. Constance told her close friend and distant relative Lady Mount-Temple that Oscar wrote:

> To you the Cathedral is dedicated. The individual side chapels are to other saints. This is in accordance with the highest ecclesiastical custom! So accept the book as your own and made for you. The candles that burn at the side altars are not so bright or beautiful as the great lamp of the shrine which is of gold, and has a wonderful heart of restless flame.[45]

The first story, 'The Young King', dedicated to Margaret, Lady Brooke [Renee of Sarawak], had appeared in the Christmas number of *The Lady's Pictorial* in 1888. It describes a dandyish young prince on the eve of his coronation who worships beauty above all else. In a series of disturbing dreams, he is confronted with the misery his impoverished subjects experience in their efforts to provide the luxury he takes for granted. Once he shuns earthly riches, he is adorned by the heavens instead.

Lady Brooke led a fascinating life that was marred by tragedy. Her exotic title was the result of her marriage to Charles Brooke, English-born Rajah of Sarawak, a sovereign state on the Island of Borneo granted to the Brooke family by the Sultan of Brunei in 1842. Although Margaret found life in Sarawak restrictive and difficult, she taught herself Malay and found friends among the indigenous women. Tragedy struck when her first three children died of cholera within six days of each other during a return voyage to England; their tiny bodies were released into the Red Sea. Pleading failing health, Margaret returned to Europe. She left a record of her experiences in *My Life in Sarawak* (1913). Although friendly with Oscar, she grew particularly close to Constance and provided great support during the most challenging period of her life.

The richly symbolic second story, 'The Birthday of the Infanta' appeared simultaneously in English and French as 'The Birthday of the Little Princess', in *Paris Illustré* on 30 March 1889. An ungainly dwarf is taken from his forest home to the Spanish royal court, where he is required to dance at the birthday party of the Infanta. He misinterprets her mocking laughter for love, and dies of grief when confronted with his own reflection. The princess is utterly unmoved: 'For the future, let those who come to play with me have no hearts', she pouts. In some sense, the dwarf shared the fate that befell his creator. Although society was charmed by him, they considered him an outsider and condemned him as grotesque when he contravened their rules.

Oscar told Ettie that he was dedicating a story 'about the little pale Infanta whom Velasquez painted' to her 'as a slight return for that entrancing day at Taplow'.[46] The dedication reads: 'Mrs William II. Grenfell of Taplow Court'.* Ettie delighted in Oscar's antics. In a letter to Helen, Lady Tree, who would play Mrs Allonby in the first run of *A Woman of No Importance*, she reminisces about an incident when he stepped 'in mid-river from my punt to the one you were in with Willie [Ettie's husband] – with heavy oscillations'.[47] Yet, while she enjoyed his wit, Ettie was far less enthusiastic about Oscar's writing. Describing him as a 'queer kind of literary acrobat', she confessed to absolutely hating his 'horrible *Dorian Gray*', and she thought *Salomé* 'repulsive'.[48] The ease with which she abandoned Oscar when he needed her support demonstrates how astute he was in his choice of story for her.

* She was married to William Henry Grenfell, later 1st Baron Desborough (1905).

Oscar dedicated the third story, 'The Fisherman and his Soul' to 'H.S.H. Alice, Princess of Monaco', telling her it was the best of the four. Alice Heine, the cultured, American-born daughter of a wealthy French banker was the second wife of Prince Albert I of Monaco. She met Oscar at a dinner organised by Frank Harris at Claridges in 1891, when his talk was described as being 'of the most extraordinary brilliancy'. The next morning, Alice sent Oscar her portrait accompanied by a note that read, 'Au vrai Art, A Oscar Wilde'. [49] One day, she would show great kindness to his son Vyvyan.

In her story, a young fisherman snares a beautiful mermaid in his net and refuses to release her unless she promises to sing for him every day to entice fish into his nets. Inevitably, he falls in love and begs her to marry him. The mermaid agrees on condition that the fisherman relinquishes his human soul. Matters proceed badly. Although this tale reads like a reversal of Hans Christian Andersen's *The Little Mermaid*, written more than half a century earlier, it also calls to mind Friedrich de la Motte Fouqué's novella *Undine* and 'The Dead Soldier', a folk tale included in his mother's collection of *Ancient Legends*, which describes a mermaid seducing a young fisherman with her song. Oscar may also have been influenced by Jane's poem 'The Fisherman', in which a young man almost drowns while under a spell cast by the song of a sea nymph.

In her memoirs, socialite Margot Tennant, by then the wife of Scottish Liberal MP Herbert Asquith, wrote: 'On 7th December [1891] I received a letter from Oscar Wilde, saying he had dedicated his new story The Star Child to me'. [50] This tale appears to borrow from Irish mythology, since Oscar's charmed child possesses some of the qualities associated with the Sidhe, a fairy race described by Jane in *Ancient Legends, Mystic Charms, and Superstitions of Ireland*. [51] Two poor woodcutters happen upon a beautiful infant who seems to have fallen from the heavens. Although he grows up to be cruel and haughty, the boy is redeemed once he passes through a series of trials designed to confront him with his wickedness. Oscar's tales rarely have unambiguously happy endings; although the young man becomes king, his munificence barely touches the unequal society he rules for three years before being replaced by a series of despots. The message appears to be that, no matter how beneficent the ruler, the people cannot progress without self-determination.

Margot Asquith was close to the seat of power. Within months of the publication of *A House of Pomegranates*, her husband was appointed Home Secretary; it was in this role that he would act as Oscar's prosecutor. Oscar and Margot met at a garden party given by Lady Archibald Campbell. She remembered him as a 'large, fat, floppy man, in unusual clothes sitting under a fir tree surrounded by admirers'.[52] Oscar was recounting a 'brilliant monologue' in which he playfully compared himself to Shakespeare and Margot felt compelled to join his circle. Afterwards, they struck up a great friendship while strolling around Janey Campbell's lovely gardens.

Recalling a 'brilliant luncheon' hosted by Margot and her husband, poet Wilfrid Scawen Blunt wrote: 'Afterwards, when the rest had gone away, Oscar remained, telling stories to me and Margot'.[53] During the autumn of 1889, Margot invited Oscar to stay at Glen, her family's country estate, but she believed that he disliked the countryside and recalled him spending 'most of his time in the house,' where he 'wrote several aphorisms and poems on loose sheets of paper'.[54] The fact that she managed to lose these sheets is indicative of the poor regard she developed for his work: 'Speaking for myself', she confessed, 'I do not think his stories, plays, or poems will live'.[55] Margot, a distant relative by marriage of Lord Alfred Douglas, would have nothing to do with Oscar when he needed her most yet she remained a loyal friend to Robbie Ross.

Although no evidence exists to suggest that Oscar matched each story to its target, W. B. Yeats observed astutely:

> if he did dedicate every story in *The House of Pomegranates* to a lady of title, it was but to show that he was Jack and the social ladder his pantomime beanstalk.[56]

Certainly, he hoped to reach a more discerning audience. Responding to a review in the *Pall Mall Gazette*, he explained, 'in building this *House of Pomegranates* I had about as much intention of pleasing the British child as I had of pleasing the British public'.[57] He delighted one woman: Jane Wilde praised *A House of Pomegranates* lavishly, describing her son's stories as 'jewels of thought set in the fine gold of the most exquisite words!'[58]

Varied reviews, a prohibitively high selling price and a mishap in the printing process that left some of the illustrations looking washed out ensured that *A House of Pomegranates* sold poorly. Much of the stock ended up in the remainders bin, a fate that did it no justice. These stories are beautiful, complex and intriguing, and they showcase Oscar's sophisticated use of symbolism.* One reviewer in the *Pall Mall Gazette* compared

---

* The pomegranate is a symbol of prosperity and ambition in ancient Egypt, and is present throughout the mythology of ancient Greece. Believed by many

them to stories written two hundred years earlier by the Countess d'Aulnoy, a leader of the women's salons in Paris.[59] This is an interesting observation. Like Oscar, the Countess told her witty and complex stories in conversational style as they would have been heard by those gathered at her salon. By describing them as 'contes de fees', she originated the term fairytales. Her stories, which, like Oscar's, were not intended for children, explored the inequalities of power and gender.

Oscar's story 'The Portrait of Mr. W. H.' was rejected by the *Fortnightly Review* but published instead in *Blackwood's Edinburgh Magazine* in July 1889. This fictionalised account of young Willie Hughes, the boy actor in Shakespeare's company who was said to have inspired many of his sonnets, explores Oscar's fascination with the venerable love that an older man might feel for a younger. To his great frustration, the extended version he planned did not appear during his lifetime. The theory of Willie Hughes was not of Oscar's invention, but had been suggested decades earlier by Classical scholar Thomas Tyrwitt MP. It is not certain whether Oscar fully believed it or not: 'You must believe in Willie Hughes,' he once said, 'I almost do myself'.[60] Inevitably, his theme caused unease. Frank Harris claimed that it 'did Oscar incalculable injury,' adding, 'it gave his enemies for the first time the very weapon they wanted and they used it unscrupulously and untiringly with the fierce delight of hatred'.[61] Jane, who was never scandalised by anything Oscar wrote, said of it: 'Your essay on Shakespeare is learned, brilliant, flashing with epigrams and mostly perfectly written'.[62]

Oscar had hundreds of stories to tell. Robbie Ross described how those that 'unfortunately exist only in the memories of friends' were:

> . . . invented on the spur of the moment, or inspired by the chance observation of someone who managed to get the traditional word in edgeways; or . . . developed from some phrase in a book Wilde might have read during the day.[63]

After he was imprisoned, Oscar's friend Adela Schuster believed that his stories might save him and asked:

> Could not Mr. Wilde now write down some of the lovely tales he used to tell me? . . . I think the mere reminder of some of his tales may set his mind in that direction and stir the impulse to write.[64]

---

to be the forbidden fruit from the Garden of Eden, it appears in Christian iconography, often in the hands of the Virgin Mary or her son, Jesus. In pagan tradition, it is associated with fertility and female sexuality.

She recalled in particular one concerning 'a nursing sister who killed the man whom she was nursing' and a second about 'two souls on the banks of the Nile'. To these another friend, More Adey, added 'the moving sphere story and the one about the Problem and the Lunatic'.[65] In a letter to Robbie Ross, dated May 1898, Oscar wrote 'I really must begin "The Sphere"'; Frank Harris published a version as 'The Irony of Chance (after O.W.)'.[66] As time went on, Oscar found it increasingly difficult to commit his stories to paper. When Adela Schuster reminded him of one in particular, he replied:

> I wish I could write them down, these little coloured parables or poems that live for a moment in some cell of my brain, and then leave it to go wandering elsewhere. I hate writing: the mere act of writing a thing down is troublesome to me.[67]

While he was editing *The Woman's World*, Oscar told James Stanley Little, executive secretary of the Society of Authors: 'I wish that I could write a novel, but I can't!'[68] All around him were those who could and many contributed to his magazine. He had been generous in promoting their literary offerings. Now that the responsibilities of an editor were behind him, he published one of his own.

Chapter 14

IN THE FOOTSTEPS OF OUIDA

> I have no desire to be a popular novelist. It is far too easy.
> OSCAR WILDE before writing *The Picture of Dorian Gray.*[1]

Although journalism provided the greater part of Oscar's income for years, it was not a métier he occupied comfortably. Responding to a request for a biographical profile, he took pains to point out: 'I write only on questions of literature and art – am hardly a journalist'.[2] He insisted that he wrote for his own pleasure and told the editor of the *Scots Observer*: 'I have no desire to be a popular novelist. It is far too easy'. Yet, the enormous fortunes accumulated by the more successful writers must have seemed desirable to a man with a troublesome bank balance. Several novelists, including Julia Constance Fletcher and Olive Schreiner, contributed to *The Woman's World* and Oscar promoted their work enthusiastically. Anyone as closely involved with the publishing trade as he must have noticed the emergence of a thriving market for affordable literary escapism, much of it written by women.

As the nineteenth century progressed, population growth, a marked improvement in literacy rates, and an increase in disposable income, fed into an upsurge in demand for reasonably priced novels that allowed readers to escape the mundanity of their daily lives. Those without the wherewithal to buy a book could borrow one instead. In 1894, novelist and journalist Walter Besant observed:

> People read faster as well as more; they devoured books. No purse was long enough to buy all the books that one could read; therefore they lent to each other; therefore they combined resources and formed book clubs; therefore the circulating libraries came into existence.[3]

Readers benefitted from the introduction of more efficient printing presses and cheap, machine-manufactured paper. The launch of the artificially expensive three-volume novel, the triple-decker, at the instigation of Charles Edward Mudie, obliged readers to borrow their escapism from his lending library instead. After one year, publishers cashed in by combining all three volumes into one cheap paperback. Canny authors began rejecting one-off payments in favour of royalty-based arrangements that allowed them to share in the success of their creations. For a fortunate few, writing became a viable profession rather than a vocation, and the most successful of these elite was Oscar's erstwhile friend Marie Corelli, who outsold her rivals, male and female.

Corelli's origins are shrouded in mystery. Born in London on or around 1 May 1855, a date she rarely admitted to, she was almost certainly the daughter of Elizabeth Mills, lover and later second wife of the journalist Charles Mackay, who was believed to be Corelli's father. Known affectionately as 'Minnie', she reinvented herself as Marie di Corelli in order to earn a paltry living giving piano recitals in private homes. Her first novel, *A Romance of Two Worlds*, was published in February 1886. It struck a chord and a second novel, *Vendetta*, appeared later that year. By June 1887, Corelli had published a third, *Thelma*, to great acclaim. Ellen Terry, who lived six doors down from her on Longridge Road, Kensington, adored her books. Lillie Langtry asked if she might dramatise them. Oscar would have sympathised to hear that she was snubbed by Rhoda Broughton, whom she had been particularly keen to meet.

Marie Corelli was enormously popular. As novelist and poet Arthur St John Adcock pointed out: '[M]any of her most enthusiastic admirers are men of the professional classes – doctors, barristers, lawyers, writers, men of education and intelligence'.[4] Although her mystical, melodramatic novels were admired by Gladstone and Tennyson, and Queen Victoria had all her books sent to Balmoral, Corelli attracted the scorn of critics. Grant Allen in *The Spectator* called her:

> . . . a woman of deplorable talent who imagined that she was a genius, & was accepted as a genius by a public to whose commonplace sentimentalities & prejudices she gave a glamorous setting.

Some branded her 'the idol of suburbia – the favorite of the common multitude'.[5] Yet, Oscar, who started out as a fan, assured her that he had 'read the book [*A Romance of Two Worlds*] over again,' adding, 'you certainly tell of marvelous things in marvelous ways'. Advising her to ignore her detractors, he said: 'Such a lot of talking-about-you does more good than an infinite number of reviews'.[6] Corelli appears to have heeded his counsel. In the foreword to *The Sorrows of Satan*, she wrote:

> No copies of this book are sent out for review. Members of the Press will

therefore obtain it (should they wish to do so) in the usual way with the rest of the reading public – i.e. through the Booksellers and Libraries.[7]

Corelli was no feminist, proto or otherwise; she celebrated the frailty of women in her novels and opposed the extension of voting rights to them. Yet Oscar persuaded her to write a speculative article on 'Shakespeare's Mother' for *The Woman's World*. He admired her success, but would hardly have wished to emulate her style, which he grew to dislike. Years later, when a prison warder in Reading Jail asked him his opinion of Corelli, he replied: 'Now don't think I've anything against her *moral* character, but from the way she writes she ought to be *here*'.[8] They had fallen out by then and she had lampooned him mercilessly in *The Silver Domino, or Side Whispers, Social and Literary*, published anonymously in 1892, characterising him as a lumbering elephant who was guided through life by a dainty fairy, a thinly disguised Constance. Although Corelli dismissed Constance as 'a charming little Radical,' she found her compelling, considering her 'one of the prettiest things alive' and 'infinitely more interesting than the Elephant himself'. Corelli never discussed her sexuality, and was almost certainly lesbian; she never married, wrote ambiguous love poems and cohabited happily for decades with her companion Bertha Vyver, who referred to her as 'beloved wee pet'.

Other women made excellent livings from their pens. The philanthropic but rather po-faced Mary Augusta Ward, founding president of the Women's National Anti-Suffrage League and a niece of poet Matthew Arnold, enjoyed huge success writing as Mrs Humphry Ward. Her instructive triple-decker *Robert Elsmere* earned her almost £3,000, over £300,000 in today's terms, in fourteen months. With the generous advance for her next book, she bought a country house. Oscar considered *Robert Elsmere* 'deliberately tedious'. In 'The Decay of Lying', he has his character Cyril describe it as 'Arnold's *Literature and Dogma* with the literature left out'.[9] His opinion may have been influenced by Ward's parody of him as egotistical poet Mr Wood. Although he included her on his list of possible contributors to *The Woman's World*, she never obliged, which was probably for the best as anything from her pen might have jarred with the general tone.

If Oscar aimed to write a novel straddling high culture and mass appeal, he did not have to look far for someone to emulate. One of the more prolific contributors to *The Woman's World* inhabited a rarefied world of beauty and luxury, in literature and in life. Her decadent novels celebrated a lush aristocratic existence and her aesthetic style represented a

kick against the fetters imposed by Victorian notions of prudence, ratio-
nality and worth. She pioneered a new style of language, studded with
witty epigrams that allowed her characters to indulge in the most subversive behaviour imaginable. Her paeans to beauty earned her a devoted
following amongst Aesthetes and Pre-Raphaelites, yet she was also hugely
popular with the shop girls and footmen who frequented the circulating
library or saved their hard-earned shillings for the six shilling single volume reprints of her latest novel.

Maria Louisa Ramé, always known as Ouida, her own childhood mis-
pronunciation of her middle name, was one of the most successful novelists England has ever produced.* She was born in the modest home of
her maternal grandmother in Bury St Edmunds on New Year's Day 1839,
to local woman Susan Sutton and her husband, Louis Ramé, a mysterious, middle-aged native of Guernsey who made an erratic living teaching
French. Ramé was a charmer who hinted at an exotic past that included
a close friendship with Louis Napoleon, but he left his wife pregnant with
their only child as soon as he had spent her modest dowry.

Although Ramé reappeared occasionally, he was largely absent from
his daughter's life. Nevertheless, years later, when she learned that a
plaque was being unveiled at the house of her birth, Ouida snapped:
'The tomfoolery in Suffolk annoys me very much'. Explaining that she
identified with her father's 'French race and blood', she insisted on being
addressed as 'Madame de la Ramée' or 'Madame Ouida'.[10] Always ambitious, Ouida wrote in her childhood diary: 'I must study, or I shall know
nothing when I am a woman'.[11] She began writing novels in her teens.
Before a single word was published, she had convinced her mother and
grandmother to move to London on the strength of her future success.

When Ouida was nineteen, an obliging neighbour introduced her to
his cousin W. Harrison Ainsworth, proprietor of *Bentley's Miscellany*. The
reaction of Ainsworth's readers to a short story she wrote for him was so
overwhelmingly positive that he commissioned a further seventeen. He also
serialised her first novel, *Granville de Vigne: a Tale of the Day* in his *New Monthly
Magazine*. When Tinsley Brothers paid Ouida £50, almost £5,000 in
today's terms, for the right to publish 'Granville de Vigne' as *Held in Bondage*
in three volumes, it became an instant sensation. During a long literary

* Professor Talia Schaffer has written comprehensively on Wilde and Ouida in
The Forgotten Female Aesthetes: Literary Culture in Late-Victorian England (Charlottesville,
VA, University Press of Virginia, 2000).

career, she wrote more than two dozen novels, numerous short stories, volumes of essays and a collection of children's stories. All appeared under her childhood nickname: 'The public has no business with what my name is or is not', she insisted, 'Ouida is all they have a right to know'.[12]

As her celebrity grew, and with it her bank balance, Ouida took a suite of rooms in the Langham Hotel, a luxurious establishment finished to the highest standards with ornate Italianate public areas, modern plumbing and a series of 'rising rooms', hydraulic lifts that carried guests from floor to floor. Her gatherings were scandalous. Since she considered women to be 'ungenerous, cruel, pitiless!' her guest list was composed almost exclusively of men. She pursued several shamelessly and the intensity of her unrequited infatuations was nothing short of terrifying. Yet, she seemed sceptical about the merits of marriage; her novel *Moths* is hailed as the first English novel in which a divorced woman was allowed to remarry happily. Apparently, the only woman Ouida ever invited to dinner was the formidable Isabel Burton, wife of explorer Richard.[13]

Lady Jeune, who described Ouida as 'small, insignificant-looking with no pretension to beauty, her harsh voice, and manner almost grotesque in its affectation', confirmed that she 'was not charitable to her own sex, and was very intolerant of women who had made a shipwreck of their own lives'.[14] Supremely self-confident, she declared, reputedly: 'Now that George Elliott [sic] is gone, there is no one else who can write English', yet she was notorious for her bad spelling and poor grammar.[15] She loved to hold court, cutting through the chatter with a voice that was 'harsh and unpleasing'; one acquaintance likened it to 'a carving-knife'.[16] Ouida didn't seem to notice, perhaps she didn't care. When some brave soul shushed her during a musical performance, her indignant reaction was that: 'As she talked better than others, *she* ought to be listened to'.[17]

In appearance, Ouida cultivated a wildly eccentric look, allowing her mane of blonde hair to tumble down her back until she was well into her thirties. Her dresses, made to her own design by Charles Worth, had short sleeves and curtailed hemlines contrived to show her dainty hands and tiny feet to best effect. She favoured pale shades, white satin in particular, and was said to make her timid mother wear black for contrast. Ouida, dressed in white, would receive guests while seated on a red satin armchair, her feet encased in tiny, jewelled slippers and stretched out in front of her in order to display their daintiness.[18] She wrote by candlelight, propped up in bed in her suite at the Langham, scratching a goose quill dipped in violet ink across large blue sheets of paper. Often, she adopted the costume of a character in her novels, one day, a princess, the next a peasant maiden. Her love of flowers rivalled Oscar's and she accessorised with the blooms favoured by her fictional creations.

Ouida adored opulence above all else. Her extraordinary excesses were funded from the ever-increasing payments she negotiated with eager publishers, but she spent her money as soon as she got it, often on some fabulous though utterly unserviceable *objet d'art*. She collected exquisite china and served tea to her guests in priceless Capo di Monte cups, or invited them to wash down platters of uncommon delicacies with the finest vintage wines. The novelist W. H. Mallock recognised her mad extravagance as an attempt to 'live up to the standards of her heroines'. He realised that she:

> Lived largely in a world of her own creation, peopled with foreign princesses, mysterious dukes – masters of untold millions, and of fabulous English guardsmen whose bedrooms in Knightsbridge Barracks were inlaid with silver and tortoise shell.[19]

In 1871, at the height of her fame, Ouida swapped the Langham for a sprawling villa in Florence; it was falling down around her but it had belonged to one of the Medici. A visiting social columnist described her 'truly picturesque' workroom: 'Its walls are painted with exquisite old Italian frescoes, and inlaid tables laden with pots of flowers (lilies and hyacinths abounding) line the walls'. The most colourful anecdote concerned

> a priceless Persian rug before the hearthstone, where she likes to lie and dream – and sometimes to scream a little as a safety valve to her emotions.[20]

As the settings of Ouida's novels shifted from foggy London to the glorious Italian landscape, she grew protective of the peasants who worked in the fields surrounding her villa. Her campaigns on their behalf prompted John Ruskin to suggest that anyone wishing to understand the plight of the 'mountain peasantry of Tuscany and Romagna' should read Ouida's 'photographic story', *A Village Commune*.[21] Her writing style was compared to his and her biographer Elizabeth Lee wrote: 'She deplored the desecration of the Tuscan country-side and the vandalism prevailing in Italian cities with an almost Ruskinian eloquence'.[22] Ouida felt a great affinity with animals, dogs in particular. In Italy, she was known as 'la signora dei cani', and around her neck, she wore a locket containing a portrait of a favourite dog, which she would show off while insisting 'this is my hero'.[23] Her novel *Puck* is narrated by a Maltese terrier.

In Italy, Ouida formed a friendship with Oscar's old friend from Oxford, James Rennell Rodd. He recognised in her 'a passion for beauty in all forms, and a wealth of imagination'.[24] She was less keen on the formidable Jane Bigelow, Oscar's champion from New York. When Bigelow called to pay her respects, she was taken aback to hear Ouida shout: 'Tell Mrs. John Bigelow, of New York, that I don't want to see her or any other American; I don't like them'. Undaunted, as ever, Bigelow replied: 'You ought to be ashamed of yourself. We're the only fools that read your nasty books anyway'. So thoroughly charmed was Ouida by her audacity that she invited Bigelow to stay for a month.[25]

Before she met him, Ouida regarded Oscar as an authority on aestheticism. In *Princess Napraxine*, published in 1884, she had her Lady Brancepeth react to a rustic and riotously colourful house on the French Riviera by declaring that it was 'utterly wrong and would give Oscar Wilde a sick headache'.[26] In December 1886, during an extended visit to London, Ouida attended one of Jane Wilde's literary 'Wednesdays' and almost outdid her hostess in the eccentricity of her dress; an elaborately flounced mauve silk gown festooned with expensive Italian lace and topped off with a peculiar bonnet-style hat. Anna de *Brémont* reported that she was 'extremely amiable and delighted the few present with her brilliant conversation'.[27] She 'spoke in quick disjointed sentences with a peculiar accent, and constantly referred to Oscar – in fact she directed all her conversation to him'.[28] This admiration was mutual. In a letter to Fanny Bernard-Beere, he declared, 'We have no Lionne now but Ouida'.[29]

. Ouida's views on the role of women were as idiosyncratic as she was. Although the exotic women and glamorous men who populated her novels transcended the restrictive gender norms imposed by Victorian society, Ouida argued against the involvement of women in public life, which was, in her opinion, 'already overcrowded, verbose, incompetent, fussy and foolish enough'. In her defence, she was dismissive of most men too: 'The chief part of humanity is insignificant, whether it be male or female,' she insisted, adding that only those with 'great genius or great beauty' could do as they pleased. She counted herself among the former and probably the latter too. Oddly enough, the term 'New Woman' was coined in this exchange in *The North American Review* between herself and feminist writer Sarah Grand, born Frances Clarke in Ireland in 1854.[30] In 'The New Woman', Ouida criticised Grand for insisting women 'get the comforts and concessions due to feebleness, at the same time as she demands the lion's share of power'. Should this be allowed, Ouida countered, it would cause woman to become 'odious to man and in her being probably kicked back roughly by him into the seclusion of a harem'.

Grand, like Oscar, supported better access to education for women, while Ouida argued that it was 'hardening and deforming'. Yet, Grand was no fan of Oscar's. She found *The Picture of Dorian Gray* 'exasperating', and described it as:

> . . . the outcome of an unlovely mind, I should say – poor, forced stuff, conceited, untrue to all that is elevating in nature and in art, and not improved by being polished up in passages of a laboured smartness.[31]

'I know very little of him personally,' Grand declared, 'and feel now that I should certainly hate him if I knew more'.

Ouida may not have sympathised with the cause but she was happy to contribute to *The Woman's World*: 'Have you read my article on War in Oscar Wilde's magazine?' she asked a friend, adding: 'The Magazine is so good, its only defect is its title'.[32] In 'Apropos of a Dinner', Ouida argued that, although smoking was a 'silly and injurious habit', women should remain at the dinner table while men indulged. She horrified all of London by doing so. That same article suggested that the dinner party had killed the salon, characterised women as 'the foes of good conversation', and protested at the compulsion felt by everyone who dined with her to share an account of the occasion with a gossip-loving public.[33] Naturally, she named names.

In 'The Streets of London', Ouida criticised the ugliness of the city: 'the influences of beauty on the mind are never sufficiently remembered,' she warned.[34] A profusion of railings, she argued, gave 'almost every house in London the aspect of a menagerie combined with a madhouse'. She despaired of basements, 'subterranean places in which nothing but the soul of a blackbeetle can possibly delight'. In 'Field-work For Women', which she illustrated with reproductions of her oil paintings, Ouida postulated that outdoor agricultural labour was far more beneficial to women than unhealthy factory work.[35] In 'War', she denounced the evils of combat, which 'cripples and impoverishes every class of the nation', and she expressed her vehement opposition to conscription.[36]

Readers loved Ouida's novels, but reviewers often castigated them. The *Pall Mall Gazette* opined:

> . . . the taste for Ouida's novels confirms what we know from other sources of the curious ignorance and vacuity of the mind of the English middle classes of the period![37]

A particularly harsh review of *Moths*, published in the conservative *Saturday Review*, declared: 'There is much in this ignorant, dull, and disgusting story which no person whose mind is not utterly corrupt can either forgive or make a subject of laughter'.[38] This did not dent her popularity with women or men. One of Ouida's most successful novels, *Under Two Flags*, was serialised in *The British Army and Navy Review*. She had far more depth to her than many supposed and some reviewers recognised this. *The Morning Post* described *Moths*, as not only 'the author's finest work, but one which marks a new epoch in fiction'.[39] *The Times* praised the 'purple magnificence of Ouida's sensuous eloquence'.[40] In a perfect summation of her style, that newspaper declared:

> Ouida shows little of the scrupulous sensitiveness which makes most English male novelists hesitate to aborder subjects which are delicate or something more; and she has the knack of insinuating with eloquent suggestiveness what it would be bad taste and false art to express.[41]

In 'The Progress of Women in Literature', Mary St Leger Kingsley, a contributor to *The Woman's World* who wrote as 'Lucas Mallet', described Ouida as one of the greatest living women writers.[42] Mallet and other women aesthetes including Vernon Lee (Violet Paget), John Oliver Hobbes (Pearl Craigie) and Michael Field (the aunt and niece partnership of Katherine Bradley and Edith Cooper) borrowed elements of her style. In 'An Appreciation of Ouida', published in *The Yellow Book* in July 1895, literary critic George Slythe Street expressed surprise at the fact that, although many thousands of readers adored her books, reviewers 'mentioned [them] with simple merriment or a frankly contemptuous patronage'. Her two most noble attributes, he contended, were: 'a genuine and passionate love of beauty as she conceives it and a genuine and passionate hatred of injustice and oppression'.[43] He could have been writing about Oscar.

Oscar reviewed Ouida's 'amazing romance' *Guilderoy* in the *Pall Mall Gazette*.[44] Declaring her 'the last of the romantics', he praised her determination to 'make passion, imagination and poetry, part of fiction', and admired how she 'caught much of the tone and temper of the society of our day'. Since he likened *Guilderoy* to her earlier novels, he was clearly familiar with her work. Although Oscar's approval was qualified, he admired the 'ease and grace and indolence' of her characters, and was particularly taken with her 'aphorisms on women, love, and modern society'; he listed sixteen of his favourites. He may have been influenced by his mother, who surely approved of Ouida's epigrammatic language, since she believed:

> Epigram is always better than argument in conversation, and paradox is the very essence of social wit and brilliancy; the unexpected, the strange combination of opposites, the daring subversion of some ancient platitude, all are keen social weapons.[45]

Oscar's admiring verdict was: 'though she is rarely true, she is never dull'. Ouida was never troubled by pedestrian notions of accuracy; a writer as prolific as she had no time to check the minutia of every circumstance. In any case, her fans were eager for what Max Beerbohm called the 'lurid sequence of books and short stories and essays which she has poured forth so swiftly, with such irresistible élan'.[46] Readers were accommodating, but reviewers pounced on every imprecision and there were many to choose from. In her critique of Ouida's work, poet and essayist Alice Meynell pointed out that one novel had not a single sentence without error. Yet, she credited Ouida with harnessing wonderful epigrammatic language that allowed characters to defy convention: 'it would be unjust for some of us to forget Ouida,' she insisted: 'She has been teacher, mistress, and mother to some of us. She absolutely invented "paradox"'.[47]

What appealed to Ouida's fans was the unashamed glamour of her situations. The fact that her themes were deemed unwholesome only added to her appeal, even if readers felt compelled to hide her books from disapproving visitors. Seduction, adultery, voyeurism and prostitution were tackled head-on and, although she steered clear of behaviour that was overtly homosexual, her books were undeniably homoerotic. She popularised the indolent male dandy connoisseur.* Ernest, her first recognisable dandy, with his 'deep-blue, poetic, eloquent eyes'; 'rich and gold-hued' hair; and 'insouciant and epicurean' mouth, appeared in *Chandos* in 1866:

> . . . alone in his house in Park Lane, a man lay in idleness and ease, indolently smoking a narghilè from a great silver basin of rose-water. A stray sunbeam lingered here and there on some delicate bit of statuary, or jeweled tazza, or Cellini cup, in a chamber luxurious enough for an imperial bride's, with its hangings of violet velvet, its ceilings painted after Greuze,

---

* As Dr Anne Markey of Trinity College, Dublin points out, the dandy, a figure determined to make of himself and his life a work of art, is associated with Charles Baudelaire's *The Painter of Modern Life* (1863). Both Ouida and Wilde annexed Baudelaire to some extent.

its walls hung with rich Old Masters and Petit Maîtres, and its niches screening some group of Coysevox, Coustou or Canova.[48]

In *Under Two Flags*, her Bertie/Beauty, a dashing Guardsman, enjoys hunting and fighting, but has a penchant for luxury and a passionate devotion to the best friend who gives up his life for him. This novel introduced 'Cigarette', a mouthy, cross-dressing young woman who 'had a thousand lovers'. As her career progressed, Ouida's women became increasingly assertive. Her 'mondaires', strikingly beautiful and aristocratic socialites who are loyal to no one but themselves, use epigrams to express illicit notions and resemble several of the women who populate Oscar's later work. In Ouida's short play *Afternoon* (1883), tragic Claire fakes her own death before finding artistic fulfilment and taking revenge on the overbearing husband who drove her to the edge of reason. Here we find 'Aldred Dorian', collector of beautiful objects and painter of portraits.

While Ouida proclaimed 'Youth is genius', Oscar wrote, 'Youth! There is nothing like it'. Her Princess Napraxine declares that she 'would sacrifice [her] own life for an epigram', while Oscar's Dorian says, 'You would sacrifice anybody, Harry, for the sake of an epigram'. There are unmistakable similarities in their styles:

> His features were exceedingly fair, fair as the fairest girl's; his hair was of the softest, silkiest, brightest chestnut; his mouth, very beautifully shaped; on the whole with a certain gentle, mournful, love me look that his eyes had with them . . .
>
> *Under Two Flags* by Ouida (1867)

Yes, he was certainly wonderfully handsome, with his finely curved scarlet lips, his frank blue eyes, his crisp gold hair. There was something in his face that made one trust him at once. All the candour of youth was there, as well as all youth's passionate purity. One felt that he had kept himself unspotted from the world.

> *The Picture of Dorian Gray* by Oscar Wilde (1890)

Oscar often purloined ideas that took his fancy: 'Of course I plagiarise', he quipped, 'it is the privilege of the appreciative man'.[49] Elsewhere, he wrote:

> It is only the unimaginative who ever invents. The true artist is known by the use he makes of what he annexes, and he annexes everything.[50]

In 'A Note on Some Modern Poets' he insisted:

There is an element of imitation in all the arts, it is to be found in literature as much as in painting, and the danger of valuing it too little is almost as great as the danger of setting too high a value upon it.[51]

André Gide claimed that Oscar told him he wrote *Dorian Gray* 'in a few days because a friend of mine claimed that I could never write novels'.[52] This novel, in a shorter version, fulfilled a commission offered by Joseph Marshall Stoddart, managing editor of the Philadelphia-based *Lippincott's Monthly Magazine*, who met with Oscar on 30 August 1889 in the Langham Hotel. Also present was Arthur Conan Doyle, a young Scottish doctor. Both agreed to write for a new London edition of *Lippincott's Monthly Magazine*. Oscar offered 'The Fisherman and his Soul' but *The Picture of Dorian Gray* was published instead in July 1890, and was followed by Conan Doyle's second Sherlock Holmes mystery, *The Sign of Four*.

Describing *Dorian Gray* as 'an essay on decorative art', Oscar explained: 'it reacts against the cruel brutality of plain realism'.[53] He could have been quoting Ouida. His critics and confidantes recognised something of her style. Vincent O'Sullivan, his friend and biographer described Oscar as 'sympathetically nearer to Ouida, that genius among women . . .' This, O'Sullivan reasoned, was because he was 'not afraid to be sentimental'.[54] The *St James's Gazette* opined that, while 'the style [of *Dorian Gray*] was better than Ouida's popular aesthetic romances the erudition remained nonetheless equal'.[55] That same publication later declared: 'the grammar is better than Ouida's – the erudition equal, but in every other respect we prefer the talented lady . . .' Writing in *McBride's Magazine*, Julian Hawthorne, American journalist and son of Nathaniel, claimed:

Mr. Wilde's writing has what is called "colour," – the quality that forms the main-stay of many of Ouida's works, – and it appears in the sensuous descriptions of nature and of the decorations and environments of the artistic life.[56]

In *Oscar Wilde: A Critical Study*, Arthur Ransome characterised *Dorian Gray* harshly as 'a mosaic hurriedly made by a man who reached out in all directions and took and used in his work whatever scrap of jasper, or porphyry or broken flint were put into his hand'.[57] This is unfair. Although both plot and style undoubtedly contain elements of earlier works, this can be said of everything ever written. It is important not to overstate the influence that Ouida or any other author had on Oscar's work.* As W. B. Yeats declared: '*Dorian Gray*, with all its faults, is a wonderful book'.[58] Oscar incorporated elements familiar to readers but subverted them brilliantly to his own ends. While Ouida's heroes invariably find redemption, Oscar's Dorian does not. By absorbing the decay of debauchery and old age, Basil Hallward's portrait of Dorian allows its subject to remain forever young and beautiful, leaving him free to act unconscionably. He dies unrepentant. Lord Henry Wotton, the man who gives Dorian his blueprint for life, is even more despicable. At its core, this brilliant novel is Oscar's alone and it changed his life: Lord Alfred Douglas claimed to have read *Dorian Gray* 'fourteen times running' and was keen to meet Oscar on the strength of it.[59]

W. H. Smith threatened to remove *Lippincott's Magazine* from its shelves but the *Speaker* categorised *Dorian Gray*, quite correctly, as 'a work of serious art, strong and fascinating'. Even Arthur Ransome admitted it had 'an individual essence, a private perfume, a colour whose secret has been lost'. [60] While many acknowledged that Oscar's tale was exceptionally well told, some disapproved and their criticisms resemble those levelled at Ouida. The *Pall Mall Gazette* claimed:

> But for "Dr. Jekyll and Mr. Hyde" it would probably not have been written, although in reality it had a morality that was only skin deep and therefore more closely aligned with the French "Decadents".[61]

The Graphic, decried 'the twaddle of his emasculate men'.[62] The *Freeman's Journal* declared it 'unevenly written' and judged that, although some of Oscar's epigrams were 'startlingly brilliant', others were 'dull'.[63] While calling it 'undeniably amusing', the *Daily Chronicle* decided that 'dullness and dirt are the chief features of *Lippincott's* this month'. Referencing its poisonous yellow book, inspired by Huysmans' *À rebours*, *Punch* claimed *Dorian Gray* contained 'more of poison than of perfection'. Calling it 'dull and nasty', the *St James's Gazette* declared: 'The writer airs his cheap research among the garbage of the French Decadents like any drivelling pedant'.[64] This led to an exchange of letters in which Oscar declared: 'I am quite incapable of understanding how any work of art can be criticized from a moral standpoint'.[65] Yet, the morality of his novel would be

---

* The influence of Charles Maturin is detectable, giving the novel a supernatural aspect. In *Melmoth the Wanderer*, John Melmoth discovers a sinister portrait of a mysterious ancestor in a locked closet and tries to destroy it in a scene reminiscent of the climax of *Dorian Gray*.

questioned at length during the libel action he took in 1895. Most damning of all, perhaps, was a review in the *Scots Observer*:

> . . . it is not made sufficiently clear that the writer does not prefer a course of unnatural iniquity to a life of cleanliness, health, and sanity . . . Mr. Wilde has brains, and art, and style; but, if he can write for none but outlawed noblemen and perverted telegraph-boys, the sooner he takes to tailoring (or some other decent trade) the better for his own reputation and the public morals.[66]

Oscar admitted: 'Basil Hallward is what I think I am: Lord Henry what the world thinks me: Dorian what I would like to be – in other ages perhaps'.[67] When Lord Henry Wotton pokes fun at women, describing them as 'the decorative sex', these are not Oscar's sentiments but his character's shortcomings: 'Lord Henry Wotton's views on marriage are quite monstrous,' he told Arthur Fish, 'and I highly disapprove of them'.[68] Although *Dorian Gray* had been translated into thirteen languages by 1911, it was greeted with hostility at first and Constance confessed 'since Oscar wrote Dorian Gray, no one will speak to us'.[69] Jane, who always believed in her son, called it 'the most wonderful piece of writing in all the fiction of the day'.[70]

When Oscar sent Ouida a copy of *Dorian Gray*, she declared: 'I do understand it'. She was back in Florence by then and had spent more recklessly than ever during her four-month stay in London, ordering a new wardrobe from *The House of Worth* and lavishing £200 a week on 'turning her sitting room in the Langham Hotel into a glade of the most expensive flowers'. When W. H. Mallock hosted a luncheon for her in the Bachelors' Club, she arrived:

> . . . trimmed with the most exuberant furs, which, when they were removed, revealed a costume of primrose-colour   a costume so artfully cut that, the moment she sat down, all eyes were dazzled by the sparkling of her small protruded shoes.[71]

Such extravagance emptied her purse, obliging her to seek assistance from friends. In *The Real Oscar Wilde*, Robert Sherard claimed that Oscar 'furnished her with sufficient money to pay the Margaret Street people [where she had modest lodgings], and rescue her luggage, and then to return to Florence'.[72]

In Italy, she fared no better. As the lucrative deals dried up, she swapped her villa for an ever-degenerating series of lodging houses from which she was occasionally evicted by force. When news of her plight reached England, Marie Corelli, who admired her genius but considered her own books an antidote to Ouida's, proposed that the editor of the *Daily Mail* establish a fund to assist her. On discovering this, Ouida became incandescent with rage and demanded that he never print her name again. When friends petitioned the prime minister to grant her a Civil List Pension of £150 a year, she railed that this sum was 'only fit for superannuated butlers'.[73] On 25 January 1908, Ouida died of pneumonia in a modest lodging house in Viareggio. Aged seventy and a shadow of her former self, she was alone apart from her maid and her beloved dogs. Later that year Macmillan published her final novel, *Helianthus*, in its incomplete form.

Ouida was aware of the ordeal that Oscar had endured: 'I knew Oscar Wilde very well,' she told her friend Mrs H. C. Huntington,

> I do not think he is a clever man; he was a successful poseur and a plagiarist; he was essentially the cabotin. 'I have written three comedies in one year,' he said to a friend of mine, and my friend replied: 'A great exercise of memory!' The Italian papers assign him a much higher place than that which he held in London society. I am most grieved for his mother, a talented and devoted woman who has had nothing but sorrow all her life. It may be very immoral of me, but I do not think the law should meddle with these offences. The publicity caused does much more harm than the offence itself.[74]

Chapter 15

THE PERFECT SALOMÉ

The form of government that is most suitable to the artist is no
government at all. Authority over him and his art is ridiculous.
OSCAR WILDE in *The Soul of Man under Socialism*

Almost a decade had elapsed since the twin disappointments of *Vera* and
The Duchess of Padua, and Oscar's passion for theatre had not diminished.
During 1891, he worked on two plays. Although the perfect subject for
the second had been on his mind for years, Oscar's thoughts on a suitable
treatment only took shape during an extended stay in Paris towards the
end of 1891. Guatemalan writer and diplomat Enrique Gomez Carrillo,
who was eighteen when he befriended Oscar, insisted that he was 'obsessed
by the spirit of Salome':

> . . . From that time forth a day never went by when he didn't speak to me of
> *Salomé*. Sometimes women passing by in the street made him dream of the
> princess of Israel. He used to stand for hours in the main streets, looking at
> jewellers' windows and imagining the perfect jewellery for the adornment
> of his idol's body.[1]

On a summer evening back in 1890, Oscar had wandered about examining the paintings that hung in the rooms of his host, Lord Francis Hope.
Reaching one depicting Salome, he beckoned to American writer and
fellow guest, Edgar Saltus,* whose wife provided this account: 'This picture calls me,' Oscar declared, 'I am going to write a classic – a play
–"Salome". It will be my masterpiece'. 'Do so,' Saltus replied, 'and I will
write a book – "Mary Magdalen". We will pursue the wantons together'.[2]
When *Mary Magdalen: A chronicle* appeared in 1891, Oscar hailed it as 'so
pessimistic, so poisonous, and so perfect'.[3] Saltus, in return, assured Oscar
that the last line of *Salomé* made him shudder.[4]

---

* Amélie Rives Chanler claimed that Oscar told her, 'In Edgar Saltus's work
passion struggles with grammar on every page'. (Carl Van Vechten, *The Merry-go-
Round*, New York, Alfred Knopf, 1918, p. 48).

Lord Hope's painting was neither Oscar's first nor only inspiration. Salome, bloodthirsty daughter of Herodias and seductive stepdaughter of Herod Antipas, has captured the imagination of writers, painters and poets down through the centuries. In 1877, Walter Pater introduced Oscar to Gustave Flaubert's 'Hérodias', one of his *Trois Contes*: 'Je suis malade de la peur que m'inspire la danse de Salomé!' Flaubert told his niece Caroline, 'Je crains de la bâcler'.* He evoked it in stirring detail.[5] Oscar was also inspired by Heinrich Heine's epic poem *Atta Troll* (1843) in which Salome's mother Herodias demands the severed head of John the Baptist and dies demented, condemned to ride with the 'wild hunt', kissing it in perpetuity.† In February 1888, Oscar reviewed *Salome* by American dramatic poet J. C. Heywood for the *Pall Mall Gazette*. Although he found it 'very commonplace', here too he found some of the charged eroticism he sought for his own princess.[6]

In Paris, Oscar attended French Symbolist poet Stéphane Mallarmé's celebrated 'Tuesdays' at his apartment on Rue de Rome. Since he admired his host immensely, he must have been aware of Mallarmé's unfinished abstract epic *Hérodiade*. It is also believed that he looked to *La Princess Maleine*, Flemish playwright Maurice Maeterlinck's adaption of *Maid Maleen* by the Brothers Grimm, which contained the obsession, sensuality and violence he sought. When Oscar shared early excerpts from *Salome* with Graham Robertson, the artist laughed inappropriately, assuming this was some burlesque of Maeterlinck: 'One was ill prepared for Wilde's serious moods, they were so rare', he explained.[7]

The key impetus was Joris-Karl Huysmans' decadent novel *À rebours*. When Oscar read it while honeymooning in Paris, he identified strongly with protagonist Jean des Esseintes, who was obsessed with Gustave Moreau's twin paintings *Salome Dancing before Herod* and *The Apparition*. Moreau's incandescent paintings caused a sensation when they were exhibited at the Paris Spring Salon of 1876, where Flaubert saw them. Several critics believe they contributed to the emergence of a *fin de siècle* preoccupation with the notion of the wanton femme fatale who strove to destroy a righteous man, a reaction, perhaps, to the campaigns orchestrated by women agitating for minimal rights and freedoms.

Commenting on Oscar's search for his perfect Salome, Gómez Carrillo insisted: 'Only Gustave Moreau's portrait unveiled for him the soul of the

---

* 'I am sick with fear at the thought of Salome's dance. I'm afraid I'll botch it.'
† Heine's cousin Michael was father of Princess Alice of Monaco, to whom Oscar dedicated 'The Fisherman and his Soul'.

dancing princess of his dreams'.[8] Little wonder, considering Huysmans' exceptionally sensual description of Moreau's Salome:

> Her face is meditative, solemn, almost august, as she commences the lascivious dance that will awaken the slumbering senses of old Herod. Diamonds scintillate against her glistening skin. Her bracelets, her girdles, her rings flash. On her triumphal robe, seamed with pearls, flowered with silver and laminated with gold, the breastplate of jewels, each link of which is a precious stone, flashes serpents of fire against the pallid flesh, delicate as a tea-rose: its jewels like splendid insects with dazzling elytra, veined with carmine, dotted with yellow gold, diapered with blue steel, speckled with peacock green.[9]

Oscar kept changing his mind: one day his Salome was naked and wanton, the next, she was pure and chaste like a lily. What she would never be was 'dry and colourless; without lavishness, extravagance, or sin', as she was in the gospels of Matthew and Mark.[10] Every aspect of Salome drew Oscar to Paris and the language of her citizens. When Robertson wondered why he was writing *Salomé* in French, Oscar responded: 'Because a play ought to be in French'.[11] He elaborated in an interview with the *Pall Mall Gazette*:

> My idea of writing the play was simply this: I have one instrument that I know I can command, and that is the English language. There was another instrument to which I had listened all my life, and I wanted once to touch this new instrument to see whether I could make any beautiful thing out of it.[12]

One version of the birth of *Salomé* places Oscar in a Parisian cafe towards the end of 1891, telling his play to Symbolist poets Adolphe Retté and Stuart Merrill.[13] As Vincent O'Sullivan attested: 'He invented, not in silence but in talking'.[14] Afterwards, Oscar returned to the Grand Hotel on Boulevard des Capucines to scribble in a blank notebook before heading to the Grand Café, where he asked a gypsy orchestra to play the frenzied music that would invoke 'a woman dancing in the blood of a man she has craved for and slain'.[15] Three handwritten manuscripts for *Salome* exist, all in French.[*] The last of these Oscar submitted to sensual poet and novelist Pierre Louÿs, to whom he dedicated his published

---

[*] A typescript corrected by Oscar Wilde was discovered in the Free Library of Philadelphia's rare book collection in 2014.

version. Although Louÿs suggested grammatical and dramatic improvements, Oscar adopted only the former. Merrill, Retté and Marcel Schwob
also received unfinished drafts inviting their comments.

Essential to the whole enterprise was the casting of the perfect Salomé.
According to Retté, Oscar sought an actress who was also a 'first-class
dancer'.[16] It was said that he watched a Rumanian acrobat dance on her
hands like Flaubert's Salome at the Moulin Rouge; he left a card but never
traced her. Flaubert had seen Salome walking on her hands in a bas-relief
at Rouen Cathedral. In May 1892, with *Salomé* occupying his thoughts,
Oscar bumped into Sarah Bernhardt, who was appearing in a repertory
season of plays performed in French at the Royal English Opera House.
When she read *Salomé* and expressed a desire to play the lead role, Oscar
wrote excitedly to Pierre Louÿs: 'Sarah va jouer *Salomé!!*'.[17]

Rehearsals began in London in June 1892. Sarah adapted the magnificent golden robe Graham Robertson had designed for Sardou's *Cléopâtre*
and dyed her hair blue for dramatic effect. Rather than hire a stand-in,
she insisted on dancing the part of the young princess herself. Although
Oscar raised some objections to the powdering of her hair, he had no
qualms about allowing Sarah, aged forty-seven, to play his teenage seductress. A letter to publisher Leonard Smithers confirms this: 'What has age
to do with acting?' Oscar asked: 'The only person in the world who could
act Salomé is Sarah Bernhardt, that "serpent of old Nile"[from Anthony
and Cleopatra], older than the pyramids'.[18]

Two years earlier, Sarah, then a forty-five year old grandmother, had
played the titular nineteen-year-old virgin in Jules Barbier's *Jeanne d'Arc*.
Aged sixty-five, she revived the role in Émile Moreau's *Le Procès de Jeanne
d'Arc*. During the summer of *Salomé*, Ellen Terry recorded her thoughts
on the matter:

> Saturday, June 11, 1892. — To see "Miss Sarah" as "Cléopâtre" (Sardou
> superb!) . . . I went round and implored her to do Juliet. She said she was
> too old. She can never be old. 'Age cannot wither her'.[19]

She declared of Sarah: 'On the stage she has always seemed to me
more a symbol, an ideal, an epitome than a *woman*'.[20]

Sarah was an enigma who shrouded herself in layers of inscrutability;
it can be difficult to catch a glimpse of the woman behind the mystique
and the least reliable source is often her autobiography *Ma Double Vie* (*My
Double Life*, 1907). As she once told her granddaughter: 'My private life
is no one's business and I find it much funnier to invent another one'.[21]

The illegitimate daughter of a Dutch woman of Jewish origin, who was described, diplomatically, as a courtesan, what is certain is that Sarah was an outsider, just like Oscar.

Her birth certificate was destroyed in the fire that engulfed the Hotel de Ville in Paris during the Commune uprising of 1871, but it seems that Sarah was born in Paris on 28 October 1844. Biographers differ but this is the date recorded on her application to the Conservatoire de Paris, where she enrolled, aged fifteen, on 29 November 1859. She was Rosine Bernardt then but she switched to Sarah and added the 'h' to her surname shortly afterwards. What little evidence survives suggests that her mother Julie or Judith, or perhaps Youle Bernardt, was a beautiful Dutch woman who lived in Paris. Her father may have been a brilliant young law student from Le Harve, as some believe, or a naval cadet named Morel, according to others. As a child, Sarah was told that he lived in China; at least that's what she said.[22]

Sarah's flighty mother was often absent and she spent a good deal of her childhood in the care of a hired nurse. 'My mother was fond of travelling,' she explained:

> She would go from Spain to England, from London to Paris, from Paris to Berlin, and from there to Christiania [Oslo]; then she would come back, embrace me, and set out again for Holland, her native country.[23]

By Sarah's account, she was raised on a farm near the Breton town of Quimperlé until she was four years old, and was sent to Paris after suffering a childhood accident. Aged eight, she was enrolled in a boarding school in the Parisian suburb of Auteuil. Two years later, she transferred to the Lycée Notre-Dame-du-Grandchamp, an Augustine convent near Versailles. While there, she thought seriously of becoming a nun but she was accepted at the Conservatoire instead.

In 1862, while still in her teens, Sarah appeared in the title role of Racine's *Iphigénie* at the Comédie-Française, but her contract was terminated after eight months when she refused to apologise for slapping Madame Nathalie, an influential, older actress, during a ceremony to commemorate Molière's birthday. In her defence, she insisted that this 'old, spiteful and surly' woman had pushed her little sister Régine.[24] She joined the fashionable Théâtre du Gymnase-Dramatique but remained there for just one year. On 22 December 1864, Sarah gave birth to Maurice, her only child. Although she named him after her maternal grandfather Moritz Bernardt, it is possible that she never met this unreliable vagabond

who, at one stage, set himself up as an eye doctor, albeit one far less eminent than Oscar's father, Sir William Wilde. Sarah seemed refreshingly
unabashed by her status as a single mother and gave Maurice her own last
name. Although his father was widely assumed to be Belgian nobleman
Charles Joseph Eugène Henri Georges Lamoral, Prince de Ligne, Sarah
refused to be drawn and joined in with humorous speculation as to her
son's paternity.

In 1866, Sarah joined the cast at the Théâtre de l'Odéon. Extraordinarily thin and little more than five feet tall, she won huge acclaim for
her portrayal of a young boy in Racine's *Athalie*. During her six years
at l'Odéon, she charmed audiences with a voice that was described
variously as 'silvery' and like a 'golden bell'.[25] French novelist and poet
Arsène Houssaye wrote: 'her voice is sometimes a caress and again a
sword-thrust'.[26] Bram Stoker likened it, rather prosaically, to 'the cooing
of pigeons'.[27] When l'Odéon closed during the Franco-Prussian War of
1870–1, Sarah, who detested the fighting, turned the foyer into a receiving station for the wounded and stayed with her charges while the building was shelled. When l'Odéon reopened, she stunned audiences with her
performance as Doña Maria de Neubourg in a revival of Victor Hugo's
Ruy Blas; it turned her into a superstar.

Such was the extent of her triumph that she was invited to rejoin the
Comédie-Française. When administrator-general Émile Perrin had a
ferocious argument with Roselia Rousseil, the actress who was to play
the title role in a production of Racine's *Phèdre* to mark the playwright's
birthday, he sacked her and called on Sarah instead. On the point of
exhaustion, battling horribly debilitating stage fright, and given just four
days notice that she would play one of the most complex and challenging
roles in French theatre, Sarah drew on all of her considerable resources.
She was magnificent.

Robert Sherard believed that Oscar's admiration for Sarah was so great
that he 'somewhat modelled himself' on her.[28] He certainly sought her
out. Arriving at Folkestone en route to perform a repertory of plays at
the Gaiety Theatre in London during the summer of 1879, the Comédie-
Française was greeted by a crowd of admirers, among them Oscar Wilde.
Sarah recalled this 'turbulent young man' shouting 'Hip, hip, hurrah! A
cheer for Sarah Bernhardt!' As was often the case, 'the crowd responded
to his appeal'.[29]

The second act of *Phèdre* was the centrepiece of the Comédie-Française
programme; on nights when Sarah performed, guinea stalls changed

hands for five guineas each. Oscar declared her *Phèdre* 'the most splendid creation I ever witnessed'.[30] Her performance inspired a sonnet, 'To
Sarah Bernhardt', published in *The World* on 11 June 1878, and included
in *Poems* as '*Phèdre*'. Sarah's description of how she acquitted herself,
having overcome her customary bout of crippling stage fright, justifies
Oscar's delight:

> I suffered, I wept, I implored, I cried out; and it was all real. My suffer-
> ing was horrible; my tears were flowing, scorching and bitter. I implored
> Hippolyte for the love which was killing me, and my arms stretched out
> to Mounet-Sully [her co-star] were the arms of Phèdre writhing in the
> cruel longing for his embrace. The inspiration had come. When the
> curtain fell Mounet-Sully lifted me up inanimate and carried me to my
> dressing-room.[31]

During the six-week run, Sarah, accompanied by fifteen-year-old
Maurice, was welcomed into the homes of actors and aristocrats alike.
Henry Irving, who admired her as 'a colleague whose managerial work
in the theatre was as dignified as his own', sent her an enormous bouquet
with a card that read 'Welcome!'[32] Bram Stoker declared her 'a being of
incarnate grace'.[33] Ellen Terry, who thought Sarah 'remarkable', left a
description of her ethereal beauty:

> How wonderful she looked in those days! . . . She was as transparent as an
> azalea, only more so; like a cloud, only not so thick. Smoke from a burning
> paper describes her more nearly! She was hollow-eyed, thin, almost con-
> sumptive-looking. Her body was not the prison of her soul, but its shadow.[34]

Sarah moved in Oscar's circles and they soon became friends. Visiting
his Salisbury Street home, she demonstrated her high kicks and autographed his white, wood-panelled wall. When Oscar moved with Frank
Miles to the house on Tite Street, he spent five guineas at Whistler's bankruptcy sale on a portrait described as 'Sarah Bernhardt, seated, holding a
book'. Although Sarah signed it for him and commented on what a good
likeness it was, the portrait was not of her but of artist Maud Franklin,
Whistler's muse and mistress. In 1895, Whistler arranged for it to be
bought back on his behalf.

As he was undoubtedly aware, Oscar's association with the most celebrated actress in the world was hugely beneficial. Fêted onstage for her
talent, Sarah's flamboyant private life was documented exhaustively.
An accomplished artist, she studied sculpture under both Franchesci

and Mathieu-Meusnier, and was invited to exhibit at the Paris Salon. In London, she bought several exotic creatures for her private zoo, including a cheetah and a wolfhound, using the proceeds of the sale she conducted at the William Russell Galleries; she had hoped to purchase two lions and a dwarf elephant. An extraordinary photograph showing Sarah lying fully dressed in a coffin with her eyes shut tight gave rise to a rumour, which she did nothing to dispel, that this was where she slept.[35] Her daring ballooning escapade during the Universal Exhibition of 1878 was hailed as a heavenly triumph.

On 18 April 1880, less than a year after she had conquered London, Sarah parted company with the Comédie-Française for a second time. The split was acrimonious. Sarah sent a letter to administrator-general Émile Perrin, with whom she had a fractious relationship, claiming that he was working her to illness and exhaustion; she shared this letter with several newspapers. In response, Perrin sued her for damages and withheld money she was owed for their London tour. Sarah retaliated by forming her own company and returning to London before embarking on a triumphant tour of America, followed by an equally successful tour of Europe. The French press turned against her. Auguste Vitu, eminent critic at *Le Figaro*, terminated a bitter article by declaring:

> But we have heard enough, surely, of Mlle. Sarah Bernhardt! Let her go abroad with her monotonous voice and her funereal fantasies! Here we have nothing new to learn from her talents or her caprices . . .[36]

Always an outsider, and with no proof of her French citizenship, Sarah was welcomed more warmly outside her native France for a time. In time, she won her compatriots over with her talent. In 1883, Oscar took Robert Sherard backstage at the Vaudeville Theatre in Paris during the interval in Sardou's *Fédora* and Sarah peeped out from behind her dressing room curtain to welcome 'mon cher Oscar'. Sherard believed she was genuinely delighted to see him.[37] Sarah's long collaboration with Sardou, which began in 1884, led to some of her most memorable roles. As well as the wronged Russian Princess Fédora, she played a homicidal Byzantine Empress in *Théodora*, inspired Puccini with her portrayal of diva Floria Tosca in *La Tosca*, and made a 'profound impression' on a critic from *The New York Times* in *Cléopâtre*.[38]

Oscar took Constance to see Sarah play Lady Macbeth during their honeymoon in Paris. Sarah too was married by then. One year earlier, she had proposed to Aristidis Damala, an aristocratic Greek army officer and playboy twelve years her junior. Her son, Maurice, despised him and thought him an absolute scoundrel. Damala had ambitions to act but no company would hire him, so Sarah took over the Théâtre de l'Ambigu and made him her leading man. The whole enterprise was a disaster. Sarah lost a fortune. Damala, who had taken to calling himself Jacques by then, developed a voracious addiction to morphine and embarked on a very public affair with his leading lady. In 1889, Sarah threw him out, but she took him back to nurse him as he lay on his deathbed at the age of thirty-four. The most interesting legacy he left is his possible influence on *Dracula*. When Bram Stoker dined with Damala backstage at the Lyceum, he wrote:

> I sat next to him at supper, and the idea that he was dead was strong on me. I think he had taken some mighty dose of opium, for he moved and spoke like a man in a dream. His eyes, staring out of his white, waxen face, seemed hardly the eyes of the living'.[39]

Oscar had long expressed a desire to write something for Sarah. He thought of casting her as Queen Elizabeth I* 'in monstrous dresses covered with peacocks and pearls'.[40] She undoubtedly inspired *Vera*, since he declared

> the heroine who gives the name to the play is conceived in all the many moods of passion that a study of Sarah Bernhardt could suggest.[41]

More interesting perhaps is her association with Moreau's Salome paintings. In an article published in *L'Événement* in November 1887, Symbolist poet Jean Lorraine wrote:

> Yes, the enigmatic Sarah is certainly the daughter of Gustave Moreau, the sister of Muses carrying decapitated heads, of Orpheus and of slim and bloody Salomes.[42]

Yet, when an article in *The Times* stated that *Salomé* had been written for Sarah, Oscar was quick to refute this:

> The fact that the greatest tragic actress of any stage now living saw in my play such beauty that she was anxious to produce it, to take herself the part of the heroine, to lend to the entire poem the glamour of her personality,

---

* As it happens, *Les Amours de la Reine Élisabeth* (1912), a silent film based on Émile Moreau's play of the same name, was to be Sarah's most successful feature film.

and to my prose the music of her flute-like voice – this was naturally, and always will be, a source of pride and pleasure to me, and I look forward with delight to seeing Mme. Bernhardt present my play in Paris, that vivid centre of art, where religious dramas are often performed. But my play was in no sense of the words written for this great actress. I have never written a play for any actor or actress, nor shall I ever do so. Such work is for the artisan in literature, – not for the artist.[43]

Even so, Sarah assumed ownership of *Salomé*: 'But the role is mine,' she declared, 'Mr. Oscar Wilde has given it to me, and nobody else can perform it'.[44]

Oscar regarded the stage as the meeting place of all the arts, and the site of 'the return of art to life'.[45] Determined to make *Salomé* an immersive experience, he spent hours ensuring the lighting and sets were flawless; his lighting directions alone called for 'torchlight', 'moonlight', 'starlight', 'darkness' and 'a moonbeam'. At one point, he suggested placing braziers of perfume in the orchestra pit so that he could waft scents that matched the emotions on stage throughout the theatre, but Graham Robertson persuaded him that even a genius could not prevent them from coalescing into something noxious. Oscar credited Sarah with making every rehearsal 'a source of intense pleasure': 'To hear my own words spoken by the most beautiful voice in the world has been the greatest artistic joy that it is possible to experience', he declared.[46]

Disaster struck when, two weeks into rehearsals, Edward F. Smyth-Pigott,* the Examiner of Plays, refused to licence *Salomé*. As justification, he invoked a little-used sixteenth-century law forbidding the depiction of biblical figures on the English stage. Privately, Smyth-Pigott described *Salomé* as 'a miracle of impudence,' characterising it as 'half Biblical, half pornographic'.[47] Oscar was stung and declared Smyth-Pigott 'a commonplace official . . . who panders to the vulgarity and hypocrisy of the English people'.[48] He told the *Pall Mall Gazette* that censorship in England was 'odious and ridiculous'. Filled with bravado, he declared:

> What I do care about is this, that the Censorship apparently regards the stage as the lowest of all the arts, and looks on acting as a vulgar thing.[49]

Insisting, 'I will not consent to call myself a citizen of a country that shows such narrow mindedness in its artistic judgements,' Oscar declared,

* Opinion on Smyth-Pigott was divided. After his death, George Bernard Shaw described him as 'a walking compendium of vulgar insular prejudice'.

'I am not English; I'm Irish, which is quite another thing'. This was undoubtedly true. Years later, reviewing Oscar's short life, his compatriot George Bernard Shaw declared:

> It must not be forgotten that though by culture Wilde was a citizen of all civilized capitals, he was at root a very Irish Irishman, and, as such, a foreigner everywhere but in Ireland.[50]

This was not the end of *Salomé* as far as Oscar was concerned. He declared his intention of staging his premiere in Paris rather than London, and envisaged Sarah performing as Salomé in her native city. He saw himself there too. In a letter to William Rothenstein, Oscar castigated the 'vulgarity and hypocrisy of the English people'.[51] That same month, he told Arthur Fish that he was 'very much hurt not merely at the action of the Licenser of Plays, but at the pleasure expressed by the entire Press of England at the suppression of my work,' adding, 'the Press only represents the worst side of English life'.[52] Several newspapers picked up on his threat to leave. *The New York Times* reported: 'All London is laughing at Oscar Wilde's threat to become a Frenchman'.[53]

Sarah too spoke to the *Pall Mall Gazette*, explaining that, while she respected the decision of the censor, she did not agree with it: 'Religion is not outraged in this piece,' she declared, adding: 'It's not a religious play. It deals with love, passion, nature, the stars, the moon'.[54] She described *Salomé* as 'an artistic work in every sense of the word', yet her backing lacked immediacy: 'I shall play the piece in Paris at some time or another', she declared.[55] She never did.

In *The Soul of Man under Socialism*, Oscar contended that 'The form of government that is most suitable to the artist is no government at all,' and added that: 'Authority over him and his art is ridiculous'. It perplexed him that his play had been refused a licence in an environment where it was perfectly permissible for writers and painters to depict biblical events without interference: 'The insult in the suppression of *Salomé* is an insult to the stage as a form of art and not to me', he declared.

He was supported in this by theatre critic William Archer, a devotee of Ibsen and a translator of his works. Describing *Salomé* as an 'oriental Hedda Gabler', high praise indeed, Archer raged: 'A serious work of art, accepted, studied, and rehearsed by the greatest actress of our time, is peremptorily suppressed'. England needed Oscar, Archer insisted, 'to aid in the emancipation of art from the stupid meddling of irresponsible officialdom'.[56] Oscar's hopeful response to his defender was to describe the whole travesty as 'a great triumph for the Philistine, but only a momentary one'.[57]

In February 1893, Oscar brought out a French edition of *Salomé* in Paris and London at his own expense and sent several copies to friends. To 'My dear Florence,' he wrote:

> Will you accept a copy of Salomé – my strange venture in a tongue that is not my own, but that I love as one loves an instrument of music on which one has not played before.[58]

The response to this printed version was not universally positive. *The Times* called it: 'An arrangement in blood and ferocity, morbid, *bizarre*, repulsive, and very offensive in its adaptation of scriptured phraseology to situations the reverse of sacred'.[59] Oscar asked his by-then beloved Bosie to translate it from French to English, a decision that caused great friction between them. Unhappy with the result, he left his young lover's name off the title page but dedicated the volume to him instead, writing: 'To my friend Lord Alfred Bruce Douglas, the translator of my play'.[60] Later, when the scales had lifted momentarily from his eyes, he railed against Bosie for causing scenes when he objected to 'schoolboy faults' in his translation.[61]

Oscar's involvement with Bosie, which dated back to a meeting in June 1891 and developed from friendship to love, coincided with his growing disenchantment with the tedium of family life. In this and in many other ways, Sarah and he were remarkably similar. A letter she wrote to her unadventurous lover and leading man Mounet-Sully could so easily have been written by Oscar: 'You must realize that I am not made for happiness,' she beseeched:

> It is not my fault that I am constantly in search of new sensations, new emotions. That is how I shall be until my life is worn away. I am just as unsatisfied the morning after, as I am the night before. My heart demands more excitement than anyone can give it. My frail body is exhausted by the act of love. Never is it the love I dream of.[62]

How close this is to Oscar's prison declaration: 'Tired of being on the heights,' he declared, 'I deliberately went to the depths in search of new sensations'.[63]

Sarah's respect for Oscar stemmed from his treatment of her 'as a fellow-artist, as a comrade'. It delighted her that he never treated her as a potential conquest; she told Robert Sherard:

Most men who are civil to actresses and render them services have an arrière-pensée [ulterior motive]. It was not so with Oscar Wilde. He was a devoted attendant, and did much to make things pleasant and easy for me in London, but he never appeared to pay court.[64]

There is in existence a copy of the limited edition of *Poems*, published in 1892, which is inscribed: 'A Sarah Bernhardt, hommage d'Oscar Wilde. *"Comme la Princesse Salomé est belle ce soir." Londres, '92.'*

The tragedy was that, although Oscar's friend Ada Leverson was certain that he cared little for any of his plays except *Salomé*, he never saw it performed. It was staged during his lifetime: When Aurélien Lugné-Poe, founder of the Theatre de l'Oeuvre, arrived in London after Oscar had been imprisoned, he was taken aback at how stunned and apathetic his supporters seemed to be. In response, he staged the world premiere of *Salomé* in Paris on 11 February 1896, performing the role of Herod himself. Salome was played by former dancer Lina Munte, who was praised in *La Matin* for her 'ferocious sensuality'. As the legality of the production was questionable under English law, Oscar received no payment, but he told Bosie:

> All I want is to have my artistic reappearance, and my own rehabilitation through art, in Paris, not in London. It is a homage and a debt I owe to that great city of art.[65]

Perhaps things would have gone better for Oscar had he taken out French citizenship as he threatened. Although her behaviour was just as outré as his, Bernhardt was acclaimed for the remainder of her life. In 1914, she was made a Chevalier of France's Legion of Honour. She was active in the war effort, visiting French soldiers on the Western Front and appearing in the propaganda film, *Les Mères Françaises*. Aged seventy, she toured America one last time and urged audiences to join the Allies. She gave a benefit performance in 1922 to generate funding for Marie Curie's laboratory even though, by then, she had lost a leg to gangrene that set in after an injury sustained while performing *Tosca* in Rio de Janeiro in 1905. What is particularly striking about her life in this context is her friendship with French impressionist painter Louise Abbéma, which was so close and passionate that they were rumoured to be lovers; nobody seemed to mind. On 26 March 1923, Sarah Bernhardt suffered kidney failure and died. She is buried in Père-Lachaise cemetery, close to Oscar.

One interesting footnote to *Salomé* concerns a British feminist production staged privately before an almost exclusively female audience by the New Stage Players at the Court Theatre on 27 and 28 February 1911. It was still banned, and this was the first time the play was staged in a proper theatre in Britain. The part of Salomé was played by Adeline Bourne, honorary secretary of the Actresses' Franchise League, an organisation that campaigned for the enfranchisement of women through education and performance.* What is intriguing is that while Salomé is often regarded as a sexually voracious woman who is dangerous to men, these emancipated women regarded her as a feminist heroine. This production was not particularly well received. Describing Bourne's performance as 'interesting', *The Playgoer and Society* said:

> Hers was not a seductive Salome. It was not always attractive. But it was well thought out. Miss Adeline Bourne is an actress – not a dancer – and is to be congratulated upon the success of a noble effort to give colour to a part for which she was not particularly suited.[66]

* The Court Theatre production was a private one and did not therefore need a licence from the Lord Chamberlain, whose ban was not lifted until 1931. The first 'open' production in Britain was in Edinburgh in August 1931 (see *Intentions* 83 from the Oscar Wilde Society).

Chapter 16

DEADLY SERIOUS SOCIAL COMEDIES

He disliked hypocrisy in social intercourse, he glorified individualism, he denied the moral right of the community to sacrifice
the life of any member of it.
VINCENT O'SULLIVAN on Oscar Wilde[1]

While working on *Vera*, Oscar had revealed his approach to playwriting
to Marie Prescott: 'Success is a science,' he explained, 'if you have the
conditions, you get the result.'[2] The formula for popularity suggested by
Lord Illingworth in *A Woman of No Importance,* a character Oscar likened
to himself, is more forthright: 'To get into the best society, nowadays, one
has either to feed people, amuse people, or shock people – that is all!'
With *Salomé*, Oscar was certain to shock and the refusal of a licence in
the summer of 1892 was an affront to his belief in artistic freedom. Yet,
earlier that year, he had enjoyed huge theatrical success with an outwardly
conventional drawing room comedy, *Lady Windermere's Fan*. By throwing
a cloak of blithe humour over his critique of Victorian society, Oscar
could entertain audiences while at the same time confronting them with
the absurdity of their most firmly held beliefs. As progressive Austrian
playwright and critic Herman Bahr recognised: 'his paradoxes rest upon
a profound insight into humanity'.[3]

By adopting this approach, Oscar was heeding his mother's counsel.
Jane considered paradox 'the very essence of social wit and brilliancy',
insisting that 'the unexpected, the strange combination of opposites; the
daring subversion of some ancient platitude are all keen social weapons'.
She added a warning:

> only assured celebrity makes society pardon originality . . . for people gen-
> erally resent being suddenly lifted out of their old groove by the intellectual
> dynamite of some audacious thinker and talker who has no respect for the
> laws of social routine.[4]

In a letter to artist Philip Houghton, Oscar explained how he disguised
solemnity behind a mask of impudence:

To the world I seem, by intention on my part, a dilettante and dandy merely – it is not wise to show one's heart to the world – and as seriousness of manner is the disguise of the fool, folly in its exquisite modes of triviality and indifference and lack of care is the robe of the wise man. In so vulgar an age as this we all need masks.[5]

Although Oscar's comedies were widely admired, several critics dismissed them as conventional or derivative, and catalogued works they believed he had drawn upon. Describing his plays as 'dominated by myself', Oscar was scathing about those who shouted 'plagiarism'.[6] In *The Critic as Artist*, he looked to ancient Greece to make his argument:

. . . the accusations of plagiarism were endless, and such accusations proceed either from the thin colourless lips of impotence, or from the grotesque mouths of those who, possessing nothing of their own, fancy that they can gain a reputation for wealth by crying out that they have been robbed.[7]

Since Oscar landed his blows with a velvet glove, many critics failed to recognise his carefully constructed attacks on proscriptive and often nonsensical Victorian morality; his celebration of the cult of individuality; and his anarchic advocacy for the rejection of all forms of authority. Oscar's wit, according to Vincent O'Sullivan, was 'full of tolerance and good humour and high spirits, as the man was himself'.[8] O'Sullivan believed that, although he regarded his plays as his most important work, Oscar 'resigned himself to being the amuser from fear of being the bore'.[9] Perhaps Oscar expressed his motivation best in 'The Nightingale and The Rose' when he counselled 'if you want to tell people the truth, make them laugh, otherwise they'll kill you'.

Essentially, he understood that drama could have a transformative effect: 'Life imitates art far more than art imitates life', he insisted.[10] Presenting 'A Good Woman' to George Alexander in October 1891, Oscar described it as 'one of those modern drawing room plays with pink lampshades'.[11] This play, which became *Lady Windermere's Fan*, was so much more than that. It exposed the ludicrously duplicitous sexual code that led 'good' women to accept oppression and enthusiastically police a patriarchal society that kept them down, enforcing rules that elevated them as pure yet disadvantaged them by limiting their freedom. Characters like Mrs Erlynne surely represent a gesture of fellowship towards autonomous women who rebelled against social conventions and forswore orthodox motherhood, as was true of several of Oscar's friends.

In *Lady Windermere's Fan,* Oscar's critique of marriage is characteristically caustic. The meddling Duchess of Berwick, who is determined to marry off Lady Agatha, her submissive daughter, expects women to be pure but men to behave badly. Like her successor Lady Bracknell, she treats marriage as a social and financial contract that takes no account of love or compatibility. Lady Plymdale extols the usefulness of a mistress who will keep a bothersome husband occupied. Lord Darlington advises ingénue Lady Windermere that, since infidelity in marriage is inevitable, the best one can hope for is discretion. And although Lady Windermere prides herself on living by a rigid moral code, she comes dangerously close to abandoning it with hardly a thought when she suspects her husband of having an affair.

Oscar's own marriage, weakened by a series of liaisons with young men, was about to face its greatest threat. In June 1891, eight months before the premiere of *Lady Windermere's Fan,* he had met Lord Alfred Douglas. Known affectionately as 'Bosie', this undergraduate at Magdalen College, Oxford had borrowed *The Picture of Dorian Gray* from his cousin and former schoolmate Lionel Johnson[*] and become 'Passionately absorbed' in it. He claimed to have read it 'fourteen times running'.[12] When Johnson, who knew Oscar socially, declared his intention of visiting the author, Bosie was eager to tag along.

The three men chatted over tea in Oscar's study before joining Constance: 'I was always on the best of terms with Mrs. Wilde,' Bosie declared. 'I liked her and she liked me. She told me about a year after I first met her that she liked me better than any of Oscar's other friends'.[13] Later, he admitted:

> Mrs. Wilde . . . began to say that I took up a great deal too much of Oscar's time, and Wilde once told me that she had made difficulties about our being so much together.[14]

Constance told Robert Sherard that Bosie had 'marred a fine life'.[15] Although Oscar had been linked with several young men, his most serious dalliance involving the extraordinarily handsome Aesthetic poet John Grey,[†] he had managed to compartmentalise his life and danger did not

[*] The third son of an Irish army officer and one of Britain's best-known decadent poets.

[†] At that time Grey was an object of infatuation for teenager Olive Custance, who also admired Oscar and would go on to marry Bosie. Recognised as one

seem imminent that day. Undoubtedly, he was drawn to this blond-haired, blue-eyed young man whose surface charm belied an erratic temperament, but this attraction was not reciprocated and their relationship remained casual until the spring of 1892.

Nevertheless, Oscar's increasing absence from the family home prompted his mother to intervene. Jane wrote to him in Paris in December 1891: 'Do come home,' she begged. 'She [Constance] is very lonely & mourns for you'.[16] Oscar returned to spend a family Christmas at the magnificent pre-Raphaelite home of Lady Mount-Temple, a distant and elderly relative of Constance's and a close confidante of hers. It was in this grand house – perched atop an arboreal cliff overlooking Babbacombe Bay on the south coast of Devon – that he finished both *Lady Windermere's Fan* and *Salome*. When the former opened on 20 February 1892, it thrilled audiences, divided critics and excited an appetite for more of the same from Oscar's pen. He might have alienated some of his newfound fans had *Salome* appeared in the summer of 1892, as was intended. Crushed by rejection but having defended his play robustly, Oscar travelled to the fashionable spa resort of Bad Homburg in Germany. He may have neglected to mention to Constance that he was joining Bosie there.

The nature of Oscar's relationship with Bosie changed in the spring of 1892 after he received 'a very pathetic letter' from his young friend, who was being blackmailed on account of an indiscreet letter he had written to another young man.[17] In response, Oscar spent a weekend with Bosie in Oxford and ensured that his solicitor George Lewis resolved the matter swiftly and discreetly. Although their friendship deepened into romance, Oscar recognised the idiosyncrasies in Bosie's character and described him as: 'a wilful, fascinating, irritating, destructive, delightful personality'.[18] To his friend Reggie Turner, he declared 'without him my life was dreary'.[19] That was the crux of the matter really.

Oscar returned from Bad Homburg feeling refreshed and enthusiastic about his next play, provisionally titled 'Mrs. Arbuthnot' and promised to Herbert Beerbohm Tree at the Haymarket Theatre. As Constance had nursed Cyril and Vyvyan through a bout of whooping cough and needed a break, the couple rented a delightful farmhouse in the village of Felbrigg in Norfolk and sent their sons to recuperate in Hunstanton forty miles away on the West Norfolk coast. At Grove Farm, their days

---

of the foremost female aesthete poets, she had a fluid sexuality and engaged in several affairs with women too.

fell into a restful pattern: Oscar worked mornings and evenings and spent each afternoon with Constance and Cyril too when he joined his parents for a week. When Oscar joined the local golf club, Constance joked that she was in danger of becoming a golf widow, but she must have been delighted to see him doing so well.[20]

Any prospect of tranquility was shattered when Bosie telegraphed early in September to announce his imminent arrival. Constance and he over-lapped for a week before Oscar, with an eye to his deadline, insisted on being left alone for the final week to finish his play. Once Constance was with their children, she was told by Oscar that Bosie had become too ill to travel. She offered to return but it seems she was not needed. In spite of Bosie's distracting presence, Oscar completed *A Woman of No Importance* by mid-October. He put a final polish on it while spending a few days at the Reading home of his good friends, Walter Palmer, son of the founder of Huntley & Palmer biscuit manufacturers, and his wife Jean, a literary woman and an accomplished hostess who Oscar called 'Moonbeam'.

In Reading, Oscar read an act of his new play and moved the gathering to tears. Fellow guest Louise Jopling wrote: 'On such occasions one ought to be equipped with a hidden phonograph, to keep indelible records of all the brilliant things spoken'.[21] Oscar then punctured the mood by announc-ing that he had taken his inspiration from an article in *The Family Herald*, a cheap and cheerful domestic magazine aimed firmly at the lower end of the market. It must have been during this stay that he signed the visitors' book in the biscuit factory on 22 September 1892; Louise Jopling's signa-ture is on the same page.[22]

Oscar dedicated *A Woman of No Importance* to the outrageous and extra-ordinarily beautiful 'Gladys, Countess de Gray', who maintained a public façade as a perfectly well-behaved aristocrat but behaved exactly as she wished in private. A pivotal member of the elite Marlborough House set[*] and a keen patron of the arts, Gladys helped rejuvenate the opera scene in London and restored the Royal Opera House at Covent Garden. She shocked polite society by throwing her home open to singers and per-formers who were invited as friends rather than entertainers. As a result, she was credited with contributing to the dismantling of social barriers that once stood between aristocrats and celebrities. She developed a close

---

[*] A circle of mostly aristocratic, fast-living friends who coalesced around Bertie, Prince of Wales and were dubbed the 'Marlborough House Set' after his London residence.

friendship with soprano Dame Nellie Melba, whom she introduced to Oscar at her house in Paris. Melba claimed that Oscar made her feel uneasy, but she admired his 'brilliant fiery-coloured chain of words'.[23]

Gladys was six feet tall and so extraordinarily beautiful that writer E. F. Benson insisted anyone seen with her looked like 'they needed a touch of the sponge and the duster'.[24] Her house parties were legendary and she made sure that her guest list included friends whose partners were occupied elsewhere. Naturally, she had no shortage of sexual partners and she liked to display their photographs on her mantelpiece. It was said she was one of the first people in London to have a telephone installed, since she believed that this removed the risk of servants discovering incriminating love letters. Gladys was far more Mrs Allonby than Mrs Arbuthnot.

Oscar's new play featured several strong female characters. When, a young actor named Oswald Yorke petitioned for a part, he received a categorical reply: 'In my new play,' Oscar informed him, 'there are very few men's parts – it is a woman's play'.[25] Perhaps Yorke felt appeased in 1938, when he played Mr Justice Wills, the man who sentenced Oscar to two years hard labour, in an all-male production of *Oscar Wilde* in the Fulton Theatre, New York. Oscar's great friend Mrs Bernard 'Bernie' Beere, who should have been Vera, played Mrs Arbuthnot and Lord Illingworth was played by Herbert Beerbohm Tree, who was in the habit of suggesting that Oscar had written the part for him.[26] In fact, Oscar expressed doubts about Tree's suitability to play this 'witty aristocrat', declaring: 'He is certainly not natural. He is a figure of art. Indeed, if you can bear the truth, he is Myself'.[27]

A Woman of No Importance opened at the Haymarket Theatre on Wednesday 19 April 1893, and ran almost continuously until 16 August, with a break of four nights, three of which were given over to Ibsen's *An Enemy of the People*. Although Oscar's play appeared to have little of Ibsen about it, he did admire the Norwegian playwright's work, in particular the way it was interpreted by Elizabeth Robins, a young American actress he had met in July 1888 at the home of Lady Seton. When Robins expressed a desire to break into English theatre, Oscar had advised her to give a matinee performance and promised to speak to Herbert Beerbohm Tree on her behalf, which he did. He helped Robins to secure an agent and introduced her to George Lewis, who became a firm friend. When he introduced her to his mother, Jane declared that Robins had 'a dramatic face'.[28]

On seeing Robins in *The Real Little Lord Fauntleroy*, a stage version of Frances Hodgson Burnett's classic, early in 1889, Oscar assured her:

. . . you have definitely asserted your position as an actress of the first order, and revealed yourself as an artist of a very rare and sensitive tempera- ment, and of quick imaginative insight into the dramatic modes by which life can find expression . . . Your future on our stage is assured.[29]

The course of Robins' life changed when she travelled to Norway and studied the works of Henrik Ibsen, a playwright sympathetic to the plight of women. In his notes for *A Doll's House*, Ibsen asserted:

A woman cannot be herself in contemporary society, it is an exclusively male society with laws drafted by men, and with counsel and judges who judge feminine conduct from the male point of view.[30]

Robins grew determined to end the stranglehold actor-managers had on English Theatre and the resultant exploitation of women, who were undervalued as actors, writers and producers. When she sought subscrib- ers to fund a series of twelve of Ibsen's plays at the Opera Comique, Oscar stepped forward with alacrity: 'The English stage is in her debt,' he declared, 'I am one of her warmest admirers'.[31] Although audiences found the realism of Ibsen's plays alarming, Oscar assured his friend: 'I count Ibsen fortunate in having so brilliant and subtle an artist to inter- pret him'.[32]

When Katherine Bradley and Edith Cooper, the aunt and niece duo who wrote as Michael Field and lived as husband and wife, saw Oscar among the audience for Ibsen's *The Master Builder*, they noted that he watched 'impassively but with intentness'.[33] He described a matinee per- formance of the first English production of *Hedda Gabler*, featuring Robins in the title role, and staged in collaboration with fellow American actress Marion Lea as 'a real masterpiece of art'.[34] He told a fellow enthusiast: 'I felt pity and terror, as though the play had been Greek'.[35] He was not so kind about the audience, describing them to Ettie Grenfell as 'sad vegetar- ians . . . men in mackintoshes and women in knitted shawls of red wool'.[36] Oscar had a habit of telling his patrons what they wanted to hear.

Robins, grateful for Oscar's support, acknowledged:

. . . he was then at the height of his powers and fame and I utterly unknown on this side of the Atlantic. I could do nothing for him; he could and did do everything in his power for me.[37]

Sometimes his guidance, though well-intended, was misplaced. On one occasion, he advised Robins to emulate Lillie Langtry: 'It seemed useless to point out that while I obviously couldn't imitate Mrs. Langtry, I didn't want to,' she wrote. 'I wanted to act'. Yet, she realised he was not being frivolous since he was 'as intent on being the centre of attraction as any professional beauty'. In Robins' astute opinion: 'Oscar Wilde was born more a creature of the theatre than most actors are. He needed an audience'.[38]

On 17 May 1892, Robins met with Oscar over tea and cigarettes to discuss their 'visions of the Theatre of the Future'. Although he appeared enthusiastic, his proposed involvement came to nothing. Perhaps the status quo suited him well since he was able to subvert it. Certainly, Yeats saw through the surface conventionality of his compatriot's plays: 'the famous paradoxes, the rapid sketches of men and women of society, the mockery of most things under heaven, are delightful', he declared. Yet he realised that the only real people in *A Woman of No Importance* were the villains and non-conformists; the 'tragic and emotional people, the people who are important to the story, Mrs Arbuthnot, Gerald Arbuthnot, and Hester Worsley, are conventions of the stage', he declared.[39]

The play is set, for the most part, at a house party hosted by Lady Hunstanton. Gerald Arbuthnot, a young bank clerk, is offered the post of secretary to fellow guest Lord Illingworth.* Delighted with his good fortune, he shares this news with his mother, a pious woman of apparently excellent character. When Mrs Arbuthnot meets Lord Illingworth, she realises that he is Gerald's father. Hester Worsley, a wealthy young American who is attracted to Gerald, casts a cold, puritanical eye over proceedings. She has many of the characteristics ascribed by Jane in 'American Traits: Women and Society in the States': the 'frank fearless candour of the American girl', her 'mercilessness' is 'uncompromising'.[40] The witty and audacious Mrs Allonby interferes with disastrous consequences. Rather than insisting that men be held to unrealistic standards, as Hester does, she believes that women should enjoy the same freedom.

What ensues is a tussle between mother and father, between Puritanism and dandyism, between freedom and dependence. The action reaches a melodramatic climax when Illingworth, in fulfilment of a bet he makes with Mrs Allonby, attempts to kiss Hester Worsley. By flying into rage and threatening to kill Illingworth, Gerald obliges his mother to reveal the truth. Selfishly, Gerald proposes that his parents marry in order to

* On seeing the 1907 revival, Lytton Strachey decided that Illingworth's interest in Gerald was sexual. Illingworth has no idea that the young man is his son and scenes deleted by Oscar make this seem even more plausible. Also, Oscar did invite young Fred Atkins to accompany him to Paris as his 'secretary'.

legitimise him. Although Illingworth is willing, Mrs Arbuthnot is aghast. For two decades, she has successfully kept her secret and constructed a façade of respectability. She has sacrificed any possibility of enjoying life, but she refuses to feel shame since Gerald is the result of her fall. Since Mrs Arbuthnot uses her suffering as a method of control, her love for her son is stifling. When Hester, who would once have judged her harshly, agrees to marry Gerald, all three depart for America, rendering Illingworth a 'man of no importance'.

Oscar declared Puritanism 'the real enemy of modern life, of everything that makes life lovely and joyous and coloured for us'.[41] Although conservatism appears to triumph in the battle between the Puritan and the dandy, the dandies, the rebels, the individualists, male and female, always have the better lines. In contrast, characters who should exemplify the values society wishes to uphold are disappointingly dull. Gerald eschews a 'very brilliant future' to become dependent on an authoritarian wife. His mother clings to her bitterness and continues to smother him. Although audiences sympathised instinctively with Mrs Arbuthnot, they were drawn to Lord Illingworth on account of his intelligence, vitality and wit. The outrageously nonconformist Mrs Allonby is his sparkling counterpart: 'We have a far better time than men have', she claims, 'There are far more things forbidden to us than are forbidden to them'.

The sting is removed from Hester Worsley's excoriating attack on the indolent upper class when she is exposed as a naive, judgemental young woman who insists that the sins of a parent should be visited on their children yet abandons this position once her own intended is implicated. Although earlier drafts went even harder on Hester, she remains humourless and hard-line. Since she is constantly reminded that she is an outsider who doesn't understand the social mores, she is undermined at every turn. Although she appears victorious, her prize is a regretful and dependent husband. She feels a downbeat kinship with Mrs Arbuthnot, declaring 'in her all womanhood is martyred'; yet, much of Mrs Arbuthnot's pious and self-denying behaviour is self-imposed.

Hester Worsley sees herself as a defender of women: 'you are unjust to women in England,' she declares, 'and till you count what is a shame in a woman to be an infamy in a man, you will always be unjust'. By condemning the system of 'one law for men and another for women', she echoes feminist reformer Josephine Butler. Hester's declaration that 'immoral men are welcomed in the highest society and the best company' parodies Butler's assertion that dissolute men were:

received in society and entrusted with moral and social responsibilities,
while the lapse of a woman of the humbler class . . . is made the portal for
her of a life of misery and shame.[42]

Laudable as this seems, Oscar was utterly opposed to such thinking.
When interviewed about *A Woman of No Importance*, he contended:

> Several plays have been written lately that deal with the monstrous injustice
> of the social code of morality at the present time. It is indeed a burning
> shame that there should be one law for men and another law for women. I
> think . . . I think there should be no law for anybody.[43]

This was not new thinking on Oscar's part. Describing the doctrine of
'sheer individualism' in a speech he gave to the Royal General Theatrical
Fund on 26 May 1892, he insisted:

> It is not for anyone to censure what anyone else does, and everyone should
> go his own way, to whatever place he chooses, in exactly the way that he
> chooses.[44]

Gender relationships are frequently inverted in *A Woman of No
Importance*. One short exchange acknowledges that women, deprived of
legitimate power, exercise it more subtly: 'Dear Mr. Cardew is ruining the
country. I wonder Mrs. Cardew lets him,' Lady Hunstanton remarks. By
exploiting their position as the 'weaker sex', some women are complicit
in maintaining the unequal power system. In a classic subversion, Lord
Illingworth declares:

> the history of women is the history of the worst form of tyranny the world
> has ever known. The tyranny of the weak over the strong. It is the only
> tyranny that lasts.

Yet such power is attained at a cost, as Illingworth points out: 'Every
woman is a rebel, and usually in wild revolt against herself'. Mrs Allonby
criticises marriage: 'The ideal husband?' she exclaims, 'There couldn't
be such a thing. The institution is wrong'. The skewed value judgements
made when choosing a partner are lampooned in a surreal line delivered
by Lady Hunstanton. Describing the rejection of a potential mate by a
member of her gilded circle, she declares: 'her family was too big, or was
it her feet'.

Although *A Woman of No Importance* was applauded enthusiastically
on opening night, Julia Neilson, who played Hester Worsley, recalled

sustained booing from one section of the audience.[45] This must have disconcerted Oscar: 'Ladies and gentlemen,' he announced, 'I regret to inform you that Oscar Wilde is not in the house tonight'. At this, Tree stepped forward to say: 'I am proud to have been associated with this work of art'. Reviews were enthusiastic. Leading drama critic William Archer described the scene between Lord Illingworth and Mrs Arbuthnot at the end of the second act as 'the most virile and intelligent . . . piece of English drama writing of our day'.[46]

As his public acclaim grew, Oscar's private life became increasingly turbulent. By then, Bosie had introduced him to a world of casual sexual encounters. At times, he seemed uneasy and easily rattled. Although he attempted to remain discreet for the sake of his family, Nellie Melba relates an anecdote about Oscar speaking to his sons 'of little boys who were naughty and made their mothers cry'; one wondered aloud 'what punishment could be reserved for naughty papas who did not come home till the early morning and made mothers cry far more'.[47]

Constance put on a brave face, but rumours of a potentially damaging divorce were rife. On one occasion in March 1893, she was returning home, having dropped Oscar's post to the Savoy Hotel where he and Bosie had adjoining rooms, when she bumped into George Jacomb-Hood.* Feigning light-heartedness, she described how she had asked Oscar to return home and he joked that he had forgotten the number of their house. Jacomb-Hood thought her terribly upset.[48] Apparently, Pierre Louÿs had witnessed the encounter between husband and wife and his good opinion of Oscar was damaged as a result.

As well as upsetting his wife, Oscar was in danger of attracting the attention of the authorities. While *A Woman of No Importance* was in rehearsal, one casual partner, a young man named Alfred Wood, had discovered compromising letters from Oscar to Bosie in the pocket of a coat given to him by the latter. Although Wood accepted a small sum of money and disappeared to America, another young man, Robert Cliburn, sent a copy of the most damaging of these letters to Tree, who alerted Oscar. The solution he hit upon was to have Pierre Louÿs translate it into French and publish it as a prose poem in *Spirit Lamp*, a literary magazine edited by Bosie.

This brush with danger did little to cool Oscar's ardour. During the unbearably hot summer of 1893, Bosie persuaded him to rent 'Ferry

---

* He illustrated *The Happy Prince* with Walter Crane.

Cottage' at Goring-on-Thames, an idyllic spot surrounded by lush gardens and meadows that swept down to the river. Constance paid four short visits but her presence and that of their sons did nothing to dissuade a steady stream of visitors who came and went at Bosie's invitation. He also recruited a dissolute and fractious staff and ordered the finest champagnes and delicacies at Oscar's expense. All that he earned with *A Woman of No Importance* was being frittered away.

The stifling weather contributed to an atmosphere that felt oppressive and strained, and the poisonous mood was detrimental to family life. By then, Constance must have sensed that she had been thoroughly usurped by Bosie. At some level Oscar appears to have realised that this set-up was wholly inappropriate. When he asked Bosie to leave, the young man stormed out in an absolute fury. Three days later, he began sending plaintive telegrams from London but relations deteriorated further when he turned in his inadequate translation of *Salome*. Bosie's removal gave Oscar the space he needed to work on a new play, provisionally titled 'Mrs. Cheveley'; it was destined to become *An Ideal Husband* and Lord Goring was named after the place of his conception.

When Oscar decided to join Constance and the boys in the French holiday resort of Dinard, Bosie begged to accompany them, but Oscar would not hear of it. He found an unwitting ally in Bosie's father, the incendiary Marquess of Queensberry, who blamed him for his son's failure to take his degree. Oscar too found Bosie's indolence and lack of ambition worrisome. He wrote to Queensberry's estranged wife, Sybil, expressing concern over her son's fragile mental state and suggesting that she might arrange for him to be sent overseas. It seems certain, judging by Oscar's description in *De Profundis*, that Bosie was complicit in hatching this plan. He had become embroiled in a sexual scandal with a well-connected youth and come perilously close to being arrested.

Lady Queensberry arranged for Bosie to stay with Lord and Lady Cromer in Egypt. During a wonderfully calm period of productivity, Oscar ignored Bosie's letters and telegrams and completed *An Ideal Husband*. He also worked on *A Florentine Tragedy*, an intense drama that remained unfinished; and wrote a good part of *La Sainte Courtisane*, the original draft of which he later left in a taxi cab in Paris. Oscar liked to work fast and intensively. When speaking of Flaubert, he wondered how the French novelist could, 'sit down to work on the same book regularly for hours, day after day, during a year, or two or three years'. He described his own approach:

Now, when I start a thing I must write desperately day and night until it is finished, otherwise I should lose interest in it, and the first bus passing in the street would distract me from it.[49]

Such serenity was short-lived. Distressed by Oscar's silence, Bosie asked his mother to intercede. When this failed, he turned to kind-hearted Constance, who couldn't stand the thought of her husband being callous. Oscar capitulated and sent Bosie a telegram, but he insisted that he would not see him. His resolve crumbled when he received an eleven-page telegram threatening suicide. After a tearful reunion in Paris, Oscar and Bosie returned to London in March 1894. On their second day in the city, they bumped into Bosie's father at the Café Royal; he joined them for lunch and found Oscar charming. Nevertheless, he insisted that his son end the association and informed him by letter that Constance was petitioning for divorce on the grounds of sodomy. She was not.

Bosie was enraged and responded with a one-line telegram: 'WHAT A FUNNY LITTLE MAN YOU ARE'.[50] Thoroughly rattled, he left for Florence in April. Oscar joined him in May but returned to London the following month to be confronted at home by Queensberry and a 'burly friend'. A terrible row ended with Oscar banning Queensberry from entering his house again. Perhaps this encounter inspired a sentiment in *An Ideal Husband*: 'Fathers should be neither seen nor heard,' Oscar wrote. 'That is the only proper basis for family life. Mothers are different. Mothers are darlings'. When Oscar turned to George Lewis for legal advice, he learned that his solicitor and good friend had already been retained by Queensberry.

In *An Ideal Husband* Oscar examined the struggle between public and personal morality, the corrupting power of self-interest, and the role of women in society. One wonders if he was influenced by 'The Ideal Husband', a column in the progressive *Young Woman Magazine*. A contribution by Mary Jeune, who had collaborated with Oscar on *The Woman's World*, expressed the sentiments:

Woman in her new-found strength is redressing the inequalities of four thousand years, and demanding a recognition at the hands of her former lord and master of the position of equality she has taken up. The new woman has determined that she will share the man's life in every sense of the word, and that men are to lead lives surrounded with the safeguards and self-restraint that have hitherto protected women. The standard of life is to be reversed.[51]

The women in Oscar's play appear equally uncompromising, but are soon thwarted. Sir Robert Chiltern's youthful duplicity leaves him open to blackmail by scheming adventuress Mrs Cheveley, who demands that he mislead Parliament so she can profit from an unwise investment: 'Nowadays, with our modern mania for morality,' she insists, 'everyone has to pose as a paragon of purity, incorruptibility, and all the other seven deadly virtues'. Blackmail was very much on Oscar's mind at that time.

Sir Robert Chiltern sees valour in his actions: 'There are terrible temptations that it requires strength, strength and courage to yield to,' he tells his friend Lord Goring. Unwilling to jeopardise his glittering political career, Chiltern agrees to do as Mrs Cheveley asks. He never regrets his crime, only its consequences. Yet, faced with what George Bernard Shaw described as 'the mechanical idealism of his stupidly good wife', who is distraught at the loss of her ideal husband, he withdraws his cooperation.[52] He is saved when Mrs Cheveley is exposed as a common thief.

Oscar shows little sympathy towards his women in *An Ideal Husband*, with the exception of minor character Mabel Chiltern, a strong and witty individualist. Mrs Cheveley is like a pantomime villain and was regarded by Shaw as a true adventuress: 'selfish, dishonest and third rate'.[53] Lady Chiltern is described by her husband as 'pitiless in her perfection – cold and stern and without mercy'. Her moral stance prompts him to insist that 'Women think that they are making ideals of men. What they are making of us are false idols merely'. Lord Goring is unabashed in his assertion that 'a man's life is of more value than a woman's'.

Although Lady Chiltern is a member of the Women's Liberal Association, Oscar portrays her insistence on purity and transparency in public life as tedious and unsustainable. Yet, it seems reasonable to expect integrity in public office. Although Oscar admired avant-garde women, he resisted the attempts of certain 'New Women'* to hold men to a higher moral standard. His central message suggests that, by accommodating flaws and abandoning hypocrisy, society can retain otherwise gifted men. Yet, Chiltern's claim that he is motivated by love rather than a desire for high office is not credible. William Archer for one suggested that he was honest only 'so long as it is absolutely convenient'.[54]

---

* 'New Woman', the phrase coined by Ouida in her correspondence with Sarah Grand, originally described a woman who railed against the double standard inherent in Victorian marriage, which insisted on impeccable virtue in a wife but not a husband.

In constructing his plot, Oscar was surely influenced by author, art historian and campaigner for women's rights, Emilia Pattison-Strong, who stood by her fiancé Sir Charles Dilke when he was mentioned as a co-respondent in a divorce case and abandoned by Gladstone's Liberal Government. The political career of Charles Stewart Parnell, campaigner for Irish self-determination, was destroyed when he was cited as co-respondent in the divorce of Captain William O'Shea and his estranged wife Katharine, even though her relationship with Parnell was an open secret. A whispered-about scandal involving Bosie's eldest brother Francis, Viscount Drumlanrig, private secretary to Lord Rosebery, who would succeed Gladstone as Prime Minister in March 1894, may also have informed the play.[55]

Marriage is characterised as dull in *An Ideal Husband*. Just as Lady Allonby in *A Woman of No Importance* complains about her perfect, and perfectly boring, husband, Mrs Marchmont moans: 'My Reginald is quite hopelessly faultless. He is really unendurably so, at times! There is not the smallest element of excitement in knowing him'. Ludicrous value systems are exposed through surreal humour: intellectual girls are unable to marry because their noses grow long. Here too 'villains' get the most memorable lines: 'Scandals used to lend charm, or at least interest, to a man,' Mrs Cheveley reminisces, 'now they crush him'. Her description of the dangers of being 'laid open by a high-minded and vigilant press' is chillingly prophetic:

> Think of their loathsome joy, of the delight they would have in dragging you down, of the mud and mire they would plunge you in . . . Think of the hypocrite with his greasy smile penning his leading article, and arranging the foulness of the public placard.

When *An Ideal Husband* opened at the Haymarket Theatre on 3 January 1895, several critics dismissed it as predictable and commonplace, a rehash of Sardou's *Dora*. William Archer decried 'Mr. Wilde's epigram-factory'.[56] It was left to George Bernard Shaw to defend his compatriot: 'As far as I can ascertain,' he declared:

> I am the only person in London who cannot sit down and write an Oscar Wilde play at will. The fact that his plays, though apparently lucrative, remain unique under these circumstances, says much for the self-denial of our scribes.[57]

When asked what the critics had missed, Oscar replied:

. . . its entire psychology – the difference in the way in which a man loves a woman from that in which a woman loves a man; the passion that women have for making ideals (which is their weakness) and the weakness of a man who dare not show his imperfections to the thing he loves.[58]

One cannot help reading this as an assessment of his own marriage.

Chapter 17

A Less Than Ideal Husband

If ever I get married, I'll certainly try to forget the fact.
ALGERNON to Jack in the *Importance of Being Earnest*

Although she seemed endlessly accommodating, Constance must have noticed that her husband's attention had wandered since the birth of their second child. There are indications that she resented the amount of time Oscar was with Bosie, but what is not clear is whether she was aware of the nature of their relationship. She battled her jealousy, as she had promised she would during their courtship, but Oscar's late nights and long absences were causing friction. Perhaps she suspected him of having an affair with a woman. One name emerged, that of Bibidie Leonard, glamorous daughter of Young Irelander John Patrick Leonard. Born in Ireland but resident in Paris for much of his life, Leonard was a naturalised French citizen, something Oscar had threatened to become. His staunch loyalty to the nation of his birth was lauded by many of his compatriots: Charles Gavan Duffy, Jane's old editor at *The Nation*, acknowledged that this émigré:

> laboured as systematically to foster Irish interests, and spread an intelligent knowledge of Ireland in France as if he were *Chargé d'affaires* of a National Government.[1]

As members of the Young Ireland movement were wont to visit Leonard in Paris, it is eminently possible that Jane, a regular visitor to the French capital, sought him out. Undoubtedly, he would have known her as Speranza. Although little beyond anecdotal evidence exists to support any connection between Oscar and Bibidie, what is certain is that she lived in London while Oscar was there. In 1893, the *Commercial Gazette* listed a Bibidie Marie Leonard, trading as Madame Mignonne, Court Dressmaker and Milliner, from premises at 39 Welbeck Street.[2] The *Colonies and India* described her as 'a charming and accomplished lady' who used to 'review Paris fashions for the benefit of a leading ladies' paper in London'.[3] Bibidie is mentioned in *East and West: the Confessions of a Princess*, a not entirely reliable book published anonymously by a social-ite and contemporary of hers. Here, Bibidie attends 'a reception at Lady Wilde's'.[4] It seems reasonable to assume that she would have made con-tact with Jane, a woman she may have known as Speranza of *The Nation*. Bibidie held fashionable 'at homes' on Thursday afternoons and it has been suggested that Jane encouraged Oscar to call on her as she might prove a useful contributor to *The Woman's World*.[5] The author of *East and West* claimed that Bibidie had inspired several poems from Oscar's pen.[6]

In *The Life of Oscar Wilde*, Hesketh Pearson reported Oscar as saying of Bibidie: 'No, she was not in the least immoral,' before adding; 'Immoral women are rarely attractive. What made her quite irresistible was that she was unmoral'; regrettably, he gives no source.[7] To add further intrigue, several sources suggest that Bibidie operated as a German spy during World War I. In his memoir *To Leave before Dawn*, American diarist and novelist Julian Green, who wrote in French and whose work was trans-lated by Oscar's son Vyvyan Holland, claims that his Irish godmother, Agnes Farley, a close friend of Bibidie's, told him she had spied on behalf of the German authorities during the war. He too heard Bibidie described as Oscar Wilde's mistress, although that may have been from Pearson.[8]

Of course it was Bosie who was commanding increasing amounts of Oscar's time: 'I miss you so much. The gay, gilt and gracious lad has gone away – and I hate everyone else: they are tedious', Oscar assured him in April 1894.[9] By then his letters were filled with extrav-agant declarations of love punctuated by laments about his chaotic finances: 'the roaring of creditors towards dawn is frightful, he com-plained'.[10] Although aware of Oscar's financial worries, Bosie expected him to fund every aspect of their hedonistic existence: 'he came to me for everything', Oscar told his friend More Adey, 'from his morning shave to his midnight hansom I was obliged to pay for every single item in his day's expenditure'.[11] Bosie's incandescent rages preceded periods of great remorse, but no matter how unreasonably he behaved, Oscar always took him back. Life had become a switchback of elation and despair, and it seemed that turmoil was part of the attraction.

Desperate for money, Oscar promised to send George Alexander a new play by October 1894. Provisionally titled 'Lady Lancing', this 'slight' but charming comedy would become *The Importance of Being Earnest*, his most celebrated work. Oscar's productive periods often coincided with a fam-ily holiday and Constance organised for them to spend several summer weeks at 'The Haven', a modest terraced house that stood at one end of the Esplanade in the seaside resort of Worthing in West Sussex.[12] She travelled down with the boys on 7 August. When Oscar followed a few days later, he found the accommodation cramped with no dedicated writing room for him to use.

While Cyril and Vyvyan were there, much of Oscar's time was taken up with traditional seaside activities; he was an excellent swimmer who enjoyed sailing and fishing. Utterly unselfconscious, he would remove his shoes and socks, roll up his trousers and build elaborate sandcastles on the beach. In one of the most poignant passages in his memoir, Vyvyan described how his father crafted 'long, rambling castles . . . with moats and tunnels and towers and battlements', before producing 'a few lead soldiers out of his pocket to man the castle walls'.[13] A report on the Annual Lifeboat Day in *The Worthing Gazette* of 22 August, described Oscar 'flitting about' in a small rowing boat.[14] On 19 September, he presented prizes for the best-dressed vessels at a Venetian Fête. He also cultivated friendships with a trio of teenage boys – Alphonse, Stephen and Percy – taking them boating and presenting Alphonse with valuable trinkets. Once the rest of the family had returned to London, he spent a night in a hotel in nearby Brighton with this sixteen-year-old youth.*

Further distraction arrived in the form of Bosie, who paid the first of three visits to Worthing just four days after Oscar arrived, although it appears he was dissuaded from staying with the family on that occasion at least. He had become, in his own words, a 'bone of contention' between Oscar and Constance, and relations between husband and wife had deteriorated to the point that Constance, while sharing a home with a man famed for holding audiences captive with his wit, was complaining of feeling lonely and having no one to talk to.[15] It has long been speculated that sexual relations between the two had ended eight years previously when Constance was pregnant with Vyvyan: Otho Lloyd spoke of an effective divorce between his sister and brother-in-law. Poet Ernest Dowson would tell an unedifying tale of taking Oscar to a brothel in Dieppe in 1897, insisting that, on emerging, Oscar had whispered: 'The first these ten years, and it will be the last. It was like cold mutton'.[16]

Oscar still valued Constance's opinion on his work. His great friend Ada Leverson heard that he was writing a farce at Worthing and described how

---

* In *Oscar Wilde's Scandalous Summer* (Amberley 2014), Anthony Edmonds had done stellar detective work in identifying Alphonse Conway, who was later passed off as a friend of the Wilde children.

'each day, he wrote a part of it and each evening he read it to the Elect – his, wife, children and a few friends'.[17] Constance also had reason to immerse herself in Oscar's back catalogue; she was compiling *Oscariana*, a selection of excerpts and epigrams to be published privately the following year by Arthur Humphreys, senior partner and manager of Hatchards bookshop in Piccadilly. It seems likely that Humphreys and Constance became acquainted in 1888 when his firm began publishing *The Rational Dress Society Gazette*, which she oversaw. In his late twenties, this personable young man had been married to his wife, Eleanor for eight years and they had a daughter, Dorothy, aged six.[*]

Besides their professional relationship, it seems they were connected through membership of the Society for Psychical Research, which had been established in 1882 with the purpose of bringing a scientific approach to the investigation of paranormal phenomenon.[†] In *Constance: the Tragic and Scandalous Life of Mrs Oscar Wilde*, Franny Moyle quotes from a letter, dated October 1894, in which Constance appears to ask Humphreys if he planned to attend a meeting of the society.[18] In *The Importance of Being Constance*, Joyce Bentley reports that she 'was also in the habit of calling in at the shop [Hatchards] to indulge in friendly arguments of a philanthropic nature'.[19] Naturally, their collaboration on *Oscariana* drew them even closer.

Humphreys visited Worthing on Saturday 11 September, an event that became as much a social occasion as a business one. While he smoked a cigarette, perhaps in Oscar's company, Constance scribbled an effusive but comparatively chaste letter: 'I do love you dear Arthur,' she declared.[20] Given his marital status, her strengthening religious beliefs and the tone of their correspondence before and after this uncharacteristic declaration, it seems likely that there was no consummated love affair between them, yet Constance took pains to deliver her letter surreptitiously and made it clear that she was eager to receive a clandestine reply. Undoubtedly, she admired Humphreys. In an earlier letter, she declared: 'you are an ideal husband, indeed I think you are not far short of being an ideal man'.[21]

Although in no position to censure his wife, Oscar may have been suspicious about her relationship with Humphreys. Certainly, his letters to the publisher are uncharacteristically cool in tone and he expressed grave

---

* A son, Laurence was born to them in 1901.
† The list of members and associates for August 1894 includes associate member Humphreys, Arthur Lee, Half-Timbered Cottage, Pangbourne and full member Wilde, Mrs Oscar, 16, Tite Street, Chelsea.

dissatisfaction with a proof of *Oscariana*.[22] Just fifty copies of *Oscariana* compiled by 'Mrs. Oscar Wilde' came out in January 1895. A further 200 were printed in May, the same month that Humphreys published a version of Oscar's essay *The Soul of Man under Socialism*. By then, Oscar was embroiled in scandal and facing a second trial for gross indecency. Whatever his feelings for Constance, Humphreys remained loyal to her husband and sent books to him in prison, a kindness for which Oscar felt deeply appreciative.

Whether prompted by his wife's admiration for another man or his own duplicity, marital infidelity was certainly on Oscar's mind. In a letter to George Alexander, sent from Worthing, he outlined the plot for a play: 'A man of rank and fashion' grows bored with his wife, a 'simple sweet country girl – a lady – but simple and ignorant of fashionable life'.[23] The man encourages his wife to flirt with an old admirer while he indulges in an affair, the discovery of which pushes her into the arms of the other man. Pregnant with her lover's child, she renounces her undeserving husband and he kills himself.

Oscar had clear ambitions for this play: '*I want the sheer passion of love to dominate everything,*' he told Alexander; 'No morbid self-sacrifice. No renunciation'.[24] Although he never completed it, he sold the scenario to several interested parties, including Frank Harris, who worked it up into *Mr. and Mrs. Daventry*. When Harris's play opened at the Royalty theatre in London in October 1900, the *Los Angeles Herald* hailed it as 'Clever, but Daring Beyond Words'.[25] Yet, George Bernard Shaw dismissed it, claiming: 'If Oscar had written it, it would now be a classic'.[26] Although the timing is less certain, Oscar also drafted an outline for *A Wife's Tragedy*, in which an adulterous poet declares: 'Life is a wide stormy sea. My wife is my harbour of refuge'. In response, he is told 'The storm may wreck the harbour as well as the ship that would reach it'.[27]

In August 1894, Oscar wrote to Bosie: 'My play is really very funny', he declared, 'I am quite delighted with it'.[28] The play in question was *The Importance of Being Earnest*. Although he subtitled it 'a trivial comedy for serious people', it has at its core a serious message involving inversions, false identities and the necessity of leading a double life in order to do as you wish. Again, Oscar demonstrated scant regard for the traditional institution of marriage, or any other Victorian convention for that matter. It is noteworthy that two lines vehemently critical of marriage did not survive: 'My dear fellow, all women are too good for the men they marry,' declares Algernon, adding: 'That is why men tire of their wives so quickly'. Not to be outdone, Jack announces: 'No one likes to be told, in a serious voice, that he will make a good husband. It sounds so tedious and second-rate'.

Oscar described his new play as 'exquisitely trivial, a delicate bubble of fancy'.[29] Yet, according to Ada Leverson, when someone remarked, 'the farce should be like a piece of mosaic,' Oscar countered: 'no; it must go like a pistol shot'.[30] It centres around two young men: Jack Worthing, who lives in the countryside but escapes to London on the pretext that he is required by Ernest, his dissolute but fictitious younger brother; and Algernon Moncrieff, who escapes the city to stand vigil at the sickbed of his fictional country friend Bunbury. Both propose marriage to forthright young women who cling to an irrational insistence that the man they marry must be named Ernest: 'In matters of grave importance, style, not sincerity, is the vital thing', Gwendolen Fairfax declares.[31]

Whether he is Ernest, or earnest, Jack's intentions towards Gwendolen seems unlikely to be realised since her mother, the imperious Lady Bracknell, who sets herself up as the only reliable source of taste and probity, will not countenance his obscure origins. As an infant, Jack was found in a handbag in Victoria Station, a situation clearly not of his making but one which allows her to accuse him of 'contempt for the ordinary decencies of family life'. In her opinion, no matter how nonsensical the underlying value system, propriety must always supersede integrity. Lady Bracknell's insistence on upholding absurd standards while demonstrating a naked interest in wealth alone exemplifies the hypocritical social anxiety that formed the basis for many a marriage. The situation resolves itself once Jack is revealed to be Ernest, a man with a perfectly respectable lineage, and Algernon proves willing to change his name.

Gender inversion abounds. Gwendolen expresses this most explicitly by declaring:

> Outside the family circle, papa, I am glad to say, is entirely unknown. I think that is quite as it should be. The home seems to me to be the proper sphere for the man. And certainly once a man begins to neglect his domestic duties he becomes painfully effeminate, does he not? And I don't like that. It makes men so very attractive.

Cecily and Gwendolen are disarmingly frank, well-informed, intelligent and self-possessed. Jack and Algernon are portrayed as dissolute and behave in an untrustworthy fashion. The young women are forthright sexual predators who impose their will, while the men are willing to bow to the most ludicrous requests.

Marriage comes under sustained attack. Lady Bracknell is opposed to long engagements, which 'give people the opportunity of finding out each other's characters before marriage'. It is 'perfectly scandalous' for a woman to flirt with her own husband, an act described as 'washing one's clean linen in public'. Once a marriage proposal is accepted, Algernon assures Jack, the excitement is over: 'The very essence of romance is uncertainty,' he insists: 'If ever I get married, I'll certainly try to forget the fact'. Algernon declares: 'in married life three is company and two is none'. To be freed entirely from the married state seems the most desirable development: Lady Harbury looks 'twenty years younger' and her hair has turned golden since the death of her husband. It is tempting to attribute these sentiments to Oscar.

Given the delight with which *The Importance of Being Earnest* was received, it is extraordinary to think that George Alexander passed it on to Charles Wyndham at the Criterion. He asked for it to be returned once he realised that Henry James's *Guy Domville* was failing to attract an audience. Reviewers took the play at face value and detected little of substance in it. The critic from *The Daily Telegraph* found 'no trace of solemn theatrical intention'.[32] His counterpart at the *Daily Graphic* declared: 'It has not a relish of reason or a sparkle of sanity; it is absurd, preposterous, extravagant, idiotic, saucy, brilliantly clever, and unedifyingly diverting'.[33] William Archer at *The World* called it: 'Nothing but an absolutely wilful expression of an irrepressibly witty personality'.[34]

Surely they were missing its subversive essence. While H. G. Wells described it as 'very good nonsense', George Bernard Shaw was probably closer to the mark when he recognised it as Oscar's 'first really heartless play'.[35] Beneath the lightness of touch and surrealism of its situations, *The Importance of Being Earnest* is an anarchic commentary on the damaging duplicity of Victorian society. According to Robert Sherard, Oscar said: 'the first act is ingenious, the second beautiful, the third abominably clever'.[36] Preposterous reversals poke fun at marriage, religion, family, property and everything held dear by an intolerant populace that would countenance no deviation; a narrow-mindedness that Oscar would soon fall foul of. While he was in favour, he was indulged. Yet, once he was deemed to have transgressed, all latitude afforded to him was whipped away. Towards the end of his life, he told Frank Harris:

while the public like to hear of my pain . . . I am not sure that they will welcome me again in airy mood and spirit, mocking at morals, and defiance of social rules.[37]

In view of Bosie's tempestuous behaviour during September and October 1894, it is testament to Oscar's drive and brilliance that he completed his play at all. Constance and the boys left Worthing to prepare for the beginning of the new school year on 12 September and Bosie was invited down the very next day.[38] There was another pressing reason to return to London. Jane Wilde, aged seventy-four by then, was terribly frail and Constance, caring and attentive as ever, called on her often, and helped her with her finances in what small way she could. By then, she was hampered by serious health issues of her own.[*] Constance had experienced lameness in her right leg as early as 1889, and had been beset periodically by severe pains ever since. Although bedridden from time to time, she dismissed her condition as 'rheumatism' or 'neuralgia' and got on with looking after those who needed her.[39] Jane was grateful for the care her daughter-in-law provided, but her low spirits were compounded by disappointment that her sons were on very poor terms. Relations between Oscar and Willie had deteriorated to the extent that a decidedly ambivalent review of *Lady Windermere's Fan* published anonymously in *The Daily Telegraph* on 27 February 1882, and characterising it as 'brilliantly unoriginal', was attributed to Willie, former drama critic with that newspaper.

Although Willie's animosity was almost certainly born of jealousy at Oscar's success, Frank Harris suggested that he had told his boyhood friend Edward Sullivan that the breach was provoked by Oscar's 'inordinate vanity' and the manner in which he surrounded himself 'with a gang of parasites who praised him all day long, and to whom he used to give his cigarette-cases, breast pins etc., in return for their sickening flattery'.[40] Whatever its origin, this hostility upset Jane dreadfully and she pleaded with Oscar to make peace with his brother: 'You will both have to meet by my coffin & I want you to meet before that in friendly feeling,' she implored.[41]

A further source of disappointment for her was the failure of Willie's marriage to her friend Miriam Florence Folline, more commonly known

---

[*] A superb analysis of Constance's illness was completed recently by Ashley H. Robins and Merlin Holland; 'The art of medicine: The enigmatic illness and death of Constance, wife of Oscar Wilde', published in *The Lancet*, Vol. 385, 3 January 2015, pp. 21–2, attributes her dreadfully debilitating symptoms to Multiple Sclerosis.

as Mrs Frank Leslie, the wealthy American widow and brilliant business-woman who had suggested Oscar should tour America back in 1882.* On the evening of 4 October 1891, Willie Wilde, aged thirty-nine, had become the fourth husband of Mrs Frank Leslie, sixteen years his senior, at the aptly named Church of the Strangers in New York. The *New York Herald* described the bride as 'the well known publisher of this city' and the groom as 'one of the editors of the *London Telegraph* and brother of Oscar'. As their best man was humorist Marshall P. Wilder, *Town Topics* magazine took the opportunity to quip that the groom was wild, the best man wilder, but the bride wildest of all. The quiet Sunday evening ceremony was followed by supper in Delmonico's and a honeymoon at Niagara Falls, an ironic choice in the light of Oscar's comment:

> Every American bride is taken there, and the sight of the stupendous waterfall must be one of the earliest, if not the keenest, disappointments in American married life.[42]

In a gushing account of this transatlantic alliance, *The New York Times* described Jane as a 'close and respected friend' of Mrs Leslie's. The *Los Angeles Herald* reported that Miriam attributed her decision to marry Willie in no small measure to her 'devotion to Lady Wilde'.[43] The *Topeka State Journal* quoted her as saying:

> Lady Wilde is so charming that it had a great deal to do with my marrying her son, I think. I have tried to profit by her acquaintance, and hope some day to be in New York what she is in London.[44]

They had much in common. Well schooled in literature and the classics, Miriam spoke French, Spanish, Italian, German and Latin. She, like Jane, had translated the work of Alexandre Dumas, fils. Miriam had high

---

* At seventeen, Miriam had married jewellery shop clerk David Charles Peacock under duress. They vowed to live apart for the remainder of their lives. After the marriage was annulled, Miriam toured with the notorious Lola Montez, making up one half of the Montez sisters before meeting her second husband, archaeologist E. G. Squier. Frank Leslie, born Henry Carter, hired Squier to edit his *Illustrated Newspaper*, and asked Miriam to fill in as editor of his *Lady's Magazine*. She was a great success. After separating from his wife, Leslie moved in with the Squiers and lived with them for more than a decade before easing Squier aside to become Miriam's third husband. Financial collapse followed by Frank's death from throat cancer in 1880, left Miriam a widow at forty-three. She paid off the debts she had inherited and changed her name legally to Frank Leslie in order to perpetuate the brand.

hopes for Willie, but her plans to install him as a charming companion and lynchpin in her publishing empire in New York came to nothing when it became clear that his preferred haunt was the fashionable Lotos Club, which was frequented by Mark Twain amongst others. While his new wife worked tirelessly at the helm of her business, Willie could be found drinking, gossiping and reciting parodies of Oscar's poems: 'You know, Oscar had a fat, potato-choked sort of voice,' one fellow Lotos Club member recalled, 'and to hear Willie counterfeit that voice and recite parodies of his brother's poetry was a rare treat.'[45] Another member remembered him as 'the most thoroughgoing night owl that ever lived,' and confirmed that he 'positively hated daylight'.[46]

Willie and Miriam's marriage was doomed. During a visit to London, Miriam hired a private investigator to report on Willie's activities. Confronted with evidence of his boorish behaviour and unfortunate habit of frequenting the city's brothels, she started divorce proceedings, charging him with drunkenness and adultery. The marriage was dissolved on 10 June 1893; Judge C. F. Brown declared that Willie was 'addicted to habits of gross and vulgar intemperance, and to violent and profane abuse of and cruel conduct to the plaintiff'.[47] Describing it as 'a funny sort of match from the start,' the *Morning Call* decided that their relationship would make a delightful social comedy. That same newspaper revealed that the bride had never altered her name, although 'at times she would let "Wilde" be tacked on with a hyphen'.[48]

Willie claimed, rather disingenuously: 'The man who marries for money jolly well earns it'.[49] When asked why he had married Miriam, his supposed reply was ''Pon my soul. I don't know. Do you? I really ought to have married Mrs. Langtry, I suppose'.[50] Ironically, Miriam reportedly declared: 'I really should have married Oscar'.[51] Yet, after their divorce, she told a reporter from the *Evening World*: 'I have only feelings of pity and sorrow for Mr. Wilde,' adding, 'I cherish no resentment towards him. He is a remarkably brilliant man of culture, but intemperance has demoralised him'. She was even kinder about Jane: 'Lady Wilde is one of the loveliest of women and extraordinarily intelligent, and there is still the best of feeling existing between us', she insisted.[52] Robert Sherard believed that the marriage had been disastrous for Willie: 'He went out to America a fine, brilliantly clever man, quite one of the ablest writers on the Press,' he noted before observing that he came back to England 'a nervous wreck, with an exhausted brain and a debilitated frame'.[53]

Although she had plenty of suitors, Miriam never married again. When she died in 1914, she left the bulk of her fortune to suffragist Carrie Chapman Catt in order that it would be used for the promotion of the cause of women's suffrage. A staunch champion of women's rights, she had once declared:

> The old order is changing and the new coming. Woman must open her eyes to it and adapt herself to it, she must free herself from her swaddling clothes and go out into the world with courage and self-reliance. Oh, what a noble woman the woman of the future may become![54]

While she was married to Willie, Miriam felt a duty of care to her impoverished mother-in-law and offered her an allowance of £400 a year. Jane, who was perhaps a little embarrassed at being financially dependent on another woman, would accept only £100, justifying this as the cost of maintaining a London home for the couple. Once the divorce was finalised, Miriam stopped Willie's allowance, leaving him with no option but to join his mother in genteel poverty in her Oakley Street home. Poor Jane lived in constant fear of bailiffs arriving at her door to collect on Willie's debts. When she cabled Miriam for help, her friend paid up grudgingly but broke with the family as a result.

In January 1894, six months after his divorce was finalised, Willie Wilde married Dublin-born Sophia Lily Lees. Always known as 'Lily', the new Mrs Wilde – aged thirty-five and with hardly a penny to her name – was considered to be a person of somewhat dubious respectability.[55] Yet, Lily was not entirely without prospects: her deceased father, William Armit Lees had made her ample inheritance subject to the life estate of his second wife, who was Lily's stepmother. As she was not inclined to advance a sum that would allow Lily to marry Willie, they married in secret, hopeful perhaps that Mrs Lees would come around in time. No cash was forthcoming.

Before they married, the couple had cohabited and for a time Lily believed she was pregnant, a circumstance that caused a good deal of upset to Jane, who was certain that not only was there no baby, there would also be no wedding once Lily was found out. Several accounts exist of Lily asking Jane's housekeeper Mrs Faithful for a 'powder' to remedy the situation.[56] Whether this was true or not, no baby was born at that time and their only child, Dorothy Ierne Wilde did not arrive until July 1895. Realising that she would have to share her home with Willie and his new wife, Jane complained to Oscar:

Miss Lees has but £50 a year and this just dresses her. She can give nothing to the house, and Willie is always in a state of utter poverty. So all is left <u>upon me.</u> I sometimes think of taking apartments for myself, and leaving them the house and furniture. For I have an immense dislike to sharing the house with Miss Lees, with whom I have nothing in common. The idea of having her here is quite distasteful to me.[57]

Lily may have contributed little to the household finances but she was a kindly and practical woman who made life considerably more comfortable for her mother-in-law: 'Willie and his wife get on very well here,' Jane informed Oscar. 'Mrs. Willie is sensible and active in arranging in the house and is very good-tempered'.[58] Yet, good temper would not pay the bills and Jane found herself staring into the abyss of abject poverty. Her pride prevented her from accepting help from anyone but Oscar or Willie and friends worried that she might starve. Henriette Corkran, bearing a large plum cake, made her way to Oakley Street in the company of American writer Gertrude Atherton: 'Lady Wilde is frightfully poor,' she explained.

> Her sons do little or nothing for her. Her friends don't dare offer her money or real food, for she's very proud, so we always take her a cake, which we beg her to "try, as we have made it ourselves". I only hope the gas isn't turned off, and you will be able to see her.[59]

The women spent an 'uncomfortable hour' in Jane's tiny drawing room, which they found stuffy and ill lit by three tallow candles that glimmered feebly on the mantle. Atherton recorded her impressions of Jane:

> In her day she must have been a beautiful and stately woman; she was still stately, heaven knew, but her old face was gaunt and gray, and seamed with a million criss-crossed lines; etched by care, sorrow, and, no doubt, hunger.[60]

Yet, in defiance of her reduced circumstances, Jane adopted a manner that was 'lofty and detached, almost complacent'. Although her voice was weak and quavering, Jane cast a spell on Atherton, who observed that:

> . . . the walls seemed to expand until the dingy parlor became a great salon crowded with courtiers, and the rotting fabric of her rag-bag covering turned by a fairy's wand into cloth of gold, shimmering in the light of a thousand wax candles.[61]

Judging by Jane's attitude, 'she might have been a queen graciously giving a private audience'.[62]

Jane saw much of Constance during the latter half of 1894 but little of Oscar. Although she was reluctant to ask him for money, she had very few options, since she struggled to pay her rent and faced the prospect of losing her home. Robert Sherard describes how she took to keeping her bills tucked into a small lacquer rack over the mantelpiece. During his rare visits, Oscar would examine them and decide which were most urgent. In reality, his largesse amounted to little more than a pittance, since the better part of his income was going elsewhere.

On 4 October 1894, Oscar and Bosie swapped Worthing for Brighton and booked into the Metropole Hotel. When Bosie fell ill with influenza, Oscar nursed him patiently for days. Hoping to complete some work, he took lodgings in the town and continued to watch over his lover. When Oscar fell ill, Bosie, who was much recovered by then, demonstrated no interest in nursing him. After an incendiary row, he stormed out and returned to London, from where he sent a petulant letter: '*When you are not on your pedestal, you are not interesting,*' he whinged. '*The next time you are ill I will go away at once*'. This callous missive reached Oscar on the day of his fortieth birthday. He resolved to break with Bosie for good.[63]

Days later, on 18 October, Oscar's resolve was undermined by news of the death of Bosie's eldest brother Francis, Viscount Drumlanrig, who was heir to his father's title of Marquess of Queensberry. While ostensibly a shooting accident, it was speculated that Drumlanrig, who was private secretary to Lord Rosebery, the man who had succeeded Gladstone as prime minister in March 1894, had been driven to end his life by the fear that he might be blackmailed over his relationship with the older man. The possibility that Rosebery was sexually involved with Drumlanrig enraged Queensberry beyond endurance and it is possible that he used what knowledge he had of an affair to ensure that the authorities dealt harshly with Oscar, who was, in his opinion, leading another of his sons astray.[64]

The relationship between Oscar and Bosie was attracting attention by then and the tide of public opinion was turning against them. A caricature published in *Punch* on 10 November, titled 'The Decadent Guys (A Colour Study in Green)', depicted them as two guys ready for burning, who expressed an unhealthy interest in their 'youthful disciples'. What seemed to offend people most was Oscar's flagrancy in flaunting his 'unwholesome' lifestyle. Perhaps the most damning description of his sleek and self-indulgent persona was recorded by Elizabeth Robins, recently disappointed by his failure to embrace her progressive plans for theatre reform. It seemed to her as if Oscar had been 'stuffed with spices and caviar'. She warmed to her theme, declaring: 'Poke him and he would bleed absinthe and clotted truffles'.[65]

Although Constance must have felt humiliated and betrayed by Oscar's deteriorating reputation and behaviour, she helped him maintain the *façade* of a conventional marriage. When she gave an innocuous interview to *To-Day Magazine* in November 1894, she shared with their reporter the romantic dedication Oscar had written in her autograph book:

> I can write no stately proem,
> As a prelude to my lay;
> From a poet to a poem,
> That is all I say.

That same month, he signed a letter to Bosie: 'Ever, with much love, yours. Oscar.'[66]

Chapter 18

THE WITTIEST WOMAN
IN THE WORLD

People do not as a rule object to a man deserving success, only to
his getting it.
    ADA LEVERSON on Oscar Wilde[1]

During his darkest days, Oscar depended on the practical and emotional
support offered by a woman he befriended in 1892. Oscar met Ada
Leverson at a party in the home of Margaret 'Meta' Crawfurd, whose
husband Oswald, editor of the illustrated weekly periodical *Black & White*,
was having an affair with Violet Hunt.* At the time, he was basking in the
success of *Lady Windermere's Fan* and mulling over the plot of *A Woman of
No Importance;* Ada almost certainly inspired Mrs Allonby, a female dandy
and one of the wittiest and most recognizably Wildean characters in any
of his plays. Since Oscar's name was on everyone's lips, Ada knew him by
reputation: 'Everyone was repeating his *mots*,' she recalled. 'Society at the
moment was enthusiastic about the rarest of human creatures, a celebrity
with good manners'.[2] Yet, she was unprepared for the reality: 'Old legends heard in the schoolroom still hung like a mist over Oscar Wilde when
I met him,' she wrote:

> I was half surprised not to see him 'wan and palely loitering' in knee-
> breeches, holding that lily on the scent of which he had been said to sub-
> sist. But he had long given up the 'aesthetic' pose of the eighties . . .[3]

They had much in common. Born on 10 October 1862 to Zillah and
Samuel Beddington, Ada, the eldest of their nine children, demonstrated an
early passion for literature and shared Oscar's enthusiasm for the poetry of
John Keats. Like Oscar, she was an accomplished linguist; her enlightened
but authoritarian father, a prosperous wool merchant, had arranged for her

---

* Osbert Sitwell suggested that Ada Leverson told him she met Oscar when he
sought her out after her parody of *Dorian Gray* appeared in *Punch* at the end of
1893, yet a telegram from Oscar dated 28 June 1893 exists.

to be instructed in Latin and Greek as well as the more commonplace French and German. The Beddingtons placed a high value on the acquisition of knowledge but Ada found family life stifling. Aged nineteen and in defiance of her father's wishes, she married Ernest Leverson, aged thirty-one and the son of a prosperous diamond merchant, in a bid to find some measure of independence. Although unrelated, the cynical observation imparted by Oscar's Lord Henry Wotton in *Dorian Gray* summed up their disappointing alliance: 'Men marry because they are tired,' he declared, 'women, because they are curious. Both are disappointed'. Samuel Beddington had good reason to object to his son-in-law. Leverson was a compulsive gambler and philanderer who had neglected to mention a daughter, Ruth, who was being raised in a convent in Paris while her father courted Ada.

Ada and Ernest had little in common and theirs was not a particularly successful coupling. Yet Ada embraced her fate with good humour, deciding that it was: 'better to have a "trying" husband than none'.[4] She had an exceptionally clear-eyed view of Victorian marriage, accepting that it was imperative for a woman but offered no real advantage to a man: 'Marriage is not his profession, as it is his wife's,' she declared. 'He is free in every way before marriage, tied in every way afterwards – just the reverse with her'.[5] Oscar would surely have endorsed this view. Her life was blighted by tragedy when her infant son George died of meningitis in 1888. A daughter, Violet, was born eighteen months later.

Ada was witty and exceptionally clever but she lacked confidence. Although she contributed anonymously to publications including *Black & White*, *The Yellow Book* and *Punch*, she seemed content to act as a muse to others until late in her life. Grant Richards, who would publish the novels she wrote between 1907 and 1916, saluted her as:

> . . . the woman whose wit provoked wit in others, whose intelligence helped so much to leaven the dullness of her period, the woman to whom Oscar Wilde was so greatly indebted.[6]

Robert Ross described her as 'a friend to whom Oscar Wilde owed, and gave, the homage of his intellect'.[7] She lauded him as chief among the 'many devoted friends' who remained loyal to Oscar.[8] Ada and Oscar took to each other immediately. He enjoyed sparring with her and she adored his flamboyance, recognising him as a 'spectacular genius', endowed with 'superb vitality'. In *Letters to the Sphinx from Oscar Wilde*, published three decades after his death, Ada described him as: 'The most soft-hearted, carelessly-generous and genial of men'.[9] Yet, recognising his tendency to take 'a short-sighted joy in living for the moment', she feared that, for all his brilliance, his character was blighted with 'a fatal want of judgement'.[10] Even when Oscar's popularity seemed universal, Ada realised that the conventional classes longed for his down-fall. Her own words express this best:

"To meet Mr. Oscar Wilde" was put on the most exclusive of invitation cards, yet every omnibus conductor knew his latest jokes. If he were cav-iar to the general he was gentleman's-relish to the particular. His greatest pleasure was to amuse the mob, to frighten the burgess and to fascinate the aristocrat. With his extraordinary high spirits and love of fun, he appealed to the lower classes; his higher gifts enchanted the artistic and such of the great world as wanted to amuse themselves; and with the sincere artist he was most himself. But the lower-middle classes never liked him, always distrusted him and disliked his success. People do not as a rule object to a man deserving success, only to his getting it.[11]

Oscar was in the habit of sending Ada dozens of telegrams. Dubbing him 'a master of the wire as a literary medium', she declared her inten-tion of bringing out *The Collected Telegrams of Oscar Wilde*. He never wasted a clever improvisation, she noted, whether his own or someone else's. On occasion, her wit matched his: 'Nothing spoils a romance more than a sense of humour in woman and the lack of it in a man,' she quipped. He purloined this for an exchange between Lord Illingworth and Mrs Allonby in *A Woman of No Importance*.[12]

Dozens of wags wished to emulate Oscar's sparkling wit. Ada detested the 'plethora of half-witted epigrams and feeble paradoxes by the mimics of his manner'.[13] Yet, both regarded skilful parody as a form of hom-age: 'One's disciples can parody one,' Oscar insisted, 'nobody else'. He listed the ingredients of a worthy parody: 'a light touch, and a fanciful treatment and, oddly enough, a love of the poet whom it caricatures'.[14] Ada had each in abundance and delighted in parodying Oscar's work, displaying an uncanny talent for sending up any hint of pomposity. She populated her high-spirited pastiche 'An Afternoon Party', published in *Punch* in 1893, with several of his most recognisable characters: Salomé, Mrs Arbuthnot, Lady Windermere, Lord Illingworth and Lord Henry Wotton. They are joined by Nora from Ibsen's *A Doll's House*, Sardou's *Dora*, Brandon's farcical *Charley's Aunt*, Pinero's Mrs Tanqueray and others Oscar had been accused of plagiarising. A passage delivered by Princess Salomé is pitch-perfect:

I think it is mayonnaise. I am sure it is mayonnaise. It is mayonnaise of salmon, pink as a branch of coral which fishermen find in the twilight of the sea, and which they keep for the King. It is pinker than the pink roses that bloom in the Queen's garden. The pink roses that bloom in the garden of the Queen of Arabia are not so pink.[15]

Oscar adored this, and her 'New Year's Eve at Latterday Hall'. Of this, he enthused:

Your sketch is brilliant, as your work always is . . . It is quite tragic for me to think how completely he [Dorian Gray] has been understood on all sides![16]

Of 'Overheard Fragments of a Dialogue', Ada's imagined conversation between Lord Illingworth and Lord Goring, Oscar declared: 'Your dialogue is brilliant and delightful and dangerous,' adding: 'No one admires your clever witty subtle style more than I do. Nothing pains me except stupidity and morality'.[17] Of their matched temperaments, he quipped: 'Everyone should keep someone else's diary; I sometimes suspect you of keeping mine'.[18] Ironically, at least one of Ada's parodies in *Punch* reached a far wider audience than Oscar's original work. While his poem 'The Sphinx' was brought out in a beautiful, limited edition numbering just two hundred copies, her parody, 'The Minx' reached 30,000 readers of *Punch*, drawing attention to his less widely known original.[19] Ada transformed Oscar's student interrogation of the inscrutable sphinx into a society newspaper interview with a sphinx who answered back.[20] Oscar approved: 'I delight in your literary minx,' he declared and he dubbed her 'Sphinx', occasionally adding the adjective 'gilded'.[21]

Although he enjoyed them, *Punch* editor F. C. Burnand felt somewhat uncomfortable that Ada's parodies were rooted in affection for their target: '. . . I don't want to *revive* any "cult" of *him*,' he warned in November 1893, 'it seems for the general public the "craze" which this illustrates is a bit out of date'.[22] For a time, Oscar suspected that Ada was the author of *The Green Carnation*, published anonymously in September 1894. In truth, this biting if uncannily accurate portrait of Oscar's relationship with Bosie was far too cruel and damaging to have come from Ada's pen, and she is almost certainly satirised as 'Mrs Windsor'.

The creator of the dissolute 'Esmé Amarinth' and 'Lord Reginald (Reggie) Hastings', instantly recognisable as Oscar and Bosie, was English journalist and satirist Robert Hichens, who had garnered much of the material for *The Green Carnation* when he spent time with Bosie in Egypt.

Such was the public fascination, and for the most part repulsion, at the novel's frank treatment of what they regarded as wanton immorality that Oscar felt obliged to deny authorship in the *Pall Mall Gazette*, describing the book as 'middle-class and mediocre'; he was snubbed in public nonetheless.[23]

Ada always enjoyed the company of witty and exuberant gay men. Although she was fond of Constance, she encouraged Oscar to bring his young lovers to dinner at her home. She remembered Bosie with fondness.* Of him, she wrote:

> Very handsome, he had a great look of Shelley. Not only was he an admirable athlete, he had won various cups for running at Oxford, but he had a strong sense of humour and a wit quite of his own and utterly different from Oscar's. His charm made him extremely popular, and he wrote remarkable poetry. Nor was Oscar indifferent to the romance of his ancient Scottish lineage.[24]

Although neither Bosie nor Constance was present, Ada was among the 'distinguished audience' that attended the opening performance of *The Importance of Being Earnest* at the St James's Theatre on 14 February 1895. Her lovely tribute to that brilliant night, confirms that she saw no reason to believe 'the gaiety was not to last, that his life was to become dark, cold, sinister as the atmosphere outside'.[25] There had been a ferocious snowstorm that day and the street was blocked with carriages as patrons stepped down into a bitterly cold wind. These inclement conditions did nothing to deter the 'Wilde fanatics' who treated the arrival of his audience as an essential part of the performance. Describing how they 'shouted and cheered the best known people,' Ada recalled that 'the loudest cheers were for the author who was as well-known as the Bank of England'.[26]

Oscar, recently returned from Algiers where he had holidayed with Bosie, appeared suntanned and prosperous, and had dressed with what Ada described as 'elaborate dandyism and a sort of florid sobriety'.[27] His outfit included the following: a coat with a black velvet collar, a green carnation blooming at the buttonhole; a white waistcoat, from which he had hung a large bunch of seals on a black moiré ribbon watch-chain; and

---

* The fact that Bosie was notoriously litigious may have had a bearing on this. He approved of Ada's *Letters to the Sphinx* and told her he would have written an introduction had she asked.

white gloves, which he held in his hand, leaving his beloved large green scarab ring visible to all. On any other man, Ada admitted, this ensemble might be taken for fancy dress, but Oscar 'seemed at ease and to have the look of the last gentleman in Europe'.[28]

Flamboyant as ever, Oscar declared lily of the valley to be the flower of the evening 'as a souvenir of an absent friend' – Bosie that was, not Constance – and those gathered sported delicate sprays of that lovely flower. Ada declared:

> What a rippling, glittering, chattering crowd was that! . . . they were certain of some amusement, for if, by exception they did not care for the play, was not Oscar himself sure to do something to amuse them?[29]

His play did not disappoint. Irene Vanbrugh, who played Gwendolen Fairfax, confirmed that it 'went with a delightful ripple of laughter from start to finish'.[30] She admired Oscar's 'charm of manner and his elegance' during the short time she knew him: 'No one was too insignificant for him to take trouble to please,' she recalled, 'and I felt tremendously flattered when he congratulated me at one of the rehearsals'.[31]

As the curtain fell, Oscar stepped forward and was greeted with an ovation. He stood smoking while he waited for the applause to subside; the evening was a triumph. When *The Importance of Being Earnest* was published in 1899, Oscar dedicated a presentation copy:

> To the Wonderful Sphinx, to whose presence on the first night the success of this comedy was entirely due, from her friend, her admirer, who wrote it, Oscar Wilde.[32]

Yet, that night, a dangerous drama was unfolding elsewhere in the vicinity of the theatre. The Marquess of Queensberry, who had grown increasingly frantic in his efforts to stop Bosie seeing Oscar, had taken to threatening restaurant and hotel managers with beatings if he discovered the couple on their premises.

That night, he planned to make a public protest by throwing a grotesque tribute, a bouquet of rotting vegetables, onstage. Oscar was tipped off and foiled his nemesis by persuading George Alexander to revoke Queensberry's ticket and organise for a cordon of policemen to surround the theatre. Thwarted, Queensberry hung around outside for hours, muttering with fury, before delivering his monstrous bouquet to the stage door. Four days later, on 18 February, Queensberry called at the Albemarle Club, where Oscar and Constance were members, and left his infamous card for all to read: 'For Oscar Wilde, posing as a somdomite [sic]'. Ten days elapsed before Oscar received this incendiary communication. 'I don't see anything now but a criminal prosecution,' he told Robbie Ross; 'My whole life seems ruined by this man'.[33] Egged on by Bosie, he decided to prosecute Queensberry for libel.

As was increasingly his habit, Oscar was not living at home at the time. On returning from Algiers, he had taken up residence at the Avondale Hotel in Piccadilly. From there, he sent a note to Constance advising her that he would call that evening to discuss an important matter. Although he signed off, 'Ever yours, Oscar', the couple had drifted far apart by then. Increasingly debilitated by poor health, Constance had returned that day from a recuperative month with Lady Mount-Temple in Torquay. She knew her husband had been overseas, but had no idea where and had asked Robbie Ross to inform him that she was desperately short of money. Realising that she would miss the first night of *The Importance of Being Earnest*, she also asked for newspaper accounts of what she expected would be another triumph.

That evening, after what must have been a desperately unhappy couple of hours with his wife, Oscar headed to the Avondale to discuss the best course of action with Robbie Ross, who was growing increasingly hesitant. When Bosie joined them, he urged Oscar to confront his accuser head-on. The following morning, since George Lewis was unavailable, all three headed for Holborn to consult with solicitor Charles Humphreys, who had been recommended by Ross. Oscar assured Humphreys that there was no truth in Queensberry's allegation and they accompanied him to Great Marlborough Street Police Station where a warrant was issued for Queensberry's arrest.

With two plays running concurrently in West End theatres, Oscar was undoubtedly the most successful playwright in London, yet he could not afford to mount this prosecution. While audiences flocked to his plays, the manager at the Avondale had confiscated his luggage for non-payment of his bill. When this lack of resources caused Oscar to hesitate, Bosie, who was determined to exact revenge, removed this obstacle by assuring him that his mother and older brother, who had suffered for years at the hands of his father, would fund the action. As Lady Queensberry and her son Lord Douglas of Hawick were out of the country, Oscar was obliged to borrow £500 from Ernest Leverson.

Ada Leverson's final parody of her friend's work, 'The Advisability of Not Being Brought up in a Handbag: A Trivial Tragedy for Wonderful

People' appeared in *Punch* on 2 March 1895, the day the Marquess of Queensberry was arrested at Oscar's instigation. Queensberry was taken from Vine Street Station to Marlborough Police Court, where he was charged with libel. Bosie made sure to alert the press. Ominously, during the committal proceedings, George Lewis announced that his client would plead justification. Humphreys testified that Oscar, a married man beyond reproach, lived contentedly with his wife and two sons. Sydney Wright, porter at the Albemarle Club was called to describe the note, which Queensberry insisted read 'posing as a somdomite' rather than 'ponce and somdomite', a far graver accusation but one that would have been more difficult to prove. At the end of this process, Queensberry was committed for trial and released on bail of £1,500. Lewis returned his brief.

That evening, Queensberry called a press conference, insisting that his actions were contrived to bring matters to a head. In advance of his trial, he engaged Edward Carson QC, Oscar's old acquaintance from Trinity College, Dublin, and set about compiling a solid defence by hiring private detectives to nose out incriminating evidence. He found little to bolster his defence until he was approached by Charles Brookfield, a disgruntled actor and playwright with a small part in *An Ideal Husband*, who appeared to have developed a morbid jealousy of Oscar's success. In 1892, Brookfield had lampooned *Lady Windermere's Fan* in a burlesque titled *The Poet and the Puppets*. Now, he took it upon himself to pass on to Queensberry's legal team the names of Alfred Taylor and several of his associates; men who could testify to the illegality of Oscar's lifestyle.

While Queensberry gathered damning evidence, Oscar and Bosie left on an ill-advised trip to Monte Carlo. There, Bosie refused to discuss the case and spent his time gambling at the casino, an activity that held absolutely no interest for Oscar and one he could ill-afford. Constance, who was not privy to her husband's whereabouts once more, asked Robbie Ross to inform him that she had been forbidden to walk in advance of an operation intended to alleviate her persistent lameness and had gone to stay with her aunt Mary Napier. Kind-hearted as ever, she took the trouble to express concern about Jane's well-being and to organise for someone to look in on her. She even offered to defer her surgery should Oscar wish to return home in advance of the trial: 'We are very worried just now', she confessed to novelist Marie Belloc Lowndes.[34]

Oscar appeared to share little of Constance's concern. He returned to London full of swagger, having told Ada Leverson that he was ready to 'fight with panthers'.[35] Apparently unwilling to accept responsibility for their fate, he and Bosie had their palms read by Mrs Robinson. Afterwards, Oscar sent Ada a telegram: 'We have been to the Sibyl Robinson,' he declared. 'She prophesied complete triumph and was most wonderful'.[36] Ada recognised his ebullience as entirely characteristic: 'Generally he was extremely optimistic,' she confirmed, 'firmly believing in the palmist's prophecy of triumph'.[37] Yet, Oscar's joviality was punctured when he met Frank Harris and George Bernard Shaw at the Café Royal and both advised him to abandon the case, flee abroad and take Constance with him. Left to his own devices, he might have been persuaded, but his resolve was bolstered by Bosie, who arrived late and reacted to the suggestion with disgust, accusing Harris of being a poor friend to Oscar. Both men stormed out with the result that Oscar, who had persuaded Harris to testify to the literary worth of *Dorian Gray*, never called on him. Harris had been willing but had warned him that no jury in England would give a verdict against a father who was attempting to protect his son.[38]

On 1 April, two days before the case against Queensberry opened at the Old Bailey, Constance dined conspicuously with Oscar and Bosie. Afterwards, all three occupied a box at the St James's Theatre to watch *The Importance of Being Earnest*. This offstage performance was part of a carefully contrived plan intended to portray Bosie as a family friend who enjoyed Constance's endorsement. During the interval, Oscar went backstage to see George Alexander, who was playing Jack Worthing. Alexander too urged him to drop the case and flee. As they left, Bosie noticed that Constance was 'very much agitated' and when he turned to wish her goodnight he saw tears glistening in her lovely eyes.[39] Although neither realised it, that was the last time they would meet.

On the morning of 3 April 1895, Oscar, carefully yet flamboyantly dressed, arrived at the Old Bailey in a hired carriage and pair.* He took his seat in the packed and stifling courtroom and listened as the unwitting Sir Edward Clarke QC prosecuted the case on his behalf. Clarke had only recently been made aware of the list of young men with whom Queensberry was accusing Oscar of having consorted, so his focus was on justifying his client's literary work and the letters he had written to Bosie. In the run-up to the trial, Clarke had issued a warning:

* Two books that provide comprehensive details of the libel and subsequent criminal trials are: Merlin Holland, *Irish Peacock & Scarlet Marquess* (London, Fourth Estate, 2003); and Michael S. Foldy, *The Trials of Oscar Wilde* (New Haven, CT, Yale University Press, 1997).

I can only accept this brief, Mr. Wilde, if you assure me on your honour as an English gentleman that there is not and never has been any foundation for the charges that are made against you.[40]

In response, Oscar, who was an Irishman of course, swore that Queensberry's allegation was 'absolutely false and groundless'. Armed with this assurance, Clarke portrayed Oscar as a family man who enjoyed an artistic friendship with Bosie and was also on intimate terms with the young man's mother, a woman who had received harsh treatment at the hands of her belligerent former husband.

Having been lulled by the gentle questioning put to him by his own counsel, Oscar was flummoxed when Edward Carson opened his cross-examination by wrong footing him for lying about his age under oath. Carson proceeded to probe Oscar's attitude towards various avant-garde literary works, including *The Picture of Dorian Gray*, a novel he portrayed as being indicative of unwholesome predilections. This line of questioning, though rapid-fire and tortuously tricky, seemed harmless enough and led to several witty exchanges. When Carson turned his attention to blackmail and enquired as to the nature of Oscar's relationship with several young men it became clear that Queensberry planned to mount a vociferous defence. Carson was clearly well-informed. Particularly damning was his theatrical flourishing of the gifts Oscar had presented to young Alphonse Conway: a cigarette case, a silver-topped cane, a book and a photograph inscribed 'Alfonso Conway from his friend Oscar Wilde'.

Oscar and Bosie had planned to dine triumphantly with Ada Leverson that evening, but they were rattled by Carson's line of questioning and realised that victory was not certain. They sent their regrets, assuring her: 'Everything is very satisfactory'; nothing could have been further from the truth.[41] On the second day, Carson continued in the same vein and there was little Clarke could do to salvage Oscar's credibility in response. Opening for the defence, Carson insisted that Queensberry, his client, was motivated by a determination to rescue his son from the clutches of this degenerate man. He listed the names of ten men he planned to put in the witness stand in order that they might testify to the lewd acts Oscar had coerced them into performing. Realising that all was lost, Clarke advised his client to withdraw from the prosecution.

On day three, 5 April 1895, the courtroom was packed with reporters and voyeuristic members of the public who had queued for hours to gain admittance. Carson had continued his opening speech for twenty minutes or so before Clarke signalled his desire to confer with his opposite number. Afterwards, he announced his client's intention of withdrawing and submitting a verdict of not guilty. He had hoped this verdict could be limited to the literary element of the evidence presented, but Queensberry refused to allow this. As directed by Mr Justice Collins, the jury returned a 'Not Guilty' verdict and awarded costs against Oscar, a decision that was greeted with raucous cheering from the public gallery. While Queensberry left in triumph, Oscar slipped out a side door, in little doubt, surely, that the danger he faced was grave.

Oscar attempted to explain his actions to a largely unsympathetic press as a gallant attempt to protect Bosie from having to testify against his father. Queensberry, feeling utterly vindicated, issued a warning: 'If the country allows you to leave, all the better for the country!' he declared, 'But, if you take my son with you, I will follow you wherever you go and shoot you!'[42] He ensured this would not be necessary by having his solicitor, Charles Russell, send the witness statements he had gathered to Director of Public Prosecutions, Hamilton Cuffe. Rather than return home, Oscar sent a note to Constance urging her to admit no one but the servants to his bedroom or study, and to speak only to friends. It was left to Robbie Ross to call on her and break the devastating news. Desperately distressed, she pleaded with Ross to persuade Oscar to flee. Convinced at last that this was necessary, Ross rushed to the Cadogan Hotel in Slone Street, where Oscar was drinking himself into a stupor, but to no avail. The debate as to whether Oscar Wilde was shocked into inertia or determined to defend what he characterised as the devotion of an older man for a younger that was rooted in intellectualism, rages to this day. In a letter to Bosie, written from Ada Leverson's home, he told his young lover:

I decided that it was nobler and more beautiful to stay. We could not have been together. I did not want to be called a coward or a deserter. A false name, a disguise, a hunted life, all that is not for me . . .[43]

Yet, W. B. Yeats speculated that he might have left had his mother, veteran of an earlier libel action, not declared:

If you stay, even if you go to prison, you will always be my son, it will make no difference to my affection, but if you go, I will never speak to you again.[44]

Within hours of receiving Queensberry's damning dossier, Cuffe convened an extraordinary meeting with the Attorney General, the Solicitor

General and the Home Secretary, who was at that time H. H. Asquith, husband of Oscar's friend Margot. It was Asquith who insisted that Oscar should be stopped wherever he was found. By five o'clock that evening, warrants had been issued for the arrest of Oscar Wilde and Alfred Taylor. Although he was tipped off by a sympathetic reporter from *The Star*, Oscar refused to flee and was arrested shortly before 6.30 p.m. He was taken to Bow Street Police Court, where he was charged under section 11 of the Criminal Law Amendment Act 1885. Refused bail, he was remanded, first in Bow Street, then in Holloway Prison, for the three weeks preceding his trial, which was scheduled for 26 April 1895.

Oscar contacted the Leversons from his prison cell:

> Dear Sphinx and Ernest,
> I write to you from prison, where your kind words have reached me and given me comfort though they have made me cry, in my loneliness.

Of his motivation for taking the libel case, he explained: 'I thought but to defend him [Bosie] from his father. I thought of nothing else'.[45] Since she hated scandal, it took courage for Ada to stand up publicly for Oscar. She had once expressed a sentiment that was a close reversal of a famous quip of his: 'I am not afraid of death but I am of scandal, of which I have a special horror,' she wrote. 'The idea of being talked about is one of which I have a weak terror'.[46] Wretched and dreadfully lonely, Oscar opened his heart to her. At times, his desperation was heart-wrenching: 'I don't know what to do,' he cried; 'My life seems to have gone from me. I feel caught in a terrible net. I don't know where to turn'.[47] During these dark days, while lamenting his separation from Bosie, he never lost sight of the importance of Ada's friendship, assuring her:

> . . . you will always remain in a niche of a heart – half broken already – as a most dear image of all that in life has love and pity in it.[48]

With Oscar in Holloway and Constance finding some comfort at the home of her aunt Mary Napier, it was left to Robbie Ross to remove valuable or potentially compromising letters and manuscripts from the couple's deserted Tite Street home. The near-complete manuscript of *La Sainte Courtisane* was entrusted to Ada. Meanwhile, Mary Napier, who was desperately worried for her niece, confided in Adrian Hope, her nephew by marriage. Laura, his wife by then, recorded their encounter in her diary:

> A most trying visit from Mrs. William Napier in a most frantic state about

her poor niece Constance Wilde as the whole verdict has gone against her monstrous husband – the whole episode most terrible.[49]

Although she had been cruel in the past, Laura felt desperately sorry for Constance, who she described as 'the most miserable woman in London'. Her diary reveals that Bosie turned up the following day to ask Hope if he would post bail for Oscar. He refused, as did theatre managers George Alexander and Lewis Waller. Having extracted a promise from her son that he would leave for France, Robbie Ross's mother, Eliza, agreed to contribute £500 towards Oscar's defence, and to keep an eye on Jane, whose health was failing fast.

Constance was determined to protect her children from the opprobrium that their father's arrest had attracted, and removed them from their respective preparatory schools. Vyvyan, aged eight, stayed with her while Cyril, almost ten, was sent to relations in Ireland. It was too late to protect him from the unfolding tragedy; a placard announcing the arrest of his father had excited his curiosity and, once he reached Ireland, he had access to newspapers that revealed the details of the case in a most lurid and sensationalist fashion. As she had so often in the past, Constance sought refuge in Lady Mount-Temple's home at Babbacombe. From there, she wrote a heart-wrenching letter to Mrs Robinson, the palmist who had offered false hope to Oscar: 'What is to become of my husband who has so betrayed and deceived me and ruined the lives of my darling boys?' she asked. Yet she felt great sympathy for Oscar and closed by lamenting: 'What a tragedy for him who is so gifted'.[50] Robinson's reply, promising better days ahead, although well-intended, was hopelessly optimistic and wholly inaccurate.

Although he had been so ruinously misled, Edward Clarke offered to waive his fee and lead Oscar's defence, which was just as well, since Oscar could not have afforded him. Sensing that there was little likelihood of their accounts being settled, his many creditors were pressing for a sale of his property. Queensberry forced the issue by demanding immediate payment of his costs, which amounted to £600. A bankruptcy sale of Oscar and Constance's possessions was held at their Tite Street home on 24 April, two days before the opening of Oscar's first trial. Many items were pilfered during the ensuing melee; these included Oscar's poignant letters to Constance, which she kept in a blue leather case. Several irreplaceable manuscripts also disappeared. Those items that were sold achieved far less than their true value. One Irish-born publisher gave an account of proceedings to Robert Sherard:

I went upstairs and found several people in an empty room, the floor of which was strewn, thickly strewn, with letters addressed to Oscar mostly in their envelopes and with much of Oscar's easily recognisable manuscript. This looked as though the various pieces of furniture which had been carried downstairs to be sold had been emptied of their contents on to the floor.[51]

The sacking of the Wildes' Tite Street home was a terrible humiliation. Ada believed that many of those in attendance that day delighted in Oscar's downfall:

It was already well known that Oscar had bitter enemies as well as a large crowd of friends . . . And if his chief enemy was eccentric, many of his jealous rivals were quite unscrupulous.[52]

Oscar's prized books, numbering around two thousand volumes, were bundled together and offered at knockdown prices, making just £130.[53] Whistler sent representatives to buy back a number of his works for less than £40. The nursery was raided and toys belonging to Cyril and Vyvyan were sold, a loss that caused them great distress. In all, the sale raised just £230.

Ernest Leverson was present that day and managed to acquire a full-length portrait of Oscar by Harper Pennington for £17. Oscar joked about the corrupting influence this work might have on visitors to the Leversons' home, writing:

I was quite conscious of the very painful position of a man who had in his house a life-sized portrait, which he could not have in his drawing-room as it was obviously, on account of its subject, demoralising to young men, and possibly to young women of advanced views.[54]

Public opprobrium was swift and brutal: Oscar's name was obliterated from the programmes and posters for *The Importance of Being Earnest* at the St James's Theatre, although George Alexander claimed his intention was to keep the play running, since Oscar needed the money.* His name did remain on the programmes for *An Ideal Husband* at the Haymarket, and at the Criterion, where it transferred. Within weeks, both plays were taken

---

* Although he did discuss the possibility of giving Oscar some money, Alexander did little to help him at the time. On his death in 1917, Alexander bequeathed the rights to *The Importance of Being Earnest* to Vyvyan Holland.

off. In America, English-born actress Rose Coghlan,* who Oscar had once suggested as a possible lead in *Vera*, was staging the first American production of *A Woman of No Importance*, and playing the part of Mrs Arbuthnot herself. When news of Oscar's arrest reached her, she ended the run and denounced him from the stage, declaring:

> This is the last time I will ever present that piece, I cannot take Wilde's name off the bills without breaking my contract, and I shall simply drop the play entirely.[55]

Oscar's books were removed from the shelves of bookshops and libraries. Little did those who wished to obliterate all trace of him realise that they were contributing to his lasting renown.

---

* Coghlan was the daughter of Francis Coghlan, a Dubliner with impeccable literary connections who founded *Coghlan's Continental Dispatch*, published *Coghlan's Continental Guides*, and counted Charles Dickens as a friend.

Chapter 19

'DEATH MUST BE SO BEAUTIFUL'

Life is such a mournful mystery.
Letter from JANE ELGEE to John Hilson[1]

The trial of Oscar Wilde and Alfred Taylor opened on 26 April 1895, in a gloomy courtroom at the Old Bailey, the Central Criminal Court, which was housed at the time in a dispiriting building adjacent to Newgate Gaol. Both men faced counts of gross indecency and conspiracy to procure the commission of acts of gross indecency, although the conspiracy charges were later withdrawn. They had been charged in accordance with Section 11 of the Criminal Law Amendment Act 1885, commonly referred to as the Labouchère Amendment, which contained no definition of gross indecency and, as a result, outlawed a broad spectrum of homosexual behaviour that was considered less serious than sodomy but was easier to prove. It was regularly exploited by blackmailers.

Women were exempt from such ludicrous strictures. In 1921, the House of Commons voted in favour of an 'Acts of Gross Indecency by Females' clause being added to the Criminal Law Amendment Act of 1885. Frederick Macquister, the Tory MP who proposed this extension, contended that lesbianism, which he saw as an abnormality of the brain, threatened the birth rate, debauched young girls and induced neurasthenia and insanity into British society. His clause got through the House of Commons but was not ratified by the House of Lords, whose members believed that silence and secrecy was a preferable approach. Insisting that the vast majority of women had no knowledge of these practices, the Lord Chancellor decried the notion that 'the taint of this noxious and horrible suspicion' would be imparted to thousands of naive women.[2] As a result, no such restrictions were ever enforced.

Damaging evidence was presented against Oscar during three committal hearings and a subsequent trial. In exchange for their testimony, several witnesses for the prosecution were offered immunity, and a number were rewarded handsomely by Queensberry, and possibly the Crown.[3] Bosie, who appeared to misconstrue the issue at hand, offered to take the stand and testify to the irrationality of his father's behaviour; this was no longer of relevance of course. He sailed for France once Edward Clarke convinced him that his presence in court would damage Oscar's case.

One by one, each witness for the prosecution attempted to seal Oscar's fate. Charlie Parker claimed that he and his brother William had been procured by Taylor for Oscar's pleasure, and that Oscar had performed an act of sodomy on him. Alfred Wood admitted to committing 'an act of grossest indecency' with Oscar at his Tite Street home.[4] Fred Atkins informed the court that Oscar had taken him to Paris as his secretary and 'made improper proposals', an irrelevancy since this incident, which was not prohibited under French law, was beyond the jurisdiction of the English courts, a point later acknowledged by trial judge Justice Charles. Edward Clarke exposed all three men as disreputable blackmailers. When Edward Shelley, a more credible witness on paper, took the stand, he came across as neurotic and slightly unhinged.

Several women offered rather flimsy evidence against Oscar. Jane Cotter, a chambermaid at the Savoy Hotel, testified that she had called the attention of the housekeeper to peculiar stains on Oscar's bed sheets. She also claimed to have seen 'a boy of eighteen or nineteen years of age' in his room.[5] Lucy Rumsby, who let a room to Charlie Parker, insisted that Oscar had once called for him there. Margery Bancroft, a neighbour of Parker's, thought she might have seen Oscar. She recognised him, she said, because he had been pointed out to her previously. Ellen Grant, Taylor's former landlady, admitted that, although she had never seen Oscar, her tenant had spoken to someone he referred to as Oscar. Sophia Grey, another of Taylor's landladies, testified that Oscar had visited him, but admitted that he had stayed for just a few minutes.[6]

Oscar, looking careworn and dishevelled, took the stand and denied all charges. Clarke's defence rested on the supposition that only a madman, or an innocent one, would have proceeded with the libel action against Queensberry when confronted with the details of his 'justification' defence. When prosecutor Charles Gill asked Oscar to comment on Bosie's poetry, specifically the 'love that dare not speak its name', he used the opportunity to describe the splendour and legitimacy of the 'great affection' an older man might feel towards a younger, finishing with a rousing justification:

> It is beautiful, it is fine, it is the noblest form of affection. There is noth-
> ing unnatural about it. It is intellectual, and it repeatedly exists between
> an elder and a younger man, when the elder man has intellect, and the

younger man has all the joy, hope and glamour of life before him. That it should be so the world does not understand. The world mocks at it and sometimes puts one in the pillory for it.[7]

Oscar's bold declaration was greeted with loud applause, interspersed with isolated hissing, from the public gallery.

On day six, the jury retired, only to return after three hours and forty-five minutes deliberation to inform the court that they were unable to reach a verdict on the charges against Oscar.[8] This collapse and subsequent press coverage provided an opportunity for the Crown to end the matter, but a retrial was requested instead. At that point, Clarke applied, successfully, for his client to be released on bail of £5,000, half of which was put up by Oscar himself, the remainder being provided jointly by the Reverend Stewart Headlam and Bosie's brother, Lord Douglas of Hawick. Headlam, a pioneer of Christian socialism and member of the Fabian Society, knew Oscar only slightly and was motivated by a strong sense of justice. He regarded Oscar's decision to stay for the trial as a declaration of honour and contended that he had been judged harshly by the press and the public in advance of due process. Inevitably, his stance attracted a degree of opprobrium.

Oscar was released on bail on 7 May 1895, and headed for the out-of-the-way Midland Hotel adjacent to St Pancras Station, where a suite of rooms had been reserved in his name. Almost immediately, he was asked to leave by the manager, who had been threatened by Queensberry's heavies. This pattern was repeated at a number of establishments. Near midnight, Oscar arrived at his mother's Oakley Street home in a state of utter exhaustion. Willie answered his brother's knock: Oscar came 'tapping with his beak against the window-pane,' he claimed, 'and fell down on my threshold like a wounded stag'.[9] When Robert Sherard arrived from Paris to lend his support, he described the 'poorly furnished room, in great disorder' that Oscar was given:

> He was lying on a small camp-bedstead in a corner between the fireplace and the wall . . . His face was flushed and swollen, his voice was broken, he was a man altogether collapsed.[10]

Yet, even *in extremis*, Sherard noted that his friend was as kind and gentle as ever.

While Oscar was at Oakley Street, Jane remained confined to her room; her bed, if Robert Sherard is to be believed. By then, the once glorious

Speranza had dwindled to a 'pathetic, faded old lady', a shadow of her former self.[11] Her 'glorious dark eyes' had lost their lustrous shine and she had abandoned all interest in the wider world.[12] Throughout her life, Jane's disposition had swung from high exuberance down to debilitating lassitude. She entered her final months confronting the certainty that the glittering future she had envisaged for both her talented sons was fatally compromised. Succumbing to a profound melancholy, she scrawled a note in her untidy handwriting: 'Life is agony and hope, illusion and despair – all commingled, but despair outlasts all'.[13]

On the rare occasions when she ventured out, Jane had taken to wearing 'a double white gauze veil drawn close like a mask over her features'.[14] Three years earlier, she had given up her celebrated 'At Homes', telling Oscar that she was 'too weary of life'.[15] Although she revived them sporadically, attendance had thinned to a trickle of faithful habitués and Oscar rarely came. Her newfound seclusion contrasted starkly with the social whirl she had enjoyed for much of her life, yet it echoed the isolation she had embraced as a girl who devoted her time to writing.

By now, arthritis had crept into her fingers, twisting them out of shape and impeding her handwriting, which had been 'a marvel of unsightliness' at the best of times.[16] It mattered little: demand for her output had dried up and her poems and essays were being returned by uninterested editors. Even her publishers, Ward and Downey, no longer wished to hear her ideas for the books she might write. With no income from writing and no rent from Moytura, all Jane had to live on was her annual Civil List pension of £70, which she had secured with Oscar's help. Little wonder she advocated the government exempt 'the race of the gifted from taxation'.[17]

Early in 1893, Jane's precarious finances had been thrown into crisis. As 146 Oakley Street was subsiding and needed extensive repairs, she was obliged to relocate to number 26 for two months. Afterwards, she was horrified to receive a summons from the letting agent, seeking compensation for damage he attributed to her. Dreadfully upset, she dashed off a twelve-page letter detailing the poor condition of number 26 when she had taken occupancy. Particularly poignant was her insistence that, since there had been no traffic through the hall, she could not have damaged the hall mats.[18] This was a far cry from the days when dozens of London's boldest and brightest inhabitants attended Lady Wilde's 'Saturdays'. In the end, Oscar settled the agent's bill, possibly because he was anxious to avoid a costly and embarrassing court case. Jane was effusive in her thanks, declaring him: 'Best & most generous of sons!'[19] They had always been close: 'Come home with me,' he had told a friend, years earlier, 'I want to introduce you to my mother. We have founded a Society for the Suppression of Virtue'.[20]

As a result of Mrs Frank Leslie stopping her allowance, Jane was utterly destitute by March 1894: 'I am in dreadful financial difficulties,' she told Oscar, '& have literally not a shilling in the world'.[21] With his own finances creaking under the weight of a hedonistic lifestyle, Oscar claimed that a contributory factor to his lack of funds was the requirement that he maintain his mother's household as well as his own; in truth, what assistance he offered her was erratic and she was often obliged to beg when a bill fell due.

In April, Jane tendered her resignation from the Irish Literary Society, an organisation she had helped found just two years earlier. Although she pleaded ill-health, it seems likely that she could no longer afford the subscription. Aware of her straitened circumstances, fellow members, an illustrious group that included W. B. Yeats and Charles Gavin Duffy, the Society's first president, made her an honorary member. Her note of thanks expressed regret that 'very uncertain health' would prevent her from attending 'Lectures and Receptions illustrated by so many distinguished representatives of Irish genius'.[22] Evidently, Jane was not without influence amongst the Irish community in London.

In Ireland, coverage of Oscar's trial in quality newspapers like *The Irish Times*, while comprehensive, was discreet and non-sensationalist in deference to Jane's standing. The high regard in which she was held by her compatriots persuaded T. M. 'Tim' Healy MP, former parliamentary correspondent for *The Nation* and the man who would become first Governor-General of the Irish Free State, to intervene in an attempt to save her son. When petitioning the Solicitor General, Frank Lockwood, to desist from proceeding with a second trial, Healy explained: 'I wished the mother should be spared further agony'. In response, Lockwood sighed and admitted: 'I would not but for the abominable rumours against __ [Rosebery]'.[23]

Several of Oscar's supporters called on him at Oakley Street, including one veiled woman who brought a bouquet of violets, the symbol of faithfulness, and a horseshoe for luck. She was later identified by Lawrence Irving, son of Henry, as Ellen Terry. Another woman who was exceptionally generous at this time was Adela Schuster, daughter of Leo Schuster, a

wealthy Frankfurt banker who was director of the Union Bank of London
and Chairman of the London and Brighton Railway. Adela and Oscar
are thought to have met late in 1892. He took to calling her 'Miss Tiny',
and sometimes 'the Lady of Wimbledon', a reference to the fact that she
lived in some style in that leafy suburb.

From the outset, Adela was effusive in her admiration for Oscar's work.
On reading *Lady Windermere's Fan*, she told him: 'It so enchanted and elec-
trified me . . . it is admirable, it is perfect'.[24] In a letter to their mutual
friend More Adey, she described the 'real affection' she felt for Oscar and
her 'immense admiration for his genius', adding:

> I do and always shall feel honoured by any friendship he may show me . . .
> Personally I have never known anything but good of O . . . and for years
> have received unfailing kindness and courtesy from him – kindness because
> he knew how I loved to hear him talk, and whenever he came he poured
> out for me his lordly tales & brilliant paradoxes without stint and without
> reserve. He gave me of his best, intellectually, and that was a kindness so
> great in a man so immeasurably my superior that I shall always be grateful
> for it.[25]

In *Oscar Wilde: His Life and Confessions*, Frank Harris described how
Adela offered assistance to Oscar when it was needed most:

> . . . a very noble and cultured woman, a friend of both of us, Miss S—, a
> Jewess by race tho' not by religion, had written to him asking if she could
> help him financially, as she had been distressed by hearing of his bank-
> ruptcy, and feared that he might be in need.[26]

Once she realised that Oscar was 'in uttermost distress', Adela sent him
a check for £1,000, 'declaring that it was only inadequate recognition of
the pleasure she had had through his delightful talks'.[27] In order to evade
his voracious creditors, Oscar entrusted this money to Ernest Leverson,
an arrangement that lead to great disharmony between them.

When Ernest and Ada called to see Oscar, they were horrified by his
reduced circumstances and palpable unhappiness. Their offer to take
him into their home was accepted with gratitude but, before he arrived,
they offered a month's wages to any servant who wished to avoid scandal
by leaving their employment. Each in turn declared their intention of
remaining and all agreed to keep his presence a secret: 'I never believed a
word against Mr Wilde,' declared Ada's old nurse, Mrs Field, 'He's a gentleman, if ever there was one'.[28] The coachman alone was given holidays,

as it was feared that he might indulge in loose talk in the public houses he frequented.

Oscar remained upstairs in the nursery, which had been allocated to him, until six o'clock each evening, when he would emerge for dinner immaculately dressed and with a flower in his lapel. Afterwards, he chatted with Ada for hours. 'When we were alone,' she remembered:

> . . . he would walk up and down the room, always smoking a cigarette, talking in the most enchanting way about everything except his trouble. Sometimes he would improvise prose poems, like those published in his works. Once he asked for writing things, to note down one of these improvisations. I could not find any. "You have all the equipment of a writer, my dear Sphinx, except pens, ink and paper".[29]

When Constance called to speak with her husband, they were left alone for two hours: 'I loved her very much,' Ada wrote, 'and was grieved to see her leave in tears'.[30] Afterwards, she discovered that Constance had pleaded with Oscar to take flight but he had ignored her. Ada too believed Oscar should leave England before his second trial, but when she sent up a note to that effect, he returned it, chastising: 'That is not like you, Sphinx', before turning the conversation to books.[31]

Ada noted the 'look of immovable obstinacy' that crossed Oscar's face whenever there was any suggestion of flight, writing:

> Nothing on earth would induce him to leave, though he knew that every facility was given to him. His mother told him it would be dishonourable for him to leave. Moreover, he never expected anything in his life to turn out badly.[32]

Before leaving for the Old Bailey on the morning of 22 May, Oscar turned to Ada and asked in a faltering voice: 'If the worst comes to the worst, Sphinx, you'll write to me?'[33] Two years would elapse before she saw him again.

Alfred Taylor was tried first and found guilty on two counts of indecent acts with the Parker brothers but not of procuring. Sentencing was deferred until Oscar had been tried. He faced eight counts of gross indecency: four with Charles Parker, two with persons unknown in the Savoy Hotel, one with Edward Shelley, and one with Alfred Wood at Tite Street. Once again, Edward Clarke did as well as he could, exposing several witnesses as blackmailers, characterising Shelley as a neurotic and violent young man, proving that the chambermaid at the Savoy could recognise no one without her glasses, and demonstrating that Wood could not corroborate his presence at Oscar's home.

Yet, although the evidence was far from overwhelming, the jury took just two hours to find Oscar guilty on all counts save that in relation to Shelley. Summing up, Mr Justice Wills described the case as the worst he had ever tried: 'People who can do these things must be dead to all sense of shame,' he declared, 'and one cannot hope to produce any effect upon them'.[34] He sentenced both men to two years imprisonment with hard labour, a punishment that was, in his opinion, totally inadequate under the circumstances.

On hearing this, Oscar turned pale and seemed on the point of fainting. Several people sitting close by heard him murmur: 'And I – May I say nothing, My Lord?' Some of those present had the decency to cry 'shame' in protest at the fact that Oscar had been convicted of acts deemed crimes under English law just ten years earlier, acts that were not prohibited in most European countries, among them France. Once he was transferred to Pentonville Prison, Oscar was stripped of his personal possessions, immersed in a vat of disinfected water, dressed in a prison uniform marked with broad arrows to signify that he was the property of the Crown for the duration of his sentence, shorn by the prison barber, and ushered into a spartan cell containing a bed of bare wooden planks and a bucket that required slopping out each morning. His fall was swift and brutal.

In Pentonville, Oscar was treated as an ordinary prisoner and allowed no communication with the outside world. His health deteriorated rapidly and he developed the symptoms of fatigue, malnutrition and chronic diarrhoea, a catastrophic combination that caused rapid weight loss. When R. B. Haldane, a member of the Home Office Committee investigating prisons, visited him on 12 June, at the urging of Margaret Brooke, Ranee of Sarawak, he was shocked by this decline and organised a transfer to Wandsworth Prison where conditions might be marginally more tolerable.

In Wandsworth, Oscar was visited by Otho Holland, who warned him that Constance was being advised to obtain a divorce, an eventuality that Oscar was anxious to avoid. The contrite letter he wrote in an attempt to dissuade her was treated as an affront by Bosie, who told Ada Leverson:

> I am so upset and perplexed by it all. It seems to me quite inconceivable that he should prefer to correspond with his 'family' than with me without

some very strong reason of which I know nothing.[35]

In the same letter, he declared: 'I really wish Oscar and I were both dead'.

As Oscar grew increasingly disillusioned with Bosie, who he had taken to calling 'Douglas', he developed a new closeness with Constance, who had decided that her husband was 'weak rather than wicked'.[36] Sherard had seen Oscar the previous month and had found him deeply depressed yet stoic. Determined to repair the relationship between Oscar and Constance, Sherard warned Oscar that Bosie planned to publish some of his love letters in *Mercure de France*, an act that would jeopardise any rapprochement with his wife. When Oscar learned that Bosie planned to dedicate a book of poetry to him, he asked Robbie Ross to prevent this. Ultimately, a rather self-serving article entitled 'Introduction to my Poems, with some remarks on the Oscar Wilde case' appeared in *La Revue Blanche* on 1 June 1896.

Bosie's crass attempts to publish Oscar's letters against his wishes could not have contrasted more markedly with the good wishes sent by Adela Schuster. When she suggested, through More Adey, that Oscar might resume his stories, he wrote:

I was greatly touched by the extract from the letter of the Lady of Wimbledon. That she should keep a gracious memory of me, and have trust or hope for me in the future, lightens for me many dreadful hours of degradation or despair.[37]

The enduring tribute he paid to her in *De Profundis* is both moving and profound; she was, he wrote:

. . . one of the most beautiful personalities I have ever known: a woman, whose sympathy and noble kindness to me both before and since the tragedy of my imprisonment have been beyond power of description: one who has really assisted me, though she does not know it, to bear the burden of my troubles more than anyone else in the whole world has: and all through the mere fact of her existence: through her being what she is, partly an ideal and partly an influence, a suggestion of what one might become, as well as a real help towards becoming it, a soul that renders the common air sweet, and makes what is spiritual seem as simple and natural as sunlight or the sea, one for whom Beauty and Sorrow walk hand in hand and have the same message.[38]

What a pity Oscar did not receive such staunch support from Willie, who could be insensitive in his defence. When George Bernard Shaw approached him to discuss the circulation of a petition for Oscar's release, Willie, showing little enthusiasm, allegedly quipped: 'Oscar was NOT a man of bad character: you could have trusted him with a woman any-where'.[39] Oscar's monstrous fate contrasted sharply with the lofty ideals his mother had clung to when she counselled him to stand firm and defend his good name. The consequences of this appalled her and hastened a decline that was already well underway.

In his memoir *Son of Oscar Wilde*, Vyvyan Holland recollected that, when he was a very small boy, Jane seemed 'a terrifying and very severe old lady sitting bolt upright in semi-darkness . . . while the sun shone brilliantly outside'.[40] He recalled her being 'dressed like a tragedy queen, her bodice covered with brooches and cameos'. Although she was kind-hearted, Jane was formidable and Vyvyan protested whenever Constance proposed a visit to her home. Long after his grandmother's death, he lived for a time on Oakley Street, and experienced a 'sense of foreboding' every time he passed her former home.[41]

In reality, Jane was exceptionally fond of her daughter-in-law and her two young grandsons. Her warm affection radiates from the regular letters she wrote to Constance, a woman she relied on for friendship and financial support. Naturally, she was desperately unhappy when Constance informed her that she was separating from Oscar and intended to change her name, and that of her sons, from Wilde to Holland: 'I do not like the idea of the boys changing their names,' Jane complained. 'It would bring them much confusion'.[42]

In June 1892, with characteristic wit, Jane had christened her home 'Oakley Hermitage' in recognition of her unwillingness to leave it.[43] Oscar's *Lady Windermere's Fan* was the toast of London at the time; his mother devoured the reviews and assured him that she was immensely proud of him, but she never saw a single one of his plays. Her increasing reluctance to venture outside was matched by her determination to suppress any rogue shafts of daylight that might filter in. She had always favoured candlelit gloom, regardless of the season or time of day. Now, thick velvet curtains in a deep vermillion shade were drawn permanently across her windows.

Desperately sad and devoid of her legendary garrulousness, Jane retreated to her gloomy bedroom and refused to admit anyone outside of her immediate family. In August 1895, when Ernest Leverson sent word of Oscar's circumstances, she thanked him but explained that she was very poorly and confined to her room. Such isolation obliged the trickle of well-wishers who continued to call on her to drop inadequate words of comfort through her letterbox instead, where they joined the demand notices for rates and taxes that arrived from the Chelsea munici-pal authorities. At least Jane's rent was being paid out of Adela Schuster's £1,000.

Oscar was declared bankrupt in November 1895 and the two hearings he was obliged to attend at the London Bankruptcy Court were hideously humiliating. In September, he had been taken from Wandsworth Prison by public transport, handcuffed and guarded by two policemen. Although he was jeered at by passers-by, Oscar's spirits were lifted by Robbie Ross, who waited outside the courtroom and raised his hat as he passed. As a result of his bankruptcy, he was increasingly dependent on Adela's lar-gesse. As well as supporting Jane, her money paid for Lily Wilde's confine-ment when she gave birth to her first child, Oscar's only niece, Dorothy Ierne Wilde, who was born on 11 July 1895.

In return for this kindness, Lily had written to the governor of Pentonville Prison asking that Oscar be given her fondest love, and that he be assured his mother was 'wonderfully well', although this was far from true. Two months after Dorothy's birth, Lily visited Oscar in the prison infirmary at Wandsworth; she was shocked by the deterioration in his health. Jane's health was declining rapidly too. Towards the end, Oscar was the only person she wanted to see. She watched for a letter with a prison postmark: 'I thought that Oscar might perhaps write to me after the three months,' she lamented, 'but I have not had a line from him, and I have not written to him as I dread my letters being returned'.[44]

In November 1895, while Oscar was being transferred to HM Prison Reading, he was made to stand on the central platform at Clapham Junction, handcuffed and dressed in prison garb 'for the world to look at'.[45] He carried hideous memories of being 'surrounded by a jeering mob'. Two months later, in January 1896, Jane, desperately ill by then, wrote to Henry B. Isaacson, the irascible governor of HM Prison Reading, ask-ing that Oscar be allowed to visit her at home.[46] Since Isaacson, whom Oscar, using a borrowed phrase from Tennyson's 'Lucretius', described as a 'mulberry-faced dictator', refused her this comfort, she never again saw the son who, decades earlier, she had predicted would 'turn out something wonderful'.[47]

During the dark days of January 1896, as winter drew to a close, Jane caught a chill and could not summon the resources to fight it: 'How can people weep at Death?', she once asked her friend John Hilson; 'To me it is the only happy moment of our miserable, incomprehensible existence'.[48] On 3 February 1896, Lady Jane Francesca Wilde died of 'acute bronchitis'. Willie mourned her passing: 'My dear mother was more than a mother to me,' he told More Adey. 'She was the best and truest and most loyal friend I had on earth'. He described her death: 'Her end was perfect peace,' he wrote. 'She was quite conscious up to an hour before her passing'. He also broached the subject of Oscar's imprisonment and the effect it had on his mother:

> It is useless to disguise from you and Oscar's friends that his sad fate saddened her life. With all his faults and follies he was always a good son to her, and even from the prison walls managed to help and assist her, as he always did when he was among us all. This much will stand to his credit.[49]

Three days later, on the afternoon of 6 February 1896, the remains of Jane Wilde were taken by hearse to the sprawling cemetery at Kensal Green. According to Henriette Corkran, her friend 'loathed the idea of being buried in a London cemetery, perhaps near some common tradesman'. She had hoped instead that her body would be 'thrown in the sea, or buried near a rock on some wild coast'.[50] In the end, she had no say in the matter and was interred in plot 147 in a remote part of the cemetery; this plot, unmarked for decades, was later classified as a public grave. Her funeral expenses were paid by Oscar via Ernest Leverson, out of the money donated by Adela Schuster.* In accordance with Jane's instructions that she 'be buried *quite privately* and for no one to come to her funeral', only Willie and Lily were there to mark her passing.[51]

A sympathetic obituary in *The Athenaeum* paid tribute to Jane, declaring: 'Under the mark of brilliant display and bohemian recklessness lay a deep and loyal soul and a kindly and sympathetic nature'.[52] The *Freeman's Journal* lauded her as 'almost the last of that brilliant circle of poets and writers who, fifty years ago, gave to the "Young Ireland" movement a world-wide celebrity'.[53] She was described in the *Virginia Enterprise* as 'a brilliant woman who had contributed much to literature and social life in England and Ireland'. Paying tribute to her as 'a confirmed woman's rights woman', that newspaper lauded the movement she had inaugurated with Lady Henry Somerset, 'the object of which was to secure from

---

* In 2000, an anonymous donor funded the erection of a monument over Jane's unmarked grave.

the crown honorific distinctions and titles for women, similar to those bestowed upon men for notable deeds'. [54]

A fortnight passed and Oscar remained unaware of his mother's death. As Willie was certain that his brother had no desire to see him, Lily and he contacted Constance and suggested that she might travel from Italy, where she was staying with Margaret Brooke, to deliver the dreadful news. Although she was debilitated by health issues of her own by then, she visited Oscar on 19 February; a full sixteen days after Jane had died. It would be the last time they met. Although Oscar was devastated by the news, he acknowledged Constance's generosity, writing:

> My wife, at that time kind and gentle to me, rather than that I should hear the news from indifferent or alien lips, travelled, ill as she was, all the way from Genoa to England to break to me herself the tidings of so irreparable, so irremediable a loss. [55]

Oscar swore that he had received portents of bad news in the hours before Jane's passing. He reacted with horror when a warder killed a spider while sweeping out his cell, declaring that he now expected to hear 'worse news than any I have yet heard'. On the night Jane died, Oscar insisted that he heard the cry of the banshee.* Later, he told Vincent O'Sullivan that Jane had appeared to him in his cell, dressed in outdoors clothes. When he asked her to remove her hat and coat, and to sit down, she shook her head sadly and vanished. He was to dream of her several times afterwards, telling Robbie Ross:

> My dream was that my mother was speaking to me with some sternness, and that she was in trouble . . . I quite see that whenever I am in danger she will in some way warn me. [56]

In *De Profundis*, Oscar likened his fall, and Jane's sorrow, to the crucifixion of Jesus in front of his mother, Mary: 'Her death was so terrible to me,' he admitted, 'that I, once a lord of language, have no words in which to express my anguish and my shame'. [57] He regretted besmirching her name:

> She and my father had bequeathed me a name they had made noble and

---

* In *Ancient Legends, Mystic Charms and Superstitions of Ireland*, Jane described how 'the cry of this spirit is mournful beyond all other sounds on earth, and betokens certain death to some member of the family whenever it is heard in the silence of the night' (p. 260).

honoured not merely in Literature, Art, Archaeology and Science, but in the public history of my own country in its evolution as a nation. I had disgraced that name eternally. I had made it a low byword among low people. I had dragged it through the very mire. I had given it to brutes that they might make it brutal, and to fools that they might turn it into a synonym for folly.[58]

Prison life took a terrible toll on Oscar's health. In a chilling aside, Major J. O. Nelson, the humane but pragmatic man who succeeded Isaacson as governor of HM Prison Reading, remarked to Robbie Ross: 'He looks well. But like all men unused to manual labour who receive a sentence of this kind, he will be dead within two years'.[59] Oscar lasted his full sentence and survived for three and a half years more, outliving Constance by almost three years.

Chapter 20

NOT MUCH TO LAUGH ABOUT

If we had only met once, and kissed each other.
OSCAR WILDE to Carlos Blacker, discussing his wife,
Constance Wilde[1]

With Oscar in prison, Constance was placed in the invidious position of needing to distance her children and herself from the opprobrium attached to his name while simultaneously reconciling her conflicting emotions. Although deeply distressed by her husband's betrayal, and determined to divorce him at first, she remained hugely sympathetic to his plight, as she told her friend Emily Thursfield:

> People have been so kind to me, but you know I am quite broken-hearted . . .
> It is so terrible to be here free in the heavenly air, and to think of those four
> walls round him.[2]

Those who understood her best, Lady Mount-Temple in particular, did not press her to divorce Oscar. Others, including her aunt Mary Napier, felt her shame more keenly and urged her to cut all ties with him.

Several decades earlier, the law had changed in her favour. By moving jurisdiction to the civil courts, the Matrimonial Clauses Act of 1857 widened the availability of divorce and created the notion of legal separation. As it also protected a woman's property rights, this legislation would allow Constance to regain her legal identity and recover the entitlements she had before marriage. Yet, since adultery alone was not sufficient grounds for a woman to divorce her husband – although it was adequate for a man to divorce his wife – Constance would have to cite examples of qualifying behaviour, which included sodomy. This would be disastrous for Oscar, since it would leave him open to future prosecutions. A judicial separation was a less ruinous option.

On the advice of her solicitor George Lewis, Constance decided to change her name and that of her sons to Holland, a Lloyd family name that had been adopted by her brother Otho several years earlier when he faced financial ruin. Keen to safeguard the boys' future, she came to the conclusion that the wisest course of action was to send them abroad, at least temporarily. On a bleak day towards the end of April, or possibly early in May 1895, Cyril, aged almost ten, and Vyvyan, aged eight, left London in the company of Mademoiselle Schuwer, a French Governess who was paid for out of funds raised by friends. Constance remained in London to settle her affairs and do what she could for Oscar but she planned to join them as soon as she could. Since her Tite Street home was no longer accessible, she was taken in by sympathetic friends; she found some stability at 'The Grange', a detached villa on Clapham Common that was home to Eva Roller, an older widowed friend who was admired by Lady Mount-Temple and knew John Everett Millais and John Singer Sargent through her artist son George.

Details of the boys' arduous journey to the picturesque Alpine village of Glion, a popular but isolated holiday resort, are recorded with admirable wryness in Vyvyan Holland's memoir, *Son of Oscar Wilde*. Both boys took an instant dislike to Mademoiselle Schuwer, a devout Catholic who spoke hardly a word of English and was horribly seasick during the crossing from Dover to Calais, as a consequence of which they were given nothing to eat. Cyril had discovered a good deal about their father's plight but was determined to protect his little brother and said little for fear of giving something away. Inevitably, Vyvyan noticed that his normally ebullient brother appeared uncharacteristically drawn and anxious. Neither boy would see his father or paternal grandmother again.

Once they reached the Hôtel du Righi Vaudois in Glion, Mademoiselle Schuwer demonstrated little interest in her charges, allowing them to roam free and do as they wished. They befriended two fellow guests: a pair of ancient, chain-smoking sisters, Russian countesses who swathed themselves in shawls and huddled by a fire that blazed perpetually. These eccentric yet kind-hearted old ladies pressed sweets and stamps on the boys and, as a special treat, allowed them to stuff paper cigarette tubes with pungent Russian tobacco. Once Constance arrived, late in June, she dispatched the unpopular governess and fell into the habit of taking tea with the countesses. To the boys, it must have seemed like an extended summer holiday. However, once news of the unfortunate circumstances of their being there reached the disapproving hotel manager, it became impossible for them to stay.[3]

In early September, Constance took the boys to stay with her brother, Otho, his second wife, Mary, and their children in the Swiss village of Bevaix, near Lake Neuchâtel, where they rented the upper half of a modest two storey chalet; Madame Benguerel, their landlady, lived down-stairs. With Otho's assistance, Constance coached her sons in the use of their new surname, asking Vyvyan to adopt the more conventional spelling of his first name and to drop Oscar, his middle name, entirely. Otho had obtained permission to visit Oscar the previous month, and had warned him that Constance had been advised to seek a divorce. Realising this was something his brother-in-law wished to avoid, he urged him to address the one letter he was entitled to write at the end of his first three months of incarceration to his wife. As a result of Otho's intervention, Constance too received permission to visit Oscar on 21 September 1885.

By then, her stance towards her husband had softened considerably. She had received his letter and been touched by his eloquent expressions of devotion and remorse, sentiments that Otho assured her were sincerely held. Further corroboration arrived by way of a letter from Robert Sherard. He too had seen Oscar and was convinced that reconciliation with Constance was the key to his friend's salvation. A third and most unlikely advocate for reconciliation emerged in the form of J. S. Hargrove, who had acted as Lloyd family solicitor for three decades. Hargrove, who was advising Constance, had urged her to seek a divorce, but he too was moved by the expressions of abject remorse in Oscar's letter. Late in August 1895, he had travelled to Switzerland to advise his client that divorce might be avoided, although he warned her that reconciliation would oblige the family to live in exile.

Won over by these expressions of support, and confident that Oscar was truly repentant, Constance decided to take him back: 'I think we women are meant for comforters, she told Emily Thursfield, 'and I believe no-one can really take my place now, or help him as I can'.[4] Inevitably, her encounter with Oscar was distressing: 'I could not see him and I could not touch him, and I scarcely spoke', she told Robert Sherard.[5] She returned to Switzerland, heartbroken at having seen her husband brought so low and convinced that he had been gripped by madness for the three years running up to his trial. Oscar seemed determined to break with Bosie for good, understanding at last, as he told Robbie Ross, that the man he loved had 'played dice with his father for my life, and lost'.[6]

Although Constance planned to return to England in the spring of 1896, as winter approached she travelled south to the market town of Nervi on the Italian Riviera, less than a mile from the winter villa of Margaret Brooke, Ranee of Sarawak. Delighted to learn of her friend's imminent arrival, Margaret found her an apartment in nearby Sori, a picturesque fishing village on the Mediterranean coast. Although her desire to escape the harsh Swiss winter was reason enough, another likely motive for Constance's move to Sori was its proximity to Genoa, the location of a private clinic run by the charismatic Luigi Maria Bossi, professor of gynaecology at Genoa University and a fellow of the British Gynaecological Society. Well regarded at the time, Bossi was later discredited for championing risky and ineffective surgery targeted at what he characterised as 'pelvic madness', the belief that many ailments specific to women were rooted in uterine disorder.* This theory, which had its origins in the Ancient Greek notion of hysteria and the wandering womb, may sound ludicrous today but it was accepted by male doctors for centuries.

Convinced by Bossi's assurances that an operation at his clinic followed by complete bed rest would improve her creeping paralysis, Constance checked into his clinic shortly before Christmas 1895. Since she was probably suffering from multiple sclerosis, as established recently by Ashley H. Robins and Merlin Holland, this risky procedure was completely ineffective.[7] Yet, satisfied that his intervention had cured her, Bossi discharged his patient in January 1896. By April, her symptoms were worse than ever. On the advice of a German 'nerve doctor', she resorted to a variety of primitive alternative therapies including hot baths and galvanism, a treatment that involved the stimulation of muscles through the administration of an electric current. By October, a tremor had crept into her right arm and affected her handwriting to the extent that she soon resorted to using a typewriter.

As if her health problems were not troublesome enough, Constance faced fresh worries in relation to Oscar. It perturbed her that he had maintained his association with friends like More Adey, 'old infamous companions' whom she believed had a bad influence on him.[8] In fact, Adey and Robbie Ross were true friends who had Oscar's best interests at heart and were keen to keep him from Bosie. Constance was also confronted with a vexatious financial dilemma. As a consequence of Oscar's bankruptcy, the life interest in her private income, an annuity designed to transfer her income to Oscar should she predecease him, had been placed with the Official Receiver to sell to the highest bidder. As one unthinkable

---

* In 1918, Bossi was suspended from practicing at the Institute for Gynaecology and Obstetrics of the University of Genoa for two years when his 'moral character' was called into question. The following year, he was shot dead in his consulting room by the jealous husband of a patient with whom he had apparently become romantically involved.

possibility involved Queensberry purchasing this interest and strengthening his hold over Oscar, it was imperative that Constance or Oscar should reassume control of it.

When she visited Oscar in February 1896, to inform him of his mother's death, Constance expressed her desire to acquire this life interest in order to settle her income on their sons. In return, she assured Oscar that she would make provision for him. Recognising the generosity of this arrangement, Oscar agreed to her terms. Directly afterwards, Constance drew up a new will placing all of her assets under the control of Adrian Hope, nephew by marriage of her aunt Mary Napier, who was also appointed executor of her estate. In the event of her death, Hope was instructed to realise everything, invest the proceeds and hold this in trust for her sons. This new will contained her 'earnest wish and desire' that Hope be appointed the boys' guardian.[9]

In April 1896, Constance, Cyril and Vyvyan moved to the German university town of Heidelberg, a romantic baroque-style settlement nestled on both banks of the River Neckar. Plans to return to England that spring had come to nothing, possibly because the headmasters of that nation's schools were reluctant to accommodate Cyril and Vyvyan. Just as the puritanical Hester Worsley had advocated in *A Woman of No Importance*, it may have been the case that the sins of the father were visited on his sons; at least Hester had the grace to change her stance. Heidelberg was chosen for several reasons, not least of which was Margaret Brooke's intention to rent a villa there, since her son Harry Keppel Brooke wished to improve his German. The town also offered an array of excellent schools and the possibility of frugal living. One further incentive was the distance Constance would put between herself and Bosie, who was living in Genoa at the time.

Cyril and Vyvyan were enrolled in a regimental German school, but both were expelled after Vyvyan was struck with a ruler by one of the masters, prompting Cyril to rush to his aid. After they were expelled from a second German school for fighting with their classmates, Constance enrolled them in Neuenheim College, a small English school established to provide the benefits of a British education to the town's small ex-pat community. As Neuenheim College placed a strong emphasis on sport and introduced rugby into Germany, it seems that Cyril was far better suited to this rough and tumble establishment than gentle Vyvyan, who was desperately unhappy there.

With the boys settled in school, Constance moved into a modest pension nearby and took up quiet pursuits: taking charge of the flowers in her local English church, brushing up on her German and developing a keen interest in photography. Increasingly, her activities were curtailed by poor health and impaired mobility. Using a line of communication that ran from Margaret Brooke to Adela Schuster and on to More Adey, she expressed frustration at attempts made by Oscar's friends to buy the life interest in her income, and what she saw as their implied mistrust of her motives. By then Adey was taking a completely contrary stance to her. Only Adela Schuster, who had agreed to finance the purchase of the life interest should it be appropriate for her to do so, was reluctant to go along with Ross and Adey unless she was satisfied that their actions were in accordance with Oscar's wishes and would not harm Constance.[10]

When Oscar learned that Ross and Adey proposed resettling the life interest on him, he asked them not to oppose Constance: 'She was gentle and good to me here, when she came to see me,' he told Ross, 'I have full trust in her'.[11] In defiance of his wishes, his friends bid £75, three times the amount Constance had offered, a tactic she assumed had Oscar's endorsement. When Robbie Ross wrote to her in June 1896, assuring her of his continuing friendship, she expressed incomprehension at his decision to act against her. Shocked by the deterioration in Oscar's health, More Adey wrote to her in July, asking that she support his efforts to petition for her husband's early release. Her agreement was conditional on Adey desisting from interfering in her affairs. When Adey showed this letter to Adela Schuster, she urged him once again in the strongest terms not to go against Constance's wishes.[12] She also wrote to inform Constance of her support for her position.[13]

Incensed by Adey's behaviour and what she interpreted as Oscar's intransigence, Constance reduced the annual allowance she was prepared to pay him from £200 to £150. Hargrove, her solicitor warned that it would be withdrawn entirely should the life interest be denied her.[14] He also informed Oscar that legal action was being taken regarding the guardianship of his children. Distressed by this change in attitude, Oscar blamed his friends for alienating his wife. They meant well and were motivated by loyalty, but they were misguided and it never seemed to occur to them that, should Oscar acquire the life interest, it might be seized by creditors at any time. In any case, it would be rendered null and void should Constance decide to divorce him or obtain a legal separation.

Before 1839, divorced or separated mothers had no rights to their children whatsoever. A campaign led by Caroline Norton, who wished to

leave her violent husband and take her children with her, led to the passing of the Custody of Infants Act of 1839, permitting a mother who was
not guilty of adultery to petition the courts for custody of her children
aged up to seven, and for access to her older children. The Infant Custody
Act of 1873 heralded a radical change by signifying that the appropriate
principle for deciding custody was the need of the child rather than the
rights of either parent, thus allowing mothers to petition for custody of
children below the age of sixteen. As the century came to a close, it had
become routine to award custody to the mother, in accordance with the
notion that a woman's place was in the domestic sphere. On 12 February
1897, Mr Justice Kekewich heard Constance's action in the Chancery
Division and awarded custody of Cyril and Vyvyan Wilde to her. She was
also appointed joint legal guardian with Adrian Hope.

In May 1897, days before Oscar's release, Hargrove brought a Deed of
Separation to HM Prison Reading for him to sign. By doing so, he relin-
quished custody of his children and gave Constance control of the life
interest in her income. In return, he was granted an allowance of £3 per
week, although the deed contained a clause ensuring that he would forfeit
this if he was found guilty of 'annoying or molesting' Constance or keeping company with 'evil or disreputable companions'.[15] Oscar appeared to
believe that this was a reasonable outcome: 'Whether I am married or not
is a matter that does not concern me,' he told Robbie Ross; 'For years I
disregarded the tie. But I really think that it is hard on my wife to be tied
to me'.[16]

As More Adey had created the false impression that friends had raised a
considerable sum of money for him to live on until he could resume writing, Oscar had no notion that he was entirely dependent on Constance.
Yet, he was grateful once he found out: 'I shall owe to her [Constance]
my first cup of tea or dish of food,' he told More Adey, 'it will taste all the
sweeter to me for it'.[17] To Robbie Ross, he wrote: 'she kissed me: she comforted me: she behaved as no woman in history, except my own mother
perhaps, could have behaved'.[18]

Although Oscar was anxious to re-establish good relations with
Constance, he was perturbed by the draconian terms of their separation:
'My life is to be ruled after a pattern of respectability,' he told Robbie
Ross. 'My friends are to be such as a respectable solicitor would approve
of'.[19] Had the couple reunited, one imagines the arrangement would have
required a fine act of balancing their individual needs, something that
would surely have been impossible even for a wife as accommodating as

Constance. While admitting that Constance had been 'wonderfully loyal', Oscar confessed to Robbie: 'She could not understand me, and I was bored to death with the married life'.[20]

Having applied for and been refused a reduction in his sentence, Oscar was released on 19 May 1897. Since regulations stipulated that a prisoner must be discharged from the place of his original incarceration, he was transferred back to Pentonville Prison on the eve of his release. By being permitted to leave that institution first thing in the morning, he avoided the attentions of a rapacious press. He was met by More Adey and the Reverend Stuart Headlam, who had put up one quarter of his bail in 1895, and taken to the Bloomsbury home of the latter, where he was greeted by a small band of friends, among them Ada Leverson: 'We all felt intensely nervous and embarrassed,' she admitted:

> We had the English fear of showing our feelings. He came in and at once put us at our ease. He came in with the dignity of a king returning from exile. He came in talking, laughing, smoking a cigarette, with waved hair and a flower in his buttonhole, and he looked markedly better, slighter, and younger than he had two years previously.[21]

Brimful of characteristic bonhomie, Oscar's first words to her were:

> Sphinx, how marvellous of you to know exactly the right hat to wear at seven o'clock in the morning to meet a friend who has been away! You can't have got up, you must have sat up.[22]

His delight at seeing Ada was genuine; he wrote to tell her so the next day, admitting:

> I often thought of you in the long black days and nights of my prison life, and to find you just as wonderful and dear as ever was no surprise; the beautiful are always beautiful.[23]

Inevitably, such bravado was unsustainable. When conversation turned to his future, Oscar decided, apparently on impulse, to contact the Jesuit Church of the Immaculate Conception on Farm Street in Mayfair to ask if he might enter a six-month retreat. On being refused, 'he broke down and sobbed bitterly'.[24]

Rejected by the Jesuits, Oscar decided to travel to Dieppe instead. At 4.30 on the morning of 20 May 1897, he was met off the night boat by Robbie Ross and Reggie Turner. After a few days at the Hotel Sandwich in Dieppe, Oscar moved to the Hotel de la Plage in the nearby village of

Berneval-le-Grand, before renting the Chalet Bourgeat from mid-June. In sleepy Berneval, he found the tranquillity he needed to write his last great work, *The Ballad of Reading Gaol*. He had hardly settled into the Hotel de la Plage when the first in a flurry of letters arrived from Bosie; this one expressing concern that he was no longer loved and begging Oscar to meet with him. Assuring him: 'Of course I love you more than anyone else', Oscar told Bosie that their lives were 'irreparably severed'.[25] Yet, within a fortnight, they had arranged a clandestine meeting, which Oscar cancelled once he learned from his solicitor that he would have to forfeit his allowance from Constance. He also learned that Queensberry was not done with him yet.

As Oscar attempted a gentle rehabilitation under the name Sebastian Melmoth, he found that life in France could be desperately lonely. Although nearby Dieppe played host to a sizable British community, many of his former acquaintances shunned him after his release. One who did not was Henrietta Eliza Vaughan Stannard, the immensely successful, Yorkshire-born novelist who wrote as 'John Strange Winter', a name she borrowed from a character in her first book, *Cavalry Life* (1881), after she was informed by her publisher that no reader would believe it was not written by a man.* One anecdote has it that, when Henrietta observed several of her compatriots snubbing Oscar, she crossed the street and exclaimed: 'Oscar, take me to tea!'[26]

Well regarded in journalistic circles, Henrietta Stannard played a pivotal role in convincing the Society of Authors to allow the election of women to official positions within that organisation. She also helped establish the Writers' Club, a rival women-only body, and was appointed its first president in 1892. She had moved to Dieppe on account of the poor health of her husband and youngest child. An enthusiastic ex-pat, she is credited with turning the town into a popular tourist resort through her glowing accounts of its many charms. On her return to London in 1901, she was elected president of the Society of Women Journalists.

Stannard had many admirers, among them John Ruskin, who was godfather to two of her children. As the sole supporter of her family, she earned a good income from her writing, which she later supplemented through the sale of cosmetic preparations of her own devising. One matter on which Oscar, Constance and she agreed was the imperative of campaigning for

---

* Michael Seeney's 'John Strange Winter and Dieppe', *The Wildean* No. 23, July 2003, gives an excellent account of Henrietta Stannard's life and her encounters with Oscar Wilde in 1897.

rational dress. In 1892, Henrietta established the Anti-Crinoline League, a crusade against 'ridiculous, vulgar, inelegant, and ungraceful' skirts that were so voluminous they presented a danger to the wearer.[27] Such skirts had contributed to the deaths of Emily and Mary Wilde decades earlier.

One anecdote often told concerns a prison warder with literary aspirations asking Oscar his opinion on John Strange Winter. Oscar replied: 'A charming person . . . but a lady you know, not a man,' adding, 'Not a great stylist, perhaps, but a good, simple storyteller'.[28] In response to a 'very sympathetic and touching message' asking him to call on her, Oscar told Henrietta:

> I was leading a life quite unworthy of a son of my dear mother whose nobility of soul and intellect you always appreciated, and who was herself always one of your warmest and most enthusiastic admirers.[29]

The Stannards called on Oscar at Berneval and he breakfasted with them in their home in Dieppe on a number of occasions. This show of support from such a prominent Englishwoman was greatly appreciated. Although he cared little for her writing, it seems likely that Henrietta immortalised Oscar in a kindly fashion in her novel *A Seaside Flirt* (1897), as epigram-spouting Irishman Vivian Dermott.[30]

Oscar soon turned his attention to the plight of others. He had encountered several child convicts in HM Prison Reading, and had been affected particularly by the plight of three young lads convicted of snaring rabbits; he secured their release by arranging for their fine to be paid. From Dieppe, he wrote a long letter highlighting the cruel treatment meted out to children held in English prisons and protesting at the dismissal of Warder Thomas Martin, whose only transgression had been to show kindness towards the youngest of the three little rabbit-poachers. He telegraphed this to Henry William Massingham, editor of the *Daily Chronicle*, who published it in full on 28 May 1897. Evidence of the importance he attached to Constance's good opinion is found in his request that a copy be sent to her.* Keen to hasten a reunion, he had written her a letter 'full of penitence' within days of arriving in France.[31]

Constance was understandably tentative in response. A note that accompanied photographs of Cyril and Vyvyan expressed her cautious

---

* A second letter from Oscar, published in the *Daily Chronicle* under the heading 'Don't Read This if You Want to be Happy To-day' during the week that the Prison Reform Bill was debated, outlined 'what reforms in our present stupid and barbarous system are urgently necessary'. Many of his suggestions were adopted.

agreement, but stopped short of suggesting a date for a meeting. By then, she was dreadfully ill and was staying with Margaret Brooke at her villa in Nervi. Compounding the difficulties she was experiencing with her mobility were profound fatigue, alarming headaches that lingered for days, a tremor in her right arm, and a left facial palsy.[32] When she stayed with Carlos and Carrie Blacker in Freiburg, her host was so shocked by her condition that he informed Oscar at once. In response, Oscar declared himself 'terribly distressed' since he had 'no idea it was so serious'.[33] In a second letter, he admitted: 'I don't mind *my life* being wrecked – that is as it should be – but when I think of poor Constance I simply want to kill myself'.[34] When he offered to visit, Blacker advised him to stay away.

On account of her health, Constance had gently batted away a suggestion that she travel to Dieppe, proposing instead that Oscar come and see her and their sons in Nervi as soon as she had rented a villa there. Once she had settled into the Villa Elvira, she was perfectly happy, eager even, to receive him. Unfortunately, her reasonable caution could not have contrasted more markedly with Bosie's ardour. While she was prudent, he was all spontaneity. Of course, that was Oscar's nature too: 'I must love and be loved, whatever price I pay for it', he told Robbie when justifying his actions.[35] For a time he even held Constance responsible for pushing him back towards Bosie.

When Oscar and Bosie met in Rouen late in August 1897, they concocted a plan to live together in Naples, although they postponed this since Bosie was due to travel with his mother, who was funding his lifestyle. Oscar had grown disillusioned with the solitude of Berneval and left for Paris on 15 September, but within a week, he had joined Bosie in Italy. When he wrote to Constance, postponing his visit until late October, when the boys would be back in school, she was desperately upset. Concerned by the fact that his letter had been sent from Naples, she expressed her fear to Carlos Blacker that Oscar had reunited with Bosie. She was incensed when Blacker confirmed this and she wrote to Oscar immediately; he quoted her words in a letter to More Adey:

> I forbid you to see Lord Alfred Douglas . . . I forbid you to return to your filthy, insane life. I forbid you to live at Naples. I will not allow you to come to Genoa.[36]

In November 1897, Constance stopped Oscar's allowance by invoking the terms of their separation, but kindness overcame her and she sent money anonymously via Robbie Ross. Unaware of her generosity, Oscar condemned his wife for having no imagination, and expressed a desire for her to leave him alone. In *Oscar Wilde: A Summing Up*, published in 1940, Bosie would accuse Constance of being 'far from generous' with her money and of letting Oscar down.[37] In *Without Apology* (1938), he wrote:

> If she had treated him properly and stuck to him after he had been in prison, as a really good wife would have done, he [Oscar] would have gone on loving her to the end of his life.[38]

Once he was deprived of a regular income, life became increasingly difficult for Oscar: 'I am face to face with starvation,' he told Ada Leverson, 'not in any rhetorical sense, but as an ugly fact'.[39] Perhaps this made it inevitable that he would accept the offer extended by Bosie's mother, Sibyl, that she would settle Bosie's debts and give Oscar £200 if they agreed to part; had they refused, she would have stopped Bosie's allowance of £8 a week. Whether this financial inducement convinced them or whether the lustre had gone from their relationship is unclear but what is certain is that Bosie moved out early in December 1897.

Although Cyril spent Christmas 1897 with Constance, Vyvyan was obliged to stay at the Jesuit College in Monaco, where he had been enrolled in order that he would be near Princess Alice of Monaco, who undertook to keep an eye on him. Constance spent a happy week with him in mid-February instead. By then, her attitude towards Oscar was softening once more. By March, she had restored his allowance and written a codicil to her will ensuring he would continue to receive it after her death. Early in April, she wrote to Vyvyan:

> Try not to feel harshly about your father . . . remember that he is your father and that he loves you. All his troubles arose from the hatred of a son for his father, and whatever he has done he has suffered bitterly for.[40]

In April, desperate to address her increasingly poor health, Constance returned to Professor Bossi's clinic, where he diagnosed and removed benign uterine fibroids. Within four days of this hazardous surgical procedure, Constance was vomiting unremittingly and had became severely dehydrated. In the absence of any effective intervention, she lost consciousness and died on 7 April 1898; she was thirty-nine years old. Otho, who was heartbroken, arranged for his sister to be buried in a section of the Campo Santo in Genoa set aside for Protestants. A marble cross inlaid with dark ivy leaves read: 'Constance Mary, daughter of Horace Lloyd, Q.C.', followed by a verse from Revelation.[*]

Oscar learned of Constance's death by telegram on 12 April: 'Am overwhelmed with grief,' he told Otho. 'It is the most terrible tragedy'.[41] He told Carlos Blacker: 'It really is awful. I don't know what to do. If we had only met once, and kissed each other'.[42] In a telegram to Robbie Ross, he wrote: 'Am in great grief'.[43] It is odd, therefore, that Ross told Leonard Smithers: 'Oscar of course did not feel it at all'.[44] Ada Leverson believed that 'he felt most of all the death of his wife,' adding: 'This was the greatest blow to Oscar'.[45] Robert Sherard agreed. In *The Life of Oscar Wilde*, he wrote of Constance:

> She was a simple, beautiful woman, too gentle and good for the part that life called upon her to play. She was a woman of heart whom kindlier gods would never have thrown into the turmoil and stress of an existence which was all a battle. Her death was to Oscar Wilde's affectionate heart a sorrow which accentuated his despair.[46]

Countering a prevailing view of his mother as serious and sombre, Vyvyan wrote of her: 'She may not have had much sense of humour, but then she did not have very much to laugh about'.[47]

As they mourned their beloved mother, Cyril and Vyvyan were given to understand that their father was dead also. They returned to England during the summer of 1898. Cyril was enrolled in Radley College, where he proved to be an outstanding athlete.[†] Vyvyan stayed with the Napiers, who were kind but never mentioned Oscar. On their bookshelves, he discovered a copy of *The Happy Prince* but was shocked to see that his father's name had been scored off the cover and erased inside. As expected, Adrian Hope, who administered their small estate, took no interest in their well-being. When Vyvyan wrote to tell him that he had won prizes for mathematics and classics and for coming top of the school, Hope never even acknowledged the letter. Later, Vyvyan was prevented from continuing his school study of Greek, a subject in which he excelled, as his father had, and he assumed that this was Hope's doing.

---

[*] The words 'Wife of Oscar Wilde' were added by her descendants in 1963.

[†] On 9 May 1915, Captain Cyril Holland, aged twenty-nine, was shot dead by a German sniper during the Battle of Festubert, which took place in the Artois region of France. Vyvyan Holland studied law and became an accomplished writer and translator. He lived until he was eighty. His warm memoir *Son of Oscar Wilde* received huge acclaim.

In February 1899, en route to Lake Geneva, Oscar drove out to the Campo Santo in a ramshackle little green cab, clutching an armful of red roses to place on Constance's grave. Although 'deeply affected', he told Robbie Ross that he was keenly aware of 'the uselessness of all regrets'.[48] Oscar, a passionate individualist, refused to adhere to the nonsensical sexual code imposed upon him. Yet, Constance had demonstrated an extraordinary degree of compassion and tolerance for a man who, although extraordinarily harshly treated by society, had behaved very badly towards his wife no matter what his nature and motivation.

Chapter 21

'The World Rings with His Infamy'

Is there on earth a crime so terrible that in punishment of it a father can be prevented from seeing his children? OSCAR WILDE to Claire de Pratz[1]

At the height of his success, when his epigrams were on everyone's lips, Oscar could count on the encouragement of a succession of accomplished and entertaining women. Now that he had fallen out of favour, he must have wondered who would stand by him. Ada Leverson and Adela Schuster offered him staunch support during his trials and imprisonment, and Henrietta Stannard extended non-judgemental friendship during the early days of his post-prison life. Constance, his wife, strove to do what was best for him until the end of her life despite his often callous disregard for her happiness.

Not every woman was so accepting. The primitive and intolerant moral code that refused to accommodate anything beyond a heterosexual orientation led to widespread condemnation. Among those who sympathised, there were several who regretted only that Oscar had been singled out. Feminist social reformer Josephine Butler, whose sentiments had been parodied by Oscar in *A Woman of No Importance*, expressed such qualified sympathy: 'I am so sorry for Oscar Wilde,' she told her son Stanley, 'because he has to bear the loathing and contempt alone which many others rightly should share with him'.[2]

This harsh sentiment was echoed by poet Alice Meynell who, on learning of Oscar's sentence, exclaimed: 'As *seclusion* two years are far too little. As punishment one wishes they might be made more tolerable,' adding: 'But while there is a weak omnibus horse at work or a hungry cat I am not going to spend feeling on Oscar'.[3] Two years earlier, in her collection of essays *The Rhythm of Life* (1893), she had described his 'The Decay of Lying' as a 'witty and delicate series of inversions'.[4] Now she attempted to have Oscar's name excised from her book: 'I am sure that you will agree with me,' she told her publisher, John Lane, 'that the mention of Oscar Wilde by name is impossible'.[5]

Many women, including Constance for a time, believed that Oscar was afflicted by madness. In *Aspects of Wilde*, a biographical treatment that was deemed reliable by Florence Stoker, Vincent O'Sullivan describes a scheme devised by one woman:

> . . . the wife of a rich baronet, and ex-actress, who wrote to the Home Secretary offering to install Wilde in the lodge at the gates of her park, where he would be carefully guarded by two strong nurses brought from the nearest asylum.[6]

According to O'Sullivan, Oscar was 'greatly amused' by this. When seeking early release, he too had pleaded 'sexual madness' to the Home Secretary in mitigation of his 'terrible offences', but to no avail.[7]

Some, who may have sympathised privately, remained publically silent. When Willie explained to Bram Stoker that his brother had been led astray by 'his Vanity – & conceit', he finished: 'Am sure you & Florence must have felt the disgrace of one who cared for you both sincerely'.[8] Although Florence appears to have done little to help him at the time, a rumour surfaced that Bram, encouraged by Florence, had travelled to Paris with money for Oscar after his release. This seems to have originated in an account given by Ann Stoker, Florence's granddaughter, who claimed she heard it from her own mother.[9] Years later, Florence expressed a desire to meet Vyvyan and told her sister Philippa, 'I wanted him to come & see me, being so fond of his Father'.[10]

Many women kept their thoughts to themselves. Art historian Mary Berenson, who thought he 'talked like an angel' admitted in her diary that the treatment of 'poor Oscar' made her miserable, adding, 'It is horrible to think what his feelings must be'.[11] Clara Morris, whom Oscar had offered the lead role in *Vera* in 1882, also confined her thoughts to a diary entry for 6 April 1895:

> Oh! Oscar Wild [sic] lost his case! All England, America – the world rings with his infamy . . . his name is stricken from the play bills . . . Poor old Lady Wilde – Oh the mother wife & little sons – They are to be pitied. Oh it is too dreadful – he is arrested now.[12]

There were others who defended him more openly. At a dinner hosted by Mary Jeune, Frank Harris spoke up for Oscar when several guests remarked that he had got what he deserved: 'I'm glad to hear you say you are a friend,' Lady Dorothy Nevill, a contributor to *The Woman's World*, assured him, adding 'I am, too, and shall always be proud of having known him, a most brilliant, charming man'.[13] When Harris announced his intention of holding a dinner for Oscar on his release, Lady Dorothy expressed the hope that she would be invited, insisting 'I always admired and liked him; I feel dreadfully sorry for him'.[14]

There were women who suffered by association. Some commentators linked Oscar's fate to the New Woman movement and rushed to pin the blame for what they regarded as deviant behaviour in men on the rise of strong, forthright, often sexually-aware women. The conservative *Reynold's Newspaper* opined: 'in the era of the "New Woman," it is not astonishing to discover that the sex-Problem is putting on a new face, and making a new course for itself'.[15] A condemnatory opinion piece in *The Speaker* insisted:

> For many years past Mr. Wilde has been the real leader in this country of the 'new school' in literature . . . The new criticism, the new poetry, even the new woman are all, more or less, the creatures of Mr. Oscar Wilde's fancy.[16]

In December 1895, *Punch* announced 'The End of the New Woman'.[17]

This association was detrimental to publications associated with the movement, most notably *The Yellow Book*, a decadent hardback quarterly that promoted New Woman writers. Ironically, it was a misinterpreted line from *Dorian Gray* that led to this spurious link: 'His eyes fell on the Yellow Book that Lord Henry had sent him'. The book in *Dorian Gray* was fictitious and resembled Huysmans' *À rebours* more than any other. In fact, Oscar detested *The Yellow Book* and was never invited to contribute to it: 'The *Yellow Book* has appeared,' he told Bosie; 'It is dull and loathsome, a great failure. I am so glad'.[18] He expressed his displeasure to Ada Leverson too: 'Have you seen *The Yellow Book*?' he inquired. 'It is horrid and not yellow at all'.[19] Leverson was surely more enthusiastic, since she contributed several short stories, one of which, 'Suggestion' is reminiscent of *The Picture of Dorian Gray*.[20]

When John Lane, publisher of *The Yellow Book*, arrived in New York in April 1895, he was confronted with newspaper headlines announcing: 'Arrest of Oscar Wilde, Yellow Book under his arm'.[*] Although this was not the case, Lane realised the implications and despaired: 'It killed *The Yellow Book* and it nearly killed me', he claimed.[21] Without delay, he telegraphed his office manager and instructed him to remove Oscar's books

---

[*] Margaret D. Stetz and Mark Samuels Lasner have identified this book as a yellow-bound copy of *Aphrodite* by Pierre Louÿs.

from sale. By then, several authors were threatening to boycott the Bodley Head, the publishing house established by Lane in partnership with Elkin Mathews, since it employed Edward Shelley, who had testified to a sexual relationship with Oscar. On 5 April 1895, the Bodley Head premises at Vigo Street were attacked by a stone-wielding mob.

When Lane removed Aubrey Beardsley as art editor of *The Yellow Book* as a result of his association with Oscar, W. B. Yeats claimed this was done at the insistence of 'a popular novelist, a woman who had great influence among the most conventional part of the British public'.[22] This was surely Mrs Humphry Ward, who had encouraged poet William Watson to write to Lane and threaten to change publisher unless *The Yellow Book* was discontinued. Volume five was halted mid-production when Alice Meynell's husband, Wilfred, applied similar pressure, although it did appear a fortnight later and the publication limped along for another two years.

Lane, a pioneer of New Women's writing, also published the contentious *Keynotes*, which took its name from the first in the series, a collection of musings by Mary Chavelita Dunne, who wrote as George Egerton. Dunne, a contributor to *The Yellow Book*, was closely associated with the Decadent movement. Her *Keynotes* (1893) caused a sensation by tackling controversial themes including female sexuality, sexual freedom, alcoholism and suicide. The daughter of an Irish army officer, Dunne described herself as 'intensely Irish'. By echoing Oscar's style and quoting him in an epigram to 'A Little Gray Glove', she reinforced his association with New Women's writing. Several passages in 'A Cross Line' imagine a dance in a 'dream of motion', and take much from *Salomé*:

> She can see herself with parted lips and panting, rounded breasts, and a dancing devil in each glowing eye, sway voluptuously to the wild music that rises, now slow, now fast, now deliriously wild, seductive, intoxicating, with a human note of passion in its strain.[23]

Dunne suffered personally from her association with Oscar, whose sad fate she mourned. She loathed the duplicity of Victorian society, which she summed up sardonically in a letter to her father: 'sin as you please but don't be found out. It's all right so long as you don't shock us by letting us know'.[24] The parody of *Keynotes* that appeared in *Punch* as 'She-notes' by Borgia Smudgiton was a sure indication of the anxiety mainstream society felt when confronted with her themes and she never replicated the success of *Keynotes*.[25]

Unlike Dunne, several women benefitted from Oscar's influence. One was novelist and dramatist Pearl Craigie, who wrote as John Oliver Hobbes and claimed to be: 'the only person in London who could sign her name to Wilde's plays and be believed'.[26] Vincent O'Sullivan described Craigie as 'Wilde's sole disciple of any significance among the young writers of the time,' adding, 'All her plays are influenced by Wilde, and her early novels'.[27] Craigie's epigrams in particular were comparable to his. In *The Sinner's Comedy* she wrote, 'Men heap together the mistakes of their lives, and create a monster they call destiny'.[28] Recognising the similarity, Oscar playfully inscribed a copy of *The Sinner's Comedy*, 'From the Author, August, 1892 to dear Edward Shelley'.[29] Craigie's most successful play *The Ambassador* was produced by George Alexander at the St James's Theatre in 1898.

Other women were inspired to write about his plight. In their youth, Oscar and Willie had played tennis with Dublin-born Julia Davis, a friend of Ada Leverson's, and her sister, fashion columnist Eliza Davis Aria. In *My Sentimental Self*, Eliza described: 'Oscar in a high hat with his frock-coat tails flying and his long hair waving in the breeze'.[30] Their connection did not end there. When Eliza became involved in a long-term affair with Henry Irving, she suggested, to no avail, that he stage *The Duchess of Padua*. In 1906, Julia, writing as Frank Danby, published *The Sphinx's Lawyer*, which Eliza described as an attempt 'to defend the undefendable Oscar Wilde'.[31]

In an astonishing preface addressed to her brother Owen Hall,* Julia declared, 'Because you "hate and loathe" my book and its subject, I dedicate it to you'. Oscar appeared in the guise of Algernon Heseltine, a man treated unjustly by society because he 'was not as others' on account of his genius: 'the applause changed to low suspicious muttering', she observed. Yet, although Julia lauded Oscar's genius and described him as a martyr, *The Sphinx's Lawyer* was not a vindication since she suggested that Heseltine was mad and should 'have been placed in safety, kept from spreading his disease, from working evil'.[32]

High profile women had their reputations to protect and often, those who showed Oscar greatest kindness were ordinary working-class women. In *The Real Oscar Wilde*, Robert Sherard quoted a cook from Tite Street, a long time employee of the Wildes, who declared: 'Bless his sweet face, he was the kindest gentleman that ever lived'.[33] Oscar described his landlady

---

* This is the pen name of Irish-born racing correspondent, theatre critic and solicitor, James 'Jimmy' Davis. He was once friendly with Oscar and it is not known why they fell out.

at the Hotel de la Plage as 'a perfect dear, who wants me to live always at Berneval!'[34] Kindest of all perhaps was restaurateur Madame Bechet, who kept a table at the back of Chez Bechet for Monsieur *Sébastien*. Each day, she prepared special dishes, ensuring that Oscar ate them by chiding: 'Come, Monsieur *Sébastien*, you must not give up!'[35]

Some of those who demonstrated kindness had scarcely known him in the days before his release. In a letter to Decadent publisher Leonard Smithers, who brought out *The Ballad of Reading Gaol*,* Oscar mentioned Smithers' wife, Alice 'whose sweetness and kindness to me I shall never forget'.[36] When she invited him to a Christmas party in 1898, he sent his apologies from Naples: 'I am a wretched walker and would probably not arrive till midsummer,' he wrote, before inviting Leonard and herself to join him in Italy.[37] Although *The Ballad of Reading Gaol* sold well during Oscar's lifetime, the first six editions omitted his name, using C.3.3., his prison designation, instead. Oscar made sure that Constance received a copy; she thought it wonderful but desperately sad.

In order to maximise profits, Oscar's pioneering American agent, Elizabeth Marbury, an astute and energetic businesswoman, immensely confident and capable, was charged with selling the rights in the US.† A frequent visitor to Paris, Marbury maintained an office in the city and represented the crème of literary France, including playwright Victorien Sardou. She was progressive in her views on sexuality and her lifelong companion was the celebrated American actress and interior designer Elsie de Wolfe.

Lizzie Marbury first met Oscar during his tour of America at the home of a Professor Doremus. He was holding a cup of tea at the time and endeared himself by offering it to her. Ever the publicist, she realised that his eccentric appearance was 'well conceived and of value in stimulating

---

* *The Ballad of Reading Gaol* was inspired by the execution of Charles Thomas Wooldridge for the murder of his wife Laura, a punishment administered on Saturday 7 July 1896, while Oscar was incarcerated in the same institution. Initially, Smithers offered Oscar all profits but they agreed to share them at Oscar's insistence (James G. Nelson, *Publisher to the Decadents: Leonard Smithers in the Careers of Beardsley, Wilde, and Dowson*, Penn State Press, 2010, p. 177).

† Marbury was business manager to Frances Hodgson Burnett and represented George Bernard Shaw. In 1903, she helped establish the Colony Club, the first women's social club in New York. During World War I, she undertook relief work for the French and American troops, working in military hospitals in France and addressing the troops. In time she would pioneer the American musical comedy, collaborating with Jerome Kern and Cole Porter.

curiosity and in providing copy for the press'.[38] As she got to know him better, Marbury summed Oscar up perfectly, observing: 'His wit scintillated incessantly. His joy in the phrases he compiled was always evident though never offensive'.[39]

In *My Crystal Ball*, her somewhat fanciful memoir, Marbury described Oscar holding court at his Tite Street home and thinking aloud the plots of his plays:

> I remember one terrible tragedy, brutally conceived, which revolved around a most revolting theme . . . It took me many days before I could prove to him that despite the dramatic value of the story that the managers and public would never tolerate the motive.[40]

Marbury believed Oscar 'was so devoid of any ethical sense' that he remained unconvinced. 'Form and treatment were everything to him,' she insisted. 'Matters and morals meant nothing'.[41]

Although tears rolled down her cheeks when she read *The Ballad of Reading Gaol*, Marbury told Smithers: 'Nobody here seems to feel any interest in the poem'.[42] Hardly surprising, given that the prevailing view of sexual relationships between men that were held up to public scrutiny led cross-dressing lesbian novelist Willa Cather to write in her book column that Wilde:

> is in prison, most deservedly so. Upon his head is heaped the deepest infamy and the darkest shame of a generation. Civilization shudders at his name, and there is absolutely no spot on earth where this man can live.[43]

Marbury finally secured $250 for it from the *New York World*. In her memoir, she describes how she also attempted to divert royalties from Oscar's plays to Constance, but was instructed to go through official channels instead. In any case, his plays were out of favour; Rose Coghlan had ended her run of *A Woman of No Importance* by denouncing him from the stage. Marbury's insistence that theatrical impresario Charles Frohman had authorised her to pay $500 to Oscar for a new comedy seems unlikely; when Frohman sold his rights to *Lady Windermere's Fan* to his brother Gustave in 1894, he was at pains to stress that this play was no longer under his supervision.[44]

Towards the end of his life, Marbury encountered Oscar in Paris, 'unkempt, forlorn and penniless', and living in 'a wretched room in the attic of a squalid little hotel'.[45] The Hotel d'Alsace was shabby, but it was not squalid. Whatever the accuracy of her memoir, she was effusive in her praise for Oscar's talent, considering *De Profundis* to be his 'masterpiece and a rich contribution to the treasure house of English literature'. As it was 'conceived and written *in* the depths,' she wrote, '[i]t was given to the world as Oscar's last message to save others *from* the depths'.[46]

Realising that his extended letter to Bosie laid bare his innermost thoughts, Oscar entrusted the manuscript to Robbie Ross, who named it *De Profundis*. He asked Ross to send excerpts to actress Frances (Frankie) Forbes Robertson and Adela Schuster, as 'both those sweet women will be interested to know something of what is happening to my soul'.[47] In May 1899, Oscar wrote to 'My dear, sweet, beautiful Friend', Frankie, to congratulate her on her recent wedding. He enclosed a vellum-bound copy of *The Importance of Being Earnest* as a gift. His letter, though characteristically cheerful, contains a fanciful lament about the state of his finances: 'Like dear St Francis of Assisi I am wedded to Poverty,' he wrote:

> but in my case the marriage is not a success: I hate the Bride that has been given to me: I see no beauty in her hunger and her rags: I have not the soul of St Francis: my thirst is for the beauty of life: my desire for its joy.

He closed by writing, 'I live now on echoes as I have little music of my own'.[48]

All Oscar could give to friends was his work. He presented Ada Leverson with a copy of *The Ballad of Reading Gaol*, dedicated, 'To the Sphinx of pleasure from the singer of pain'. She was frequently on his mind: 'Bosie and I often talk over your delightful sayings, and your brilliant and beautiful personality – unique, troubling and imaginative,' he told her.[49] While Oscar was in Naples in October 1897, Ada lent him her copy of *Salomé*, which he hoped to have translated and performed; it was not to be. She also returned to him the almost completed manuscript of *La Sainte Courtisane*, which Robbie Ross had rescued from Tite Street. When Oscar left it in a cab in Paris, he laughed that this was the proper place for it.*

In 1898, when Ada visited Oscar in Paris, she found him 'leading the life of a student in a tiny room at the Hotel d'Alsace'.[50] Yet, she noted, he had retained the 'power of making people fond of him' and had persuaded Jean Dupoirier, proprietor of the hotel, to settle his debts.[51] Ada

---

* Robbie Ross attempted to restore this play from odd leaves of a first draft. It concerns Honorius, a hermit who falls in love with a courtesan and reveals to her the secret of the love of God, which she embraces. When the reformed courtesan is murdered, the hermit loses his faith and returns to Alexandria to pursue a life of pleasure.

had problems of her own by then; her marriage to Ernest was failing. Having lost the bulk of his fortune, he argued with his wife over her profligacy, which, in his defence, was prodigious. Nonetheless, Ada stood by him when he was cited as co-respondent in a divorce case in May 1897.*

In an interview she gave to Léon Guillot de Saix in *L'Européen* and in her memoir, *France from Within*, London-born journalist Claire de Pratz, née Zoe Clara Solange Cadiot, offers fascinating insights into the final months of Oscar's life.† On graduating from the Sorbonne, Claire, whose mother was Professor of French Literature at Queens College, worked as an English teacher before becoming a correspondent with *Le Petit Parisien* and the *Daily News*. In July 1889, when she was seventeen, she had written 'Pierre Loti and His Works' for *The Woman's World*. When she met Oscar in Paris, she reminded him that he was her first editor. They struck up a friendship as a result and he christened her 'the good goddess', 'la bonne déesse'.[52]

According to Claire, Oscar often spoke of his mother but never of his trials and imprisonment, although he was clearly devastated by the consequences of his conviction: 'Is there on earth a crime so terrible that in punishment of it a father can be prevented from seeing his children?' he asked her.[53] When she invited him to tea in February 1900, he declined on the grounds of ill-health. Apparently, it was to Claire that Oscar said of the wallpaper in his room at the Hotel d'Alsace – chocolate flowers on a blue background – 'my wallpaper and I are fighting a duel to the death. One or the other has to go'.[54]

As Oscar hated to be alone, he took to frequenting several of the bars and cafes that studded the French capital: Cafe de la Paix, the Grand Cafe, Cafe Julien or Bar Calisaya. In each one, he would regale what audience he could assemble with stories, outlines of plays and plans for the future. Vincent O'Sullivan remembered him reminiscing about his mother on many occasions. He also spoke of his plan to write a play called 'Isabel', based on the story of Jezebel, which he insisted he would write for Sarah Bernhardt.[55] His intention, he said, was to 'bring out that Queen Jezebel was not the "bedizzened hussy", termagant and shrew, which her

---

* In time, Ernest left England to work in the lumber trade in Canada, where he was joined by his daughter Ruth. Ada stayed in London but was obliged to leave her home. She wrote a woman's column, 'White and Gold', for *The Referee* under the name Elaine. Her first novel, *The Twelfth Hour*, was published in 1907.

† Claire de Pratz attained a Professorship in English language in a state Lycee for women. She wrote several books, fiction and non-fiction, including 'A Frenchwoman's Notes on the War'.

name connoted in the popular estimation'.[56]

Although Oscar hoped to collaborate with Sarah, she was far more reticent. Earlier, when Robert Sherard, at Oscar's suggestion, had offered her the rights to *Salomé* for £400, she 'wrung her hands, and her wonderful eyes moistened with real emotion' as she spoke of the calamity that had befallen her 'good friend'. She promised to do what she could, and to write to Oscar soon, yet she never did and she was 'out' when Sherard called by appointment.[57] Oscar was not at all surprised: 'I suppose Sarah is hopeless', he wrote.[58] Yet, he had been grateful that she cared at all and, at the time of his arrest, had expressed relief that 'Sarah, and Goncourt, and other artists are sympathising with me'.[59]

While Oscar was in Nice in December 1898, he saw Sarah perform in Sardou's *La Tosca*. He described their touching reunion to Robert Ross: 'I went round to see Sarah and she embraced me and wept, and I wept, and the whole evening was wonderful'.[60] Later, he told Vincent O'Sullivan: 'the three women I have most admired are Queen Victoria, Sarah Bernhardt, and Lily Langtree [sic]. I would have married any one of them with pleasure'.[61] He was laughing as he said this. Lillie was living in America at the time and had a ready excuse not to go to his aid, although, according to O'Sullivan, she 'pretended she had hardly known him'.[62] Years later, when she lived in Monaco, it was said that she kept an empty seat at her dining table in his memory.[63] It was an empty gesture really.

Although Oscar sought consolation from friends, as was typical of his nature, it was often he who offered comfort to others. In August 1897, impresario Augustus Daly offered Oscar an advance to write a play for his lead actress Ada Rehan, who was at the height of her popularity at the time. No agreement was made and Daly died in Paris on 7 June 1899. For Ada Rehan, as shy and retiring offstage as she was forceful onstage, this was as much a personal tragedy as a professional one. She was touched by Oscar's kindness in the wake of her loss: 'Oscar Wilde came to me and was more good and helpful than I can tell you – just like a very kind brother', she wrote; 'I shall always think of him as he was to me through those few dreadful days'.[64]

In February 1900, Oscar agreed to terms with Ada Rehan to write 'a new and original comedy, in three or four acts', which, he assured her, he would finish by 1 June. It was to be produced anonymously 'in London at a first-class West-End theatre'.[65] In return, Ada paid him an advance of £100 with the promise of £200 on acceptance. Once Oscar realised his deadline was wildly optimistic, he offered to return the advance but asked that he be given some time. Ada, though disappointed, agreed to this delay, but Oscar never did manage to return her money.

Ada Rehan was not the only woman to commission this never-to-materialise play, which was based on the scenario outlined to George Alexander in August 1894. An exasperated letter from American actress Cora Brown Potter, dated 22 March 1900, asks: 'When will you give me over my play? Don't you think I have been very patient with you about it?'[66] When Frank Harris developed Oscar's scenario into *Mr & Mrs. Daventry*, he was obliged to pay off five claimants who had paid advances to Oscar.* Desperate for money, it's hardly surprising that Oscar did what he could to raise funds, although it seems unlikely he would resort to outright begging, as claimed by Nellie Melba.

Although Melba was not a close friend to Oscar, her description of his insatiable desire for cigarettes, and her claim that she knew he had called by the quantity of cigarette ends in her fireplace suggest they knew each other reasonably well. On one occasion, she remembered him producing six cigarette cases from about his person, although they may have been intended as gifts. In *Melodies and Memories*, Melba writes of walking through Paris when Oscar lurched around a corner with a 'hunted look in his eyes'. She describes how she was about to walk past when he stopped her: 'Madame Melba – you don't know who I am? I'm Oscar Wilde', he said, perhaps assuming she did not recognise him, before continuing, 'I am going to do a terrible thing. I'm going to ask you for money'.[67] Hardly able to look at him, she emptied her purse. He almost snatched the money, muttered his thanks and was gone.

It is a testament to Oscar's generosity that, desperately short of funds, he still tried to help others. On 13 March 1899, Willie Wilde, aged forty-six, succumbed to complications related to alcoholism. When Robbie Ross wrote to inform Oscar of his brother's death, he replied:

> I suppose it had been expected for some time. I am very sorry for his wife, who, I suppose, has little left to live on. Between him and me there had been, as you know, wide chasms for many years. Requiescat in Pace.[68]

Oscar did try to help Lily by exploring the option of selling Moytura and giving her some of the proceeds.[69] This necessity was removed by her second

---

* A letter from Ross to More Adey claimed that Harris had to pay £100 each to the five people who said Oscar had sold them the rights. They were: Horace Sedger, Leonard Smithers, Kyrle Bellew, Cora Brown-Potter and Louis Nethersole.

marriage to Dutch translator Alexander Teixeira de Mattos, who had been a witness when she married Willie. In October 1900, while honeymooning in Paris, Lily and her new husband called on Oscar. Shortly beforehand Lily had signed a letter: 'Your most affectionate sister, Lily Wilde'.[70] She had kept in touch with Constance too, expressing concern for her 'sad and lonely' state and her 'shocking state of health' just weeks before her death.[71]

Like Willie, Oscar too found solace in alcohol and towards the end, his consumption was prodigious; Jean Dupoirier reported that a litre of cognac 'would hardly see him through the night'.[72] This was, by all accounts, supplemented by day with quantities of champagne, wine and absinthe, which, he told Frank Harris, had about it 'the seduction of strange sins'.[73] In Robert Sherard's assessment, 'the poor fellow was seeking through drink to create for himself an artificial paradise in the real and palpable hell of his existence'.[74] Aside from his drinking, Oscar's general health was poor. For much of his adult life, he had suffered from deafness and infections of his right ear. When this condition flared up in prison, it was inadequately treated. In September 1900, he fell ill once again, to the extent that his right ear was operated on in his hotel room. Although the procedure seemed effective, by mid-November, he had suffered a relapse and was confined to bed.

During the final weeks of his life, Oscar was nursed lovingly by his great friends Robbie Ross and Reggie Turner. On 29 November, Ross, a convert to Catholicism since 1894, sent for Father Cuthbert Dunne, a priest attached to the Passionist Church of St Joseph's in Paris. Although incapable of speech at that point, Oscar was conditionally baptised into the Catholic faith, an act, Ross assured Ada Leverson, that was in accordance with Oscar's long-held wishes. Early on the morning of 30 November, a change came over Oscar and his breathing became laboured. Shortly before two o'clock, he heaved a great sigh and breathed his last.* Ross found two Franciscan nuns to watch over his friend's laid-out body while he informed the authorities of his death.

An exceptionally mean-spirited memorial notice printed in *The Guardian* declared:

Wilde's life is one of the saddest in English literature. His abilities were

---

* In their paper 'Oscar Wilde's terminal illness: reappraisal after a century', Ashley H. Robins and Sean L. Sellars concluded, based on medical evidence, that Oscar Wilde died of meningoencephalitis secondary to chronic right middle-ear disease (*The Lancet*, Vol 356, 25 November 2000, pp. 1841–3).

sufficient to win him an honoured place as a man of letters, but they struggled in vain against his lack of character.[75]

The *Pall Mall Gazette* concluded: 'Mr. Wilde had a wonderful cleverness, but no substantiality,' adding, 'nothing that he ever wrote had strength to endure'.[76] Across the Atlantic, *The New York Times* alluded to suicide and damned him with faint praise, declaring: 'As a dramatist, Wilde was hampered by his utter lack of sincerity and his inability to master the technical side of play-writing,' before adding: 'But his wit, his pleasing literary facility, and his droll views of life made some of his plays rather effective with a limited audience'.[77]

On 3 December, a funeral mass was read by Fr. Dunne at the church of Saint-Germain-des-Prés in the presence of fifty-six people, among them 'five ladies in deep mourning'.[78] Robbie Ross identified four: Anna de Brémont* and her maid; Mme Stuart Merrill, wife of the American Symbolist poet who had raised a petition for Oscar's release; and 'an old servant girl of Oscar Wilde's wife'.[79] Richard Ellmann identified the fifth as Miriam Aldrich, although Horst Schroeder disputes this.[80] When Oscar was buried at Bagneux cemetery on 3 December 1900, Bosie turned up as chief mourner.[†] At the head of Oscar's coffin, Ross placed a wreath of laurels, inscribed 'A tribute to his literary achievements and distinction'; it bore the names of 'those who had shown kindness to him during or after his imprisonment', among them Ada Leverson and Adela Schuster.[81]

Afterwards, Adela received a detailed letter from Ross describing Oscar's final months. She remained loyal to his memory for the rest of her life and, when Frank Harris published *Oscar Wilde: His Life and Confessions* in 1916, she took exception to his characterization of her friend: 'Miss Schuster objects, and rightly, to my saying that Oscar was very cold and hard and incapable of friendship,' Harris wrote.[82] Robbie Ross dedicated *The Duchess of Padua* to Adela Schuster in fulfilment of Oscar's desire to express gratitude for her 'infinite kindness'. Oscar had wished for something better, declaring 'it is unworthy of her and unworthy of me'.[83]

Although Cyril and Vyvyan were not told of their father's death, Robbie

---

* Anna de Brémont confirms her presence in *Oscar Wilde and his Mother*.
† Two years later he married poet and heiress Olive Custance. When she left him, his father-in-law obtained custody of their son, who suffered from schizophrenia and died in 1964. Bosie was declared bankrupt after losing a libel action he took against Arthur Ransome. He was sued for libel by Winston Churchill in 1923, and served six months in Wormwood Scrubs. He died of congestive heart failure in March 1945.

organised for flowers to be sent in their name. Oscar had approached Adrian Hope through More Adey in the hope of getting a message to his sons, but Hope insisted that any letters he sent would be destroyed. This was the man of whom Oscar had written: 'with him Cyril and Vyvyan have a good chance of a beautiful future'.[84] When Ross bought the rights to Oscar's work from the receiver, it was his intention to clear Oscar's debts and give what remained to his children. To do so, he needed Hope's permission since, as trustee of Constance's estate, he was a principle creditor; Hope refused to allow the boys to benefit in any way from their father's work.

On 1 December 1908, a group of Oscar's friends gathered in the Ritz Hotel to honour Robbie Ross and celebrate the publication of the *Collected Edition of the Works of Oscar Wilde*, which he had edited. In his speech that day, Ross announced that an unnamed benefactor had donated £2,000 to fund the relocation of Oscar's remains from Bagneux to Père Lachaise cemetery and the commissioning of a suitably imposing tomb from sculptor Jacob Epstein. This donor was Oscar's great friend and admirer Helen Carew, to whom Ross dedicated *Volume XIII: Reviews* of his *Collected Edition* (1908) and also *Intentions* (1909).

Helen was the widow of James Lawrence Carew, an Irish nationalist MP, who had attended Trinity College, Dublin at the same time as Oscar. She owned a copy of *The Happy Prince and Other Tales* inscribed: 'to the happy princess from the unhappy prince, with the devotion of the author, Oscar Wilde'.[85] In 1907, when Helen's son Sir Coleridge Kennard took his friend Vyvyan Holland to meet her, she used the opportunity to speak in glowing terms of his father. She took Vyvyan to the Hotel d'Alsace and Bagneux Cemetery, and organised for him to meet Robbie Ross, thus opening up a world of admiration for Oscar.[86] Ross in turn took him to see Adela Schuster, whose beautiful home he had visited as a child. When Vyvyan met Ada Leverson, he noted: 'She was a fascinating person, still very beautiful with the aureole of gold-tinted hair from which derived the name my father had given her'.[87]

One woman who never forgot Oscar was Ellen Terry. When she visited Paris in 1900 with Amy Lowther, they had spotted him, much diminished, gazing longingly through the window of a patisserie and biting his fingers with hunger. They invited him to eat with them and were much relieved when he 'sparkled just as of old', but neither ever saw him again.[88] After Oscar's death, Ellen stopped Robert Sherard 'to talk of Wilde and to say many beautiful and kind things about him'.[89] When speaking at a dinner held in her honour by the Gallery First-Nighters' Club in 1905, she included 'the late Oscar Wilde' in a list of people seen regularly 'in the gallery and pit at the dear old Lyceum'.[90] Yet, when writer and poet Richard Le Gallienne asked her to write a foreword to a memorial edition of *The Complete Works of Oscar Wilde*, it seems she never responded.[91]

In *Works and Days* – the journal co-authored by Katherine Bradley and her niece Edith Cooper, the two halves of 'Michael Field' – Cooper, on reading of Oscar's death, deplored the 'foolish punishment' meted out to him for 'an odious offence that sh'd never have been made public or lighted up by law'. This despair at the public airing of what were regarded by many women as private matters was a common theme. Although Bradley and Cooper effectively lived as a married couple, they were not subject to public scrutiny or opprobrium, since women, often considered asexual, were encouraged to form companionships with each other. Yet they sympathised enormously and Cooper expressed particular regret that the punishment imposed had 'killed Oscar's mother, his wife, indirectly his Brother, + now himself; while leaving his children orphans branded outrageously'. She went on to write in glowing terms of Oscar: 'Now I can think of nothing but the quality that was in him – the pleasurableness,' she recalled.[92]

Lesbian women were not always safe from condemnatory finger-pointing. An extraordinary posthumous tale concerning Oscar Wilde involves Marie Corelli, who had fallen out with him and never displayed any sympathy for his plight. Corelli, who was almost certainly a lesbian, may have been fearful for her own reputation.* Believing that the New Woman movement was misguided and that women should embrace their 'simple womanliness', Corelli campaigned against women's suffrage, arguing:

> if she has the natural heritage of her sex, which is the mystic power to persuade, enthral and subjugate man, she has no need to come down from her throne and mingle in any of his political frays.[93]

In 1918, she spotted a small advert in *The Sunday Times* announcing two private performances of *Salomé* at the Prince of Wales Theatre starring dancer Maud Allan. Linking this to a conspiracy that suggested the existence of a black book containing 47,000 names of homosexuals who operated as German agents, Corelli wrote to Noel Pemberton Billing MP,

---

* She lived with Bertha Vyver for more than forty years and left her fortune to her.

editor of *Vigilante*, expressing concern at 'this new "upholding" of the Wilde "cult"'.[94]

As it happened, Billing had heard rumours that Allan was involved in a lesbian affair with Margot Asquith, dedicatee of 'The Star Child' and wife of the prime minister during the early war years. Margot had disowned Oscar, writing:

> To me, he appeared like something monstrous and unreal thrown into a world of human beings ready to applaud, but not to accept any of his views upon life.[95]

When Billing published 'The Cult of the Clitoris', accusing Allan of participating in a homosexual conspiracy intended to undermine the war effort, she sued him for libel. Allan, represented by Travers Humphreys, who had been Oscar's junior counsel, lost her case at the Old Bailey, just as Oscar had twenty-three years earlier.

Billing, who represented himself, persuaded his lover, Eileen Villiers-Stuart, to testify that she had seen the Asquiths' names in the black book. He also persuaded the jury to find for him by discrediting Allan, attacking her morals, and her long association with *Salomé*, and pointing out her relationship to her murderous brother.* Fortunately, there were no dire consequences of this verdict for Allan since expressions of lesbian orientation had not been outlawed, although the suggestion that they should be was mooted in 1922, when the notion was rejected by the House of Lords in a paternalistic attempt to protect women's innocence.

One of the witnesses who testified in Billing's defence was Lord Alfred Douglas, Oscar's lover and inept translator of the original *Salomé*. During his testimony, Bosie described Oscar as a sexual and moral pervert who had 'a diabolical influence upon everyone'. Calling him 'the greatest force for evil that has appeared in Europe during the last 350 years', he went on to say:

> He was the agent of the devil in every possible way. He was a man whose whole object in life was to attack and to sneer at virtue, and to undermine it in every way by every possible means, sexually and otherwise.[96]

This bizarre set of circumstances calls to mind a line from *De Profundis*,

---

* In 1895 Allan's brother, Theodore Durrant, was charged with the brutal murders of Blanche Lamont and Minnie Flora Williams. He was executed on 7 January 1898. In an attempt to distance herself from Durrant, his sister changed her name to Allan.

in which Oscar told Bosie:

> I thought life was going to be a brilliant comedy, and that you were to be one of many graceful figures in it. I found it to be a revolting and repellent tragedy . . .[97]

A WILDE LEGACY

Her words flew out like soap bubbles.
BETTINA BERGERY on her friend Dolly Wilde[1]

On 10 April 1941, when the chambermaid who serviced the block of flats located at Twenty Chesham Place in Belgravia, used her pass key to gain entry to number 83, she must have been horrified to discover the lifeless body of a woman in her mid-forties slumped half in and half out of her bed. Although the occupant, recently arrived, had a history of suicide attempts, and several bottles labelled paraldehyde, an over-the-counter depressant of the central nervous system used to treat alcoholism and chronic insomnia, were discovered in her flat, there was no evidence to suggest she had deliberately ingested an overdose. For that reason, Coroner Mr Neville Stafford recorded an open verdict, declaring that this 'independent spinster', as she was described on her death certificate, 'came to her death through causes unascertainable'.[2]

The dead woman was Dorothy 'Dolly' Wilde, daughter of Willie and niece of Oscar. At the time, she was undergoing treatment for breast cancer, diagnosed two years earlier, and was under the care of several eminent doctors. Although her doctors advocated it strongly, Dolly had prevaricated about surgery, preferring a combination of pharmaceutical and New Age treatments that included a heroin cure and a brief pilgrimage to Lourdes. As a result, the cancer had metastacised and an autopsy revealed traces in her lungs. Fatally self-destructive, Dolly had also battled several addictions; years of prodigious drug and alcohol consumption had compromised her health. She tried to conceal her worst excesses, but anecdotes described her slipping a syringe from her handbag and injecting herself in the thigh under the table at dinner parties, or emerging from a variety of bathrooms with telltale traces of white powder under her nose.[3]

Dolly Wilde was born into chaos and poverty to a father lost to alcohol and a mother whose inability to cope led her to abandon her infant daughter in a 'country convent'.[4] From the day of her birth, three months after the imprisonment of her Uncle Oscar, her life was governed by turmoil and impulsiveness. In adulthood, she was so outrageous that had she been fictional she would have lacked credibility. While in her teens, she ran away to war-torn France, where she drove an ambulance and developed a taste for fast cars and foreign women. One early paramour was her Montparnasse flat mate, Joe Carstairs, the cross-dressing Standard Oil heiress who later seduced Marlene Dietrich. Afterwards, Dolly drifted through her twenties, living out of a suitcase in a series of hotel suites, spare bedrooms and borrowed apartments. Since she hated 'flat reality', the antidote she seized upon was to live hard and travel constantly, a lifestyle that took a toll on her well-being.[5]

An incorrigible womaniser, Dolly specialised in 'emergency seductions' and went through a string of lovers.[6] She once made a pass at Zelda Fitzgerald, much to Scott's annoyance; he captured her in an unflattering cameo in *Tender is the Night* as incorrigible lesbian seductress Vivien Taube, but he deleted the passage from the published version.[7] She had a passionate affair with Russian-American actress Alla Nazimova, who produced and starred in a silent film adaptation of *Salomé* (1923), which drew heavily on Aubrey Beardsley's illustrations for Oscar's book. Dolly prided herself on her irresistibility to women and men; although she showed no interest in anything beyond friendship, several men proposed marriage to her.

Dolly was always promiscuous, but the love of her life was Natalie Clifford Barney, two decades her senior and a woman with a self-professed fascination with Oscar. Natalie's decision to install Dolly in her 'blue bedroom' at 20 Rue Jacob, where she hosted her celebrated Friday salon may have been influenced by her resemblance to her iconic uncle. In 1882, when six-year-old Natalie was holidaying at Long Beach with her mother Alice, she was chased by a pack of taunting boys. She ran headlong into Oscar, who scooped her onto his knee and comforted her by telling her a wonderful tale.[8] At ten, she insisted on being painted as his happy prince, dressed exotically in medieval green and gold. In her teens, she wrote a letter of sympathy to him in HM Prison Reading, and she served on committees that commemorated his birth and his death. As an adult, Natalie had a fling with poet Olive Custance, Oscar's one-time rival for the affections of poet John Grey. Through her, she befriended Lord Alfred Douglas. Her ultimate Wildean trophy was Dolly.

Although Dolly never met her famous uncle, her pale, elongated face, remarkable blue-grey eyes, shock of dark hair and affected pose, conjured him up for all who met her. She inherited too his 'clear, low, musical voice', insatiable appetite for cigarettes and inability to regulate her chaotic finances.[9] While her friends nicknamed her 'Oscaria', Dolly herself declared: 'I am more like Oscar than Oscar himself'.[10] In her 'Letter from Paris' column in July 1930, Janet Flanner, Paris correspondent for *The New Yorker*, described Dolly attending a *bal masqué* dressed as Oscar, 'looking both important and earnest'.[11] When H. G. Wells bumped into her at the Paris PEN Club, he declared himself delighted to meet at last a feminine Wilde.

Everyone who knew Dolly said she should write. Days after her birth, her grandmother Jane declared her 'magnificent!!!', and described her as: 'A force of intellect and power'. Dolly, she assured her daughter-in-law Constance, would 'most certainly write books'.[12] When she was almost four, her mother, Lily, told Oscar that little Dolly, had 'a fair share of the family brains'.[13] This weight of expectation overshadowed her life. Although she left scant evidence to support it, a hyperbolic obituary written by her great friend Victor Cunard, diplomat and *The Times* correspondent in Venice, stated that Dolly 'carried on with undiminished wit the family tradition of conversational brilliance,' concluding that 'Epigram and paradox are the weapons of the Wilde family, and none of its members has used them more humanely nor more effectively than Dorothy'.[14]

There is little to indicate that Dolly shared any measure of Oscar's brilliance; wishful thinking may simply have projected his wit onto the blank canvas that she supplied. She left nothing more tangible than personal letters, and many of the testimonies collected in a posthumous tribute, *In Memory of Dorothy Ierne Wilde: Oscaria*, published privately by Natalie Clifford Barney ten years after Dolly's death, suggest that what wit she possessed was ephemeral. Her friend Bettina Bergery wrote of her, 'she scintillated with so many epigrams, all delivered at once – that no one had time to remember any . . . Her words flew out like soap bubbles'.[15] Yet she had some ability to charm. Cartoonist Osbert Lancaster called her 'irrepressible and wholly delightful'.[16] Her last lover, actress Gwen Farrer, described her as a 'jolly and high spirited woman, with many friends'.[17] Ironically, one friend, novelist Rosamond Harcourt-Smith, likened her to a panther.[18]

Dolly's first cousin Vyvyan Holland discovered her existence when she was brought to his house by a mutual friend; she was twenty-two years old by then and he was thirty-one. She never met Cyril, who died in the war she had been so eager to join. Vyvyan's relationship with Dolly was an uneasy one; she must have been infuriating at times with her posing and her insistence in finding refuge behind a narcotic fog. She could be a messy drunk. On one occasion the manager of the luxurious Hotel Montalembert on Saint Germain des Prés, Dolly's favourite Parisian hotel, contacted Natalie Clifford Barney, who was probably paying the bill, complaining of piercing cries and heart-wrenching groans that were disturbing his other guests, and asking her to please remove Dolly to a sanatorium. Undoubtedly, she knew anguish and she almost succeeded with at least one of her four recorded suicide attempts. She left little trace of her life, just a bundle of letters and an ambiguous turn as 'Doll Furious' in *Ladies Almanack*, an obscure novel celebrating the splendid lesbian cult of Clifford Barney. It was written by her friend Djuna Barnes, whose grandmother, the irrepressible Zadel Turner Barnes, used to attend Jane Wilde's Saturdays.

ACKNOWLEDGEMENTS

Throughout his short life, Oscar Wilde formed hugely rewarding relationships with dozens of remarkable women, all of them deserving of biographies in their own right. Therefore, in writing this book, I have looked to a vast range of information sources and I am enormously grateful to the many individuals who shared their time, expertise and resources with me.

As is so often the case, particular thanks must go to Merlin Holland for his generosity in allowing me to quote from the many illuminating letters written by his grandfather, grandmother and great-grandmother. I am also grateful to him for allowing me access to photographs and images from his private collection, and for his warmth and affability in all our dealings.

I must also thank the Stoker family, in particular Noel Dobbs and Robin MacCaw, who expressed their delight at my interest in their much admired great-grandmother, Florence Balcombe, and who granted me access to the Stoker family papers, which are held in Trinity College, Dublin. Paul Murray, author of *From the Shadow of Dracula: A Life of Bram Stoker*, was also very helpful in providing information on Florence.

It is always delightful to have an excuse to spend time in our beautiful National Library of Ireland, and, as many of the sources referenced here are held in this treasured repository of Irish literature and life, I spent much time there with my head bowed over something wonderful. Hugely valuable collections of material relating to Oscar Wilde are also held in the William Andrews Clark Memorial Library, UCLA; the Lady Eccles Oscar Wilde Collection at the British Library; the University of Reading, Special Collections; and the National Library of Sweden, among others.

Eternal gratitude is owed to Michael Seeney, Deputy Chairman of the Oscar Wilde Society, and to Dr Anne Markey of the School of English, Trinity College, Dublin. Both agreed to read my manuscript, and this book has benefitted greatly from their expertise and scholarship. My agent, Andrew Lownie of the Andrew Lownie Literary Agency, has been enormously supportive, as ever. Both Andrew Lockett and Jane Rogers of Duckworth Overlook, a publishing house with a humbling pedigree, have guided me with great patience through the process of producing a first book. Thanks are due also to Josh Bryson, who edited my manuscript so expertly and who must have been channelling Oscar Wilde as he added and removed commas.

Final thanks must go to my husband, Derek, and my sons, Alex and Ewan, for their unfailing love and encouragement in this and every other project I undertake.

Selected Bibliography

Amor, Anne Clark (1983), *Mrs. Oscar Wilde: A Woman of Some Importance* (Sidgwick & Jackson).

Asquith, Margot (1933), *More Memories* (London, Cassells & Company).

Atherton, Gertrude (1932), *Adventures of a Novelist* (London, Jonathan Cape).

Auberon, Reginald (pseudonym of Horace Wyndham)(1922), *The Nineteen Hundreds* (London, George Allen & Unwin Ltd.).

Belford, Barbara (1990), *Violet: The Story of the Irrepressible Violet Hunt and her Circle of Lovers and Friends – Ford Madox Ford, H. G. Wells, Somerset Maugham, and Henry James* (New York, Simon and Schuster).

Belford, Barbara (1996), *Bram Stoker and the Man Who Was Dracula* (New York, Alfred A. Knopf).

Bernhardt, Sarah (1907), *My Double Life: Memoirs of Sarah Bernhardt* (London, William Heinemann).

Bigland, Eileen (1950), *Ouida: the Passionate Victorian* (London, Jarrolds).

Black, Helen C. (1906), *Notable Women Authors of the Day (London, McLaren & Company).*

Bristow, Joseph (ed.)(2013), *Wilde Discoveries: Traditions, Histories, Archives (Toronto, University of Toronto Press).*

Clayworth, Anya (2004), *Oscar Wilde: Selected Journalism (Oxford, Oxford University Press).*

Coakley, Davis (1994), *Oscar Wilde, the Importance of Being Irish (Dublin, Town House).*

Corkran, Henriette (1902), *Celebrities & I* (London, Hutchinson).

Dearinger, Kevin Lane (2009), *Marie Prescott: A Star of Some Brilliancy* (Madison, NJ, Fairleigh Dickinson University Press).

De Brémont, Anna (1914), *Oscar Wilde and his Mother: A Memoir* (London, Everett & Co.).

De Pratz, Claire (1912), *France from Within* (London, Hodder & Stoughton).

De Vere White, Terence (1980), 'Speranza's Secret', *Times Literary Supplement,* 21 November.

Dibb, Geoff (2013), *Oscar Wilde A Vagabond With a Mission* (London, The Oscar Wilde Society).

Douglas, Lord Alfred (1914), *Oscar Wilde and Myself* (New York, Duffield & Company).

Edmonds, Antony (2014), *Oscar Wilde's Scandalous Summer* (Stroud, Amberley Publishing).

Ellmann, Richard (1988), *Oscar Wilde* (London, Penguin Books).

Eltis, Sos (1996), *Revising Wilde: Society and Subversion in the Plays of Oscar Wilde* (Oxford, Clarendon Press).

Field, Michael (1933), *Works and Days: From the Journal of Michael Field*, eds, T. and D. C. Sturge Moore (London, John Murray).

Furniss, Harry (1923), *Some Victorian Women, Good Bad and Indifferent* (London, John Lane, The Bodley Head).

Gagnier, Regenia (1986), *Idylls of the Marketplace: Oscar Wilde and the Victorian Public* (Stanford, CA, Stanford University Press).

Gavan Duffy, Charles (1883), *Four Years of Irish History 1845–1849* (London: Cassel, Petter, Galpin & Co.).

Gavan Duffy, Charles (1898), *My Life in Two Hemispheres Volumes I & II*, (New York, MacMillan Co.).

Glover, James M. (1912), *Jimmy Glover, His Book* (London, Methuen & Co. Ltd.).

Gold, Arthur and Robert Fizdale (1991), *The Divine Sarah: A Life of Sarah Bernhardt* (New York, Alfred A. Knopf).

Graves, Robert Perceval (1889), *Life of Sir William Rowan Hamilton Volume III* (Dublin, Hodges Figgis).

Grossman, Barbara Wallace (2009), *A Spectacle of Suffering: Clara Morris on the American Stage* (Carbondale, IL, Southern Illinois University Press).

Hamilton, C. J. (1900), *Notable Irishwomen* (Dublin, Sealy, Bryers & Walker).

Hanberry, Gerard (2011), *More Lives than One: The Remarkable Wilde Family Through the Generations* (Cork, The Collins Press).

Harris, Frank (1916), *Oscar Wilde: His Life and Confessions*, Vols. I & II (New York, The Author).

Holland, Merlin (1997), *The Wilde Album* (London, Fourth Estate).

Holland, Merlin and Rupert Hart-Davis (eds)(2000), *The Complete Letters of Oscar Wilde* (London, Fourth Estate).

Holland, Vyvyan (1999), *Son of Oscar Wilde* (Carroll & Graf; Revised edition).

Hope, Adrian and Laura Troubridge (2002), *Letters of Engagement*, (London, Tite Street Press).

Hunt, Violet (1926), *The Flurried Years* (London, Hurst & Blackett).

Hunter Blair, Rt. Rev. Sir David (1939), *In Victorian Days & Other Papers* (London; New York, Longmans, Green & Co.).

John, Angela V. (1995), *Elizabeth Robins: Staging a Life* (London & New York, Routledge).

Jopling, Louise (1925), *Twenty Years of My Life 1867–1887* (London & New York, John Lane).

Kingston, Angela (2007), *Oscar Wilde as a Character in Victorian Fiction* (New York, Palgrave Macmillan).

Langtry, Lillie (2005), *The Days I Knew: An Autobiography* (North Hollywood, CA, Panoply Publications).

Lee, Elizabeth (1914), *Ouida: A Memoir* (London, T. F. Unwin).

Leverson, Ada (1930), *Letters to the Sphinx from Oscar Wilde: With Reminiscences of the Author* (London, Duckworth).

McKenna, Neil (2004), *The Secret Life of Oscar Wilde* (London, Arrow Books).

Maguire, J. Robert (2013), *Ceremonies of Bravery: Oscar Wilde, Carlos Blacker and the Dreyfus Affair* (Oxford, Oxford University Press).

Marbury, Elizabeth (1923), *My Crystal Ball* (New York, Boni & Liveright).

Mason, Stuart (1907), *A Bibliography of the Poetry of Oscar Wilde* (London, E. Grant Richards).

Mason, Stuart (1914), *Bibliography of Oscar Wilde* (London, T. Werner Laurie Ltd.).

Masters, Brian (1978), *Now Barabbas was a Rotter* (London, H. Hamilton).

Melba, Nellie (2011), *Melodies and Memories* (Cambridge, Cambridge University Press).

Melville, Joy (1994), *Mother of Oscar* (London, John Murray).

Mikhail, E. H. (1979), *Oscar Wilde: Interviews and Recollections,* (London, Macmillan).

Montgomery Hyde, Harford (1973), *The Trials of Oscar Wilde* (New York, Dover Publications).

Morris Jnr, Roy (2013), *Declaring his Genius: Oscar Wilde in North America* (Cambridge, MA, Harvard University Press).

Morse, W. F. (1907), 'American Lectures', Chapter IV, *The Writings of Oscar Wilde* (London & New York, Keller-Farmer Co.).

Moyle, Franny (2012), *Constance: The Tragic and Scandalous Life of Mrs. Oscar Wilde* (London, John Murray).

Mulholland Gilbert, Rosa (1905), *Life of Sir John Gilbert LL.D., F.S.A., Irish Historian and Archivist, Vice-President of the Royal Irish Academy, Secretary of the Public Record Office of Ireland, by his Wife Rosa Mulholland Gilbert* (London, Longmans, Green & Co.).

Murray, Paul (2004), *From the Shadow of Dracula: A Life of Bram Stoker* (London, Random House).

O'Donoghue, David (1896), *Life of William Carleton Volume II* (London, Downey & Co.).

O'Sullivan, Vincent (1936), *Aspects of Wilde* (London, Constable & Company).

Pearson, Hesketh (1946), *The Life of Oscar Wilde* (London, Methuen).

Powell, Kerry (1990), *Oscar Wilde and the Theatre of the 1890s* (Cambridge, Cambridge University Press).

Rennell Rodd, James (1922), *Social and Diplomatic Memories 1884–1893* (London, Edward Arnold & Co.).

Ricketts, Charles (1932), *Recollections of Oscar Wilde* (London).

Robertson, W. Graham, (1933), *Time Was* (London, H. Hamilton Ltd.).

Robins, Elizabeth (1940), *Both Sides of the Curtain* (London, W. Heinemann Ltd.).

Saltus, Marie (1925), *Edgar Saltus: the Man* (Chicago, IL, Pascal Covici).

Schaffer, Talia (2000), *The Forgotten Female Aesthetes* (Charlottesville and London, University Press of Virginia).

Schenkar, Joan (2000), *Truly Wilde: The Unsettling Story of Dolly Wilde, Oscar's Unusual Niece* (London, Virago).

Schroeder, Horst (2002), *Additions and Corrections to Richard Ellmann's Oscar Wilde* (Braunschweig Selbstverl).

Shaw, George Bernard (1916), *Dramatic Opinions and Essays, Volume 1* (New York, Brentano's).

Sherard, Robert Harborough (1905), *The Story of an Unhappy Friendship*, (London, Greening & Company Ltd.).

Sherard, Robert Harborough (1906), *The Life of Oscar Wilde* (New York, Mitchell Kennerley).

Sherard, Robert Harborough (1916), *The Real Oscar Wilde* (London, T. W. Laurie).

Showalter, Elaine (ed)(1993), *Daughters of Decadence: Women Writers of the Fin-de-Siècle (London, Virago).*

Sloan, John (2003), *Authors in Context: Oscar Wilde (Oxford, Oxford University Press).*

Smyth, Dame Ethel (1946), *Impressions that Remain* (New York, Alfred A. Knopf).

Snel, Harmen (2007), *The Ancestry of Sarah Bernhardt* (Amsterdam, Jewish Historical Museum).

Speedie, Julie (1994), *Wonderful Sphinx: The Biography of Ada Leverson* (London, Virago).

Spencer, Walter T. (1923), *Forty Years in my Bookshop* (Boston, MA, Houghton Mifflin).

Stanford, W. B. and R. B. McDowell (1971), *Mahaffy: A Biography of an Anglo-Irishman* (London, Routledge & Kegan Paul).

Stern, Madeleine B. (1953), *Purple Passage: The Life of Mrs. Frank Leslie* (Norman, OK. University of Oklahoma Press).

Stoker, Bram (1907), *Personal Reminiscences of Henry Irving* (London, W. Heinemann).

Stokes, John (1996), *Oscar Wilde: Myths, Miracles and Imitations* (Cambridge, Cambridge University Press).

Swanwick, H. M. (1935), *I Have Been Young* (London, Victor Gollancz).

Terry, Ellen (1908), *The Story of My Life: Recollections and Reflections* (New York, Doubleday).

Troubridge, Laura (1999), *Life Amongst the Troubridges: Journals of a Young Victorian, 1873–1884*, ed., Jacqueline Hope-Nicholson (London, Tite Street Press).

Tydeman, William (1996), *Wilde Salome* (Cambridge, NY, Cambridge University Press).

Tynan, Katherine (1913), *Twenty-five Years: Reminiscences*, (London, Smith, Elder & Co.).

Ward, Genevieve and Richard Whiting (1918), *Both Sides of the Curtain* (London, Cassell & Company).

Wilde, Lady Jane (1864), *Poems* (Dublin, James Duffy).

Wilde, Lady Jane (1884), *Driftwood from Scandinavia* (London, R. Bentley and Son).

Wilde, Lady Jane (1890), *Ancient Cures, Charms, and Usages of Ireland: Contributions to Irish Lore* (London, Ward & Downey).

Wilde, Lady Jane (1891), *Notes on Men, Women, and Books* (London, Ward & Downey).

Wilde, Lady Jane (1893), *Social Studies* (London, Ward & Downey).

Wilde, Oscar (1881), *Poems* (London, David Bogue).

Wilde, Oscar (1988), *Wilde: The Complete Plays* (London, Methuen).

Wilde, Oscar (1991), *The Complete Illustrated Works of Oscar Wilde* (Chancellor Press, London).

Wilde, Oscar (2005), *The Prose of Oscar Wilde* (New York, Cosimo).

Wilde, Oscar and Stuart Mason (ed.)(1906), *Impressions of America* (Sunderland, Keystone Press).

Wilson, T. G. (1942), *Victorian Doctor, Being the Life of Sir William Wilde* (New York, L. B. Fischer).

Wood, Marilyn (1993), *Rhoda Broughton: Profile of a Novelist* (Stamford, Paul Watkins).

Yeats, J. B. and Joseph M. Hone (ed.)(1944), *John Butler Yeats Letters: Letters to his Son W. B. Yeats and Others, 1869–1922* (London, Faber & Faber Ltd.).

Yeats, W. B. (1922), *The Trembling of the Veil* (London, Werner Laurie).

Yeats, W. B. *Letters to the New Island*, (Cambridge, MA, Harvard University Press, 1934)

Yeats, W. B. (1892), *United Irishman*, 19 January.

ARCHIVES

Ann Stoker Collection, Trinity College, Dublin, The

BL Eccles

Elizabeth Robins Papers 1803–1963, MSS 002, Fales Library and Special Collections, New York University

Ellen Terry and Edith Craig Archives

Gilbert and Sullivan Collection, Pierpont Morgan Library, New York

Harry Ransom Research Center, University of Texas at Austin, Olive Schreiner Letters Project Transcription

Henry W. and Albert A. Berg Collection of English and American Literature, The New York Public Library, The

National Library of Ireland

National Library of Sweden

Oxford University, Magdalen College Archives, Diary of Anna Florence Ward, MS 618

Robert Young Collection relating to William Winter, Folger MS Y.c.61 (36)

Schlesinger Library, Radcliffe Institute, Harvard University, Cambridge, MA

Women's Library, The

University of Reading, Special Collections, MS 559

Violet Hunt Papers, 1858–1962, Collection Number 4607, Cornell University Library

Violet Hunt Diaries 1858–1962, Olin Library, Cornell, Collection Number: 4607

William Andrews Clark Library

NEWSPAPERS & JOURNALS

Athenaeum Magazine, The
Belfast Morning News
Birmingham Daily Mail
Birmingham Post
The Bookman
Boston Evening Transcript
Cassell's Weekly
Century Magazine
Century Illustrated Monthly Magazine
Chicago Tribune
Colonies and India, The
Commercial Gazette, The
Cornhill Magazine, The
Daily Charlotte Observer, The
Daily Telegraph
Dayton Daily Democrat
Dramatic Review
Dublin Evening Mail
Dublin Historical Record
Dublin Journal of Medical Science
Dublin Review
English Illustrated Magazine
The Era
Fortnightly Review
Freeman's Journal
Guardian, The
Harper's Weekly
Irish Times, The
Journal of the Eighteen Nineties Society
Kottabos Volume II
Lady's Pictorial

Lancet, The
Lewiston Saturday Journal
Los Angeles Herald
Morning Post, The
New York Daily Graphic
New York Dramatic Mirror
New York Herald
New York Mirror
New York Times, The
New York World
Pall Mall Gazette
North American Review, The
Nation, The
Philadelphia Press, The
Police Gazette
Punch
Queen
Scots Observer
Sketch, The
Spectator, The
Spirit of the Times
Stage, The
St James's Gazette
Sunday Times, The
Times, The
Times-Picayune, The
Tuapeka Times
Wildean, The
Woman's World, The
World, The
Yellow Book, The

NOTES AND REFERENCES

INTRODUCTION
1 O'Sullivan, Vincent (2010), *Aspects of Wilde* (Portsmouth, Callum James Books), p. 39.
2 Ibid., p. 56.

CHAPTER 1
1 'Oscar Wilde's New Play' (1892), *The New York Times*, 28 February.
2 Letter from Oscar Wilde to George Alexander, 2 February 1891, in Merlin Holland and Rupert Hart-Davis (eds)(2000), *The Complete Letters of Oscar Wilde* (London, Fourth Estate) p. 463.
3 Letter to George Alexander, Summer 1891, *Complete Letters*, p. 486.
4 Letter to George Alexander, mid-February 1892, *Complete Letters*, p. 516.
5 Scott, Clement (1892), 'Blue Button-hole Buffoonery', *The Stage*, 8 March.
6 Kaplan, Joel H. (1992), 'A Puppet's Power: George Alexander, Clement Scott, and the Replotting of *Lady Windermere's Fan*', *Theatre Notebook* 46:2, 59–72.
7 'Mr Oscar Wilde Explains' (1892), a letter to the editor of the *St James's Gazette*, 27 February, reprinted in Stuart Mason (1914), *Bibliography of Oscar Wilde* (London, T. Werner Laurie Ltd.), p. 390.
8 Jopling, Louise (1925), *Twenty Years of My Life 1867–1887* (London & New York, John Lane) p. 81.
9 Blathwayt, Raymond (1898), 'Does the Theatre make for Good?: An interview with Mr Clement Scott', *Great Thoughts* (London, A. W. Hall).
10 *The Sunday Times*, 21 February 1892, quoted in William Tydeman (1982), *Wilde: Comedies: Lady Windermere's Fan; A Woman of No Importance; An Ideal Husband; The Importance of Being Earnest: A Casebook* (London, Macmillan), p. 47.
11 Letter from Henry James to a friend written on 23 February 1892, quoted in Daniel Karlin, 'Our precious *quand même*': French in the Letters of Henry James », *Cahiers victoriens et édouardiens* [En ligne], 78 Automne | 2013, mis en ligne le 01 septembre 2013, accessed on 2 March 2015. http://cve.revues.org/945.
12 Jopling, *Twenty Years of My Life 1867–1887*, p. 81.
13 Letter to Augustin Daly, September 1891, *Complete Letters*, p. 489.
14 Letter to Augustin Daly, August 1897, *Complete Letters*, p. 928.
15 Langtry, Lillie (2005), *The Days I Knew: An Autobiography* (North Hollywood, CA, Panoply Publications) p. 85.
16 This and all quotes taken from Oscar Wilde's 'Lady Windermere's Fan' in *Wilde: The Complete Plays* (London, Methuen), p. 96.
17 Wilde, Oscar (1882), 'Mrs. Langtry as Hester Grazebrook', *New York World*, 7 November, reproduced in *Miscellanies* (London, David Price, 1908).

18 Langtry, *The Days I Knew*, p. 76.

19 Troubridge, Laura (1999), *Life Amongst the Troubridges: Journals of a Young Victorian, 1873–1884*, ed., Jacqueline Hope-Nicholson (London: Tite Street Press), p. 152.

20 Langtry, *The Days I Knew*, p. 85.

21 *Punch*, 31 December 1881, Vol. 81, p. 309.

22 Langtry, *The Days I Knew*, p. 140.

23 Ibid., p. 85.

24 Ibid.

25 Ibid., p. 124.

26 Beatty, Laura (1999), *Lillie Langtry Manners Masks and Morals* (London, Chatto), p. 236.

27 'The Haymarket Theatre: "She Stoops to Conquer"', *The Times*, 16 December 1881, p. 6.

28 Menzies, Stuart (1915), *Further Indiscretions by a Woman of No Importance* (Oscarside Press)(Reprint), p. 11.

29 'The Haymarket Theatre: "She Stoops to Conquer"', *The Times*, 16 December 1881, p. 6.

30 Letter to an unidentified correspondent, February 1893, *Complete Letters*, p. 553.

31 Most notably the Magdalen College Manuscript 300 as outlined by Sophie Duncan, in 'Oscar Wilde's 'A Good Woman': A Bibliographical Investigation into Magdalen College Manuscript 300. Bodleian Library, Oxford.

32 Langtry, *The Days I Knew*, p. 77.

33 Included in the Introduction to *Wilde: The Complete Plays*, (London, Methuen, 1988) pp. 2–3.

34 Yeats, W. B. (1934), *Letters to the New Island*, (Cambridge, MA, Harvard University Press) p. 77.

35 *De Profundis*, Letter to Lord Alfred Douglas, January-March 1897, *Complete Letters*, p. 736.

CHAPTER 2

1 Graves, Robert Perceval (1889), *Life of Sir William Rowan Hamilton Volume III* (Dublin, Hodges Figgis) p. 497.

2 Edward Carson QC, a childhood acquaintance and fellow student at Trinity College, Dublin, challenged him on his assertion that he was thirty-nine years old as he knew him to be forty.

3 Letter in the possession of 'Mrs Richard Elgee' quoted in Joy Melville (1994), *Mother of Oscar* (London, John Murray), p. 18.

4 Application Form, Lady Jane Francesca Wilde in the British Library Western Manuscripts collection, Loan 96 RLF 1/2290/4.

5 From *The Life of Sir John T. Gilbert LL.D., F.S.A., Irish Historian and Archivist, Vice-President of the Royal Irish Academy, Secretary of the Public Record Office of Ireland, by his Wife Rosa Mulholland Gilbert* (London, Longmans, Green & Co., 1905) p. 253.

6 *The Philadelphia Press*, 2 March 1877.

7 One example is James Bentley Gordon (1803), *History of the Rebellion in Ireland in the Year 1798* (Dublin, T. Hurst), p. 176. An article in the Belfast Newsletter of 12 March 1824 repeats this version. Elgee undoubtedly had a connection with Wexford Gaol: Parliamentary records suggest that he acted as prison inspector and procured supplies for the prisoners. Details of payments to purchase provisions, along with an application for a salary on behalf of Rev. John Elgee are included in accounts presented to the House of Commons from the East India Company, printed in 1808, p. 429.

8 Wilde, Lady Jane (1890), *Ancient Cures, Charms, and Usages of Ireland: Contributions to Irish Lore* (London, Ward & Downey) pp. 228–9n.

9 'Tithe case Before the Privy Council', *Waterford Mirror,* 24 January 1825, p. 3.

10 Wilde, Lady Jane, *Ancient Cures, Charms, and Usages of Ireland*, pp. 229–30.

11 From *Lady Morgan's Memoirs: Autobiography, Diaries and Correspondence. Second Edition, Revised*, 2 volumes (London, Wm. H. Allen & Co., 1863), p. 154.

12 Information included in her obituary in *The Guardian* on Wednesday 12 February 1896, p. 3, and *The Times* 7 February 1886, p. 6, and often mentioned in local histories of the county.

13 *Freeman's Journal* (1825), 4 February 1825, p. 4.

14 An obituary for John Kingsbury Elgee's son, Charles Le Doux Elgee, contained in the *Report of the Secretary, Class of 1856, Harvard* and published in Boston by Geo. C. Rand & Avery in January 1865 (p. 16) reported that 'John was educated in his early youth by his mother, until at the age of fifteen, he entered the University of Dublin. On account of domestic difficulties, he left the university before receiving his degree'. This report also suggests that Jane's father, Charles had 'some connection with the East-India Company' before his death.

15 Part of a flippant questionnaire he completed in 1877 in *Mental Photographs, An Album for Confessions of Tastes, Habits and Convictions*. Reproduced in Merlin Holland (1997), *The Wilde Album: Public and Private Images of Oscar Wilde* (London, Fourth Estate), p. 45.

16 Listed in *Alumni Dublinenses* (London, Burtchaell and Sadler, 1924).

17 See note 14.

18 They are listed in the *Passenger List Quarterly Abstracts* for New Orleans. They sailed from Belfast on *The Planter*. After Matilda's untimely death in 1834, John married Marie Francoise Laulette Ledoux, a wealthy widow who was seventeen years his senior, but their marriage was not a success and they lived apart for much of it. During the Civil War, his plantation house was annexed by the Union. John Kingsbury Elgee was aware of Oscar's existence, since Emily sent him a newspaper cutting reporting his nephew's birth. In 1882, when Oscar visited Louisiana during his extensive lecture tour of America, *The Daily Charlotte Observer*, 29 January 1882 (p. 1), reported that he was investigating, '. . . if he cannot recover possession of' the valuable plantation left by his uncle John. Reputed to be worth almost $1 million at the time, it had long been the subject of litigation

19 Terence de Vere White, 'Speranza's Secret', *The Times Literary Supplement* (1980), 21 November.

20 Letter from Oscar Wilde to his mother, 5 September 1868, *Collected Letters*, p. 4. He asks if she has written to Aunt Warren, 'on the green notepaper', a playful reference to Emily's disapproval of Jane's politics.

21 Quoted in Judith Harford and Clare Rush (2009), *Have Women Made a Difference?: Women in Irish Universities, 1850–2010* (Oxford; New York, Peter Lang), p. 58.

22 *Hearth and Home*, 30 June 1892, reproduced in the *Freeman's Journal*, 6 February 1896, p. 5.

23 Obituary in *The Times*, 7 February 1896, p. 6; *Hearth and Home*, 30 June, reproduced in the *Freeman's Journal*, 6 February 1896, p. 6

24 Letter to Mr D. J. O'Donoghue, 1888, quoted in Robert Harborough Sherard (1906), *The Life of Oscar Wilde* (London, T. W. Laurie), p. 78.

25 O'Sullivan, T. F. (1944), *The Young Irelanders* (Tralee, The Kerryman Ltd.).

26 Yeats, W. B. (1947), *Tribute to Thomas Davis* (Cork, Cork University Press), p. 17. By coincidence Dr William Wilde was present at Davis's funeral in his capacity as

member of the Royal Irish Academy. Years later he was invited to head a committee formed to commemorate Davis, and it was he who commissioned the marble figure of Davis by sculptor John Hogan that stands in Dublin's City Hall.

27　The details of this lecture, during which he read several of his mother's poems and spoke admiringly of her are contained in Michael J. O'Neill (1955), 'Irish Poets of the Nineteenth Century: Unpublished Lecture Notes of a speech by Oscar Wilde at San Francisco', in *University Review*, 1, 4, pp. 29–33.

28　Wilde, Lady Jane (1890), *Ancient Cures, Charms, and Usages of Ireland: Contributions to Irish Lore* (London, Ward & Downey), p. 173.

29　Ibid., p. 236.

30　Sherard, *The Life of Oscar Wilde*, p. 46.

31　'How Lady Wilde Became a Nationalist' excerpts from an interview with *Hearth and Home* (1892), 30 June, reproduced in *The Times-Picayune* (1892), Sunday 14 August, p. 18.

32　Duffy, Charles Gavan (1883), *Four Years of Irish History 1845–1849* (London: Cassel, Petter, Galpin & Co.) p. 94.

33　Ibid., p. 448.

34　Wilde, *Ancient Cures, Charms, and Usages of Ireland*, pp. 173–4.

35　Duffy, *Four Years of Irish History*, p. 95.

36　Letter to Charles Gavan Duffy, Letters to Charles Gavan Duffy from people prominent in literary and political affairs, 1840–1854, National Library of Ireland, Mss. 5756–5757.

37　A. M. Sullivan was an Irish nationalist politician, lawyer and journalist. This quotation is from his *New Ireland* (Glasgow, Cameron & Ferguson, 1877), p. 75.

38　From 'Forward!' by Jane Wilde, originally titled 'To My Brothers' in *Poems by Speranza* (Dublin, James Duffy, 1864), p. 35.

39　Duffy, Charles Gavan, *My Life in Two Hemispheres Volume I*, (New York, The McMillan Co., 1898), pp. 286–7.

40　In a letter to William Carleton quoted in David O'Donoghue, *Life of William Carleton Volume II* (London, Downey & Co., 1896) p. 139.

41　Wilde, Lady Jane (1893), *Social Studies* (London, Ward & Downey), p. 23.

42　Several newspaper accounts suggest that she attempted this but was silenced.

43　*Reports of State Trials* (1896), HM Stationery Office, p. 923.

44　Letter to John Hilson, April 1849, University of Reading, Special Collections, MS 559.

45　Duffy fared better. In 1852 he was elected to Parliament for New Ross, County Wexford but his efforts to reform land ownership were thwarted and, in 1855, he sold *The Nation* and left for Australia, where he entered politics and served as prime minister of Victoria in 1871–72. He returned to Europe, and was knighted for his services to the Empire. He renewed his acquaintance with Jane and was introduced to Oscar, who considered him a friend. He died in Nice in 1903, aged eighty-six.

46　Wilde, *Ancient Cures, Charms, and Usages of Ireland*, p. 175.

47　National Library of Ireland, Mss 10, 517.

48　Letter to John Hilson, 1850, University of Reading, Special Collections, MS 559.

49　Ibid.

50　Ibid.

51　*The Nation*, 6 April 1850, p. 506.

52　National Library of Ireland, Mss 10, 517.

53　*The Nation*, 6 April 1850, p. 10.

54 O'Donoghue, David (1896), *Life of William Carleton Volume II* (London, Downey & Co.) p. 165.

55 Phrases, Aphorisms and Fragments of Verse – Wilde 672, 1M3 P576, Clark Library.

56 Letter to John Hilson, November 1852, University of Reading, Special Collections, MS 559.

57 Letter to John Hilson, 13 January 1849, University of Reading, Special Collections, MS 559.

58 Letter to John Hilson, 1850, University of Reading, Special Collections, MS 559.

59 Wilde, *Social Studies*, p. 16.

60 Letter to John Hilson, 1850, University of Reading, Special Collections, MS 559.

61 *The Nation*, 15 September 1849.

CHAPTER 3

1 This quote and all of the information concerning the details of Jane and William's wedding day comes from a letter sent by John Elgee to Emily Warren. This letter was shown to Terence de Vere White and he quotes from it in 'Speranza's Secret', *Times Literary Supplement*, 21 November 1980.

2 Letter to John Hilson, 14 February 1849, University of Reading, Special Collections, MS 559.

3 Letter to John Hilson, 1852, University of Reading, Special Collections, MS 559.

4 Wilde, W. R. W., and Charles George Perceval (1843), *Narrative of a Voyage to Madeira, Tenerife and Along the Shores of the Mediterranean: Including a Visit to Algiers, Egypt, Palestine, Tyre, Rhodes, Telmessus, Cyprus, and Greece* (Dublin, W. Curry, Jr. & Co).

5 This letter is included in John Butler Yeats (1944), W. B. Yeats and Joseph M. Hone, *John Butler Yeats Letters: Letters to his Son W. B. Yeats and Others, 1869–1922* (London, Faber and Faber Ltd.), p. 277.

6 Mulholland Gilbert (1905), *Life of Sir John Gilbert*, p. 77.

7 Ibid., p. 81.

8 Wilde MD, Sir William (1880), *Memoir of Gabriel Béranger, and his Labours in the Cause of Irish Art and Antiquities, From 1760 to 1780* (Dublin, M. H. Gill & Son), p. 141.

9 Wilde, William R. (1849), *The Beauties of the Boyne, and its Tributary, the Blackwater* (Dublin, James McGlashan), in Preface, p. viii.

10 Wilde, W. R. (1852), *Irish Popular Superstitions* (Dublin, James McGlashan), p. 25

11 Letter to John Hilson, dated 1852, University of Reading, Special Collections, MS 559.

12 Letter from Constance Wilde to Oscar Wilde, BL Eccles MS 81690.

13 Tynan, Katherine (1913), *Twenty-five Years: Reminiscences*, (London, Smith, Elder & Co., 1913), p. 41.

14 Letter to John Hilson, dated May 1850, University of Reading, Special Collections, MS 559.

15 Letter to John Hilson, dated November 1852, in *Lady Jane Wilde's Letters to Mr. John Hilson, 1847–1876*, p. 58.

16 Letters to John Hilson dated June 17 1855 and November 1852, University of Reading, Special Collections, MS 559.

17 Letter to John Hilson, dated 1852, University of Reading, Special Collections, MS 559.

18 Letter to John Hilson, dated November 1852, University of Reading, Special Collections, MS 559.

19 Letter to John Hilson, dated 1852, University of Reading, Special Collections, MS 559.

20 Wilde, *Social Studies*, p. 69.
21 Ibid., p. 94.
22 Ibid., p. 50.
23 Letter to John Hilson, 22 November 1854, University of Reading, Special Collections, MS 559.
24 Letter to John Hilson, 17 June 1855, University of Reading, Special Collections, MS 559.
25 Ibid.
26 Letter to John Hilson, 22 November 1854, University of Reading, Special Collections, MS 559.
27 Wordsworth, William (1876) *The Prose Works of William Wordsworth, Vol. III* (London, Edward Moxton, Son, & Co.), pp. 318–19.
28 Letter from William Rowan Hamilton to Augustus de Morgan, 4 May 1855, quoted in Robert Graves, *Life of Sir William Rowan Hamilton, knt., LL. D., D.C.L., M.R.I.A., Andrews professor of astronomy in the University of Dublin, and royal astronomer of Ireland, etc.: including selections from his poems, correspondence, and miscellaneous writings. Volume III*, (Dublin, Hodges, Figgis, & Co., 1882–89), pp. 496–7.
29 Hamilton, Eliza Mary (1838), *Poems*, (Dublin, Hodges & Smith).
30 Graves (1889), *Life of Sir William Rowan Hamilton Volume III*, p. 497.
31 Ibid., p. 230.
32 Letter from William Rowan Hamilton to Jane Wilde, 30 June 1855, quoted in Terence de Vere White (1967), *The Parents of Oscar Wilde* (London, Hodder and Stoughton), p. 136.
33 Graves (1889), *Life of Sir William Rowan Hamilton Volume III*, p. 80.
34 Ibid., p. 26.
35 Ibid., p. 40.
36 Ibid., p. 604n.
37 Wilde, *Social Studies*, pp. 108–9.
38 Letter to John Hilson, 17 June 1855, University of Reading, Special Collections, MS 559.
39 Ibid.
40 Ibid.
41 Letter to Lotten von Kraemer, 23 March 1861, National Library of Sweden.
42 Corkran, Henriette (1902), *Celebrities & I* (London, Hutchinson), p. 138.
43 Ibid., pp. 137–8.
44 Letter Lotten von Kraemer, 17 February 1858, National Library of Sweden.
45 Wilde, *Social Studies*, pp. 45–6.
46 Lotten von Kraemer, 'Författaren Oscar Wilde's Föräldrahem i Irlands Hufvudstad' *Ord och Bild Illustrerad Månadsskrift*, Vol. 11, 1902, pp. 429–35, http://runeberg.org/ordochbild/1902/0473.html accessed on 10 January 2015.
47 Wilde, Lady Jane (1884), *Driftwood from Scandinavia* (London, R. Bentley and Son), p. 201.
48 Letter to Lotten von Kraemer, 20 December 1858, National Library of Sweden.
49 Letter to Lotten von Kraemer, 21 December 1858, National Library of Sweden.
50 Letter to Lotten von Kraemer, 3 December 1859, National Library of Sweden. Later, Jane returned to Sweden with William, who was to receive the prestigious Nordstjärneorden (Order of the North Star) from King Karl XV.
51 Wilde, *Driftwood from Scandinavia*, p. 275. Oscar appears to have inherited her low opinion of Germans (see *Complete Letters*, p. 409).

52 Ibid., p. 196.

53 Letter to Lotten von Kraemer (fragment)(1860), National Library of Sweden.

54 Letters to Lotten von Kraemer, 19 March and 22 April 1862, National Library of Sweden.

55 Letter to John Hilson, 10 February 1859, University of Reading, Special Collections, MS 559.

56 *Athenaeum* (magazine), quoted in Victoria Glendinning, 'Speranza', in Peter Quennell (1980), *Genius in the Drawing-Room* (London, Weidenfeld & Nicolson), p. 103.

57 'The Literati of Dublin', *Irish Times*, March 1878.

58 Wilde, *Social Science*, p. 74.

59 Mulholland Gilbert, *Life of Sir John Gilbert*, p. 78.

60 Corkran, *Celebrities & I*, p. 141.

61 Letter to Lotten von Kraemer, 22 April 1863, National Library of Sweden.

62 Glover, James M. (1912), *Jimmy Glover, His Book* (London, Methuen & Co. Ltd.), p. 34.

63 Wilde, Jane Francesca (1864), *Poems* (Dublin, James Duffy).

64 'Recent Irish Poetry', *Dublin Review* (1865), Vol. IV, p. 315.

CHAPTER 4

1 Letter to Lotten von Kraemer, 16 April 1867, National Library of Sweden.

2 *Freeman's Journal*, Wednesday 14 December 1864, p. 4.

3 'The Extraordinary Libel Case', *The Morning Post*, Friday 16 December 1864, p. 2.

4 *The London Review of Politics, Society, Literature, Art, & Science*, Vol. 9, 24 December 1864, p. 684.

5 'Law Courts – Yesterday', *Freeman's Journal*, Tuesday 13 December 1864, p. 4.

6 Mentioned in Melville, *Mother of Oscar*, p. 102.

7 *Dublin Evening Mail*, Thursday 15 December 1864, p. 3.

8 Ibid.

9 *Freeman's Journal*, Saturday 17 December 1864, p. 3.

10 Letter allegedly from William Wilde to Mary Travers, 12 December 1862, read out in court and reprinted in *The Morning Post*, Friday 16 December 1864, p. 2.

11 *The London Review of Politics, Society, Literature, Art, & Science*, Vol. 9, 24 December 1864, p. 684.

12 Ibid.

13 *Belfast Morning News*, Saturday 17 December 1864, p. 4.

14 All of these details are recorded in various newspaper reports of the subsequent libel trial.

15 *Freeman's Journal*, Saturday 17 December 1864, p. 3.

16 *Dublin Evening Mail*, Thursday 15 December 1864, p. 3.

17 *Freeman's Journal*, Friday 16 December 1864, p. 4.

18 *Dublin Evening Mail*, Thursday 15 December 1864, p. 3.

19 *Dublin Evening Mail*, Tuesday, 13 December 1864, p. 3.

20 *Freeman's Journal*, Thursday 15 December 1864, p. 4.

21 *Freeman's Journal*, Friday 16 December 1864, p. 4.

22 *Dublin Evening Mail*, Tuesday 13 December 1864, p. 3.

23 'Law Courts – Yesterday' in *Freeman's Journal*, Tuesday 13 December 1864, p. 4.

24 *Irish Times*, Tuesday 13 December 1864, p. 4.

25 Murphy, William Michael (2001), *Prodigal Father: The Life of John Butler Yeats (1839–1922)*, (New York, Syracuse University Press), p. 551, n. 75.

26 'Law Courts – Yesterday', *Freeman's Journal* (1864), Tuesday 13 December, p. 4.

27 *The Solicitors' Journal and Reporter*, Vol. 9, 17 December 1864, p. 147.

28 *Freeman's Journal*, Friday 16 December 1864, p. 4.

29 *Dublin Evening Mail*, Thursday 15 December 1864, p. 3.

30 Ibid.

31 de Vere White, Terence (1967), *The Parents of Oscar Wilde: Sir William and Lady Wilde*, (London, Hodder & Stoughton), p. 189.

32 Letter to Rosalie Olivecrona, 1 January 1865, National Library of Ireland, Ms. 15, 281.

33 Quoted in James Comyn (1981), *Irish Law: A Selection of Famous and Unusual Cases* (London, Secker & Warburg), p. 119.

34 Letter to Rosalie Olivecrona, 1 January 1865, National Library of Ireland, Ms. 15,281.

35 Letter to Lotten von Kraemer, 10 July 1866, National Library of Sweden.

36 Letter to Lotten von Kraemer, 16 April 1867, National Library of Sweden.

37 Letter to John Hilson, 2 September 1870, University of Reading, Special Collections, MS 559.

38 'E.R.F' in the *New York Herald*, 18 August 1881.

39 Sherard, Robert (1905), *The Story of an Unhappy Friendship*, (London, Greening & Company Ltd.), p. 79.

40 Sherard, Robert (1916), *The Real Oscar Wilde* (London, T. W. Laurie), p. 250; the envelope is illustrated in colour in Holland, *The Wilde Album*.

41 Letter to W. B. Yeats, 1894, in *Complete Letters*, p. 605.

42 *Birmingham Post*, 27 December 1906.

43 There are various accounts of the reaction of their host, Mr Andrew Nicholl Reid, but this is the account given by Dr T. G. Wilson in his biography of William Wilde (1942), *Victorian Doctor, Being the Life of Sir William Wilde* (New York, L. B. Fischer).

44 Letter to W. B. Yeats, May 1921 in J. B. Yeats & Joseph M. Hone (eds)(1944), *John Butler Yeats Letters: Letters to his Son W. B. Yeats and Others, 1869–1922* (London, Faber & Faber Ltd.), p. 277.

45 Coroner's Inquisition Book: Vol. 2 (1856–1876) Commenced 1 January 1856, (Monaghan Ancestry 090/1/4). Details of the tragedy and of both enquiries are contained in a paper compiled by Theo McMahon for the *Clogher Record*, Vol. 18, No. 1 (Clogher Historical Society, 2003), pp. 129–45.

46 Coroner's Report Book (Inquiry 4, 9 November 1871), p. 316.

47 Yeats and Hone (eds), *John Butler Yeats Letters: Letters to his Son W. B. Yeats and Others, 1869–1922*, p. 277.

48 Mulligan, Eamonn, and Fr. Brian McCluskey (1984), *"The Replay" – A Parish History* (Monaghan, Sean McDermott's G.F.C.), pp. 90–1.

CHAPTER 5

1 Letter to Ellen Terry, 3 January 1881 in *Complete Letters*, p. 107.

2 Harris, Frank, *Oscar Wilde: His Life and Confessions*, Vol. I (New York, The Author, 1916), p. 37.

3 Tyrrell, Robert Yelverton (ed.), *Kottabos Volume II* (Dublin, William McGee, 1877), p. ii; the poems were submitted after he left Trinity College, Dublin.

4 Letter to Oscar Wilde from Jane Wilde, quoted in Davis Coakley (1994), *Oscar Wilde, The Importance of Being Irish* (Dublin, Town House), p. 149.

5 David James O'Donoghue was an Irish biographer and editor, who featured Jane's work in his *Irish Poetry of the Nineteenth Century* (1894).

6 Sherard, *The Real Oscar Wilde*, p. 148.

7 Stanford, W. B., and R. B. McDowell (1971), *Mahaffy: A Biography of an Anglo-Irishman* (London, Routledge & Kegan Paul), p. 39.

8 Ibid., p. 87.

9 Letter from Louis Claude Purser to A. J. A. Symons quoted in Coakley, *Oscar Wilde, The Importance of Being Irish*, p. 150.

10 O'Neill, Michael J., 'Irish Poets of the Nineteenth Century: Unpublished Lecture Notes of Oscar Wilde', *University Review*, Vol. 1, No. 4, Spring 1955, pp. 29–32.

11 Vernier, Peter, 'Oscar at Magdalen; "The Bad Boy doing so well in the end!"' in *Magdalen College Record*, 2000.

12 Hunter Blair, Rt. Rev. Sir David (1939), *In Victorian Days & Other Papers* (London; New York, Longmans, Green & Co.) p. 116.

13 Ibid.

14 Ibid., p. 117.

15 Letter Jane Wilde to Rosalie Olivecrona, 31 December 1875, National Library of Ireland.

16 Sherard, *The Real Oscar Wilde*, pp. 31–2.

17 Ibid., p. 32.

18 Letter to Sir Thomas Larcom, 25 April 1876, National Library of Ireland, MS 7482.

19 Wilde MD, Sir William (1880), *Memoir of Gabriel Beranger, and his Labours in the Cause of Irish Art and Antiquities, From 1760 to 1780*, (Dublin, M. H. Gill & Son), p. 176.

20 *The London Gazette*, 11 January 1876, p. 100. Although alternative sources suggest that it was his son, also James, who occupied this post, Lt. Gen. H. J. Warre (1878), *The Historical Records of the Fifty Seventh, or, West Middlesex Regiment of Foot*, (London, W. Mitchell & Co.)(p. 282) states that, on retirement, James Balcombe accepted the post of Secretary to the Commissioners of Clontarf Township Office.

21 Warre C. B., Lt. Gen. H. J. (1878), *The Historical Records of the Fifty Seventh, or, West Middlesex Regiment of Foot* (London, W. Mitchell & Co.), pp. 281–2.

22 Letter to Reginald Harding, August 1876, *Complete Letters*, p. 29.

23 *The Era*, 6 July 1897, p. 12.

24 Du Maurier said this to fellow cartoonist John Bernard Partridge as recounted by E. V. Lucas in the *London Times* 4 May 1895; Barbara Belford (1996), *Bram Stoker and The Man Who Was Dracula* (New York, Knopf), p. 131.

25 *The Era*, Saturday 18 March 1895, p. 15.

26 Auberon, Reginald (pseudonym of Horace Wyndham)(1922), *The Nineteen Hundreds* (London, George Allen & Unwin Ltd.), p. 128.

27 Letter in the Stoker Family Papers, Trinity College, Dublin, TCD MS 11076

28 Ibid.

29 Neil McKenna (2004) suggests a sexual relationship between Wilde and Miles in *The Secret Life of Oscar Wilde* (London, Arrow Books), pp. 14–17.

30 Letter in the Stoker Family Papers, Trinity College, Dublin, TCD MS 11076.

31 Belford, Barbara (1996), *Bram Stoker and The Man Who Was Dracula* (New York, Knopf), p. 85.

32 When he was staying in Clonliffe House in Longford, he completed a page in an album called *Mental Photographs: An Album for Confessions of Tastes, Habits, and Convictions* and it is here that he recorded his favourite girl's name as 'Florence'. Reproduced in Holland, *The Wilde Album*, pp. 44–5.

33 Letter to Florence Balcombe, April 1878, *Complete Letters* p. 66.

34 Letter to Reginald Harding, 15 May 1877, *Complete Letters* p. 47.

35 Letter from Denis Florence McCarthy to John Gilbert, July 1877, in *Life of Sir John T. Gilbert*, p. 262.

36 Letter to Florence Balcombe, April 1878, *Complete Letters*, pp. 66–7.

37 In an appendix to his *Narrative of a Voyage to Madeira, Teneriffe and Along the Shores of the Mediterranean*, William wrote: 'It has long been incumbent on the British government to bring one or other of the Alexandrian Obelisks, called Cleopatra's needles, to England . . .' (p. 449).

38 Murray, Paul (2004), *From the Shadow of Dracula: A Life of Bram Stoker* (London, Random House), p. 65.

39 Wilde, *Ancient Legends, Mystic Charms & Superstitions of Ireland Volume I*, p. 242; Elements of *The Snake's Pass*, appear to draw on her description of serpent worship in ancient Ireland.

40 Stoker, Bram (1907), *Personal Reminiscences of Henry Irving* (London, W. Heinemann), p. 21.

41 Ibid., p. 39.

42 Letter to Florence Balcombe, September 1878, *Complete Letters*, p. 71.

43 Letter to Florence Balcombe, September 1878, *Complete Letters*, pp. 71–2.

44 Letter to Florence Balcombe, September 1878, *Complete Letters*, p. 72.

45 Letter to Florence Balcombe, September 1878, *Complete Letters*, p. 73.

46 The following day, a notice appeared in the *Irish Times* announcing the betrothal of: Bram Stoker MA, the second son of the late Abraham Stoker of the Chief Secretary's Office Dublin Castle, to Florence, third daughter of Lieut-Col Balcombe, late of the 57th regiment and Royal South Down Militia.

47 Letter, 21 October 1900, in Gilbert and Sullivan Collection, Pierpont Morgan Library, New York, Record ID: 76160.

48 On 13 April 1887, while Florence and Noel, aged seven, were sailing to Dieppe, a thick fog descended and their ship hit some jagged rocks at 3 a.m. The bow was ripped open and the ship sank in two hours with twenty people drowned. There were only four inadequate lifeboats and there was a scramble to get to them – Florence and Noel made it on to the third. They were at sea for a further 12 hours before being picked up by a steam tugboat.

49 Murray, *From the Shadow of Dracula*, p. 221.

50 Violet Hunt's Diary, 8 August 1890, in Violet Hunt Papers, 1858–1962, Collection Number 4607, Cornell University Library.

51 Letter in the Stoker Family Papers, Trinity College, Dublin, TCD MS 11076.

52 Letter to Thornley Stoker, 11 January 1911, quoted in Belford, *Bram Stoker*, p. 315.

53 Hall Caine in the *Daily Telegraph*, 24 April 1912, p. 16.

54 Stoker, Bram (1914), *Dracula's Guest and Other Weird Stories* (London, George Routledge & Sons, Ltd.).

55 Letter to Ellen Terry, January 1881, *Complete Letters* p. 107.

56 Wilde, Oscar (1881), 'Her Voice' in *Poems* (London, David Bogue).

The wild bee reels from bough to bough
  With his furry coat and his gauzy wing.
Now in a lily-cup, and now
  Setting a jacinth bell a-swing,
    In his wandering;
Sit closer love: it was here I trow
    I made that vow,

Swore that two lives should be like one
   As long as the sea-gull loved the sea,
As long as the sunflower sought the sun,—
   It shall be, I said, for eternity
     'Twixt you and me!
Dear friend, those times are over and done,
   Love's web is spun.

Look upward where the poplar trees
   Sway and sway in the summer air,
Here in the valley never a breeze
   Scatters the thistledown, but there
     Great winds blow fair
From the mighty murmuring mystical seas,
   And the wave-lashed leas.

Look upward where the white gull screams,
   What does it see that we do not see?
Is that a star? or the lamp that gleams
   On some outward voyaging argosy,—
     Ah! can it be
We have lived our lives in a land of dreams!
   How sad it seems.

Sweet, there is nothing left to say
   But this, that love is never lost,
Keen winter stabs the breasts of May
   Whose crimson roses burst his frost,
     Ships tempest-tossed
Will find a harbour in some bay,
   And so we may.

And there is nothing left to do
   But to kiss once again, and part,
Nay, there is nothing we should rue,
   I have my beauty,—you your Art,
     Nay, do not start,
One world was not enough for two
   Like me and you.

57 Wilde, Oscar (1881), 'My Voice' in *Poems* (London, David Bogue).

Within this restless, hurried, modern world
   We took our hearts' full pleasure—You and I,
And now the white sails of our ship are furled,
   And spent the lading of our argosy.
Wherefore my cheeks before their time are wan,
   For very weeping is my gladness fled,
Sorrow hath paled my lip's vermilion,
   And Ruin draws the curtains of my bed.
But all this crowded life has been to thee
   No more than lyre, or lute, or subtle spell

Of viols, or the music of the sea
    That sleeps, a mimic echo, in the shell.

58 Wilde, Oscar, 'Silentium Amoris'.

As often-times the too resplendent sun
Hurries the pallid and reluctant moon
Back to her sombre cave, ere she hath won
A single ballad from the nightingale,
So doth thy Beauty make my lips to fail,
And all my sweetest singing out of tune.
And as at dawn across the level mead
On wings impetuous some wind will come,
And with its too harsh kisses break the reed
Which was its only instrument of song,
So my too stormy passions work me wrong,
And for excess of Love my Love is dumb.
But surely unto Thee mine eyes did show
Why I am silent, and my lute unstrung;
Else it were better we should part, and go,
Thou to some lips of sweeter melody,
And I to nurse the barren memory
Of unkissed kisses, and songs never sung.

59 Miller, Elisabeth, and Dacre Stoker (eds)(2012), *The Lost Journal of Bram Stoker* (London, The Robson Press), p. 46.

CHAPTER 6

1 Douglas, Lord Alfred (1914), *Oscar Wilde and Myself* (New York, Duffield & Company), p. 38.
2 Ellmann, Richard (1988), *Oscar Wilde* (London, Penguin Books, 1988), p. 56n.
3 As outlined by A. J. A. Symons (1969), 'Wilde at Oxford' in *Essays and Biographies* (London, Cassell), p. 161. The letter was from an Edith J. Kingsford of Brighton and is in the William Andrews Clark Memorial Library.
4 Information contained in Oxford University, Magdalen College Archives, Diary of Anna Florence Ward, MS 618; Letter to Reginald Harding, June 1876, *Complete Letters*, p. 17.
5 Letter to Reginald Harding, July 1876, *Complete Letters*, pp. 21–2.
6 Hamilton, Walter (1882), *The Aesthetic Movement in England*, third edition (London, Reeves and Turner), p. 100.
7 Hunter Blair, *In Victorian Days & Other Papers*, p. 117.
8 Ibid., pp. 119–20.
9 A comprehensive description of the poor relationship between Oscar Wilde and Rhoda Broughton is contained in Marilyn Wood (1993), *Rhoda Broughton: Profile of a Novelist* (Stamford, Paul Watkins).
10 Black, Helen C. (1906), *Notable Women Authors of the Day (London, McLaren & Company), p. 41.*
11 *Athenaeum*, 2060, 20 April 1867, pp. 514–15.
12 Rodd, James Rennell (1922), *Social and Diplomatic Memories 1884–1893* (London, Edward Arnold & Co.) p. 9.
13 Trollope, Anthony (1905), *An Autobiography*, (New York, Dodd Mead & Co.), p. 224.

14 Wood, *Rhoda Broughton*, p. 57.
15 Maugham, William Somerset (1998), 'The Round Dozen' in *Short Stories* (London, Vintage Books), p. 301. This story is also known as 'The Ardent Bigamist'. By kind permission of United Agents LLP on behalf of The Royal Literary Fund.
16 Arnold, Ethel M. (1920), 'Rhoda Broughton as I Knew Her', *Fortnightly Review* 114 (20 August), p. 265.
17 Woods, M. L. (1941), 'Oxford in the "Seventies"', *Fortnightly Review*, Vol. 156 (London, Chapman and Hall), p. 281.
18 'New Novels' (1886), *Pall Mall Gazette*, 28 October, p. 5.
19 Douglas, *Oscar Wilde and Myself*, p. 38.
20 Letter to A. H. Sayce, June 1878, *Complete Letters*, p. 68.
21 This relationship is mentioned in Robert Browning, Sarah Anne Elizabeth Purefoy (ed.) and Jervoise FitzGerald (ed.)(1966), *Learned Lady; Letters from Robert Browning to Mrs. Thomas FitzGerald, 1876–1889* (Boston, MA, Harvard University Press) p. 108n8.
22 Fleming, George (1878), *Mirage* (Boston, MA, Roberts Brothers) p. 153.
23 Letter to William Ward, July 1877, *Complete Letters*, p. 58.
24 Letter to William Ward, August 1877, *Complete Letters*, p. 61.
25 Letter from Julia Constance Fletcher to Oscar Wilde in Clark, Finzi 920.
26 Letter from Jane Wilde to Oscar Wilde, 11 June 1878, Eccles Bequest, British Library.
27 *The Nation* (1878), 15 June, p. 8.
28 *The Oxford and Cambridge Undergraduate Journal*, reprinted in Stuart Mason (1907), *A Bibliography of the Poetry of Oscar Wilde* (London, E. Grant Richards), pp. 4–5.
29 '"George Fleming" novelist and dramatist', *The Times*, 11 June 1938, p. 14.
30 Swanwick, H. M. (1935), *I Have Been Young* (London, Victor Gollancz), p. 65.
31 Ibid.
32 *Complete Letters*, p. 83n1.
33 Swanwick, *I Have Been Young*, p. 65.
34 Ibid., p. 67.
35 Ibid., p. 138.
36 Ibid., p. 68.
37 Hunter Blair, *In Victorian Days & Other Papers*, p. 122.
38 Letter to Herbert Warren, October 1885, *Complete Letters*, p. 265.
39 Letter to Bouncer Ward, December 1878, *Complete Letters*, p. 77; the description of himself as 'A Professor of Aestheticism, and a Critic of Art' is one he recorded in Joseph Foster's *Alumni Oxonienses*.
40 Letter from Vernon Lee to her mother, quoted in Vineta Colby, *Vernon Lee: A Literary Biography* (Charlottesville, VA, University of Virginia Press, 2003), p. 80.
41 Lee, Vernon (1937), *Vernon Lee's Letters with a Preface by her Executor I. C. Willis* (London, Privately Printed), p. 65.
42 Lee, Vernon (1884), *Miss Brown Volume II* (Edinburgh, William Blackwood & Sons), p. 8.
43 Letter to William Ward, March 1877, *Complete Letters*, p. 42.
44 From the unpublished memoirs of Harry Marillier, in *The Wildean*, No. 28, January 2006, p. 2.
45 Langtry, *The Days I Knew*, p. 54; Letter to Harold Boulton, 23 December 1879, *Complete Letters*, p. 85.
46 Wilde, Oscar (1913), 'London Models' in *English Illustrated Magazine*, January 1889, reproduced in *Essays and Lectures* (London, Methuen), p. 213.

47 Holland, Evangeline, 'The Professional Beauties', http://www.edwardianprome-nade.com/women/the-professional-beauty/ accessed on 12 January 2015

48 Wilde, Oscar, 'London Models', p. 213.

49 Troubridge, *Life Amongst the Troubridges*, p. 152.

50 Jopling, *Twenty Years of My Life 1867–1887*, p. 78.

51 Ibid., p. 64.

52 Belford, Barbara (1990), *Violet: The Story of the Irrepressible Violet Hunt and her Circle of Lovers and Friends – Ford Madox Ford, H. G. Wells, Somerset Maugham, and Henry James* (New York, Simon and Schuster), p. 44.

53 From *My Oscar* quoted in Robert Secor, 'Aesthetes and pre-Raphaelites: Oscar Wilde and the Sweetest Violet in England', *Texas Studies in Language and Literature*, Vol. XXI, No. 3 (Fall 1979), p. 402.

54 Letter to Mrs Alfred Hunt, March 1880, *Complete Letters*, pp. 88–9.

55 Hunt, Violet (1926), *The Flurried Years* (London, Hurst & Blackett), p. 173.

56 Violet Hunt's Diary, 30 July 1891, Violet Hunt Papers, #4607. Division of Rare and Manuscript Collections, Cornell University Library.

57 Quoted in Belford, *Violet*, p. 53.

58 Quoted in John Sutherland (2011), *Lives of the Novelists: A History of Fiction in 294 Lives* (London, Profile Books), p. 250.

59 Ford, Ford Maddox (1911), *Ancient Lights and Certain New Reflections* (London, Chapman & Hall Ltd.), p. 152.

60 Hunt, *The Flurried Years*, p. 13.

61 Letter to Charlotte Montefiore, September 1879, *Complete Letters*, p. 82.

62 *Complete Letters*, p. 82n2.

CHAPTER 7

1 'In Memoriam Henry Wilson' *Dublin Journal of Medical Science*, Vol. 64, Issue 1, 2 July 1877, pp. 98–100.

2 Letter to John Hilson from Lady Jane Wilde, 16 December 1869, University of Reading Special Collections MS 559.

3 Sherard, Robert, *The Life of Oscar Wilde*. The book she was reading is likely to have been the 1874 Longmans edition of this ancient Greek tragedy with notes and expla-nations by the Reverend North Pinder M.A.

4 Glover, James M. (1912), *Jimmy Glover, His Book* (London, Methuen & Co. Ltd.), p. 31.

5 Harris, *Oscar Wilde: His Life and Confessions*, Vol. I, p. 82.

6 Smyth, Dame Ethel (1946), *Impressions that Remained* (New York, Alfred A. Knopf) p. 101.

7 Ibid., p. 102.

8 Ibid., p. 103.

9 Letter to Rosalie Olivecrona from Jane Wilde, 7 April 1879, National Library of Ireland Ms. 15, 281.

10 Binstead, Arthur Morris (1903), *Pitcher in Paradise: Some Random Reminiscences, Sporting and Otherwise* (London, Sands), p. 230.

11 Ibid., pp. 231–2

12 Ibid., pp. 232–3.

13 Jopling, *Twenty Years of My Life 1867–1887*, p. 79.

14 Letter to Norman Forbes Robertson, October 1880, *Complete Letters*, p. 99.

15 Terry, Ellen (1908), *The Story of my Life: Recollections and Reflections* (New York, Doubleday), p. 135.

16 Ibid., p. 62.

17 Ibid., p. 66.

18 Letter to Ellen Terry, July 1879, *Complete Letters*, p. 81.

19 Terry, *The Story of my Life*, pp. 198–9.

Queen Henrietta Maria (Charles I, Act III)

In the lone tent, waiting for victory,
   She stands with eyes marred by the mists of pain,
   Like some wan lily overdrenched with rain;
The clamorous clang of arms, the ensanguined sky,
War's ruin, and the wreck of chivalry
   To her proud soul no common fear can bring;
   Bravely she tarrieth for her Lord, the King,
Her soul aflame with passionate ecstasy.
O, hair of gold! O, crimson lips! O, face
   Made for the luring and the love of man!
   With thee I do forget the toil and stress,
The loveless road that knows no resting place,
   Time's straitened pulse, the soul's dread weariness,
My freedom, and my life republican!

20 'Portia' *The World*, Vol. XII, No. 289, 14 January 1880, p. 13.

I marvel not Bassanio was so bold
   To peril all he had upon the lead,
   Or that proud Aragon bent low his head,
Or that Morocco's fiery heart grew cold;
For in that gorgeous dress of beaten gold,
   Which is more golden than the golden sun,
   No woman Veronese looked upon
Was half so fair as thou whom I behold.
Yet fairer when with wisdom as your shield
   The sober-suited lawyer's gown you donned,
And would not let the laws of Venice yield
   Antonio's heart to that accursed Jew—
   O, Portia! take my heart; it is thy due:
I think I will not quarrel with the Bond.

21 Sherard, *The Life of Oscar Wilde*, p. 182.

22 *Athenaeum*, 23 July 1881, reproduced in Sherard, *The Life of Oscar Wilde*, pp. 184–5.

23 *Punch*, 23 July 1881.

24 *Time*, April 1880. The original, 'The New Helen' was in Vol. I, No. 4, July 1879, pp. 400–2

25 'Oscar Wilde's Poems' (1882), *Century Illustrated Monthly Magazine*, Vol. XXIII, November 1881 to April 1882 (New York, The Century Co.), p. 153.

26 Letter to the Librarian of the Oxford Union Society, November 1881, *Complete Letters*, p. 116.

27 Letter to Violet Hunt, July 1881, *Complete Letters*, p. 114.

28 Terry, *The Story of my Life*, pp. 239–40.

29 Ibid., p. 155.

30 As reported by G. K. Atkinson in *The Cornhill Magazine* (1925), Part 395, p. 564.

31 Modjeska, Helena, 'Mojeska's Memoirs: The Record of a Romantic Career Part V, Success in London', *The Century Magazine,* Vol. 79, p. 879.

32 Ibid., p. 883.

33 'Sen Artysty; or, The Artist's Dream' was published in Clement Scott (ed.)(1880), *The Green Room: Stories by Those Who Frequent It* (London, Routledge), pp. 66–8; http://www.helenamodjeskasociety.com/activity.html accessed on 12 January 2015.

34 Letter to Norman Forbes Robertson, October 1880, *Complete Letters,* p. 99.

35 Ricketts, Charles, *Recollections of Oscar Wilde,* first published in 1932 by the Nonesuch Press (Pallas Athene, 2011) p. 16.

36 Bernhardt, Sarah, *My Double Life: Memoirs of Sarah Bernhardt* (London, William Heinemann, 1907), p. 297.

37 Rennell Rodd, James (1922), *Social and Diplomatic Memories 1884–1893* (London, E. Arnold) p. 23; Oscar assisted Rodd in securing publication for *Rose Leaf and Apple Leaf,* his first book of verse; he even provided an introduction, but as his life became more scandalous, their friendship cooled.

38 Bernhardt, *My Double Life,* pp. 297–8.

39 Letter to Oscar Browning, June 1889, *Complete Letters,* p. 80

40 Oscar Wilde, 'Literary and Other Notes', *The Woman's World,* January 1888, in The Woman's World Volume I (London, Cassell & Company, 1888), p. 132

41 Ricketts, *Recollections of Oscar Wilde,* p. 27.

42 Rennell Rodd, *Social and Diplomatic Memories 1884–1893,* p. 23.

43 Wilde, Oscar (1912), *The Soul of Man* (London, Arthur L. Humpreys), p. 6.

44 O'Neill, M. J. (1955) 'Irish Poets of the Nineteenth Century: Unpublished Lecture Notes of Oscar Wilde', *University Review,* I, No.4, pp. 29–32.

45 Interview in *Pall Mall Budget,* 30 June 1892.

46 *De Profundis:* Letter to Lord Alfred Douglas, January to March 1897, *Complete Letters,* p. 769.

47 Letter to James Knowles, October 1881, *Complete Letters,* p. 116.

48 Rowell, George, 'The Truth About Vera', *Nineteenth Century Theatre,* 21 No. 2, 1993, p. 94.

49 *The Times,* 23 April 1878, p. 7.

50 Vera *Zasulich,* originally published in *Sbornik statei* (St Petersburg, 1907), quoted in Jay Bergman (1983), *Vera Zasulich: A Biography* (Stanford, CA, Stanford University Press), p. 27.

51 Letter to Ellen Terry, September 1880, *Complete Letters,* p. 96.

52 Ward, Genevieve, and Richard Whiting (1918), *Both Sides of the Curtain* (London, Cassell & Company), p. 89. In November 1880, Jane and Oscar had shared a box to see Ward play the lead in *Annie Mie,* a mournful Dutch play she had purchased and translated. The critics panned it, but Oscar assured her it was misunderstood, and Jane railed: 'I am *enraged* with the critics who have done it so little justice!'

53 *The Sketch* quoted in http://www.npg.org.uk/collections/search/person/mp69757/fanny-mary-bernard-beere-nee-whitehead accessed on 2 January 2015

54 'Floats and Flies', *Fun,* 30 November 1881, p. 228.

55 This notice appeared in *The World,* 30 November 1881, p. 12.

56 'The Stage', *Bells Life in London and Sporting Chronicle,* Saturday 3 December 1881, p. 11.

57 *The New York Times,* 26 December 1881, p. 1.

58 Letter to George Curzon, November 1881, *Complete Letters* p. 117.

CHAPTER 8

1 Wilde, *Social Studies*, p. 123.

2 This was reported in an interview with one Canadian newspaper but it does ring true.

3 Arthur Wisner (published under pseudonym A. L. Renner)(1896), *Sarah Bernhardt, Artist and Woman With Numerous Autograph Pages Especially Written by Sarah Bernhardt,* (New York, A. Blanck), p. 29.

4 The D'Oyly Carte Opera Company was born out of a partnership formed by Richard D'Oyly Carte with W. S. Gilbert and Arthur Sullivan. The company produced ten Gilbert and Sullivan operas in addition to many other works and companion pieces. In 1881, Carte built the Savoy Theatre in London, for the purpose of staging these productions; the company also toured extensively in Britain, America and elsewhere, generally operating several companies simultaneously.

5 Wilde, *Social Studies*, p. 91.

6 Morse, W. F., 'American Lectures', chapter IV in *The Writings of Oscar Wilde* (London & New York, Keller-Farmer Co., 1907), pp. 74–5.

7 Wilde, *Social Studies*, p. 144.

8 Wilde, Oscar (1888), in 'Literary and Other Notes', *The Woman's World,* November 1887, in *The Woman's World Volume I* (New York, Source Book Press), p. 39.

9 'Oscar Wilde's Arrival', *New York World*, 3 January 1882, p. 1.

10 Wilde, Oscar, 'Woman's Dress', *Pall Mall Gazette*, 14 October 1884.

11 Wilde, Oscar (1888), 'Literary and Other Notes', *The Woman's World,* December 1887, in *The Woman's World Volume I* (New York, Source Book Press, 1888), p. 84.

12 Wilde, Oscar (1888), 'Literary and Other Notes', *The Woman's World,* November 1887, in *The Woman's World Volume I* (New York, Source Book Press), p. 40.

13 *The Sun* (New York), Vol. XLIX, No. 125, Tuesday 3 January 1882.

14 *Truth* was a British periodical publication founded in 1877 by the diplomat and Liberal politician, Henry Labouchère, the man responsible for enacting the legislation under which Wilde would be tried in 1895.

15 Ibid.

16 'Mrs. Paran Stevens Dead', *New York Times*, 4 April 1895.

17 Jane Croly as 'Jennie June' in *Demorest's Monthly Magazine*, 15 June 1877, quoted in Roy Morris Jr., *Declaring His Genius: Oscar Wilde in North America* (Cambridge, MA, Belknap Press, 2013), p. 39.

18 *New York Tribune*, 9 January 1882, p. 5.

19 'The Throes of Art: Oscar Wilde's first lecture in New-York last evening', *The Providence Sunday Star,* 11 January 1882, p. 3.

20 Letter to Elizabeth Lewis, January 1882, *Complete Letters*, p. 124.

21 Collins Brown, Henry (1935), *Brownstone Fronts and Saratoga Trunks* (New York, E. P. Dutton & Co. Inc.), p. 261.

22 Potter, Helen (1891), *Impersonations* (New York, E. S. Werner), p. 197.

23 Reported in the *Times-Picayune*, 13 January 1882, p. 10.

24 Collins Brown, *Brownstone Fronts and Saratoga Trunks*, p. 262.

25 Letter to Mrs George Lewis, January 1882, *Complete Letters*, p. 126.

26 Quoted in David M. Friedman (2014), *Wilde in America: Oscar Wilde and the Invention of Modern Celebrity* (New York, Norton & Co., 2014), p. 76.

27 'Kate Field Dead', *New York Tribune*, 31 May 1896, p. 7; *Chicago Tribune*, 31 May 1896.

28 Aldrich, Mrs Thomas Bailey (Lillian Woodman Aldrich), *Crowding Memories* (Boston, MA, Houghton Mifflin, 1920), p. 246.

29 As outlined in a letter to the *Boston Transcript* in which he called Wilde a 'clever humbug' and declared that he was unsure whether to 'send to my tailor for buckles and breeches and hose, or to sell my house and go to the country'.

30 *New York Daily Graphic*, 11 January 1882, p. 486.

31 *Memoirs of Anne C. L. Botta, Written by Her Friends* (New York, J. S. Tait & Sons, 1893), p. 23.

32 Pennell, E. Robins, and Joseph Pennell (1914), *Our Philadelphia* (Philadelphia, PA, J. B. Lippincott Company), p. 344; 'Aesthetic: An interesting interview with Oscar Wilde', *Dayton Daily Democrat*, 3 May 1882, p. 4.

33 Pennell, E. Robins, and Joseph Pennell (1921), *The Whistler Journal* (Philadelphia, PA, J. B. Lippincott Company), p. 3.

34 James, Henry, and Rosella Mamoli Zorzi (ed.) (2012), *Letters to Isabella Stewart Gardner* (London, Pushkin Press), p. viii.

35 Schafer, Edith Nalle (2008), *Literary Circles of Washington* (Bedford, MA, Applewood Books), p. 49.

36 'What Oscar Has to Say', *Baltimore American*, 20 January 1882, p. 4.

37 *Thoron, Ward* (ed.)(2011), *First of Hearts: Selected Letters of Mrs. Henry Adams*, (San Francisco, CA, Willowbank Books), p. 113.

38 *Ibid.*, p. 109.

39 *Ibid.*, p. 113.

40 *The Baltimore Sun*, 27 January 1882.

41 Richards, Laura Elizabeth Howe, and Maud Howe Elliott (1925), *Julia Ward Howe, 1819–1910* (Boston, MA, Houghton Mifflin).

42 Clifford, Deborah Pickman (1978), *Mine Eyes Have Seen the Glory: A Biography of Julia Ward Howe* (Boston, MA, Little, Brown and Co.).

43 James and Mamoli Zorzi (ed.), *Letters to Isabella Stewart Gardner*, p. viii.

44 *Boston Evening Transcript*, 2 February 1882.

45 Clifford, Deborah Pickman (1978), *Mine Eyes Have Seen the Glory: A Biography of Julia Ward Howe* (Boston, MA, Little, Brown and Co.).

46 Higgins, Thomas Wentworth, 'Unmanly Manhood', *Woman's Journal* 13, 4 February 1882.

47 Howe, Julia Ward, *Boston Evening Transcript*, 19 February 1882, reprinted in *Encore*, Vol. 8, July 1945, p. 761.

48 Letter to Julia Ward Howe, July 1882, *Complete Letters*, p. 175.

49 Longfellow, Henry Wadsworth, and Andrew R. Hilen (ed.)(1982), *The Letters of Henry Wadsworth Longfellow, Volume 5* (Boston, MA, Harvard University Press), p. 765.

50 Wilde, Oscar, and Stuart Mason (ed.)(1906), *Impressions of America* (Sunderland, Keystone), pp. 25–6.

51 *Chicago Tribune*, 12 March 1882.

52 O'Brien, Kevin F., '"The House Beautiful": A Reconstruction of Oscar Wilde's American Lecture' in *Victorian Studies*, Vol. 17, No. 4, June 1974, pp. 395–418.

53 Cigliano, Jan, and Sarah Bradford Landau, *The Grand American Avenue, 1850–1920* (San Francisco, CA, Pomegranate Artbooks, 1994), p. 143; *Chicago Tribune*, 15 March 1882.

54 Wilde, Oscar, 'Keats Sonnet on Blue', *Century Guild Hobby Horse*, July 1886, p. 5.

55 Letter to Emma Keats Speed, March 1882, *Complete Letters*, p. 157.

56 'Oscar Lectures', *The Toronto Daily Mail*, 14 January 1882, p. 13; Gustafson, Zadel Barnes (1882), *Genevieve Ward from Original Material Derived from Her Family and Friends*, (Boston, MA, James R. Osgood & Company), p. 180.

57 *The Times of Philadelphia*, 8 January 1882, p. 4.

58 Letter from Jane Wilde to Oscar Wilde, 18 September 1882, BL Eccles 81690.

59 Pepper, Robert D. (ed.)(1972), *Oscar Wilde 'Irish Poets and Poetry of the Nineteenth Century':
A Lecture Delivered in Platt's Hall, San Francisco on Wednesday, April fifth, 1882. Edited from
Wilde's Manuscript and Reconstructed, in part, from Contemporary Newspaper Accounts, with an
Introduction and Biographical Notes* (San Francisco, CA, Book Club of California); Lewis,
Lloyd, and Henry Justin Smith (1936), *Oscar Wilde discovers America, 1882* (New York,
Harcourt, Brace), p. 270.

60 Pepper, *Oscar Wilde 'Irish Poets and Poetry of the Nineteenth Century'*.

61 Ibid.

62 Watson, Mary (1890), *People I Have Met* (San Francisco, CA, Valentine), pp. 48–52.

63 Field, Isobel Osbourne (1938), *This Life I've Loved* (New York, Longmans, Green,
1938), p. 148.

64 Fiore, Roberta et al., *Long Beach* (Charleston, SC, Arcadia Publishing, 2010), p. 18.

65 Barney, Natalie Clifford (1929), *Aventures de l'esprit* (New York, Arno Press).

66 'Rude Fashionable Women', *New Ulm Weekly Review*, 4 October 1882, Image 4.

67 'Oscar Wilde', *Chicago Tribune*, 1 March 1882, p. 7.

68 *Aurora Daily Express*, 31 October 1882.

69 *New York Dramatic Mirror*, 11 November 1882, p. 2.

70 *The New York Times*, 7 November 1882, p. 5.

71 Oscar Wilde, 'The American Invasion', *Court and Society Review*, 23 March 1887, p.
37.

CHAPTER 9

 1 Letter to Clara Morris, September 1880, *Complete Letters*, p. 97.

 2 Letter from Dion Boucicault to Oscar Wilde, September 1880 quoted in Ian Small
(1993), *Oscar Wilde Revalued: An Essay on New Materials and Methods of Research* by, ELT
Press, p. 96.

 3 While not immediately apparent from his exotic Huguenot name, Boucicault, like
Oscar, was born and brought up in Dublin. A contemporary of William and Jane,
he was almost certainly the son of the pioneering science writer and lecturer Dr
Dionysius Lardner, the lodger who had become his mother's lover while her unwitting husband remained in the family home. As well as providing his forename, Larder
supported Boucicault financially for the first years of his life. Aged seventeen and
using a false name to thwart his mother's opposition, young Dion embarked on a
career in the theatre and enjoyed early success in London. He sailed for New York in
1853, accompanied by the Scottish actress Agnes Robertson, who was the second of
his three wives. He had inherited a fortune from his wealthy and considerably older
first wife, Anne Guiot, who, it was rumoured, had died in a Swiss mountaineering
accident while she and Boucicault were holidaying together a few months into their
marriage. There were no witnesses.

 4 Letter to Colonel Morse quoted in Stuart Mason (1914), *Bibliography of Oscar Wilde*
(London, T. Werner Laurie), pp. 255–6.

 5 *Complete Letters*, p. 135, n.1.

 6 'Oscar Wilde', *Chicago Tribune*, 1 March 1882, p. 7.

 7 Hopkins McDannald, Alexander (ed.)(1926), *The Americana Annual: An Encyclopedia of
Current Events* (New York, Americana Corporation), p. 518.

 8 Modjeska, Helena, 'Modjeska's Memoirs: The Record of a Romantic Career' in *The
Century Magazine*, March 1910, p. 710.

9 Morris, Clara (1901), *Life on the Stage* (New York, McClure, Phillips & Co.), p. 2.

10 Theatre Historian George D. C. Odell quoted in Barbara Wallace Grossman (2009), *A Spectacle of Suffering: Clara Morris on the American Stage* (Carbondale, IL, Southern Illinois University Press), p. 82.

11 'A Wilde Week', *The Argonaut*, January–June 1882, Vol. 10, p. 64.

12 Reported in the *Times-Picayune*, 13 January 1882, p. 10.

13 *Cincinnati Enquirer*, 12 March 1882, p. 12.

14 'Is This Aesthetic Taffy?' *New York Herald*, Friday 13 January 1882.

15 Reproduced in 'Many Anxious Enquiries', *The New York Times*, 5 July 1881.

16 Letter to D'Oyly Carte, March 1882, *Complete Letters*, p. 152.

17 Letter to Mary Anderson, 8 September 1882, *Complete Letters*, p. 180.

18 Letter to Mary Anderson, September 1882, *Complete Letters*, p. 178.

19 Scarry, John, 'Mary Anderson and the Irish', *Dublin Historical Record*, Vol. 56, No. 2 (Autumn 2003) pp. 182–92.

20 Letter to Steele MacKaye, October 1882, *Complete Letters*, p. 184.

21 Letter to Mary Anderson, 8 September 1882, *Complete Letters*, p. 180.

22 Letter to Steele MacKaye, October 1882, *Complete Letters*, p. 184.

23 Letter to Mary Anderson, October 1882, *Complete Letters*, p. 185.

24 Letter to Steele MacKaye, October 1882, *Complete Letters*, p. 186.

25 Furniss, Harry (1923), *Some Victorian Women: Good, Bad and Indifferent* (London: John Lane [Bodley Head]), p. 62.

26 Mason, Stuart (1914), *Bibliography of Oscar Wilde* (London, T. Werner Laurie Ltd.), p. 327; However, Horst Schroeder maintains,

Though 1 March 1883 was the stipulated date in the rough draft of the agreement (Mason 327), the date set forth in the final agreement must have been 31 March 1883, as Wilde had suggested in a letter of late November 1882. Otherwise Wilde would no doubt have begun his letter of 23 March 1883 to Mary Anderson with some words of apology and not by calmly saying: "The play was duly forwarded some days ago".

27 *Complete Letters*, p. 187n2.

28 *Police Gazette*, 4 November 1882, p. 3.

29 Letter from Marie Prescott to Oscar Wilde, December 1882, quoted in Mason, *Bibliography of Oscar Wilde*, p. 258.

30 Letter Marie Prescott to Oscar Wilde, 26 February 1883, Berg Collection.

31 Mason, *Bibliography of Oscar Wilde*, p. 260.

32 *New York Dramatic Mirror*, 27 February 1885, p. 10.

33 Letter from Oscar Wilde to Marie Prescott, published in the *New York Herald*, 12 August 1883, quoted in Mason, *Bibliography of Oscar Wilde*, p. 259.

34 Mason, *Bibliography of Oscar Wilde*, p. 261.

35 Wilde, Oscar, 'The Grosvenor Gallery', *Dublin University Magazine*, Vol. XC, July–December 1877, p. 122.

36 Sherard, *The Real Oscar Wilde*, p. 235.

37 Ibid., p. 218.

38 Letter to Mary Anderson, 23 March 1883, *Complete Letters*, p. 196.

39 Ibid., p. 198.

40 Ibid. p. 203.

41 Sherard, *The Story of an Unhappy Friendship*, p. 85.

42 Ellmann, *Oscar Wilde*, p. 212.

43 Robert Young Collection relating to William Winter, Folger MS Y.c.61(36).

44 Barnes, J. H. (1914), *Forty Years on the Stage* (London, Chapman & Hall), p. 175.

45 *Stedman*, Jane (1996), *W. S. Gilbert: A Classic Victorian and His Theatre* (Oxford, Oxford University Press), p. 205.

46 Anderson, Mary (1896), *A Few Memories* (New York, Harper & Brothers Publishers), p. 204.

47 Mason, *Bibliography of Oscar Wilde*, p. 42.

48 Ibid., p. 259.

49 Ibid., p. 262.

50 Harris, *Oscar Wilde: His Life and Confessions*, Vol. I, p. 82.

51 Sherard, *The Real Oscar Wilde*, pp. 282–3.

52 Letter from Constance Lloyd to Otho Lloyd, *Complete Letters*, p. 221n1.

53 Oscar's lecture tours of Britain and Ireland are documented comprehensively in Geoff Dibb (2013), *Oscar Wilde A Vagabond With a Mission* (London, The Oscar Wilde Society).

54 *National Police Gazette*, 11 August 1883, p. 5; 1 September 1883, p. 3; quoted in Kevin Lane Dearinger (2009), *Marie Prescott: 'A Star of Some Brilliancy'* (Madison, NJ, Fairleigh Dickinson University Press), p. 135.

55 *Spirit of the Times*, 25 August 1883, quoted in Dearinger, *Marie Prescott*, p. 135.

56 Mason, *Bibliography of Oscar Wilde*, p. 272.

57 *The New York Times*, 21 August 1883, p. 7.

58 *New York Daily Tribune*, quoted in 'Mr. Oscar Wilde's Play', *North-Eastern Daily Gazette*, 2 August 1883, p. 3.

59 *New York Mirror*, 25 August 1883, p. 7, quoted in Mason, *Bibliography of Oscar Wilde*, p. 273.

60 Mason, *Bibliography of Oscar Wilde*, p. 273.

61 Reported in *The New York Times*, 22 August 1883.

62 *The New York Times*, 28 August 1883, p. 8.

63 'THE PLAY'S (NOT) THE THING', *Punch*, 1 September 1883, p. 99, quoted in Mason, *Bibliography of Oscar Wilde*, p. 274.

64 Mason, *Bibliography of Oscar Wilde*, p. 327.

65 Letter to Mina K. Gale, December 1891, *Complete Letters*, p. 508.

CHAPTER 10

1 Corkran, *Celebrities & I*, p. 141.

2 Letter to Lotten von Kramer, 1880, National Library of Sweden.

3 As overheard by Frank Harris, who reported her thoughts on Parnell in Harris, *Oscar Wilde: His Life and Confessions*, Vol. I, p. 83.

4 As confirmed in a letter Jane Wilde received from the feminist journalist Charlotte O'Connor Eccles, who wrote for the magazine. Held in the William Andrews Clark Memorial Library.

5 Hamilton, C. J. (1900), *Notable Irishwomen* (Dublin, Sealy, Bryers & Walker), p. 173.

6 Corkran, *Celebrities & I*, p. 141.

7 Glover, James M. (1911), *Jimmy Glover, His Book* (London, Methuen), p. 33.

8 Wilde, *Social Studies*, p. 22.

9 Hamilton, *Notable Irishwomen*, p. 187.

10 Yeats, W. B. (1888), *Fairy and Folk Tales of the Irish Peasantry* (London, The Walter Scott Publishing Co. Ltd.), p. xv.

11 *The Spectator*, 24 October 1891, p. 23.

12 Hamilton, *Notable Irishwomen*, p. 188.

13 Wilde, Oscar (1913), *Lord Arthur Savile's Crime, The Story of Mr. W. H., & Other Stories* (London, Methuen & Co. Ltd.), p. 3.

14 Letter to Harold Boulton, December 1879, *Complete Letters*, p. 87.

15 Reproduced in Rachel Holmes (2014), *Eleanor Marx: A Life* (London, Bloomsbury), p. 173.

16 Kapp, Yvonne (1976), *Eleanor Marx: The Crowded Years (1884–1898)* (London, Lawrence and Wishart), p. 236. Her column was called 'Missive from England' and it was published in Russkoye Bogatsvo (Russian Wealth), No. 5, 1895.

17 In a letter from Mary Gilbert to Denis Florence McCarthy, March 1881, Rosa Mulholland Gilbert, *Life of Sir John T. Gilbert*, pp. 286–7.

18 de Brémont, Anna (1914), *Oscar Wilde and his Mother* (London, Everett & Co.), p. 76.

19 Shaw, G. B., 'My Memories of Oscar Wilde' in *Oscar Wilde: His Life and Confessions Volume II*, p. 9.

20 Yeats, W. B., and Allan Wade (ed.), *The Letters of W. B. Yeats 1887–1939* (London, R. Hart-Davis, 1954), p. 80. He must have been referring to *Ancient Legends, Mystic Charms and Superstitions of Ireland*, which he admired hugely and was influenced by.

21 Yeats, W. B., *United Ireland*, 16 January 1892, p. 27.

22 Yeats, W. B. (1922), *The Trembling of the Veil* (London, Werner Laurie), p. 27.

23 Ibid., p. 26.

24 Tynan, *Twenty-five Years: Reminiscences*, p. 130.

25 Ibid., p. 127.

26 Corkran, *Celebrities & I*, p. 137.

27 Letter from Lady Jane Wilde to Oscar Wilde, Clark Library.

28 Wilde, Lady Jane (1891), *Notes on Men, Women, and Books* (London, Ward & Downey), p. 122.

29 Mikhail, E. H., *Oscar Wilde: Interviews and Recollections, Volume I* (London, Macmillan, 1979), p. 167.

30 Harris, Frank, *My Life and Loves*, Vol. II, p. 338.

31 According to *Brooklyn Life*, 3 December 1892, at http://bklyn.newspapers.com/image/83186150/, accessed on 15 February 2015.

32 *Los Angeles Herald*, Vol. 42, No. 39, 20 May 1894.

33 Hopkins, Gerard Manley (1955), *The Letters of Gerard Manley Hopkins to Robert Bridges* (London, Oxford University Press), p. 254.

34 Wilde, Oscar, 'English Poetesses', *Queen* LXXIV, 2189, 8 December 1888, pp. 742–3.

35 de Brémont, *Oscar Wilde and his Mother*, p. 46.

36 Ibid., p. 47.

37 Ibid., p. 62.

38 Sherard, *The Real Oscar Wilde*, p. 56.

39 de Brémont, *Oscar Wilde and his Mother*, p. 64.

40 Ibid., p. 58.

41 Ibid., p. 65.

42 Ibid., p. 65.

43 'Books to Read, and Others', *Vanity Fair*, 31, 19 January 1884, p. 33.

44 Hamilton, *Notable Irishwomen*, p. 186.

45 Interview with Jane Wilde published in the *Kentish Mercury*, 2 September 1892.

46 Wilde, *Social Studies*, p. 93.

47 Ibid., p. 90.

48 Ibid., p. 92.

49 Jane Wilde in a two-part article on 'The Laws of Dress', which she wrote for the *Burlington Magazine*, May and July 1881.

50 Zasulich, Vera, originally published in Sbornik Statei (St Petersburg, 1907), translation quoted in Jay Bergman (1983), *Vera Zasulich: A Biography* (Stanford, CA, Stanford University Press), p. 27.

51 Blakemore, Trevor (1911), *The Art of Herbert Schmalz*, (London, Allen). The clash with Oscar is recorded in Christie's biographical notes on Herbert Gustav Schmalz.

52 Hamilton, *Notable Irishwomen*, p. 186.

53 Corkran, *Celebrities & I*, p. 138.

54 Hartley, Harold (1939), *Eighty-Eight: Not Out: a Record of Happy Memories* (London, Muller).

55 Wilde, *Social Studies*, p .23.

56 Wilde, Lady Jane, 'A New Era in English & Irish Social Life' in *Gentlewoman*, January 1883.

57 Wilde, *Social Studies*, p. 13.

58 Quoted in Anne Varty, *A Preface to Oscar Wilde* (Routledge, 1998), p. 14.

59 Wilde, *Social Studies*, p. 95.

60 Wilde, Lady Jane, 'Clever Women', *The Queen*, 2 April 1887.

61 Wilde, *Social Studies*, p. 71.

62 Ibid., p. 93.

63 Letter from Florence Fenwick Miller to Lady Jane Wilde, 21 November 1891, quoted in Karen Sasha Anthony Tipper (2013), *Lady Jane Wilde's Letters to Constance Wilde, Friends and Acquaintances with Selected Correspondence Received* (New York, Edwin Mellen Press), p. 181.

64 Spencer, Walter T. (1923), *Forty Years in My Bookshop* (Boston, MA, Houghton Mifflin), p. 247.

65 de Brémont, *Oscar Wilde and his Mother*, pp. 80–1 (de Brémont refers to the author as 'O'Sullivan' but it was T. D. Sullivan, who knew Lady Jane Wilde well)

66 Letter from Lady Jane Wilde to Philippa Knott, Berg Collection, New York Public Library.

67 Letter from Lady Jane Wilde to Oscar Wilde, 24 April 1893, Clark Finzi 2377.

68 Spencer, *Forty Years in My Bookshop*, p. 247.

69 Hamilton, *Notable Irishwomen*, p. 188.

70 de Brémont, *Oscar Wilde and his Mother*, p. 77.

71 Ibid.

CHAPTER 11

1 From the transcript of Oscar Wilde's libel trial, 3–5 April 1895; The 'love that dare not speak its name' is a phrase from the poem 'Two Loves' by Lord Alfred Douglas

2 'After the Fall', an interview between Julia Ann Charpentier and Merlin Holland, *The Advocate*, 18 June 2008: http://www.advocate.com/news/2008/06/19/after-fall accessed on 15 February 2015.

3 Douglas, Lord Alfred (1938), *Oscar Wilde: A Summing Up* (London, Duckworth, 1940), p. 95.

4 Letter from Constance Lloyd to Oscar Wilde, 11 November 1883, BL Eccles 81690.

5 Letter from Constance Lloyd to Oscar Wilde, BL Eccles 81690, quoted in Moyle, *Constance*, p. 71.

6 Letter from Constance Lloyd to Otho Lloyd 22 November 1883, *Complete Letters*, p. 222.

7 Letter from Constance to Otho, 23 November 1883, *Complete Letters,* p. 221.

8 From the original promotional flier.

9 Letter from Constance Lloyd to Otho Lloyd 26 November 1883, *Complete Letters*, p. 222.

10 Ibid.

11 Letter from Otho Lloyd to Oscar Wilde, *Complete Letters*, p. 222n1.

12 Sherard, *Oscar Wilde: The Story of an Unhappy Friendship*, p. 91.

13 Letter from Oscar Wilde to Waldo Story, January 1884, *Complete Letters*, pp. 225–6.

14 Letter from Oscar Wilde to Lillie Langtry, January 1884, *Complete Letters*, p. 224.

15 Langtry *The Days I Knew*, p. 84.

16 Jopling, *Twenty Years of My Life 1867–1887*, p. 81.

17 Letter from Constance Lloyd to Otho Lloyd, 21 September 1878, in Merlin Holland's Collection, included in Franny Moyle, (2012), *Constance: The Tragic and Scandalous Life of Mrs. Oscar Wilde* (London, John Murray), p. 28.

18 Letter from Jane Wilde to Philippa Knott, Berg Collection.

19 Letter from Jane Wilde to Oscar Wilde, 27 November 1883, quoted in Melville, *Mother of Oscar*, pp. 191–2.

20 Wilde, *Social Studies*, p. 31.

21 Letter from Jane Wilde to Oscar Wilde, 27 November 1883, quoted in Melville, *Mother of Oscar*, pp. 191–2.

22 These sentiments were expressed in a letter from Ada Swinburne-King to Lady Jane Wilde, 30 November 1883, Clark Library, included in Moyle, *Constance*, pp. 75–6.

23 Letter to Lillie Langtry, January 1884, *Complete Letters*, pp. 224–5.

24 Letter from Constance to Oscar, British Library Eccles 81690, included in Moyle, *Constance*, p. 78.

25 From *Queen*, reprinted in *Freeborn County Standard* from Albert Lea, Minnesota, 23 July 1884, p. 7; also described in Sherard, *The Life of Oscar Wilde*, p. 258.

26 Jopling, *Twenty Years of My Life 1867–1887*, pp. 79–80.

27 *Edinburgh Evening News*, Friday 30 May 1884, p. 4.

28 Ibid.

29 *The Morning News from Belfast*, Friday 13 June 1884, p. 6.

30 *Lancaster Gazette*, Saturday 14 June 1884, p. 3.

31 *Aberdeen Evening Express*, Wednesday 4 June 1884, p. 2.

32 Sherard, *Oscar Wilde: The Story of an Unhappy Friendship*, p. 92.

33 Sherard, *The Real Oscar Wilde* p. 325.

34 Ibid., p. 318.

35 Ibid

36 Rothenstein, William (1922), *Men and Memories A History of Arts 1872–1922* (New York, Tudor Publishing Company) p. 81.

37 Letter to Constance from Willie Wilde, Clark Library.

38 de Brémont, *Oscar Wilde and his Mother*, p. 87.

39 Robertson, W. Graham (1933), *Time Was* (London, H. Hamilton Ltd., reprinted by Quartet Books, 1981), p. 233.

40 Her speech was reviewed by the Society's *Gazette*.

41 Wilde, Constance, 'Children's Dress in this Century', *The Woman's World Volume 1*, 1888, p. 417.

42 Lowndes, Susan (ed.)(1971) *Diaries and letters of Marie Belloc Lowndes 1911–1947*, (London, Chatto & Windus), p. 13; Holland, Vyvyan (1999), *Son of Oscar Wilde* (Robinson, Revised edition), pp. 34–5.

43 Potter, Beatrix, and Glen Cavaliero (ed.)(1986), *Beatrix Potter's Journal* (Harmondsworth, Warne), p. 98.

44 Ibid.

45 Hope, Adrian, and Laura Troubridge (2002), *Letters of Engagement*, (London, Tite Street Press), Diary entry for 8 July 1884, p. 6; Letter from Hope to Troubridge, 10 November 1884, p. 38.

46 *Lady's Pictorial*, 19 July 1884, quoted in Anne Clark Amor (1983), *Mrs. Oscar Wilde, A Woman of Some Importance* (London, Sidgwick & Jackson), p. 49.

47 *Lady's Pictorial*, 8 January 1887, quoted in Amor, *Mrs. Oscar Wilde*, p. 65.

48 de Brémont, *Oscar Wilde and his Mother*, p. 89.

49 Leverson, Ada (1930), *Letters to the Sphinx from Oscar Wilde: With Reminiscences of the Author* (London, Duckworth), p. 44.

50 Letter to Constance from Oscar sent from the Balmoral Hotel Edinburgh in December 1884, *Complete Letters*, pp. 241–2.

51 Letter to Nellie Lloyd, 5 June 1885, *Complete Letters*, p. 261.

52 Letter to Norman Forbes Robertson, June 1885, *Complete Letters*, p. 262.

53 Hope and Troubridge, *Letters of Engagement*, p. 134.

54 Letters to William Ward, July 1878, *Complete Letters*, p. 69.

55 Wilde, Oscar, 'Mr Froude's Blue Book', *Pall Mall Gazette*, 13 April 1889, p. 3.

56 'Mr. Oscar Wilde on Women's Dress', *Pall Mall Gazette*, 14 October 1884, p. 6.

57 Wilde, Oscar, 'Helena in Troas', *Dramatic Review*, 22 May 1886.

58 Harris, *My Life and Loves*, Vol. II, p. 486.

59 Rothenstein, *Men and Memories A History of Arts 1872–1922*, p. 133.

60 Yeats, *The Trembling of the Veil*, p. 24.

61 Holland, *Son of Oscar Wilde*, p. 53.

62 Hope and Troubridge, *Letters of Engagement*, p. 115.

63 Ibid., p. 117.

64 Ibid., p. 122.

65 Ibid., p. 125; the charity book was *In a Good Cause*, compiled by Margaret S. Tyssen Amherst and published later that year.

66 'Mrs Oscar Wilde on Women and War', *Pall Mall Gazette*, 17 April 1888, p. 8.

67 *Pall Mall Gazette*, 24 May 1889, p. 6.

68 de Brémont, *Oscar Wilde and his Mother*, pp. 97–8.

69 Sherard, *The Life of Oscar Wilde*, p. 264.

CHAPTER 12

1 Wilde, Oscar, 'Literary and Other Notes', *The Woman's World*, Vol. I, December 1887, pp. 81–5.

2 Outlined in greater detail in Cynthia L. White (1970), *Women's Magazines 1693–1968* (London, Joseph), p. 58.

3 Letter to Thomas Wemyss Reid, April 1887, *Complete Letters*, p. 297.

4 Ibid.

5 Letter to Mrs Hamilton King, November 1887, *Complete Letters*, p. 332.

6 Letter to Thomas Wemyss Reid, April 1887, *Complete Letters*, p. 297.

7 Ibid., p. 298.

8 Ibid., p. 297.

9 Harris, *My Life and Loves*, Vol. I, p. 91.

10 Letter to the Hon. Mrs Stanley (later Lady Jeune), 1881, *Complete Letters*, p. 115.

11 Doyle, Sir Arthur Conan (1924), *Memories and Adventures: an Autobiography* (London,

Hodder & Stoughton, reprinted by Wordsworth Editions, 2007), p. 232.

12 Letter to Thomas Wemyss Reid, May 1887, *Complete Letters*, pp. 299–300.

13 Letter to Thomas Wemyss Reid, September 1887, *Complete Letters*, p. 317.

14 Ibid.

15 Wilde, Oscar, 'Literary and Other Notes', *The Woman's World*, Vol. I, November 1887, p. 40.

16 Portsmith, Eveline, 'The Position of Women', *The Woman's World*, Vol. I, November 1887, p. 8.

17 Bevington, Louise S., 'Women in Germany', *The Woman's World*, Vol. I, 10 August 1888, p. 458.

18 Wedgewood, Julia, 'Women and Democracy', *The Woman's World*, Vol. I, June 1888, pp. 337–40.

19 Barnett, Henrietta O., 'The Uses of a Drawing-room', *The Woman's World*, Vol. I, May 1888, pp. 289–92.

20 Tabor, Mary C., 'The Working Ladies' Guild', *The Woman's World*, Vol. I, July 1888, pp. 423–4.

21 Black, Clementina, 'Something About Needlewomen', *The Woman's World*, Vol. I, May 1888, pp. 300–4.

22 Eccles, Charlotte O'Connor, 'The Poplin Weavers of Dublin', *The Woman's World*, Vol. I, July 1888, pp. 396–9.

23 Letter to Helena Sickert, May 1887, *Complete Letters*, p. 301.

24 Anonymous, 'The 'The Oxford Ladies' Colleges', *The Woman's World*, Vol. I, November 1887, pp. 32–5.

25 The feature appeared in *The Woman's World*, Vol. I, 1888 p. 129. He mentions the invitation in a letter to Reginald Harding, March 1877, *Complete Letters*, pp. 47–8.

26 Wilde, Oscar, 'Literary and Other Notes', *The Woman's World*, Vol. I, January 1888, pp. 135–6; Reviewed Defoe's 'The Education of Women' which is included in *English Essays from Sir Philip Sidney to Macaulay* (1910)(F. Collier & Son), p. 159.

27 Wilde, 'Literary and Other Notes', *The Woman's World*, Vol. I, December 1887, p. 85.

28 Simcox, Edith, 'Elementary School Teaching as a Profession', *The Woman's World*, Vol. I, October 1888, pp. 537–42.

29 Marshall, Mary A., 'Medicine as a Profession for Women', *The Woman's World*, Vol. I, October 1888, pp. 537–42.

30 Letter to Edith Simcox, July–August 1887, *Complete Letters*, p. 314.

31 Wilde, Oscar, 'Literary and Other Notes', *The Woman's World*, Vol. II, May 1889. p. 390.

32 Fawcett, Millicent Garrett, 'Women's Suffrage', *The Woman's World*, Vol. II, pp. 9–12.

33 Letter to Oscar Wilde reprinted in *The Story of the House of Cassell* (London, Cassell & Co, 1922), p. 139.

34 Garnett, Lucy, 'Reasons For Opposing Woman Suffrage', *The Woman's World*, Vol. II, April 1889, pp. 306–10.

35 McLaren, Laura, 'The Fallacy of the Superiority of Man', *The Woman's World*, Vol.1, December 1887, pp. 54–9.

36 Wilde, 'Literary and Other Notes', *The Woman's World Volume I*, December 1887, p. 84.

37 Carr, Alice Comyns, 'A Lady of Fashion in 1750', *The Woman's World*, Vol. II, May 1889, p. 374.

38 Wilde, 'Literary and Other Notes', *The Woman's World*, Vol. I, November 1887, p. 40.

39 Wilde, Literary and Other Notes', *The Woman's World*, Vol. I, December 1887.

40 Wilde, Oscar (2005), 'A Monstrous Fashion', reproduced in *The Prose of Oscar Wilde* (New York, Cosimo Classics), p. 445.

41 Letter to James Whistler, June 1882, *Complete Letters*, p. 174.

42 Crawford, Emily, 'Women Wearers of Men's Clothes', *The Woman's World*, Vol. II, 1889, pp. 283–6,

43 Wilde, 'Literary and Other Notes', *The Woman's World*, Vol. I, November 1887, p. 40.

44 Louise Chandler Moulton in her regular column for the *Boston Herald*, March 1889, reproduced in *The Literary World: A Monthly Review of Current Literature*, Vol. 20 (Boston, MA, S. R. Crocker, 1889), p. 123.

45 Letter to Helena Sickert, October 1887, *Complete Letters*, p. 325; Letter to Amy Levy, October 1887, *Complete Letters*, p. 326.

46 *The Woman's World*, Vol. III, 1890.

47 Yeats, W. B., *Four Years*, reprinted in Yeats, Douglas Archibald and William O'Donnell (eds)(2010), *Autobiographies* (Simon and Schuster), p. 147.

48 'The Lost' *The Woman's World*, Vol. II, 1889, pp. 145–6; 'A Dream of Wild Bees', *The Woman's World*, Vol. II, pp. 3–4; 'Life's Gifts' *The Woman's World*, Vol. II, p. 408.

49 *Olive Schreiner to Oscar Wilde, June 1888*, Harry Ransom Research Center, University of Texas at Austin, Olive Schreiner Letters Project Transcription. Lines 12 and 13.

50 Letter to George Macmillan, October 1887, *Complete Letters*, p. 327.

51 Wilde, 'Literary and Other Notes', *The Woman's World*, Vol. I, November 1887, p. 36.

52 Wilde, 'Literary and Other Notes', *The Woman's World*, Vol. II, June 1889, pp. 447–8.

53 Wilde, 'Literary and Other Notes', *The Woman's World*, Vol. I, November 1887, pp. 36–40.

54 Letter from Jane Wilde to Oscar Wilde, November 1887, Eccles MS 81690.

55 Wilde, Constance, 'Children's Dress in this Century', *The Woman's World*, Vol. I, July 1888, pp. 413–17.

56 Constance Wilde to Charlotte Carmichael Stopes, 21 March 1889, BL MS Add. 58454: f.

57 Green, Stephanie, 'The Serious Mrs Stopes: Gender, Writing and Scholarship in Late-Victorian Britain', *Nineteenth-Century Gender Studies*, Issue 5.3 (Winter 2009).

58 'Metropolitan Notes', *Nottingham Evening Post*, 28 October 1887, p. 2.

59 *The Times*, December 1888.

60 'Review of August Magazines', *St James's Gazette*, 29 July 1889, p. 6.

61 *The Spectator*, 5 November 1887, p. 25.

62 *The Spectator*, 4 February 1888, p. 22.

63 *Irish Times*, 5 November 1887, p. 7.

64 *Irish Times*, 28 June 1890, p. 7.

65 Yeats, *Four Years* quoted in Yeats, Archibald, and O'Donnell, *Autobiographies*, p. 125.

66 Fish, Arthur, 'Memories of Oscar Wilde: Some Hitherto Unpublished Letters', *Cassell's Weekly*, 2 May 1923 p. 215.

67 Letter to Wemyss Reid, September-October 1889, *Complete Letters*, p. 413.

68 Letter to Arthur Fish, October 1890, *Complete Letters*, p. 455.

69 Fish, Arthur (1913), 'Oscar Wilde as Editor', *Harper's Weekly* (Harper's Magazine Company), Vol. 58, p. 18.

70 Ibid.

71 Ibid.

72 Ibid.

73 Letter to Helena Sickert, October 1887, *Complete Letters*, p. 325.

74 Letter to William Sharp, October–November 1887, *Complete Letters*, p. 332.

75 Letter to Oscar Browning, December 1887, *Complete Letters*, p. 337.
76 Fish, 'Oscar Wilde as Editor', p. 18.
77 Ibid., p. 19.
78 Letter to Wemyss Reid, October 1888, *Complete Letters*, p. 363.
79 VanArsdel, Rosemary T. (2001), *Florence Fenwick Miller. Feminist, Journalist and Educator* (Aldershot, Ashgate), p. 130.
80 Fish, 'Memories of Oscar Wilde', p. 215.
81 Arthur Fish, *The Story of The House of Cassell*, p. 134.
82 'Reviews: Magazines of the Month', *Women's Penny Paper*, 13 September 1890, p. 557.

CHAPTER 13
 1 O'Sullivan, Vincent (1936), *Aspects of Wilde* (London, Constable & Company), p. 36.
 2 Holland, *Son of Oscar Wilde*, p. 278.
 3 Letter to Aimee Lowther, August 1899, *Complete Letters*, p. 1163.
 4 *Complete Letters*, p. 583n1.
 5 Letter to Aimée Lowther, August 1899, *Complete Letters*, p. 1164.
 6 Called 'Hazel Eyes', it was published in 1922. *Complete Letters*, p. 583n1.
 7 These, and other apocryphal stories, were published by Thomas Wright as *Table Talk: Oscar Wilde* (London: Cassell & Co., 2000).
 8 Langtry, *The Days I Knew*, p. 76.
 9 Pearson, Hesketh (1946), *The Life of Oscar Wilde* (London, Methuen & Co.), p. 205.
10 Yeats, *The Trembling of the Veil*, p. 19.
11 O'Sullivan, *Aspects of Wilde*, p. 37.
12 Wilde, Oscar (1999), '*A Woman of No Importance*' in *Wilde: The Complete Plays (Methuen, London), p. 345.*
13 Harris, *My Life and Loves*, Vol. I, pp. 134–5.
14 Robert Ross from an introduction to Oscar Wilde (1909), *Essays and Lectures* (Methuen, London), p. xii.
15 'Harry Marillier and the Love of the Impossible', Jonathan Fryer, *The Wildean*, 28 January 2006.
16 Dowson, E. C. et al. (eds)(1968), *The Letters of Ernest Dowson* (Madison, NJ, Fairleigh Dickinson University Press), p. 386.
17 Robertson, *Time Was*, pp. 130–1.
18 Letter to W. Graham Robertson, 1888, *Complete Letters*, p. 347.
19 Robertson, *Time Was*, p. 135.
20 Ibid., pp. 132–5.
21 Holland, *Son of Oscar Wilde*, p. 53.
22 Ibid., p. 54.
23 Ibid.
24 Gide, André, and Stuart Mason (trans.)(1905), *Oscar Wilde: A Study* (Oxford, The Holywell Press), p. 24.
25 From a description published in *L'Echo de Paris*, 19 December 1891.
26 Gide and Mason, *Oscar Wilde: A Study*, p. 49.
27 Gide, André, and Robert Mallet (1966), *André Gide-Paul Valéry Correspondence 1890–1942* (Chicago, IL, University of Chicago Press), p. 92.
28 Sherard, *The Life of Oscar Wilde*, p. 292.
29 A. J. A. Symons, *Horizon IV*, No. 22, October 1941, pp. 251–8.
30 Letter to William Gladstone, June 1888, *Complete Letters*, p. 350.
31 Letter to G. H. Kersley, June 1888, *Complete Letters*, p. 352.

32 Letter to Amelie Rives Chanler, January 1889, *Complete Letters*, p. 388.

33 Wilde, Oscar (1991), 'The Happy Prince', *The Complete Illustrated Works of Oscar Wilde* (Chancellor Press, London), pp. 156–7.

34 *Woman's Union Journal*, (Women's Protective and Provident League (WPPL), 1888), p. 66.

35 Wilde, Oscar (1915), *The Soul of Man under Socialism* (New York, Max N. Maisel), p. 4.

36 Wilde, Oscar, 'The Devoted Friend', *The Complete Illustrated Works of Oscar Wilde* (Chancellor Press, London), p. 182.

37 Wilde, Oscar, 'The Remarkable Rocket', *The Complete Illustrated Works of Oscar Wilde*, p. 186.

38 Letter to Thomas Hutchinson, July 1888, *Complete Letters*, p. 354.

39 From the introduction to Isobel Murray (ed.)(1979), *Oscar Wilde Complete Shorter Fiction* (Oxford, Oxford University Press), p. 9.

40 Letter to Mrs W. H. Grenfell, July 1891, *Complete Letters*, p. 484.

41 O'Sullivan, *Aspects of Wilde*, p. 35.

42 From 'The Souls', *Oxford Dictionary of National Biography*.

43 *The Times*, 21 January 1929, p. 13.

44 Blunt, Wilfrid Scawen (1921), *My Diaries: Being a Personal Narrative of Events 1888–1914 Volume I* (A. A. Knopf, New York), p. 375.

45 Letter from Constance to Lady Mount-Temple, 23 November 1891, BR 57/14/1 quoted in Moyle, *Constance*, p. 200.

46 Letter to Mrs William H. Grenfell, November 1891, *Complete Letters*, p. 493.

47 Beerbohm, Max (1920), *Herbert Beerbohm Tree: Some Memories of Him and of His Art* (New York, E. P. Dutton & Co.), p. 87.

48 Davenport-Hines, R. (2009), *Ettie: The Intimate Life And Dauntless Spirit Of Lady Desborough* (London, Weidenfeld & Nicolson), p. 58.

49 Sherard, *The Story of an Unhappy Friendship*, p. 109.

50 Asquith, Margot (1933), *More Memories* (London, Cassells & Company), pp. 115–16.

51 This and the true nature of many other influences is discussed in fascinating detail by Dr Anne Markey (2011), *Oscar Wilde's Fairy Tales: Origins and Contexts* (Irish Academic Press) p. 183.

52 Asquith, *More Memories*, p. 116.

53 Blunt, W. S. (1921), *My Diaries; being a Personal narrative of Events 1888–1914* (New York, Alfred A. Knopf), p. 145.

54 Asquith, *More Memories*, p. 116.

55 Ibid., p. 117.

56 Yeats, *The Trembling of the Veil*, pp. 27–8.

57 A letter to the editor of the *Pall Mall Gazette*, 11 December 1891, reproduced in Mason, *Bibliography of Oscar Wilde*, p. 368.

58 Letter from Jane Wilde to Oscar Wilde (Clark) quoted in Amor, *Mrs. Oscar Wilde*, p. 105.

59 'Some Illustrated Gift Books', *Pall Mall Gazette*, 30 November 1891, p. 3.

60 Pearson, *The Life of Oscar Wilde*, p. 143.

61 Harris, *My Life and Loves*, Vol. I,, p. 117.

62 Letter Jane Wilde to Oscar Wilde quoted in Melville, *Mother of Oscar*, p. 212.

63 Robert Ross from his introduction to Wilde, *Essays and Lectures*, p. xi.

64 Letter from More Adey to Oscar Wilde, 23 September 1896, *Complete Letters*, p. 663.

65 Ibid.

66 For more information on 'The Sphere' see 'The Magic Ball' in John Stokes (1998), *Oscar Wilde: Myths, Miracles and Imitations* (Cambridge, Cambridge University Press).

67 Letter to Adela Schuster, November 1894, *Complete Letters*, p. 621.
68 Letter to James Stanley Little, *Complete Letters*, p. 339.

CHAPTER 14

1 Letter to the Editor of the *Scots Observer,* July 1890, *Complete Letters*, p. 439.
2 Letter to Unknown Correspondent, 1886–7, *Complete Letters*, p. 293.
3 Besant, Walter (1894), 'The Rise and Fall of the Three Decker', *The Dial*, Vol. 17, pp. 185–6.
4 Adcock, Arthur St. John (1909), 'Marie Corelli: A Record and an Appreciation', *The Bookman*, 36, No. 212, pp. 59–60.
5 In a flattering profile included in 'Chronicle & Comment', *The Bookman*, July 1909, reproduced in *The Bookman Volume XXIX, March 1909 – August 1909* (New York, Dodd, Mead & Co., 1909), p. 461.
6 Masters, Brian (1978), *Now Barabbas was a Rotter* (London, H. Hamilton), p. 74.
7 *Reproduced in The Bookman*, Volume XXIX, p. 465.
8 *Complete Letters*, p. 905n2.
9 Wilde, Oscar (1907), 'The Decay of Lying', *Intentions: The Soul of Man under Socialism* (New York, Nottingham Society), p. 16.
10 Bigland, Eileen (1950), *Ouida: The Passionate Victorian* (London, Jarrolds), p. 13.
11 Ibid., p. 20.
12 Lee, Elizabeth (1914), *Ouida: A Memoir* (London, T. F. Unwin), p. 18.
13 Allingham, William (1908), *A Diary* (London, Macmillan), p. 193.
14 Furniss, Harry (1923), *Some Victorian Women, Good Bad and Indifferent* (London, John Lane, The Bodley Head), p. 15; Lady St. Helier (1909), *Memories of Fifty Years* (London, Edward Arnold), p. 237.
15 'Eccentric Englishwomen: IV. Ouida', *The Spectator*, 6 May 1937, p. 11.
16 Allingham, *A Diary*, p. 193.
17 Layard, George Somes (1907), *A Great "Punch" Editor* (London, Pitman & Sons), p. 410.
18 Lee, *Ouida: A Memoir*, pp. 82–3
19 Mallock, W. H. (1920), *Memoirs of Life and Literature* (London, Chapman & Hall), p. 94.
20 'Ouida at Home', *Tuapeka Times*, 15 August 1894, p. 5.
21 Ruskin, John (1884), *The Art of England: Lectures Given in Oxford* (New York, Wiley & Sons), p. 21.
22 Lee, *Ouida: A Memoir*, p. 6.
23 Allingham, *A Diary*, p. 193.
24 Rodd, *Social and Diplomatic Memories*, p. 13.
25 Exchange reported in the *Mataura Ensign*, Vol. 9, Issue 654, 25 March 1887, p. 2.
26 Ouida (1884), *Princess Napraxine*, Vol. I (London, Chatto & Windus), p. 11.
27 de *Brémont, Oscar Wilde and his Mother,* p. 75.
28 Ibid., p. 76.
29 Letter to Fanny *Bernard-Beere*, October 1887, *Complete Letters*, p. 331.
30 Ouida (1894), 'The New Woman', *The North American Review*, 158, pp. 610–19, in response to Sarah Grand (1894), 'The New Aspect of the Woman Question', *The North American Review*, 158, pp. 271–6.
31 An unpublished letter written in 1891, quoted in Elaine Showalter (2001), *Inventing Herself: Claiming a Feminist Intellectual Heritage* (New York, Scribner), p. 90.
32 Bigland, *Ouida: The Passionate Victorian*, p. 203.
33 Ouida, *The Woman's World*, Vol. I, pp. 193–4.

34 Ibid., pp. 481–4.

35 Ouida, *The Woman's World*, Vol. II, pp. 171–3.

36 Ibid., pp. 339–42.

37 'Cecil Castlemaine's Gage', *Pall Mall Gazette*, Vol. VI, 21 September 1867, p. 11.

38 *The Saturday Review, 49, 28 February 1880, p. 546.*

39 *The Morning Post*, 2 February 1880, p. 3.

40 *The Times*, 13 April 1880 p. 9.

41 *The Times*, 27 March 1880, p. 12.

42 Included in the *Universal Review* 2, October 1888, pp. 295–301.

43 Street, G. S. (1895), 'An Appreciation of Ouida', *The Yellow Book*, Vol. 6 (London, E. Mathews & J. Lane), p. 185.

44 Wilde, Oscar, 'Ouida's New Novel', *Pall Mall Gazette*, 17 May 1889, p. 3.

45 Wilde, *Social Studies*, p. 70.

46 Beerbohm, Max (1899), *More* (London, The Bodley Head), p. 198.

47 Meynell, Alice, 'The Praises of Ouida', *Pall Mall Gazette*, 16 August 1895, p. 4.

48 Ouida (1871), *Chandos: A Novel, Part I* (London, B. Tauchnitz), p. 12.

49 Ellmann, *Oscar Wilde*, p. 355.

50 Wilde, Oscar, 'Olivia at the Lyceum', *Dramatic Review*, 30 May 1885, reprinted in *Reviews* (1908), p. 29.

51 Wilde, Oscar, 'A Note on Some Modern Poets', *The Woman's World*, Vol. II, December 1888.

52 Gide, André (1926), 'In Memoriam Oscar Wilde', *Pretextes* (Paris) pp. 284–5.

53 Oscar Wilde's letter to the *Daily Chronicle*, 2 July 1890, reproduced in Stuart Mason (1908), *Oscar Wilde: Art & Morality A Defence of The Picture of Dorian Gray* (London, J. Jacobs), p. 29.

54 O'Sullivan, *Aspects of Wilde*, p. 177.

55 'A Study in Puppydom', *St James's Gazette*, 24 June, 1890, reproduced in Mason, *Oscar Wilde: Art & Morality A Defence of The Picture of Dorian Gray*, p. 9.

56 Hawthorne, Julian, 'The Romance of the Impossible', *McBride's Magazine*, Vol. 46, July-December 1890, p. 413.

57 Ransome, Arthur (1912), *Oscar Wilde: A Critical Study* (New York, Mitchell Kennerley), p. 98.

58 Yeats' Review of *Lord Arthur Savile's Crime & Other Stories, United Ireland*, 26 September 1891.

59 Lord Alfred Douglas in a letter to A. J. A. Symons, 8 July 1930, Clark Finzi 756.

60 Ransome, *Oscar Wilde: A Critical Study*, p. 105.

61 'Mr. Oscar Wilde's Dorian Gray', *Pall Mall Gazette*, 26 June 1890, p. 3.

62 *The Graphic*, 12 July 1890, p. 18.

63 *Freeman's Journal*, 16 May 1891, p. 6.

64 'A Study in Puppydom', *St James's Gazette*, 24 June 1890, reproduced in Mason, *Oscar Wilde. Art & Morality A Defence of The Picture of Dorian Gray*, p. 9.

65 Letter from Oscar Wilde to editor published in *St James's Gazette*, 26 June 1890, reproduced in Mason, *Oscar Wilde: Art & Morality A Defence of The Picture of Dorian Gray*, pp. 12–13.

66 *Scots Observer*, 5 July 1890, reproduced in Mason, *Oscar Wilde: Art & Morality A Defence of The Picture of Dorian Gray*, p. 30.

67 Letter to Ralph Payne, February 1894, *Complete Letters*, p. 585; this is possibly Ralph Stephen Hacon Payen Payne, son of author and genealogist James Bertrand Payen Payne, who at one time managed Moxon Publishing. This Ralph was sixteen years

younger than Oscar and born in Kensington. He would have been twenty-four when this letter was sent.

68 Letter to Arthur Fish on his engagement, July 1890, *Complete Letters*, p. 440.
69 Ellmann, *Oscar Wilde*, p. 302.
70 Letter from Jane Wilde to Oscar Wilde, June 1890, Ellmann, *Oscar Wilde*, p. 302.
71 Mallock, *Memoirs of Life and Literature*, p. 95.
72 Sherard, *The Real Oscar Wilde*, pp. 68–9.
73 Lee, *Ouida: A Memoir*, p. 223.
74 Ibid., p. 158.

CHAPTER 15

1 Carillo, Enrique Gomez (1902), 'Comment Oscar Wilde reva Salome', *La Plume* 14, pp. 1149–52. English translation from E. H. Mikhail (1979), *Oscar Wilde: Interviews and Recollections*, Vol. I (London, Macmillan), pp. 192–3.
2 Saltus, Marie (1925), *Edgar Saltus: The Man* (Chicago, IL, Pascal Covici), p. 51.
3 Letter to Edgar Saltus, September 1890, *Complete Letters*, p. 453.
4 Saltus, Edgar (1917), *Oscar Wilde: An Idler's Impression* (Chicago, IL, Brothers of the Book), p. 22.
5 Letter from Flaubert to his niece Caroline, 28 January 1877, Gustave Flaubert, Correspondance: Année 1877, (Édition Louis Conard), http://flaubert.univ-rouen.fr. Several English translations are available including: Gustave Flaubert, Roger Whitehouse (trans.), and Geoffrey Wall (ed.)(2005), *Three Tales* (New York, Penguin Classics).
6 'The Poets' Corner', *Pall Mall Gazette*, 15 February 1888, p. 2.
7 Robertson, *Time Was*, p. 136.
8 Carrillo, 'Comment Oscar Wilde reva Salome', pp. 1149–52.
9 Huysmans, Joris-Karl, and John Howard (trans.)(1922), *A rebour/Against the Grain* (New York, Lieber & Lewis), p. 92.
10 Carrillo, 'Comment Oscar Wilde reva Salome', pp. 1149–52.
11 Robertson, *Time Was*, p. 136.
12 'The Censure and "Salome", an Interview with Mr. Oscar Wilde', *Pall Mall Gazette*, 29 June 1892, p. 2.
13 Merrill, Stuart (1903), 'Souvenirs sur le Symbolisme', *La Plume* (Paris), pp. 107–15.
14 O Sullivan, *Aspects of Wilde*, p. 32.
15 Ibid., p. 33.
16 Mikhail (ed.), *Oscar Wilde: Interviews and Recollections*, Vol. 1, pp. 190–1.
17 Letter to Pierre Louÿs, June 1892, *Complete Letters*, p. 529.
18 Letter to Leonard Smithers, September 1900, *Complete Letters*, p. 1196.
19 Terry, Ellen (1908), *The Story of My Life: Recollections and Reflections* (New York, Doubleday), p. 239.
20 Ibid., p. 237.
21 Snel, Harmen (2007), *The Ancestry of Sarah Bernhardt* (Amsterdam, Jewish Historical Museum), p. 98.
22 Bernhardt, Sarah, *My Double Life* (London, William Heinmann, 1907), p. 1.
23 Ibid.
24 Ibid., p. 101.
25 *The Pittsburg Press*, 'I Dare Say – Two Birthdays', 17 August 1949, p. 2.
26 Arsène Houssaye quoted in Arthur Wisner (1896), *Sarah Bernhardt, Artist and Woman* (New York, Blanck), p. 62.

27 Stoker, *Personal Reminiscences of Henry Irving*, p. 344.

28 Sherard, *The Real Oscar Wilde*, p. 128.

29 Bernhardt, *My Double Life*, pp. 297–8.

30 Letter to Oscar Browning, June 1879, *Complete Letters*, p. 80.

31 Bernhardt, *My Double Life*, p. 307.

32 Terry, *The Story of My Life: Recollections and Reflections*, p. 163.

33 Stoker, *Personal Reminiscences of Henry Irving*, p. 344.

34 Terry, *The Story of My Life: Recollections and Reflections*, p. 237.

35 Bernhardt, *My Double Life*, p. 258; It was taken by Parisian photographer Melandri.

36 Ibid., p. 338.

37 Sherard, *The Real Oscar Wilde*, p. 268.

38 'The Latest "Cleopatra"', *The New York Times*, 24 October 1890.

39 Stoker, *Personal Reminiscences of Henry Irving*, pp. 345–6.

40 Ricketts, *Oscar Wilde: Recollections*, p. 16.

41 Letter to Unidentified Correspondent, September 1880, *Complete Letters* p. 97.

42 Jean Lorrain, "Une visite chez Sarah," *Événement*, 3 November 1887, quoted in Charles Bernheimer and T. Jefferson Kline (2003), *Decadent Subjects: The Idea of Decadence in Art, Literature, Philosophy, and Culture of the Fin de Siècle in Europe* (John Hopkins University Press), p. 214.

43 *The Times*, 2 March 1892, reprinted in Mason, *Bibliography of Oscar Wilde*, p. 377.

44 'The Censorship and Salome', *Pall Mall Gazette*, 6 July 1892, p. 1.

45 Wilde, Oscar (1999), 'The Truth of Masks', *Complete Works of Oscar Wilde* (New York, Harper Collins), p. 1162.

46 'The Censure and "Salome"', *Pall Mall Gazette*, 29 June 1892, p. 1.

47 Contained in a private letter, disclosed posthumously, which is held with the Lord Chamberlain's papers and correspondence in the Public Record Office (LC.1:582 27 June 1892), quoted in John Russell Stephens (ed.), *The Censorship of English Drama 1824–1901* (Cambridge, Cambridge University Press, 1980), p. 112.

48 Letter to William Rothenstein, July 1892, *Complete Letters*, p. 531.

49 'The Censure and "Salome"', *Pall Mall Gazette*, 29 June 1892, p. 1.

50 Hyde, H. Montgomery (1975), *Oscar Wilde. A Biography* (New York: Farrar, Straus, and Giroux), p. 37.

51 Letter to William Rothenstein, July 1892, *Complete Letters*, p. 531.

52 Letter to Arthur Fish, July 1892, *Complete Letters*, p. 531.

53 'Drama and Music Abroad; Oscar Wilde Covers Himself with Ridicule', *The New York Times*, 3 July 1892.

54 'The Censorship and Salome', *Pall Mall Gazette*, 6 July 1892, p. 1.

55 Ibid.

56 'Mr Oscar Wilde's New Play', *Black & White Magazine*, 11 May 1893; Letter to the editor 'Mr. Oscar Wilde and the Censorship' in 'Insurance Notes', *Pall Mall Gazette*, 1 July 1892, p. 3.

57 Letter to William Archer, July 1892, *Complete Letters*, p. 534.

58 Letter to Florence Stoker, February 1893, *Complete Letters*, p. 552.

59 'Books of the Week', *The Times*, 23 February 1893, p. 8.

60 *Complete Letters*, p. 574n2.

61 *De Profundis*: Letter to Lord Alfred Douglas, January–March 1897, *Complete Letters*, p. 692.

62 Gold, Arthur, and Robert Fizdale (1991), *The Divine Sarah: A Life of Sarah Bernhardt* (New York, Knopf), p. 117.

63 *De Profundis*: Letter to Lord Alfred Douglas, January–March 1897, *Complete Letters*, p. 730.

64 Sherard, *The Life of Oscar Wilde*, p. 181.

65 Letter to Lord Alfred Douglas, June 1897, *Complete Letters*, p. 873.

66 'Notes and Impressions', *The Playgoer and Society: Illustrated*, Vol.III, (London, The Kingshurst Publishing Company, 1911), p. 208.

CHAPTER 16

1 O'Sullivan, *Aspects of Wilde*, p. 17.

2 Letter to Marie Prescott, March–April 1883, *Complete Letters*, p. 204.

3 Henderson, Archibald (1913), *European Dramatists* (Cincinnati, OH, Stewart & Kidd Company), p. 308.

4 Wilde, *Social Studies*, p. 70.

5 Letter to Philip Houghton, February 1894, *Complete Letters*, p. 586.

6 Interview in the *St James's Gazette*, 18 January 1895, pp. 4–5.

7 Wilde, Oscar (1904), 'The Critic as Artist Part I', *Intentions* (Portland, OR, Mosher), p. 108.

8 O'Sullivan, *Aspects of Wilde*, p. 14.

9 Ibid., p. 17.

10 Wilde, Oscar (1904) 'The Decay of Lying', *Intentions* (Portland, OR, Mosher), p. 29.

11 From the introduction to *Wilde Complete Plays* (London, Bloomsbury Publishing, 2014), p. 2.

12 In a letter to A. J. A. Symons quoted in Ellmann, *Oscar Wilde*, p. 306.

13 Douglas, Lord Alfred (1929), *The Autobiography of Lord Alfred Douglas* (London, Martin Secker), p. 59.

14 Douglas, *Oscar Wilde and Myself*, p. 74.

15 Letter from Constance Wilde to Robert Sherard, 21 September 1895, Sherard, *The Real Oscar Wilde*, p. 173.

16 Letter from Jane Wilde to Oscar Wilde, 1 December 1891, Clark, Finzi 2375.

17 Letter to More Adey, April 1897, *Complete Letters*, p. 795.

18 Letter to Reginald Turner, October 1897, *Complete Letters*, p. 961.

19 Letter to Reginald Turner, September 1897, *Complete Letters*, p. 948.

20 She suggests this in a letter to Lady Mount-Temple, quoted in Moyle, *Constance*, p. 206.

21 Jopling, *Twenty Years of My Life 1867–1887*, p. 80.

22 A facsimile of this page can be seen at http://www.huntleyandpalmers.org.uk.

23 Melba, Nellie (1925), *Melodies and Memories* (Cambridge, Cambridge University Press), p. 74.

24 Benson, E. F. (1930), *As We Were: A Victorian Peep Show* (London, Green & Co.), p. 180.

25 Letter to Oswald Yorke, February 1893, *Complete Letters*, p. 558.

26 'Behold the First Lord Illingworth', *The New York Times*, 30 April 1916, Section 2, p. 7.

27 Ellmann, *Oscar Wilde*, p. 359.

28 Robins, Elizabeth, *Oscar Wilde: An Appreciation*. An unpublished memoir written around 1950 in Elizabeth Robins Papers 1803–1963, held amongst the extensive Fales Library and Special Collections in New York University. Typed Manuscript, Signed London, No Year. MSS 002 (Permission from Fales Library and Independent Age on behalf of Trustees of Backsettown).

29 Letter to Elizabeth Robins, January 1889, *Complete Letters*, p. 384.

30 McFarlane, James W. (ed.)(1961), *The Oxford Ibsen V* (London, Oxford University Press), pp. 436–7.

31 Letter to Gerald Duckworth, February 1894, *Complete Letters*, p. 584.

32 Letter to Elizabeth Robins, February 1893, *Complete Letters*, p. 551.

33 Field, Michael, *Works and Days: From the Journal of Michael Field*, quoted in Hesketh Pearson (1946), *Oscar Wilde: His Life and Wit* (New York, London, Harper & Bros.), p. 156.

34 Telegram to Elizabeth Robins, 23 April 1891, *Complete Letters*, p. 477.

35 Letter to the Earl of Lytton, May 1891, *Complete Letters*, p. 480.

36 Letter to Mrs W. H. Grenfell, April 1891, *Complete Letters*, p. 477.

37 Robins, *Oscar Wilde: An Appreciation*.

38 Ibid.

39 Yeats, W. B. (1893), 'An Excellent Talker', *The Bookman*, March 1895, *The Bookman Volumes 4–7* (London, Hodder and Stoughton), p. 182.

40 Wilde, Lady Jane, 'American Traits: Women and Society in the States', *Home Journal*, 2 May 1883.

41 Pearson, Hesketh (1971), *Beerbohm Tree: His life and Laughter* (Westport, CT, Greenwood Press), p. 69.

42 Quoted in Joseph Bristow (2003), *Wilde Writings: Contextual Conditions*, Published by the University of Toronto Press in association with the UCLA Center for Seventeenth- and Eighteenth-Century Studies and the William Andrews Clark Memorial Library (Toronto; Buffalo, NY), p. 135.

43 Burgess, Gilbert, 'A Talk with Mr. Oscar Wilde', *The Sketch*, 9 January 1895, quoted in Mason, *Bibliography of Oscar Wilde*, p. 440.

44 Ellmann, *Oscar Wilde*, p. 348.

45 Neilson, Julia (1940), *This for Remembrance* (London, Hurst & Blackett).

46 *The World*, 26 April 1883, quoted in Peter Raby (1988), *Oscar Wilde* (Cambridge University Press Archive), p. 95.

47 Melba, *Melodies and Memories*, p. 75.

48 Jacomb-Hood, G. P. (1924), *With Brush & Pencil* (London, John Murray) p. 116.

49 O'Sullivan, *Aspects of Wilde*, p. 31.

50 Harris, *My Life and Loves*, Vol. I, p. 187.

51 *Hawera & Normanby Star*, Vol. XLVIII, Issue 8965, 3 August 1905, p. 3

52 Bernard Shaw, George (1916), *Dramatic Opinions and Essays, Volume 1* (New York, Brentano's) p. 27.

53 Ibid., p. 28.

54 Archer, William, '*An Ideal Husband*', *Pall Mall Budget*, 10 January 1895.

55 McKenna, *The Secret Life of Oscar Wilde*, p. 330.

56 Archer, '*An Ideal Husband*'.

57 Shaw, *Dramatic Opinions and Essays, Volume 1*, p. 26.

58 Burgess, Gilbert, 'A Talk with Mr. Oscar Wilde', *The Sketch*, 9 January 1895, in Mason, *Bibliography of Oscar Wilde*, p. 440.

CHAPTER 17

1 Gavan Duffy, Charles (1898), *My Life in Two Hemispheres Volume II* (New York, Macmillan), p. 353.

2 *Commercial Gazette*, 23 August 1893, p. 8.

3 *The Colonies and India*, 9 July 1892, p. 28.

4 Anonymous (1922), *East and West: The Confessions of a Princess* (London, Jarrolds), p. 79.

5 Byrne, Patrick (1953), *The Wildes of Merrion Square: the family of Oscar Wilde* (London, New York, Staples Press), pp. 218–19.

6 Anonymous, *East and West*, p. 177.

7 Pearson, *The Life of Oscar Wilde*, p. 262.

8 Green, Julian (1967), *To Leave before Dawn*, (London, Peter Owen), p. 106; Also *Journal, Volume 3*.

9 Letter to Lord Alfred Douglas, April 1894, *Complete Letters*, p. 588.

10 Ibid.

11 Letter to More Adey, April 1897, *Complete Letters*, p. 795.

12 Constance announced their intention of doing so in a letter to Lady Mount-Temple, dated 30 July 1894 – as detailed in Antony Edmonds (2014), *Oscar Wilde's Scandalous Summer* (Amberley), p. 27.

13 Holland, *Son of Oscar Wilde*, p. 55.

14 Article from *Worthing Gazette* reproduced in Edmonds, *Oscar Wilde's Scandalous Summer*, p. 49.

15 Letter from Lord Alfred Douglas quoted in *Daily Telegraph*, 19 April 1913 and cited in Ellmann, *Oscar Wilde*, p. 397.

16 Yeats, *The Trembling of the Veil*, p. 203.

17 Leverson, *Letters to the Sphinx from Oscar Wilde*.

18 Moyle, *Constance*, p. 250.

19 Bentley, Joyce (1983), *The Importance of Being Constance* (London, R. Hale), p. 98.

20 Quoted in Edmonds, *Oscar Wilde's Scandalous Summer*, p. 91.

21 Edmonds, *Oscar Wilde's Scandalous Summer*, p. 93.

22 Letter to Arthur L. Humphreys, November 1894, *Complete Letters*, p. 623.

23 Letter to George Alexander, August 1894, *Complete Letters*, p. 599.

24 Ibid., p. 600.

25 'London All Agog Over a New Play', *Los Angeles Herald*, 26 October 1900, p. 1.

26 George Bernard Shaw in his Preface to the 1938 edition of Harris, *My Life and Loves*, Vol. II, p. xxv.

27 Quoted in Rodney Shewan (1983), 'Oscar Wilde and A Wife's Tragedy: Facts and Conjectures', *Theatre Research International*, 8, p. 86.

28 Letter to Lord Alfred Douglas, August 1894, *Complete Letters*, p. 602.

29 Oscar Wilde in an interview with Robert Ross, *St James's Gazette*, January 1895 reprinted in Mikhail, *Oscar Wilde: Interviews and Recollections*, Vol. I, p. 195.

30 Leverson, *Letters to The Sphinx from Oscar Wilde*, p. 31.

31 All quotes from *The Importance of Being Earnest* are taken from the three act version published in *Wilde: The Complete Plays* (London, Methuen, 1999).

32 *The Daily Telegraph*, 15 February 1895, quoted in William Tydeman (1982), *Wilde: Comedies* (London, Macmillan), p. 63.

33 Ibid., p. 64.

34 Archer, William, *The World*, 20 February 1895, in William Archer (1896), *The Theatrical World of 1895* (London, Scott) pp. 56–60.

35 *Pall Mall Gazette*, 15 February 1895, p. 4; *The New York Times*, 17 February 1895; 'Memories of Oscar Wilde', George Bernard Shaw in Harris, *My Life and Loves*, Vol. II, Appendix p. 13.

36 Sherard, *The Life of Oscar Wilde*, p. 329.

37 Letter to Frank Harris, February 1899, *Complete Letters*, p. 1124.

38 They had been due to leave on 4 September but delayed their departure, as catalogued in 'No-one to talk to' – Constance Wilde in Worthing', Antony Edmonds in *The Wildean*, No. 42, p. 46.

39 Robins, Ashley H., and Merlin Holland, 'The Art of Medicine: The Enigmatic

Illness and Death of Constance, Wife of Oscar Wilde', *The Lancet*, Vol. 385, 3 January 2015, p. 21.

40 Harris, *My Life and Loves*, Vol. I, p. 184.

41 Letter Jane Wilde to Oscar Wilde quoted in Amor, *Mrs. Oscar Wilde*, p. 141.

42 Wilde and Mason (ed.), *Impressions of America*, p. 25.

43 'Mrs Leslie Speaks', *Los Angeles Herald*, 13 February 1892, p. 10.

44 'Why Mrs. Leslie Married', *Topeka State Journal*, 11 October 1891, p. 1.

45 From 'Wilde and Willie' by Nancy Johnson (archivist) in *News and Notes from the Lotos Club*, January 2011.

46 'Dropped from the Lotos', *The New York Times*, 18 September 1893.

47 'Mrs Leslie is Free', *The Evening World*, 10 June 1893, p. 3.

48 *Morning Call*, 8 June 1893, p. 10.

49 Murray, *From the Shadow of Dracula*, p. 124. Also reported in Wyndham, *The Nineteen-Hundreds*, p. 76.

50 'Dropped from the Lotos', *The New York Times*, 18 September 1893.

51 Stern, Madeleine B. (1953), *Purple Passage: The Life of Mrs. Frank Leslie* (Norman, OK, University of Oklahoma Press), p. 162.

52 'Mrs Leslie is Free', *The Evening World*, 10 June 1893, p. 3.

53 Sherard, *The Real Oscar Wilde*, p. 323.

54 Included in Anne Commire and Deborah Klezmer (1999), *Women in World History Volume 9* (Waterford, CT, Yorkin Publications), p. 413.

55 O'Brien, Kevin (1994), 'Lily Wilde and Oscar's Fur Coat', *Journal of the Eighteen Nineties Society*, Thirtieth Anniversary Commemoration Special, No. 21, pp. 15–28.

56 One example is O'Brien, 'Lily Wilde and Oscar's Fur Coat'.

57 Lady Wilde to Oscar Wilde, 4 February 1894, Clark, Finzi, 2389.

58 Lady Wilde to Oscar Wilde, 27 February 1894, Clark, Finzi 2390.

59 Atherton, Gertrude (1932), 'Oscar Wilde and his Mother', *Adventures of a Novelist*, (London, Jonathan Cape), p. 182.

60 Ibid.

61 Ibid., p. 183.

62 Ibid., p. 182.

63 *De Profundis*: Letter to Lord Alfred Douglas, January–March 1897, *Complete Letters*, p. 700.

64 McKenna, *The Secret Life of Oscar Wilde*, p. 330.

65 Robins, *Oscar Wilde: An Appreciation*.

66 Letter to Lord Alfred Douglas, November 1894, *Complete Letters*, p. 621.

CHAPTER 18

1 Leverson, *Letters to the Sphinx from Oscar Wilde*, p. 29.

2 Ibid., p. 28.

3 Found among Ada Leverson's papers and reproduced in Julie Speedie (1994), *Wonderful Sphinx: The Biography of Ada Leverson* (London, Virago), p. 33.

4 Quoted in Speedie, p. 17.

5 Ibid.

6 Richards, Grant (1933), *Memories of a Misspent Youth 1872–1896*, (New York, Harper), p. 300.

7 Robert Ross's introduction to *Letters to the Sphinx*, p. 14.

8 Leverson, *Letters to the Sphinx from Oscar Wilde*, p. 48.

9 Ibid., pp. 23–4; p. 32.

10 Ibid.

11 Ibid., p. 29.

12 Reported by Ada's daughter, Violet Wyndham (trans.)(1969), *Philippe Jullian, Oscar Wilde* (London, Constable), p. 198.

13 Leverson, *Letters to the Sphinx from Oscar Wilde*, p. 30.

14 Letter to Walter Hamilton, January 1889, *Complete Letters*, p. 390.

15 'An Afternoon Party', *Punch*, 15 July 1893, p. 13.

16 Letter to Ada Leverson, November 1893, *Complete Letters*, p. 569.

17 Telegram to Ada Leverson, November 1893, *Complete Letters*, p. 577.

18 Letter to Ada Leverson, October 1894, *Complete Letters*, p. 618.

19 Mason, *Bibliography of Oscar Wilde*, p. 394.

20 'The Minx A Poem in Prose', *Punch*, 21 July 1894, in *Punch, or the London Charivari*, Vol. 107, 21 July 1894, p. 33.

21 Leverson, *Letters to the Sphinx from Oscar Wilde*, p. 50.

22 Letter from F. C. Burnand to Mrs. Leverson, Clark, Finzi 192.

23 Wilde, Oscar, 'The Green Carnation', *Pall Mall Gazette*, 2 October 1894, p. 3.

24 Leverson, *Letters to the Sphinx from Oscar Wilde*, pp. 57–8.

25 Ibid., pp. 26–7.

26 Ibid.

27 Ibid., pp. 33–4.

28 Ibid.

29 Ibid., pp. 26–7.

30 Vanbrugh, Dame Irene (1948), *To Tell My Story* (London, Hutchinson), p. 33.

31 Ibid., p. 34.

32 'A Remarkable Collection of the Writings of Oscar Wilde'(1911)(New York, The Anderson Auction Company), p. 37.

33 Letter to Robert Ross, February 1895, *Complete Letters*, p. 634.

34 Ellmann, *Oscar Wilde*, p. 414.

35 Letter to Ada Leverson, March 1895, *Complete Letters*, p. 635.

36 Telegram to Ada Leverson, March 1895, *Complete Letters*, p. 636. The *Sibyls* were oracular women in ancient Greece who were believed to possess prophetic powers.

37 Leverson, *Letters to the Sphinx from Oscar Wilde*, p. 41.

38 Holland, Merlin (2003), *Irish Peacock and Scarlet Marquess* (London, Fourth Estate), pp. xxv–xxvi.

39 Wilde, Oscar (2014), *Complete Plays* (London, Bloomsbury Publishing), p. 15.

40 Hyde, Harford Montgomery (1973), *The Trials of Oscar Wilde* (New York, Dover Publications), p. 87.

41 Telegram to Ada Leverson, March 1895, *Complete Letters*, p. 636.

42 Hyde, *The Trials of Oscar Wilde*, p. 149.

43 Letter to Lord Alfred Douglas, May 1895, *Complete Letters*, p. 652.

44 Yeats, *The Trembling of the Veil*, p. 167.

45 Letter to Ada and Ernest Leverson, April 1895, *Complete Letters*, pp. 641–2.

46 Letter to George Moore, quoted in Leverson, *Letters to the Sphinx from Oscar Wilde*, p. 23.

47 Letter to Ada Leverson, April 1895, *Complete Letters*, p. 645.

48 Ibid., pp. 644–5.

49 Amor, *Mrs. Oscar Wilde*, p. 171.

50 Letter from Constance Wilde to Mrs Robinson, April 1895, *Complete Letters*, p. 642.

51 Sherard, *The Life of Oscar Wilde*, p. 359–60.

52 Leverson, *Letters to the Sphinx from Oscar Wilde*, p. 35.

53 Mead, Donald, 'Heading for Disaster: Oscar's Finances', *The Wildean*, No. 46, January 2015, p. 89.

54 Letter to Frank Harris, June 1897, *Complete Letters*, p. 896.

55 'Coghlan Refuses Wilde's Play', *Boston Post*, 7 April 1895, p. 5.

CHAPTER 19

1 Letter from Jane Wilde to John Hilson, 16 December 1869, University of Reading, Special Collections, MS 559.

2 Weeks, Jeffrey (2014), *Sex, Politics and Society: The Regulations of Sexuality Since 1800* (London, Routledge), p. 131.

3 In his biography, *The Secret Life of Oscar Wilde*, Neil McKenna explores the possibility of a political conspiracy against Oscar in a very thorough fashion.

4 This and other excerpts from the trial transcripts sourced at http://law2.umkc.edu/faculty/projects/ftrials/wilde/wilde.htm – accessed on 28 January 2015.

5 http://law2.umkc.edu/faculty/projects/ftrials/wilde/wilde.htm – accessed on 28 January 2015.

6 Hyde, *The Trials of Oscar Wilde*, p. 179.

7 Ellmann, *Oscar Wilde*, p. 435.

8 Michael Foldy, *The Trials of Oscar Wilde*, p. 39

9 Sherard, *The Life of Oscar Wilde*, p. 358.

10 Sherard, *The Story of an Unhappy Friendship*, pp. 155–6.

11 Spencer, Walter T. (1923), *Forty Years in my Bookshop* (Boston, MA, Houghton Mifflin), p. 248.

12 Hamilton, *Notable Irishwomen*, p. 186.

13 MSS in Berg Collection held in the New York Public Library, quoted in Ellmann, *Oscar Wilde*, p. 467.

14 Robins, Elizabeth (1940), *Both Sides of the Curtain* (London, W. Heinemann Ltd.), p. 10.

15 Letter from Lady Jane Wilde to Oscar Wilde, February 1892, Clark, Finzi 2376.

16 Gavan Duffy, *Four Years of Irish History*, p. 94.

17 Wilde, *Social Studies*, p. 47.

18 Melville, *Mother of Oscar*, p. 239.

19 Letter from Lady Jane Wilde to Oscar Wilde, 18 September 1893, Clark, Finzi 2380.

20 Sherard, *The Life of Oscar Wilde*, p. 96.

21 Letter from Lady Jane Wilde to Oscar Wilde, 29 March 1894, Clark, Finzi 2391.

22 'O'Donoghue Papers' in *Irish Book Lover*, 12 (1921), p. 128.

23 Healy, Timothy Michael (1929), *Letters and Leaders of My Day*, Vol. II (New York, Frederick A. Stokes Company), pp. 416–17.

24 Letter from Adela Schuster to Oscar Wilde, 26 November 1893, Clark, Finzi 2022.

25 Letter from Adela Schuster to More Adey, 14 August 1896, Clark, Finzi 28, quoted in J. Robert Maguire (2013), *Ceremonies of Bravery: Oscar Wilde, Carlos Blacker and the Dreyfus Affair* (Oxford University Press), p. 67.

26 Harris, *My Life and Loves*, Vol. I, p. 289.

27 Ibid., p. 290.

28 Leverson, *Letters to the Sphinx from Oscar Wilde*, p. 38.

29 Ibid., p. 39.

30 Ibid., p. 41.

31 Ibid., p. 42.

32 Ibid., p. 41.

33 Ibid., p. 42.

34 http://law2.umkc.edu/faculty/projects/ftrials/wilde/wilde.htm – accessed on 28 January 2015.

35 Leverson, *Letters to the Sphinx from Oscar Wilde*, p. 54.

36 Letter from Constance Wilde to American evangelist and reformer, Hannah Whitall Smith, October 1895, quoted in Ellmann, *Oscar Wilde*, p. 462.

37 Letter to More Adey, September 1896, *Complete Letters*, p. 666.

38 *De Profundis*: Letter to Lord Alfred Douglas, January-March 1897, *Complete Letters*, p. 738.

39 George Bernard Shaw in Harris, *My Life and Loves*, Vol. II, p. 15.

40 Holland, *Son of Oscar Wilde*, p. 24.

41 Ibid.

42 Letter from Jane Wilde to Constance Wilde, 22 April 1895, quoted in Moyle, *Constance*, p. 273.

43 She uses this address in a letter to Oscar dated June 1892.

44 Hart-Davis, Rupert (1962), *The Letters of Oscar Wilde* (San Diego, CA, Harcourt, Brace & World, Inc.), p. 398.

45 *De Profundis*: Letter to Lord Alfred Douglas, January–March 1896, *Complete Letters*, p. 757.

46 Wilde borrowed this description from Tennyson's 'Lucretius' (1868).

47 As reported in J. Glover (1911), *Jimmy Glover – His Book* (London, Methuen & Co.), p. 34. Apparently Jane Wilde said this to George Henry Moore, father of the novelist George Moore, when he asked what she believed were her sons' prospects.

48 Letter from Jane Wilde to John Hilson, May 1850, University of Reading, Special Collections, MS 559.

49 Letter from Willie Wilde to More Adey, 4 February 1896, Clark, Finzi, 2826 quoted in Kevin O'Brien, 'Lily Wilde and Oscar's Fur Coat', *Journal of the Eighteen Nineties Society*, Thirtieth Anniversary Commemoration Special, No. 21, 1994.

50 Corkran, *Celebrities & I*, p. 140.

51 Letter from Lily Wilde to More Adey, quoted in Melville, *Mother of Oscar*, p. 273.

52 *The Athenaeum*, No. 3564, 15 February 1896, p. 220.

53 *Freeman's Journal*, 6 February 1896, p. 5.

54 'The Mother of Oscar Wilde', *Virginia Enterprise*, 10 April 1896, p. 2.

55 *De Profundis*: Letter to Lord Alfred Douglas, January–March 1896, *Complete Letters*, p. 721.

56 Letter to Robbie Ross, May 1897, *Complete Letters*, p. 858.

57 *De Profundis*: Letter to Lord Alfred Douglas, January–March 1897, *Complete Letters*, p. 721.

58 Ibid.

59 Quoted in Osbert Sitwell (1950), *Noble Essences* (London, Macmillan), p. 43.

CHAPTER 20

1 Letter to Carlos Blacker, April 1898, *Complete Letters*, p. 1055.

2 Letter from Constance Wilde to Emily Thursfield, 25 June 1895, Clark shelf mark W6711L T543, 25 June 1895.

3 Holland, *Son of Oscar Wilde*, p. 71.

4 Letter from Constance Wilde to Emily Thursfield, 25 June 1895, Clark shelf mark W6711L T543, 12 October 1895.

5 This letter is reproduced in Sherard, *The Real Oscar Wilde*, p. 173.
6 Letter to Robert Ross, May 1897, *Complete Letters*, p. 818.
7 Robins and Holland, 'The Art of Medicine', pp. 21–2.
8 Letter to More Adey, November 1897, *Complete Letters* p. 989.
9 Moyle, *Constance*, p. 290.
10 Letter from Adela Schuster to More Adey, 20 March 1896, Clark Finzi 27.
11 Letter to Robbie Ross, March 1896, *Complete Letters*, p. 652.
12 Maguire, J. Robert (2013), *Ceremonies of Bravery: Oscar Wilde, Carlos Blacker and the Dreyfus Affair* (Oxford, Oxford University Press), p. 79.
13 Letter from Adela Schuster to More Adey, 17 August 1896, quoted in Maguire, *Ceremonies of Bravery*, p. 79
14 Detailed in Ellmann, *Oscar Wilde*, p. 484.
15 Maguire, *Ceremonies of Bravery*, p. 82.
16 Letter to Robert Ross, April 1897, *Complete Letters*, p. 785.
17 Letter to More Adey, May 1897, *Complete Letters*, p. 814.
18 Letter to Robert Ross, May 1897, *Complete Letters*, p. 818.
19 Ibid., p. 817.
20 Letter to Robbie Ross, April 1897, *Complete Letters*, p. 785.
21 Leverson, *Letters to the Sphinx from Oscar Wilde*, p. 45
22 Ibid.
23 Letter to Ada Leverson, May 1897, *Complete Letters*, p. 845.
24 Leverson, *Letters to the Sphinx from Oscar Wilde*, p. 46.
25 Letter to Lord Alfred Douglas, June 1897, *Complete Letters*, p. 880.
26 Packenham, Simona (1967), *Sixty Miles from England: the English at Dieppe, 1814–1914* (London, Macmillan), p. 168.
27 Youngkin, Mollie (2007), *Feminist Realism at the fin de siècle: The Influence of the Late-Victorian Woman's Press on the Development of the Novel* (Columbus, OH, Ohio State University Press), p. 163.
28 Hyde, H. Montgomery (1978), *Oscar Wilde: The Aftermath* (Westport, CT, Greenwood), p. 53.
29 Letter to Mrs Stannard, May 1897, *Complete Letters*, p. 857.
30 Kingston, Angela (2007), *Oscar Wilde as a Character in Victorian Fiction* (New York, Palgrave Macmillan), p. 189
31 Moyle, *Constance*, p. 301.
32 Robins and Holland, 'The Art of Medicine', pp. 21–2.
33 Letter to Carlos Blacker, July 1897, *Complete Letters*, p. 920.
34 Letter to Carlos Blacker, August 1897, *Complete Letters* p. 921.
35 Letter to Robbie Ross, September 1897, *Complete Letters*, p. 942.
36 Letter to More Adey, November 1897, *Complete Letters*, p. 994.
37 Douglas, *Oscar Wilde: A Summing Up*, p. 87.
38 Douglas, *Without Apology*, p. 219.
39 Letter to Ada Leverson, November 1897, *Complete Letters*, p. 981.
40 Holland, *Son of Oscar Wilde*, p. 130.
41 Telegram to Otho Lloyd, *Complete Letters*, p. 1055.
42 Letter to Carlos Blacker, April 1898, *Complete Letters*, p. 1055.
43 Telegram to Robbie Ross, April 1898, *Complete Letters*, p. 1054.
44 Letter from Robbie Ross to Leonard Smithers, *Complete Letters*, p. 1054n2.
45 Leverson, *Letters To The Sphinx from Oscar Wilde*, p. 43.
46 Sherard, *The Life of Oscar Wilde*, p. 375.

47 Holland, *Son of Oscar Wilde*, p. 24.

48 Letter to Robert Ross, March 1899, *Complete Letters*, p. 1128.

CHAPTER 21

1 *de Saix, Guillot, L'Européen, 8* May *1929,* 'Souvenirs Inedits' referenced in Témoignages d'époque, Claire de Pratz, *Rue de Beaux Arts*, No. 37 : March–April 2011. http://www.oscholars.com/RBA/thirty-seven/37.13/epoque.htm accessed on 2 March 2015

2 Letter from Josephine Butler to Stanley Butler, 4 June 1895, The Women's Library, GB 106 3JBL/34/29.

3 Badeni, June (1981), *The Slender Tree: a life of Alice Meynell* (Padstow, Cornwall, Tabb House), p. 115.

4 Meynell, Alice (1893), 'The Unit of the World', *The Rhythm of Life and Other Essays* (London, E. Mathews and J. Lane), p. 29.

5 Letter from Alice Meynell to John Lane, 19 February 1896, *The Selected Letters of Alice Meynell*, Damian Atkinson (ed.)(Cambridge, Cambridge Scholars, 2013), p. 90.

6 O'Sullivan, *Aspects of Wilde*, pp. 110–11.

7 Letter to the Home Secretary, July 1896, *Complete Letters*, p. 656.

8 Letter from Willie Wilde to Bram Stoker, 16 July 1895, Quoted in Belford, *Bram Stoker and The Man Who Was Dracula*, pp. 245–6.

9 Murray, *From the Shadow of Dracula*, p. 123.

10 Letter from Florence Stoker to Philippa Knott, 30 January 1937, quoted in Belford, *Bram Stoker and The Man Who Was Dracula*, p. 325.

11 Entry in the diary of Mary Berenson quoted in Ray Monk (1996), *Bertrand Russell: The Spirit of Solitude, 1872–1921*, Vol. 1 (New York, Simon & Schuster), p. 107.

12 *Clara Morris Diaries, 1867–1924*; Volume 26 (1895), 5, 6 April 1895. A-168, folder 26, Schlesinger Library, Radcliffe Institute, Harvard University, Cambridge, MA.

13 Harris, *My Life and Loves*, Vol. II, p. 325.

14 Ibid., pp. 325–6.

15 Quoted in Michael Madden and Mary Ann Jensen (1995), *Oscar Wilde: A Writer for the Nineties* (Princeton, NJ, Princeton University), pp. 26–7.

16 'New Art at the Old Bailey', *The Speaker*, 13 April 1895, quoted in Sally Ledger (1997), *The New Woman: Fiction and Feminism at the Fin de Siècle* (Manchester, Manchester University Press), p. 94.

17 'The End of the New Woman', *Punch*, 21 December 1895, in *Punch Volume VIII*, p. 297.

18 Letter to Lord Alfred Douglas, April 1894, *Complete Letters*, p. 589.

19 Letter to Ada Leverson, April 1894, *Complete Letters*, p. 588.

20 Ada Leverson, 'Suggestion.' *The Yellow Book* 5 (April 1895), pp. 249–57. The Yellow Nineties Online, Dennis Denisoff and Lorraine Janzen Kooistra (eds), Ryerson University, 2011, http://www.1890s.ca/HTML.aspx?s=YBV5_leverson_suggestion.html – accessed on 3 February 2015.

21 May, J. Lewis (1936), *John Lane and the Nineties* (London, John Lane), p. 80.

22 Yeats, *The Trembling of the Veil*, p. 198.

23 Egerton, George (1893), 'A Cross Line', *Keynotes* (London, Elkin Mathews and John Lane), p. 20.

24 Letter from George Egerton to her father, 15 March 1891, quoted in the introduction to *The Marriage of Mary Ascension* (Cork, Aubane Historical Society, 2011).

25 *Punch*, 10 March 1894, Vol. III, p. 109.

26 Schaffer, Talia (2000), *The Forgotten Female Aesthetes* (Charlottesville and London, University of Virginia Press), p. 60.

27 O'Sullivan, *Aspects of Wilde*, p. 106.

28 Hobbes, John Oliver (1894), 'The Sinner's Comedy', *The Tales of John Oliver Hobbes* (London, T. Fisher Unwin), p. 147.

29 Hyde, *The Trials of Oscar Wilde*, p. 121.

30 London, Mrs Aria (1922), *My Sentimental Self* (London, Chapman & Hall), p. 16. The whole story is told in great detail in Margaret D. Stetz, 'To defend the undefendable': Oscar Wilde and the Davis Family, *Oscholars Special Issue: Oscar Wilde, Jews & the Fin-de-Siècle*, Summer 2010.

31 Ibid., p. 54

32 Danby, Frank (1906), *The Sphinx's Lawyer* (New York, F. A. Stokes Company) p. 1; p. 103.

33 Sherard, *The Real Oscar Wilde*, p. 283.

34 Letter to Robert Ross, 31 May 1897, *Complete Letters*, p. 866.

35 Holland, *Son of Oscar Wilde*, p. 4.

36 Letter to Leonard Smithers, August 1897, *Complete Letters*, p. 927.

37 Letter to Mrs Smithers, August 1897, *Complete Letters*, p. 1114.

38 Marbury, Elizabeth (1923), *My Crystal Ball* (New York, Boni & Liveright), p. 94.

39 Ibid.

40 Ibid., p. 96.

41 Ibid.

42 Letter from Elizabeth Marbury to Leonard Smithers, 25 January 1898 quoted in Mason, *Bibliography of Oscar Wilde*, p. 416.

43 Cather, Willa, 'The Passing Show', *The Courier* (Lincoln, NE), 28 September 1895, p. 7.

44 'Between the Acts', *Nebraska State Journal*, 29 April 1894, p. 13.

45 Marbury, *My Crystal Ball*, p. 98.

46 Ibid., p. 99.

47 Letter to Robert Ross, April 1897, *Complete Letters*, p. 782.

48 Letter to Frances Forbes-Robertson, May 1899, *Complete Letters*, p. 1145.

49 Letter to Ada Leverson, November 1897, *Complete Letters*, p. 981.

50 Leverson, *Letters to the Sphinx from Oscar Wilde*, pp. 46–7.

51 Ibid.

52 *de Saix, Guillot, L'Européen, 8 May 1929*, 'Souvenirs Inedits' referenced in Témoignages d'époque, Claire de Pratz, *Rue de Beaux Arts*, No. 37, March–April 2011, http://www.oscholars.com/RBA/thirty-seven/37.13/epoque.htm – accessed on 2 March 2015.

53 Ibid.

54 *Ibid.*

55 O'Sullivan, *Aspects of Wilde*, p. 117.

56 Ibid., p. 220.

57 Sherard, *The Story of an Unhappy Friendship*, pp. 136–7.

58 Letter to Robert Sherard, April 1895, *Complete Letters*, p. 644.

59 Letter To R. H. Shepherd, April 1895, *Complete Letters*, p. 643.

60 Letter to Robert Ross, January 1899, *Complete Letters*, p. 1116.

61 O'Sullivan, *Aspects of Wilde*, p. 25.

62 Ibid., p. 174.

63 'Oscar Wilde Letter to Lilly Langtry', The Oscar Wilde Fan Club, http://oscarwilde-fanclub.com/index.php/oscar-wilde-letter-to-lilly-langtry – accessed on 4 February 2015.

64 Robertson, *Time Was*, p .231.

65 Jackson, Russell (1996), 'Oscar Wilde's Contract for a New Play 1900', *Theatre Notebook*, Vol. 50, No. 2, contained in Vols. 50–52 (Society for Theatre Research), p. 113.

66 Letter to Oscar Wilde from Cora Brown Potter, 22 March 1900, *Complete Letters*, p. 1190n1.

67 Melba, *Melodies and Memories*, p. 75.

68 Letter to Robbie Ross, March 1899, *Complete Letters*, p. 1130.

69 O'Brien, Kevin, 'Lily Wilde and Oscar's Fur Coat', *Journal of the Eighteen Nineties Society*, Thirtieth Anniversary Commemoration Special, No. 21, 1994.

70 Letter from Lily Wilde to Oscar Wilde, October 1900, Clark, Finzi, 2414.

71 Letter from Lily Wilde to More Adey, 14 March 1898, Oxford; Folio 117.

72 Sherard, *The Real Oscar Wilde*, p. 132.

73 Harris, *My Life and Loves*, Vol. I, p. 129.

74 Sherard, *The Real Oscar Wilde*, pp. 79–80.

75 'Memorial Notice: Mr Oscar Wilde', *The Guardian*, Saturday 1 December 1900, http://www.theguardian.com/books/1900/dec/01/classics.fromthearchives – accessed on 2 February 2015.

76 *Pall Mall Gazette*, 1 December 1900, p. 2.

77 'Death of Oscar Wilde', *The New York Times*, 1 December 1900.

78 Robert Ross in Harris, *My Life and Loves*, Vol. II, p. 602.

79 'Robert Ross Gives a New Version of the Last Days of Oscar Wilde', *The New York Times*, 13 March 1910, http://query.nytimes.com/mem/archive-free/pdf?res-=9802E5D91139E333A25750C1A9659C946196D6CF – accessed on 17 November 2014.

80 Schroeder, Horst (2002), *Additions and corrections to Richard Ellmann's Oscar Wilde* (Braunschweig Selbstverl), p. 216.

81 Harris, *My Life and Loves*, Vol. II, p. 603.

82 Letter from Frank Harris to Robbie Ross quoted in Gary Schmidgall (1994), *The Stranger Wilde: Interpreting Oscar* (New York, Dutton), p. 291.

83 Letter from Robert Ross to Adela Schuster, Christmas 1806, included in *Complete Works of Oscar Wilde*, Vol. 8 (London, Methuen, 1908), p. 1.

84 *De Profundis*: Letter to Lord Alfred Douglas, January–March 1897, *Complete Letters*, p. 766.

85 Kennard, George (1990), *Loopy: The Autobiography of Sir George Kennard* (London, Pen and Sword Books (formerly Leo Cooper)), p. 5.

86 Holland, *Son of Oscar Wilde*, p. 194.

87 Ibid., pp. 187–8.

88 Steen, Marguerite (1978), *A Pride of Terrys* (Westport, CT, Greenwood Press), p. 206n.

89 Sherard, *The Real Oscar Wilde*, p. 304.

90 Sherard, *Life of Oscar Wilde*, p. 176.

91 Letters from Richard Le Gallienne to Ellen Terry, 25 July 1920 & 15 May 1921, Ellen Terry and Edith Craig Archives: Documents ID ET-Z1, 276 and ID ET-Z1, 275. The book, with a foreword by Le Gallienne, was published by Doubleday in 1923.

92 [EC] '30th November' / 5th December 1899, Reel 4 quoted in Charlotte Cosham (2011), *A Personal Remembering of Michael Field: A Critical Dismembering of Works and Days*, (Birmingham University of Birmingham).

93 'Miss Corelli's Attack', *The Montreal Gazette*, 26 December 1906, p. 11.

94 Tydeman, William, and Steven Price (1996), *Wilde Salome* (Cambridge and New York, Cambridge University Press), p. 80 .

95 Asquith, *More Memories*, p. 117.

96 Verbatim report of the trial of Noel Pemberton Billing, MP, on a charge of criminal libel before Mr Justice Darling at the Central Criminal Court, Old Bailey, with report of the preliminary proceedings at Bow Street Police Court, an appendix of documents referred to in the case, reference index. (London, 'Vigilante' Office, 1918), p. 287.

97 *De Profundis:* Letter to Lord Alfred Douglas, January–March 1897, *Complete Letters,* p. 705.

EPILOGUE

1 Bergery, Bettina (1952), 'What's in a Name?' *In Memory of Dorothy Ierne Wilde*, Natalie Clifford Barney (ed.)(Paris, privately printed), quoted in Joan Schenkar (2000), *Truly Wilde: The Unsettling Story of Dolly Wilde, Oscar's Unusual Niece* (London, Virago), p. 116.

2 'Death Mystery: Open verdict on Oscar Wilde's niece', *Gloucestershire Echo*, Monday 12 May 1941, p. 1.

3 This story originated with Osbert Lancaster and is reported in Schenkar, *Truly Wilde*, p. 130.

4 Letter from Lily Wilde to Oscar Wilde, 7 May 1899, Clark, Finzi 2416.

5 Schenkar, *Truly Wilde*, p. 284.

6 Ibid., p. 314.

7 Crowley, John William (1994), *The White Logic: Alcoholism and Gender in American Modernist Fiction* (Amherst, MA, University of Massachusetts Press), p. 86.

8 Recounted in Natalie Clifford Barney (1929), Aventures de l'esprit (Paris, Émile-Paul Frères).

9 Schenkar, *Truly Wilde*, p. 26.

10 Natalie Clifford Barney from *In Memory of Dorothy Ierne Wilde*, quoted in Schenkar, *Truly Wilde*, p. 239.

11 Janet Flanner, 'Letter from Paris, *The New Yorker*, 16 July 1930.

12 Letter from Lady Jane Wilde to Constance Wilde, July 1095, Eccles Collection 81731.

13 Letter from Lily Wilde to Oscar Wilde, 7 May 1899, Clark, Finzi, 2416.

14 'Miss Dorothy Wilde', *The Times*, 14 April 1941, p. 6.

15 Bettina Bergery quoted in Schenkar, *Truly Wilde*, p. 116.

16 Lancaster, Osbert (1967), *With an Eye to the Future* (London, Murray), p. 136.

17 *Daily Mail*, 12 April 1941.

18 Rosamond Harcourt-Smith from *In Memory of Dorothy Ierne Wilde*, quoted in Schenkar, *Truly Wilde*, p. 117.

INDEX